Inland Waterways of Germany

**GERMAN WATERWAYS MAP
KEY TO FIGURES**

1. Donau (Danube)
2. Main-Donau-Kanal (MDK)
3. Main
4. Rhein (Rhine)
5. Neckar
6. Lahn
7. Mosel
8. Saar
9. Ruhr
10. Rhein-Herne-Kanal (RHK)
11. Wesei-Datteln-Kanal (WDK)
12. Datteln-Hamm-Kanal (DHK)
13. Dortmund-Ems-Kanal (DEK)
14. Unter Ems
15. Ems-Seitenkanal
16. Haren-Rütenbrock-Kanal
17. Ems-Jade-Kanal
18. Nordgeorgsfehnkanal
19. Leda
20. Jumma
21. Elisabethfehnkanal
22. Küstenkanal (KK)
23. Fulda
24. Weser
25. Aller
26. Mittellandkanal (MLK)
27. Elbe-Seitenkanal (ESK)
28. Schiffahrtsweg Elbe-Weser
29. Oste
30. Nord-Ostsee-Kanal (NOK) (Kiel Canal)
31. Eider
32. Elbe-Lübeck-Kanal (ELK)
33. Elbe
34. Saale
35. Elbe-Havel-Kanal
36. Untere Havel-Wasserstrasse
37. Havelkanal
38. Havel-Oder-Wasserstrasse
39. Hohensaaten-Friedrichstaler-Wasserstrasse
40. Ruppiner Wasserstrasse
41. Finowkanal
42. Obere Havel-Wasserstrasse
44. Muritz-Havel-Wasserstrasse
45. Muritz-Eide-Wasserstrasse
46. Spree-Oder-Wasserstrasse
47. Teltowkanal
48. Muggelspree
49. Dahme-Wasserstrasse
50. Obere Spree-Wasserstrasse
51. Oder
52. Peene
53. Uecker
54. Strelasund

Inland Waterways of Germany

REVISED FIRST EDITION

Barry Sheffield

with revisions by

**Catherine and John Best
and Robert Thomas**

Published by
Imray, Laurie, Norie & Wilson Ltd
Wych House St Ives Cambridgeshire PE27 5BT England
℡ +44(0)1480 462114
Fax +44(0)1480 496109
Email ilnw@imray.com
www.imray.com
2016

All rights reserved. No part of this publication may be reproduced, transmitted or used in any form by any means – graphic, electronic or mechanical, including photocopying, recording, taping or information storage and retrieval systems or otherwise – without the prior permission of the publisher.

Revised first edition 2016

© Barry Sheffield 1995
© Catherine and John Best and Robert Thomas 2016

ISBN 978 184623 463 7

CAUTION
Every effort has been made to ensure the accuracy of this book. It contains selected information and thus is not definitive and does not include all known information on the subject in hand; this is particularly relevant to the plans, which should not be used for navigation. The author believes that his selection is a useful aid to prudent navigation, but the safety of a vessel depends ultimately on the judgement of the navigator, who should assess all information, published or unpublished.

PLANS
The plans in this guide are not to be used for navigation. They are designed to support the text and should at all times be used with navigational charts.

CORRECTIONAL SUPPLEMENTS
This pilot book will be amended at intervals by the issue of correctional supplements. These are published on the internet at our web site www.imray.com and may be downloaded free of charge. Printed copies are also available on request from the publishers at the above address.

This work has been corrected to August 2016

Printed in Britain by CPI Antony Rowe Ltd

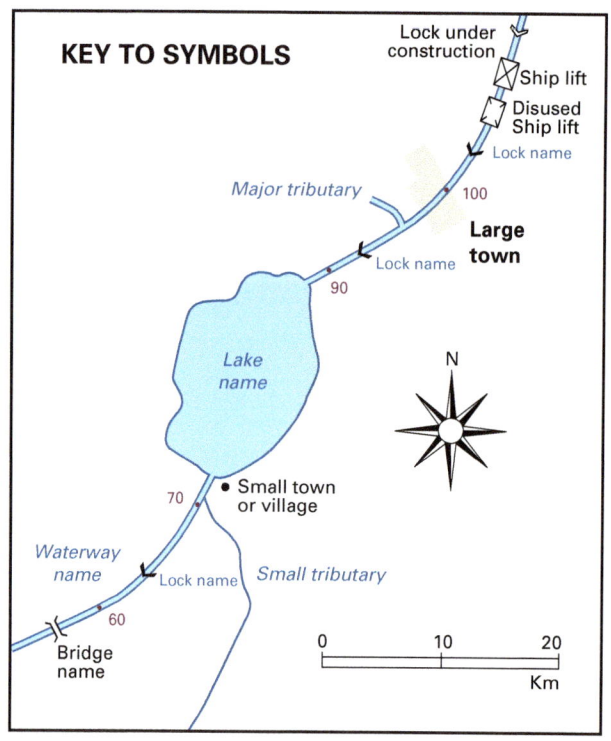

Contents

Preface	**6**
Part I. Cruising in Germany	**7**
Modern Germany	7
The German waterways	13
Administrative matters	13
Navigation	14
Locks	15
Overnight stops	17
Fuel and water	18
Channel depths	18
VHF radio	18
Boats and equipment	19
Routes	20
Part II. Waterways guide	**21**
Introduction	21
South	**21**
Donau (Danube)	21
Main-Donau-Kanal	25
Main	28
Southwest	**32**
Rhein (Rhine)	32
Neckar	45
Lahn	48
Mosel	52
Saar	57
West	**61**
Ruhr	61
Rhein-Herne-Kanal	62
Wesel-Datteln-Kanal	62
Datteln-Harmm-Kanal	63
Dortmund-Ems-Kanal	64
Unter Ems	68
Ems-Seitenkanal	70
Haren-Rütenbrock-Kanal	71
Northwest	**72**
Ems-Jade-Kanal	73
Nordgeorgsfehnkanal	76
Leda and Sagter Ems	76
Jümme	78
Elisabethfehnkanal	78
Küstenkanal and Untere Hunte	79
Middle	**80**
Fulda	80
Weser	81
Aller	84
Mittellandkanal	85
Elbe-Seitenkanal	93
North	**95**
Schiffahrtsweg Elbe-Weser	95
Nord-Ostsee-Kanal (Kiel Canal)	95
Eider and Gieselaukanal	98
Elbe-Lübeck-Kanal and Trave	98
East	**102**
Elbe	103
Saale	111
Elbe-Havel-Kanal	113
Untere Havel-Wasserstrasse	115
Havelkanal	126
Havel-Oder-Wasserstrasse	127
Hohensaaten-Friedrichsthaler-Wasserstrasse	131
Ruppiner Wasserstrasse	132
Finowkanal	133
Werbelliner Gewässer	134
Obere Havel-Wasserstrasse	134
Müritz-Havel-Wasserstrasse	141
Müritz-Elde-Wasserstrasse	144
Spree-Oder-Wasserstrasse	153
Teltowkanal	157
Müggelspree	158
Dahme-Wasserstrasse	160
Obere Spree Wasserstrasse	166
Oder	167
Peene	168
Uecker	169
Strelasund and the Bodden	170
Appendix	**172**
I. Guides and charts	172
II. Useful addresses	172
III. Speed and distance table	172
IV. Navigational marks, signs and sounds	173
V. German vocabulary	174
Index	**178**

Preface

Barry Sheffield's *Inland Waterways of Germany* was first published in 1995 shortly after the reunification of Germany. He had spent several years exploring the navigable rivers and canals by boat and car and was able to produce the first really comprehensive guide based on the same tables of distances that are a feature of Imray's guides to the waterways of France, Belgium and Great Britain. Not many British visitors cruise the German waterways but for those who do this guide is invaluable for planning and as a cockpit reference.

In the twenty years since the book was first published a lot of investment has been made in the German waterways, particularly in the East where the navigations had been allowed to fall into a poor state of repair since 1945. In particular, leisure boating, especially around Berlin, in Brandenburg and the Mecklenburg Lake District, has been keenly promoted.

Barry Sheffield died over ten years ago and since then various users of *Inland Waterways of Germany* have sent us corrections, photographs and supplementary information. Catherine and John Best lived on their boat for a number of years during the summer months and we are grateful to them for their work in completely recompiling the tables for well over half the waterways in the guide, many of them are ones that are critical to leisure boating. A lot of work went into this and bringing the information up to date. Their excellent photographs support this work.

Our original intention was to publish the Best's data as a supplement to the first edition but because it is so extensive it is now incorporated in this revised edition. Robert Thomas contributed a more general update to the first edition and has worked particularly on the introductory sections where the information about Germany was looking very long in the tooth. After 20 years the changes have been extensive.

There is still work to do on *Inland Waterways of Germany* and the reader will notice that photo coverage of some of the waterways is limited. The text for Elbe and associated waterways, Danube, Main-Danube Canal, and the Upper Rhine all stand out as being likely to benefit from up-to-date photography. Readers are therefore encouraged to assist towards the improvement of this useful handbook. Email editor@imray.com

Imray Laurie Norie and Wilson 2016

Barry Sheffield's original Preface follows:

'Germany has a thriving water transport system which exists for commercial purposes, but for those of us who cruise in small boats it also provides an extensive and up-to-date waterway network which makes it possible for us to explore an attractive country in an interesting way. It enables us to meet its people and extend our interests in history, architecture, music, wildlife, food or wine in a new context. Furthermore, occupying as they do the central part of Europe, the German rivers and canals provide through routes which make it possible to travel in comfort to new cruising areas in far-off places such as the Baltic, eastern Europe and the Black Sea.

The aim of this book is to enable more boat owners and charterers to enjoy the pleasures of cruising in Germany. Part I discusses cruising in Germany generally, provides an introduction to the German waterway system and deals with the specific issues relating to cruising in a small boat. Part II, the main bulk of the book, contains a detailed description of every navigable inland waterway route in Germany. The route descriptions in Part II are intended to provide enough information to enable the skipper of a small boat to navigate any waterway they wish. It might be considered advantageous, however, to use the book in conjunction with the appropriate sheets of the 1:200,000 general touring maps known as Die General Karte, which can be bought cheaply in almost any book shop in German.'

Acknowledgements

It would not be realistic to believe that every detail of a guide such as this could derive from personal knowledge. Although I have spent a considerable amount of time travelling the German inland waterways, I have also been fortunate in having many friends in Germany who have generously helped me by checking my material and in some cases providing additional information.

I would especially like to thank Kapitan Konrad Nussbaum in Frankfurt for spending a great deal of time checking my work so thoroughly and so diligently. I am greatly indebted to him. The late Fred Evers of Petershagen and Wolfgang Peiler from Berlin also helped me with their extensive knowledge based on practical boating experience. I would also like to thank Herr Heesch of WSD-Nord and the staff of all the other WSD regions for the helpful way they answered my queries.

Finally I would like to express my gratitude to Willie Wilson and his staff at Imray, and to Sue Pepper for her constant encouragement.

Barry Sheffield November 1995

Part I. Cruising in Germany

Modern Germany

There is something satisfactory about being in Germany. It is well organised. Everything works. The people one meets in the streets are friendly and helpful. Most of them seem to speak English. They are self-confident without being arrogant. Hardly any of them are poor. Even in eastern Germany, until recently under a corrupt totalitarian regime, conditions are improving rapidly, although (hardly surprisingly in view of the rapid pace of change) not without some degree of tension.

Perhaps the 'clean sweep' following the Second World War, with the setting up of a new system of government designed to meet present-day needs and not handicapped by history and tradition, made it possible for Germany to achieve prosperity without sacrificing good humanitarian principles. Whatever the reason, the Germans do seem to have found a way of achieving a well-balanced society, of which realism, logic and hard work seem to be the hallmarks. Their electoral system produces a legislature whose range of hues fairly reflects those of the electors. Their welfare system is effective but does not overburden the taxpayer. They understand the importance of a good infrastructure and manage to invest adequately in it. And although there is considerable delegation of power to the 16 *Länder* (semi-autonomous states), most Germans appear to recognise the importance of European collaboration and know that Germany must play its part in an increasingly united Europe.

The first thing that hits you as a visitor from Britain (at least in the former West Germany) is the feeling of prosperity. There is a noticeable absence of

old cars, poor-quality buildings or badly maintained public facilities. Town (and country) planning seems to be very effective in achieving an aesthetically pleasing environment. There is surprisingly little visible evidence of heavy or unsightly industry in spite of Germany's success as a supplier to the markets of the world. It would seem that the public want 'green' policies - and the political system is capable of translating the wishes of the public into reality.

Geography

It is possible to find almost every type of terrain in Germany. The *Bodden* (salt-water lagoons) and islands of the northern coastline exude a feeling of wildness and mystery. The beautiful lakes of Mecklenburg-Vorpommern are full of old-world charm. The low-lying agricultural lands of Lower Saxony are lush and fertile. The wooded hills and valleys of central Germany have a warmth which contrasts with the Wagnerian splendour of the hill-top castles of Rheinland, the jagged peaks of Saxony and the alpine ranges of the extreme south.

Inside the glass dome of the Reichstag, Berlin

CRUISING IN GERMANY

Check Point Charlie

History

The history of Germany effectively begins in the 9th century, when Charlemagne forced together a number of tribes in central Europe during the formation of the Holy Roman Empire. Over the following centuries the Empire became less unified and five feudal states, or duchies, emerged: Bavaria, Swabia, Franconia, Lorraine and Saxony. It is in these that some of the 16 present-day *Länder* (semi-autonomous regions similar in concept to the states in the USA) had their origins. The diagram on page 7 shows these important political regions as they are today (together with their anglicised names where these exist).

Gradually the Empire became a loose federation of German princedoms, but to create a greater collective strength an overall emperor, Albert of Habsburg, was elected in 1438. The Habsburgs held the throne almost continuously until the final dissolution of the Holy Roman Empire in 1806 following the Napoleonic wars. At this point there were some 39 German states, which became united as the German Confederation, although in practice most of the sovereignty lay in the hands of the member states.

In 1866 Bismarck, prime minister of Prussia, defeated Austria and annexed most of the northern German states. The southern states soon joined this confederation and in 1871 the German Empire was formed with King William I of Prussia as emperor. By 1900 the unified Germany had become the leading industrial nation in Europe.

At the end of the First World War William II abdicated and under the Treaty of Versailles Germany lost the overseas colonies which it had by now established. The resulting collapse of the economy and the ensuing massive unemployment and social discontent led to the rise of the National Socialist (Nazi) party. In 1933 Adolf Hitler became chancellor and a year later president of what became known as the Third Reich. Hitler's ambition and fanaticism led to Germany's defeat in the Second World War, and its occupation by the Allies in four zones. In 1949 the United States, Britain and France consolidated their zones into the Federal Republic of Germany and the Soviet Union set up the German Democratic Republic under communist rule.

West Germany very rapidly developed its industrial capabilities and achieved a leading position as a world industrial nation. East Germany meanwhile suffered severely from the corruption arising from its non-democratic totalitarian government. Civil unrest became rampant, and in 1961 the Berlin wall was built in order to reduce the number of defections to the West.

Aerial view of Museum Island with the Bode Museum on the River Spree

Following the ending of the Cold War, the Berlin wall was demolished after 1989 and Germany became reunited in 1990; with the five eastern *Länder* joining the existing 11 of the Federal Republic. However, the task of reconstructing eastern Germany is huge, and it is likely to require many further years of struggle and hardship before the people of the East gain full equality with their more fortunate compatriots of the West.

Architecture

To the visitor the visible evidence of this fascinating history is a wealth of historic buildings and other relics left behind by countless kings, princes, dukes, counts and bishops, and scattered throughout the land. There are important buildings from all ages: ruins from the times of Caesar, churches and monasteries from the period of the Holy Roman Empire, and magnificent baroque palaces and castles. There are also many uncomfortable reminders of the mass destruction of the Second World War.

Most of the beautiful old buildings are carefully preserved and often on show to visitors - as if with a sense of pride. Elegant churches, castles standing dramatically on hill tops and mediaeval houses clustered in picturesque groups just as they were centuries ago all demonstrate the rich history of the country.

In rural areas farms, equipped though they may be with the latest technology, blend architecturally with their surroundings as harmoniously as they have always done. Clearly new building is carefully controlled, with a responsible eye to the environment. While on the one hand out-and-out modern architecture is encouraged in Frankfurt, the exciting and vibrant centre of banking and commerce, on the other hand in the many historic towns and villages where new buildings need to coexist with the old there is an emphasis on traditional materials such as clay tiles and red bricks, creating a satisfactory sense of overall harmony.

Trees too are clearly a very important factor in planning, and their use to enhance modern developments almost seems obligatory. Presumably it is this same sensitivity towards the environment which also limits the extent of outdoor advertising – so disfiguring and alien to nature in many countries.

Transport

With the natural coming together of the countries of western Europe, travelling to Germany is very little different from travelling to other parts of the British Isles. There are direct flights to many German airports, travel by rail and coach is very easy and there is no difficulty in driving, crossing the Channel by ship, hovercraft or tunnel. Formalities are few, and although – as in any country – politeness requires at least some effort at speaking the language, it is possible to cope with the basic necessities of life without knowing any German at all.

Arriving by boat with the intention of cruising on the German inland waterways involves fewer options, but there are still a number of choices, depending on the departure point, the area to be explored and the type of boat. These matters will be discussed later.

For travel inside Germany, whatever your method of transport, you will find order and efficiency. The airports are designed for practicality, and domestic services are good. Rail transport is excellent: trains are comfortable, punctual and not expensive. Possibly because of this, intercity coaches are not as numerous as in some countries.

The standard of local bus and tram services in most cities is a good incentive to leave your car on the outskirts. The system is normally to buy a ticket from a kiosk or automatic machine, and to validate it by inserting it into a stamping machine as soon as you board the bus. Penalties for not doing so are quite steep, and are collected on the spot. In some areas, but by no means all, tickets can be bought from the bus driver, but still need validation.

River Mosel - 7000 tonnes of coal on the move

CRUISING IN GERMANY

The bicycle is widely accepted as a cheap, healthy, rapid and environmentally friendly method of local transport and cycling is encouraged everywhere by the provision of good cycle tracks, usually safely segregated from road traffic, with special traffic lights at crossing points and good provision for storing bicycles wherever it is needed. Indeed, outside most railway stations you will see hundreds of bicycles neatly stored in specially designed racks, often covered. Bicycles can also be hired at many railway stations.

Renting a car is very straightforward, with prices similar to those at home, but shop around: it is nearly always possible to find local rental companies whose rates undercut the well known international operators by half. Long-distance road travel is catered for by the constantly evolving autobahn network. There are often bitter battles between environmentalists and planners over new autobahn routes, and it is perhaps because of this that the end result seems to be roads which do not disfigure the countryside – at least after the inevitably ugly construction phase has been completed. Roads are generally well maintained and roadworks seldom seem to be a problem. There are no speed limits on the autobahns, and on other roads the speed limits for cars are generally 100km/h on the open road and 50km/h in built-up areas, although other limits may be indicated where appropriate. On the whole, speed limits tend to be realistic but well enforced, and road discipline is generally of a high order.

It is not only the motorist who is subject to discipline: pedestrians are forbidden to jaywalk, and anyone seen dropping litter in a public place also risks a fine.

Over 20% of heavy freight is transported by river and canal (in western Germany). This remarkable achievement, relieving the roads of a considerable volume of heavy lorries, is undoubtedly the result of strategic planning and adequate investment in the facilities which make it attractive for industry to ship its non-urgent bulk cargoes by water.

Public Holidays

New Year's Day	Neujahr	1 January
Epiphany	Heilige Drei Könige	6 January
Good Friday	Karfreitag	Variable
Easter Monday	Ostermontag	Variable
Labour Day	Tag der Arbeit	1 May
Whit Monday	Pfingstmontag	Variable
Corpus Christi	Fronleichnam	Variable
Day of German Unity	Tag der Deutschen Einheit	3 October
All Saints' Day	Allerheiligen	1 November
Christmas	Weinachten	25–26 Dec

Accommodation

There is plenty of overnight accommodation for all budgets, from youth hostels to Hilton hotels. But if the visitor wishes to get to know and understand German people there is no doubt that bed-and-breakfast accommodation in private houses (there are *Zimmer Frei* signs everywhere except perhaps in the centre of large towns and cities) offers an excellent way of gaining an insight into the everyday lives of ordinary people. This type of accommodation is also without doubt the best value for money. Do try to arrive in time for an evening meal. An attempt to speak in German, no matter how rudimentary your linguistic skills, is always appreciated.

Money

There is very little difference between arrangements for getting and spending money in Germany and the UK. ATMs are widespread and found even in smaller towns. If looking for one it may be worthwhile knowing that the German name for an ATM is *Geldautomat*.

Eurocheques are no longer used and indeed no longer accepted. Credit or debit cards are widely accepted, obviously Mastercard, Maestro or Visa cards are most widely used, American Express less so. Still, it is a good idea to be sure that cards are accepted and to ask rather than run the risk of not being able to pay, especially in restaurants where you have already eaten and cannot return the goods!

Normal banking hours are 0900 to 1230 and 1400 to 1600 with an extension until 1800 on Thursdays. Banks do not open on Saturdays. German bank holidays are listed below left.

Shopping

If, as with many people in the western world, shopping is one of your major hobbies you will not be disappointed in Germany. The range of shops and goods is enormous, although it is noticeable that the huge hypermarkets of Britain and France are slow in spreading to Germany. The big department stores of the large cities are remarkably similar to those in the high streets of our own towns, and the specialist food shops (cake shops in particular) are a sight for sore eyes. Unfortunately, with the gradual downward movement of the value of sterling over the last few decades, prices seem generally high to British eyes.

There are excellent markets in most places, and for economical shopping it is as well to locate one. The range and quality of goods is always excellent, and prices tend to be lower than in the larger stores.

Shop opening hours vary but can usually be expected to be Monday to Saturday from 0900 until 1900. Many smaller shops may close for lunch and opening hours in smaller towns may be shorter than the above.

Laundry

For boat people, the often problematic matter of laundry is easily dealt with, as there is no shortage of spotless, well equipped launderettes. Dry-cleaning shops are in every main street. Note that being seen to hang laundry on a Sunday is still frowned upon in many parts of Germany. It is always worth checking at the marinas and yacht clubs as to their guidelines for laundry.

Telecommunications

Germany's telecommunication systems are superb, as might be expected in a nation so successful in international markets.

Call boxes have all but disappeared in the meantime and mobile coverage is excellent. If in Germany for any length of time it may be worthwhile to purchase a local advance payment SIM card for your mobile phone from one of the major phone companies such as Deutsche Telekom or Vodafone. As in the UK, shops selling SIM cards or cheap mobile phones are found in all larger towns.

WIFI

Whilst WiFi is available in many of the restaurants and clubhouses at marinas and yacht clubs, its availability is not guaranteed. If access to the internet is important, it is worth considering the use of a personal mobile WiFi hub, available from all the major telecommunication shops in Germany.

Radio

If your German is good enough, there is no problem in keeping in touch with world affairs via the German broadcasting services, but even if your linguistic abilities are not up to this there is always a wide selection of broadcast music which can be heard by tuning in to local or national services.

On the western side of Germany it is very easy to pick up Radio 4 on 198Khz. As you progress eastwards, however, if your German is limited and you want to keep in touch with world and British news you will find it necessary to use the excellent shortwave broadcasts of the BBC World Service. It is well worth investing in a small transistor radio (preferably with digital tuning) capable of receiving short wave.

Food

There is a widespread myth that German food is dull. This is far from the truth. For the adventurous there is a very wide range of new tastes to try, and for the more conservative there are many traditional meat, fish and vegetable dishes. It is certainly true that the Germans eat well and heartily: you are unlikely to leave the table feeling unsatisfied – but few people will find this a matter to complain about. Desserts do not feature a great deal on German menus, although their wonderful cakes and pastries, often eaten with coffee in the morning or afternoon, more than amply make up for this.

There is a very wide choice of restaurants if you feel like eating out. Most restaurants are unpretentious but there are plenty of expensive restaurants if money is not a limitation. Most yacht clubs have a modest restaurant, and even where this is not the case it would be surprising if there were not a *Gaststätte* (a cross between a pub and a restaurant) in the locality. The *Gasthof* (guest house) usually provides good value too. Always look for the *Tagesmenu* (fixed-price menu of the day).

Wine

It is fashionable to dismiss German wines as sweet and perhaps even of poor quality. This again is quite unjust. There are of course few red German wines, but there are many magnificent whites, and by choosing with care – and perhaps a little local advice – it is possible to find wines of an almost infinite variety of tastes, including some rated amongst the best in the world. Do not think that all German wines are like the cheap *Liebfraumilch* which is sold in large volumes in British supermarkets.

Beer

Germany is often said to be the home of beer. The variety is enormous – and the arguments about the relative merits of different brands never-ending. Beer can be drunk everywhere, from the traditional *Biergarten* (beer garden) or *Bierkeller* (beer cellar) to the most sophisticated of restaurants. It is worth taking local advice on which type of beer to choose. Try to avoid sticking to the mass-produced brands;

Vineyard along the River Saar

CRUISING IN GERMANY

Wine festival in Cochem, along the river Mosel

some of the local brews are not to be missed, but as at home the smaller breweries are gradually being gobbled up by the large groups and local individual flavours are sadly disappearing.

Festivals

Wherever you are in Germany you are almost certain to stumble across a festival. There are festivals of beer, of wine, of food, and of music. For the boat traveller it can be most enjoyable to get involved in a local beer or wine festival. A small amount of alcohol works wonders with language problems and is excellent for promoting international understanding! The *Oktoberfest* (which starts in September in spite of its name) in Bavaria is probably the best-known beer festival; it is regarded as a bad year if fewer than 6,000,000 litres of beer are consumed. It is well worthwhile checking the list of festival dates at the German tourist office when deciding your cruise plan.

Culture

The popular image of Germans as excessive beer drinkers is, however, misleading. They are in fact a very cultured nation. Classical music has a much larger following than in many countries, and even medium-sized towns have opera houses and concert halls as well as art galleries. The Wagner festival at Bayreuth (July/August) is world-famous. The Bach festival at Leipzig and the Handel festival at Halle are important events in the international music calendar. There are also international drama, film and folk festivals.

Etiquette

If you are lucky enough to be invited into a German home – or boat – for a meal, you should recognise that the Germans are somewhat more formal than we are. Take flowers (preferably not roses), and do not too quickly assume that you can call your hosts by their first names.

Cost of living

Unfortunately for us, the relative prosperity of the Germans, coupled with the intermittent devaluation of sterling over the years, means that by our standards the cost of living in Germany is high. However, if care is taken to avoid some of the more expensive products, with prudent shopping in supermarkets and by eating in yacht clubs or modest restaurants it is possible to live in Germany at only a slightly higher cost than at home.

Climate

Germany's climate is not enormously different from our own. The winters are somewhat colder and the summers are perhaps slightly hotter. The rainfall is a little lower.

Wildlife

Germany is rich in wildlife of a wide variety of types, but to the boat traveller it is the birds which haunt the rivers, canals, lakes and estuaries that are a constant source of interest. Needless to say, swans and ducks (of many types) are constantly in attendance, and herons can always be seen at the water's edge. In some areas storks and egrets are much in evidence; hoopoes can be spotted amongst the trees, and on the desolate *Bodden* of the Baltic coast thousands of geese and swans collect, unapproachable by human beings. It is also a common sight whilst travelling the canals and rivers to see kites, harriers and occasionally eagles wheeling overhead in search of prey. Do not forget to take a book which will help you to identify the birds of central Europe.

Cows along the Lahn admiring the passing boat

12 INLAND WATERWAYS OF GERMANY

The German waterways

The German waterway network offers enough interest in its own right to justify many years of enjoyable cruising. It also provides opportunities for ambitious long-distance cruising. The frontispiece map shows the scope of the German waterway system itself and gives some idea of the extent of the sheltered-water cruising opportunities which exist, not only in central Europe but further afield in southern Scandinavia, Russia and the Black Sea.

The atmosphere on the *Bundeswasserstrassen* (national waterways) is one of purposefulness. The waterways are alive: they exist for a practical purpose, and the skippers and crews of the barges, push-tows, hotel ships, car transporters, tugs and ferries form a very special community. But it is far from being a closed community, and a *Sportboot* (any boat used for leisure purposes) will be readily accepted as part of this fraternity of the waterways – provided the skipper is judged to be competent. It should be remembered that barge skippers, river police and lock-keepers are professionals with a job to do and time schedules to meet. It is hardly surprising that their tolerance can easily become stretched if they discern that a *Sportboot* skipper is incompetent, or thoughtless about the needs and the problems of large unwieldy commercial vessels. Much of the pleasure of travelling on the German waterways is the satisfaction of being for a time part of this waterways fraternity.

The skippers of German pleasure boats also have a good sense of camaraderie, and this is willingly extended to visitors from other countries whom they identify as like-minded. An overnight stop at a German yacht club is usually a friendly and pleasant experience, especially if the visitor is willing to try his or her hand at speaking German.

It is noticeable that there is a very strong European feeling everywhere. A high proportion of vessels now carry the European Union ensign, with the German flag inset in the top corner, instead of their own national ensign. Clearly there is a feeling amongst the waterways community that national boundaries and excessive demonstrations of national pride have become anachronistic. The much-publicised behaviour of some of the minority nationalist groups in Germany is certainly no reflection of national attitudes.

As well as the *Bundeswasserstrassen*, there are many delightful smaller waterways, originally built for trading purposes but no longer used to any great extent by commercial ships. Nevertheless, many of them continue to be maintained for the benefit of pleasure craft. By contrast with the huge modern commercial waterways, these smaller waterways (such as the Lahn, the northwestern canals and the waterways throughout the Mecklenburg lake district) have an atmosphere not unlike that of the French canals: they are generally rural in character, provide peace and tranquillity, and the lock-keepers are friendly and helpful. That same spirit of friendship from the skippers and crews of the other pleasure craft one meets is also, pleasingly, apparent.

Barge traffic on the Rhein

Administrative matters

The German waterways are freely available to visitors. As boats will be likely arriving from one of the surrounding Schengen countries, no checks are carried out any longer at border crossings.

It is recommended to be in possession of a valid International Certificate of Competence. Even if this may not legally be necessary, it will make matters easier should you be checked by the *Wasserschutzpolizei* (Police).

In earlier publications a 15-tonne displacement limit is mentioned for pleasure vessels. The recommendations given for all UK registered boats cruising the German waterways are:

> **For vessels up to 15m LOA** German owners need a *Sportsbootfuhrerschein Binnen* and the ICC should cover this. This applies to all German inland waters and the big rivers, including the Rhine.
>
> **For vessels between 15m and 25m LOA** German owners need a *Sportsschifferzeugnis E* or a German *streckerpatent/strechennachweise* for any specific waterway. It would be unwise to expect an ICC to provide cover on the big rivers. The authorities would be quite likely to stop any vessel and possibly impose a fine if one attempted to navigate without a pilot.
>
> Anybody expecting to cruise the big German rivers for sometime might do best to take the German test and exam (in German) to navigate the Rhine, Weser, Elbe and some parts of the other big rivers. The *Sportsschifferzeugniss E* or *Sportpatent E* is a prerequisite for all additional qualifications on specific waterways. The regular number of trips up and down a specific waterway is normally 8 but if you are taught by a registered school then this is reduced to 4 trips each way.

CRUISING IN GERMANY

The Rathaus (town hall), Bernkastel

All boats must be registered, but for British boats registration on the Small Ships Register is adequate. If VAT has been paid on the vessel it is sensible to carry documentary evidence of this. If VAT has not been paid, advice should be obtained from the RYA before arrival in Germany. Boats are expected to carry normal safety equipment such as life buoys, life jackets, first-aid kit, fire extinguishers and an anchor. It is believed that at some stage a regulation will be introduced requiring all vessels using the inland waterways to have holding tanks, and discharging toilets overboard will be prohibited. There is, however, no indication as yet of when this will become a requirement.

The *Wasserschutzpolizei* (river police), or WSP, will be noticeable from time to time. Normally, however, the crews of WSP patrol vessels are nothing but helpful – and this can be very comforting to know in case of serious problems. It goes without saying, of course, that visiting leisure boats – like everyone else on the water – should be careful to take proper notice of the rules of the road, speed limits, etc. These are working waterways, and not unreasonably all users are expected to behave responsibly.

For navigation on the Rhein, vessels over 20m long are required to have on board the *Rheinschiffahrtpolizeiverordnung* (Rhine river police regulations).

The *Bundeswasserstrassen* are administered by the German ministry of transport, through the agency of the *Wasser-und-Schiffahrtsdirektion* (Water and Shipping Authority), WSD for short, which has seven regions: WSD-Nord (Kiel), WSD-Nordwest (Aurich), WSD-Mitte (Hannover), WSD-West (Munster), WSD-Südwest (Mainz), WSD-Süd (Würzburg) and WSD-Ost (Berlin). Each region of the WSD is further subdivided into smaller areas known as WSAs (*Wasser-und-Schiffahrtsamt*), each responsible for the physical maintenance of the waterway system within its own area. A list of addresses of these organisations is included in the Appendix.

There are no charges for foreign leisure boats on German inland waterways. Previous charges for single usage of locks specifically on the Mosel have been dropped. It should be noted that although use of the WSD-controlled waterways is free to foreign yachtsmen, all German yacht clubs pay a substantial fee each year towards their upkeep, and German boat owners therefore share this cost. This fact should not be forgotten when visiting yacht clubs or mixing with local boat owners.

The smaller waterways are generally not controlled by the WSD and are usually operated by the appropriate *Land*. Most *Länder* make a nominal charge for using them.

Navigation

The normal rules of the road apply to users of the German waterways. Speed limits are clearly displayed and actively enforced by the WSP. Offenders are required to pay a substantial fine on the spot. Language is no excuse, and credit cards are not taken. All requisite warnings and other items of information are displayed by means of sign boards which conform to international standards. The more important of these signs are illustrated in the Appendix.

In general there are few problems in navigating these waterways, but there are several important matters which should be borne in mind. For example, when steering along a busy river, considerable concentration is called for, not only to be constantly aware of all traffic both ahead and astern, but also to observe all oncoming ships carefully to find out as early as possible whether they are 'blue-flagging'. All commercial vessels on the Rhein and other major waterways are required to carry a large square blue board (the 'blue flag') on the starboard side of the bridge. This board is normally carried horizontally, and is therefore virtually invisible to vessels approaching in the opposite direction. Should the helmsman wish, however, he or she has the option of turning the board vertical and therefore making it visible to oncoming vessels, indicating that he or she wishes to pass starboard to starboard. This option is very commonly used on rivers, especially the Rhein, where the vagaries of current and depth may make it difficult for large vessels to stick to the normal conventions. At busy times, when there may be as many as 10 ships in your vicinity, you have to be aware not only of the channel markers (to avoid straying into shallow water), but also of the movements of all nearby ships, some of which will be blue-flagging and some not. This can cause the adrenaline to flow on occasion,

It is also important to be aware of some of the hydrographic effects of large power vessels moving through the water. When meeting a barge or other large vessel on a narrow canal, the width often dictates that you must pass within a few metres of the oncoming ship to avoid running aground. The natural reaction is to slow down to minimise the danger of grounding. However, the propeller of a large vessel creates a powerful suction, pulling water in from ahead and from both sides, ejecting it astern.

A small vessel close abeam can therefore find itself sucked into collision with the larger one, and the slower the speed of the smaller vessel the more likely this is to happen. Some degree of skill may be required to judge the speed of your boat under these conditions. In practice, it is probably best to steer as close to the bank as possible with safety and to slow down almost to a standstill before the arrival of the ship, and then to open the throttle quite hard just before its bow is level with yours. If carried out skilfully this procedure will result in the boat having minimum speed but maximum manoeuvrability during the critical seconds while the two vessels are alongside each other.

Barges and other large vessels tend to travel at 6–7kn or more through the water, and if your cruising speed happens to be a little below this you will find that from time to time you are overtaken by a large vessel. Your natural reaction is to slow down to allow the other vessel to pass more quickly, but as you may be only a few metres from the ship the suction effect of the ship's propeller can be a danger if you slow down too much and lose steerage. Sometimes in this situation the barge skipper will help by closing his throttle at the critical point when his stern is almost abeam of you, thereby reducing the suction effect – but it would be unwise to assume that this will necessarily happen.

Similarly, if you come up behind a sizeable ship which is travelling at a slightly lower speed than you and you wish to overtake it you should take into account the fact that because the ship's propeller is constantly sucking in water from abeam and ahead, as your boat comes alongside your speed over the ground will reduce because of this artificial adverse current, and unless you have enough reserve of power to accelerate you may find that overtaking is impossible. At this point you will find that you are also unable to close your throttle for fear of losing control and being sucked into the stern of the vessel you have been trying to overtake. The secret is to slow down only slightly and to wait patiently for the barge to draw ahead. But keep an eye out for the over-helpful barge skipper who, recognising your predicament, closes his throttle to help you – just at the moment when you decide to give up the attempt and slow down yourself.

It is perhaps worth pointing out that the suction from passing ships applies equally well when a small boat is anchored at the side of the stream. In the event of engine trouble, or other emergency requiring the boat to anchor, it is essential to anchor both fore and aft. Unless the river is very wide, lying to a single anchor is not sufficient, as the scope of the anchor cable may be enough to allow you to be sucked helplessly into collision with a passing barge.

Locks

On the main waterways, because of the size and cost of the locks needed to accommodate the large vessels which need to use them, the tendency is to build as few locks as possible. It follows, therefore, that the average height of the locks is quite large. Some locks are well over 20m in height, and entering one of these can be a daunting experience. In practice, however, negotiating large locks is far less frightening than it might seem at first sight.

The Germans categorise the locks according to their type, and this is often reflected in the official name of a lock, for example *Doppelschleuse* Vogelgrün or *Schleusengruppe* Griesheim, indicating that the locks are double or multiple respectively. Some of the deeper locks are of a type resembling a vertical shaft with a guillotine gate at the bottom. This type of lock is known as a *Schachtschleuse* (shaft lock), for example *Schachtschleuse* Minden. However, even though the official name may include this categorisation, unless there is a possibility of confusion it is usual to refer to the lock (for example over VHF) simply as *Schleuse* Vogelgrün or *Schleuse* Griesheim. These categorisations have therefore been ignored in the route descriptions in this book.

Major locks on the commercial waterways are equipped with red and green lights (or in a few cases semaphores) to signal the state of the lock to waiting vessels and to give permission to enter. The signals are self-evident. If your German is sufficiently fluent you can also talk to the lock-keeper on VHF to discover the state of the lock and perhaps find out how long it will be necessary to wait before entering. In most cases small boats are expected to wait until any commercial vessels have entered, and then to tuck into any available space (if any) at the back of the lock. The normal practice therefore is either to tie up to some convenient mooring place or to hover, well clear of the lock gates but near enough to be able to enter quickly if and when the opportunity occurs. Generally it is advisable to approach the lock gates whilst the last ship is entering, to be able to enter the lock as soon as the turbulence from the ship has subsided. Lock-keepers cannot wait for leisure boats if they are too far away.

A few locks have special mooring stages for leisure boats, sometimes even with their own light signals to indicate when the lock is clear for entry. Or there

Schleuse at the entrance of the Haren-Rutenbrock-Kanal

may be an extension to the lock public address system for the benefit of waiting leisure boats.

Once inside the lock, the technique used will undoubtedly vary from boat to boat according to personal preferences, although there are certain basic principles. Also, the method used when ascending will differ somewhat from that used when descending.

The locks on the main waterways are designed for large ships, with mooring bollards too widely spaced to allow a small boat to moor fore-and-aft. Instead, it is necessary to moor to a single bollard amidships. In tall locks, the mooring bollards are set in recesses in the lock wall in a vertical line, spaced at vertical intervals of about 1·5m, so that as the level of water rises or falls, the mooring warps can be shifted at intervals onto the next higher or next lower bollard. It is not difficult to develop a drill for this operation, and it is not normally hazardous except on rare occasions when strong turbulence is being experienced. Many of the larger and more modern locks are equipped with *Schwimmpoller* (floating bollards), which rise and fall with the level of the water, making life much simpler for a small craft. It should be borne in mind, however, that floating bollards have been known to stick before reaching the end of their travel, so it is wise to have some way of allowing lines to run if this should happen.

Mooring amidships is usually accomplished either by using a breast rope from a strong amidships mooring cleat or by bringing bow and stern lines together onto the same bollard. A single amidships line is undoubtedly quicker and easier to use, especially if it can be led back to a winch in the cockpit, but the strain on the fixing point can be very severe if there should be turbulence, and it may be considered prudent to use this arrangement as a convenient way of picking up the mooring, but then add bow and stern lines afterwards to ease the strain on the amidships point and to make the mooring doubly secure. Some locks, such as some of those on the Mosel, have very convenient vertical bars fixed to the stepladders which are set into the lock walls. By mooring amidships to these the mooring lines can be slid up or down, somewhat more convenient than moving them from one bollard to another as the water level changes.

When ascending, there will always be some risk of turbulence whilst the chamber is filling, and mooring lines should therefore be hauled tight before the lock starts to fill to minimise the extent to which turbulence can push the boat away from the lock wall. The engine should be kept running and if serious turbulence is experienced the strain can be reduced by engaging whichever gear is appropriate to counteract the flow of water. If the lock is an older one, the water inlet is usually via sluices in the top gate, and it is always best if going upwards to choose a bollard fairly close to the lower gate, as far away from the likely source of turbulence as possible. Even in the largest of German locks it is unusual for turbulence to be severe enough to be dangerous, but it is important to know that it can occur and that if appropriate precautions are not taken serious damage could be incurred. With many modern locks, such as those on the Main-Donau-Kanal, the water inlets are along the floor of the chamber, which usually makes for a much quieter flow. Even so it is not safe to assume that turbulence cannot exist, as water is admitted in distinct bursts, and at each burst turbulence can be created. Normal precautions should still be taken.

Descending is usually far less problematical than ascending, as the emptying of the chamber creates little turbulence within it. The biggest problem is that sometimes on entering a lock which is full (and not equipped with floating bollards) it may be difficult to know where on the lock wall the fixed bollards are located. It could be dangerous if it is discovered when the chamber starts to empty that the boat is not positioned over a line of bollards down the lock wall. If in doubt, ask – even if it is only in sign language.

Whether the lock is up or down, it is very important to be aware of the potential danger of turbulence from the propellers of large ships. The force of the water pushed out by the propeller of a 3,000-tonne ship or a powerful push-tow as it begins to move out of a lock, even under low power, is easily capable of wrenching a sturdy mooring cleat off the deck of a small boat. Do not be tempted to release mooring lines until all big ships have left the lock. Be aware also that this propeller wash can circulate from the stern of the vessel creating it around the closed end of the lock chamber and forwards along the wall opposite to the ship. This powerful reverse flow of water can take the skipper of a small boat off his or her guard and put immense strain on mooring cleats or even force the boat into collision with the lock wall.

On some rivers, for example the Mosel and the Main, many of the commercial locks have self-actuated boat locks alongside them, and leisure boats, usually up to a maximum beam of 3·5 or 4 metres, are required to use these instead of the main locks. The procedure is to enter the lock, moor to a vertical rod, then climb onto the lock side, where a control box is situated. The control box has a lever which must be moved up or down to indicate the direction of travel, and a large knob which actuates the lock. When you are ready to leave, you press the knob again to open the appropriate gate. Full instructions are displayed on the control box.

At several places where a very deep lock would have been required, a *Hebewerk* (ship-lift) has been built instead. A ship-lift is essentially a moveable dock in which several ships can be moored. The gate is closed and the whole dock, complete with water and ships, is raised or lowered to the appropriate level. The other gate is then opened and the ships continue their journey. There are four of these mammoth lifts in Germany, two on western canals and two in the east. The two western lifts are modern, but the two eastern ones are gigantic monuments to the engineering feats of the past. Nevertheless they work perfectly well and, like their western equivalents, handle very large volumes of traffic, at the same time providing an irresistible spectacle for tens of thousands of onlookers every year. For the small pleasure boat they at first sight appear to present a daunting prospect, but in fact it is normally simpler and easier to use a ship-lift than to use an equivalent lock (or series of locks). The only practical problem is that most of the lifts are extremely busy and waiting times for barges are long. The secret is to tuck into a convenient corner within earshot of the Tannoy, so that if space can be found to accommodate a small boat behind a group of commercial ships you may be lucky enough to be called into the lift well ahead of your proper place in the queue. Listen to the Tannoy or VHF for the word *Sportboot*.

In the locks on the smaller waterways the situation is somewhat similar to that in France. Most of the locks are mechanised, but they are usually operated by a lock-keeper. You simply moor to bollards on the lock side, taking care to keep as far away from the upper gate as possible if you are going upwards, and let out or take in the lines as the lock empties or fills.

Overnight stops

On some of the major waterways commercial traffic continues throughout the night. Under no account should this be attempted in a small boat. The barge skippers know the waterways intimately and understand each other's habits, but for the foreign cruising skipper, navigating at night on the Rhein (for example) in the midst of heavy barge traffic is a nightmare. On most lakes around Berlin navigation at night is forbidden for pleasure boats.

Finding a place to stop for the night sometimes requires a little planning. On the smaller and less busy waterways it is usually very easy to find a quiet corner as dusk begins to fall, but on the larger rivers and canals this cannot be relied upon. Here it is best to think ahead and aim for a known harbour or yacht club which can be reached by 1700 or 1800, and to have a contingency plan for an alternative stopping place which can still be reached during daylight hours in case there is a problem with the first choice. The problem is perhaps most acute on the more modern canals, such as the Main-Donau or the Elbe-Seiten, where there are often very long stretches without convenient moorings, and where it is forbidden to moor anywhere other than in a designated harbour. In eastern Germany too the choice of places to stop is slightly more restricted than in the western part of the country, simply because there are fewer yacht clubs. In other respects, however, the situation is similar.

Clearly the type of mooring place preferred is a matter of taste, and there is a wide variety to choose from. In the main most people find that it is best to look for a yacht club or yacht harbour away from the main stream if the waterway is likely to be in constant use during the night, for a modest fee (usually €1–€1.50 per metre per night) one gets a quiet berth, showers, the opportunity of a meal in the clubhouse and, usually, a warm welcome.

Another convenient type of overnight stop is in a harbour provided by the local town council. These are usually safe and comfortable, but the facilities are often somewhat sparse compared with those at most yacht clubs. Nevertheless, as they are often situated close to town centres they can be extremely convenient.

Some of the many harbours which exist for use by large commercial vessels can also provide a satisfactory overnight stop, but facilities for a small cruising boat are usually fairly non-existent and great care is required to find a spot in the harbour where you are unlikely to be a nuisance to larger vessels or to be damaged by them. Needless to say, one should always make an attempt to seek permission from the harbourmaster (if you can find one) before settling down for the night or leaving the boat to go to a restaurant.

There are many free moorings on certain waterways with no facilities for leisure craft, signed 'Nur fur sportsboots'. These have a maximum stay period – normally 24 hours or 3 days – which must not be exceeded.

On the main waterways there are quite often harbours operated by the WSAs (water authorities) to house their own work boats. Officially these are not available for leisure boats, but it is sometimes possible to obtain permission to stay in one of these if there are no other mooring places in the vicinity. Sometimes too it is possible simply to anchor in a lake or backwater off the main channel, or to tie up alongside a vessel which is not in use and moored in an out-of-the-way corner. Similarly there are many industrial harbours at manufacturing plants on the side of the waterway where, in an emergency, it may be possible to stay for a brief overnight stop.

Probably the most satisfactory type of stopping place, however, is the quiet rural corner of a small canal or river, perhaps tied up to a grassy quay along the bank, moored in an out-of-the-way corner near a lock or anchored in some tranquil backwater.

Guest moorings on the Havelkanal

CRUISING IN GERMANY

Except when the boat is safely in a marina berth, a white anchor light should be displayed to warn other vessels of your presence. It is not unknown for a barge to turn up mysteriously in the middle of the night, expecting its regular mooring place to be free. A small vessel without a light could be very vulnerable.

If it is required to keep the boat in one place for a longer time, perhaps even over a winter, there are excellent secure storage facilities afloat or ashore at many yacht clubs. It would be advisable, however, to make enquiries well ahead of the time when the boat is to be left, as many such places tend to become over-subscribed and last-minute arrivals may be unlucky.

Fuel and water

On the whole, throughout the former West Germany there are few problems in finding convenient supplies of diesel fuel, either from bank-side fuelling stations or from the bunker boats which exist for the benefit of commercial shipping. On the rare occasions when it is not possible to find a means of refuelling alongside, there is almost certain to be a reasonably accessible street filling station for an emergency top-up. Note that when refuelling at a bunker boat it may occasionally be found that the delivery nozzle is too large for the normal small boat, as the prime purpose of these bunker boats is the refuelling of barges and other large vessels. Nor can it be guaranteed that a bunker boat will always be on station, as from time to time they may be taken to a fuel depot to replenish their supplies.

In the former East Germany, although things are steadily improving, it is advisable to ensure that your tanks are full before entering the area. If an emergency arises and a fuelling station cannot be found, it is best to contact a yacht club and explain your predicament. It would be unusual if help were not forthcoming.

Users of petrol will find the situation more difficult, and will frequently have to rely on carrying cans of fuel from the nearest roadside filling station.

Water supplies are not a problem, and tanks can be replenished either at bunker stations whilst refuelling or from hosepipes at yacht clubs, locks or harbours. Facilities for emptying holding tanks are becoming increasingly widespread, and enquiries will usually enable the necessary service to be located (except perhaps in the former East Germany, where such facilities are less common).

Channel depths

For most of the German waterways a *Tauchtiefe* (maximum permitted draught) is stipulated, either for the whole length of the waterway or for predetermined segments of it. Waterway users are legally required to observe the *Tauchtiefen*, and failure to do so could result in insurance and legal

Pegel at Trier on the Mosel River

problems in the event of an accident in which grounding was a factor. In some cases, notably rivers subject to varying levels, *Tauchtiefen* change from day to day; they are published daily in a variety of ways, and usually related to the *Pegelstand* (level of water at a *Pegel* (depth gauge)). *Pegels* are situated at strategic intervals along each major waterway whose level is not constant.

On the Rhein, instead of quoting *Tauchtiefen* a slightly different system is used, based on a stated *Gleichwertiger Wasserstand-Fahrrinnentiefe* (normal channel depth) for each stretch of the river. It is important always to be aware of the current situation for the waterway in use, especially during dry periods when water levels are low. The system applicable to each waterway is outlined in the relevant route description in Part II.

During times of flood, all traffic may be banned if the water level exceeds a certain level. Such conditions normally occur only during winter or early spring, and if the situation arises it will be made amply evident that navigation is prohibited.

VHF radio

On all the major waterways there is a well organised *UKW* (VHF) radio communication system, heavily used by the skippers of commercial vessels.

All radios must be equipped with an ATIS function which transmits the ATIS code number every time it is used. Needless to say, the radio must be programmed with your unique ATIS number. It is not mandatory to actually have a radio but if you have one it must be tuned to Channel 10 (ship-ship) at all times except to leave the Channel for a short time to use another Channel e.g. to contact a lock, after which you must switch back to Channel 10 as soon as possible. Channel 10 has much the same function as Channel 16 at sea, i.e. it is not to be used for personal or private conversations between ships. For this Channel 77 can be used.

An important issue is that hand held radios are not allowed to be used at any time for ship-ship or ship-land communications. This is regardless of whether the hand held has an ATIS function or not. Hand held radios are only allowed on commercial barges for communication between crew on the same ship.

All radios must be restricted to 1 watt outage, 25 watt as used at sea is not allowed as it would transmit at too much range. Normally ATIS equipped radios automatically reduce to 1 watt when the ATIS function is enabled but you should check your own radio for this.

Radar is not allowed to be used on pleasure vessels even if the vessel is equipped with it. Normal yacht radars are not good enough anyway to have the resolution needed for inland waterways.

Boats and equipment

Few normal cruising boats are unsuitable for the German waterways. The ideal, perhaps, is the type of boat which has evolved over the years as almost the standard boat used by the Germans (and the Dutch). This is a steel motor cruiser, usually between 8–12m in length, with a draught of 1–1·2m, a centre bridge, an exterior steering position, a single propeller and a diesel engine giving a normal cruising speed of 7–8kn but capable of 10kn if the need arises. However, although such a boat may be most suitable, any boat with a draught of less than 1·8m and capable of sustaining a speed of 4–5kn will be able to cruise widely in Germany with only a few limitations. It is not really practicable to think of going upstream in the Rhein or the Donau in any boat which cannot cruise at a steady 8–10kn. Nor is it likely that any boat drawing more than 1·2m would be suitable for exploring a number of waterways in the eastern part of Germany in late summer.

Converted barges, ideal for inland waterway cruising in so many ways, often have a length of over 15m. Please be aware of the restrictions applying to vessels over 15m mentioned in the chapter 'Administrative matters'.

There is considerable debate about the relative merits of single- and twin-propeller configurations. The advantage of the additional manoeuvrability provided by twin propellers may be offset by the increased probability of grounding against the shelving sides of canals, especially if, as is standard practice in the building of many canals, the profile of the canal bottom is constructed of broken rocks. With the emergence of bow thrusters, however, it seems likely that the ideal configuration will become a single propeller in combination with a bow thruster.

Sailing boats with their masts carried horizontally are an increasingly common sight on German inland waters, as boat owners begin to realise that an inland route can be a more interesting and comfortable way of reaching the Baltic or eastern Europe than the usual offshore route. Provided care is taken to avoid damage to the overhanging spars there are no real problems to this. There are plenty of yacht clubs (or boatyards – but they tend to be more expensive) with cranes suitable for stepping and unstepping masts, and it is not difficult to construct two or three wooden crutches for carrying the spars horizontally.

For those who do not have the good fortune to own their own boat, or for boat owners who do not have the time for the lengthy journeys to and from Germany, it is very easy to charter a boat in Germany.

Apart from the needs of safety, mentioned earlier, there are no special requirements for boat equipment, although for long journeys involving wide rivers and perhaps lakes or coastal waters it is very useful to have an autopilot. For exploring some of the smaller canals and rivers where (as in France) there is a danger of weed blocking the cooling-water intake, some form of audible or visible engine-overheating alarm has its advantages. In any case, it makes good sense to inspect the water-intake strainer daily to guard against clogging. A horn, although not likely to be used regularly, should be instantly available for use in an emergency.

From the earlier discussion on using locks, it should go without saying that good fendering is essential. Many small boats carry several car tyres for this purpose, but unless they are suitably covered they can be very unsightly and leave almost indelible black marks on the boat's topsides. Many people prefer simply to carry several extra large conventional fenders, which may be less offensive to the eye. It is also extremely useful to carry a good strong plank with a line attached to each end. By hanging this outside the fenders it is possible to moor alongside piled walls without difficulty. Indeed, you will find occasional locks with piled walls, and without a plank there may be a considerable danger of damaging the topsides of the boat. It need hardly be mentioned that the image of a well managed boat will be enhanced if fenders are taken up and stowed on deck promptly on leaving a lock.

All cruising boats accumulate a collection of hose fittings and electrical adapters. There is, surprisingly, no sign of standardisation in Germany so far as hose fittings are concerned, but *Strom* (electricity) outlets are usually either two-pin, with earth contacts on the sides, or the blue European standard fittings.

Camping Gaz is widely available on an exchange basis, and propane cylinders can usually be refilled at major depots. The further east one goes, the less easy it is to obtain *Camping Gaz*, and it is wise to have a propane regulator on board.

It is useful but by no means essential to carry a dinghy for use on the odd occasion when it is desirable to anchor away from the shore, but by far the most useful accessory is undoubtedly the bicycle. A couple of small bikes make shopping and exploration so much easier and more enjoyable, especially as cyclists are so well catered for throughout Germany. It is quite unnecessary to invest in expensive folding bikes. The standard cheap 'shopping bicycle' is perfectly satisfactory and a good deal less attractive to potential thieves.

Routes

By general consensus, the favourite cruising grounds are (in no particular order) the Neckar, the Rhein Gorge, the Lahn, the Mosel, the Saar, the Main, the Donau, the upper Weser, the upper Elbe, Berlin, the Spree with its associated waterways, the Mecklenburg lake district and the *Bodden* of northeast Germany. In addition, there are many through routes which provide connections between these areas and also make it possible to reach the waterways of other countries.

The major through routes are:

A From the North Sea to the Baltic via the Nord-Ostsee-Kanal (fixed-mast route). A more interesting variation is to use the Eider for the first part of the journey.

B From the Netherlands upstream along the Rhein.

C From France into the Rhein via the Rhone-Rhein-Kanal, the Rhein-Marne-Kanal or the Mosel, then northwards into Holland or Routes D to I.

D From the Rhein to the Black Sea via the Main, the Main-Donau-Kanal and the Donau (Danube).

E From the Rhein to the North Sea via the Rhein-Herne or Wesel-Datteln-Kanal and the Dortmund-Ems-Kanal (masts up at Ditzum).

F From the Rhein to the Baltic via the Rhein-Herne or Wesel-Datteln-Kanal, the Dortmund-Ems-Kanal, the Mittellandkanal, the Elbe-Seiten-Kanal and the Elbe-Lübeck-Kanal (masts up in the Passathafen at Travemünde).

G From the Rhein to the Baltic via the Mittellandkanal, the Elbe, the Elbe-Havel-Kanal, the Havel-Oder-Wasserstrasse and the Oder (masts up in Marina Marco at Szczecin).

H To the Czech Republic via a modification of Route F, turning upstream in the Elbe at Magdeburg.

I To the Polish rivers via another modification of Route F, branching off at Berlin through the Spree to the Oder.

The main factors which influence the planning of routes in Germany are the currents and depths of the major rivers.

In the Rhein the current is quite strong throughout the year, and very strong in the spring. It is normally best to use the French canals in such a way as to avoid any travel upstream in the Rhein, unless of course the boat is capable of the necessary speed. A downstream passage is usually trouble-free at least up to the end of July, or even later for shallower-draught boats or in wet summers. An up-stream passage through the Rhein Gorge and further up to Iffezheim is difficult at the best of times, and for most boats impossible before the end of May, as the current along this stretch can be anything up to 10kn.

In the Donau the current is very strong in the spring, and unless speeds of 10kn or so are possible an upstream journey should not be contemplated until early July at least. For downstream passages in times of flood, it is wise to make enquiries along the river to ensure that bridge clearances are adequate.

The currents in the Elbe are on the whole less of a problem than those in the Rhein and the Donau, but in most years vessels drawing more than 1·2m may have problems above Lauenburg after about the end of June. The short stretch of the Elbe connecting the Mittellandkanal to the Elbe-Havel-Kanal may have as little as 1·2m of water by the end of July, depending on rainfall.

The length of time required for any given journey naturally depends on the speed of the boat, the length of time travelled each day, the number of locks on the route, the number of days allowed for exploration ashore and of course the assistance (or otherwise) gained from any current. As a rough guide, it should be possible to cover an average of 50km a day, given a boat capable of cruising at 5–6kn, without having to get out of bed at the crack of dawn each day. This means that in practice it is possible to travel the 320km from the Rhein to the Elbe comfortably in about six days. By contrast, with the help of a moderate current in midsummer, a journey of some 630km downstream along the Rhein from Niffer to Wesel can be accomplished in a mere five days.

Dom Cathedral as seen from the Spree-Oder-Wasserstrasse

Part II. Waterways guide

Introduction

This section of the book is made up of detailed route descriptions for every navigable waterway in Germany. The information provided should enable a small-boat skipper to navigate any waterway he or she wishes without further documentation, but it will undoubtedly be useful to use the book in conjunction with the appropriate 1:200,000 sheets of the general touring map sold under the title of *Die General Karte* and easily available in almost any book shop in Germany.

Waterways are not necessarily described in the same direction as the kilometre markings. The height of each lock is quoted as a rise or a fall according to the direction in which the waterway is described. The terms 'left bank' and 'right bank' are used in a conventional sense (i.e. when pointing downstream) in connection with rivers only. In the case of canals, where 'left' and 'right' may cause confusion, the banks are called, for example, 'north' or 'south'. All waterway features referred to in the route descriptions are identified by their kilometre locations, reflecting the fact that all waterways have clearly marked kilometre posts along their banks.

Most of the major waterways in Germany have designated *Tauchtiefen* (maximum permitted draughts), which are legal requirements, but there are slight variations in the systems used for different waterways, and for the sake of simplicity a 'maximum draught' is quoted for each waterway, whether or not this is technically a *Tauchtiefe*.

Speed limits for pleasure craft are quoted in the section on each waterway. Where not otherwise stated, the speed limit on lakes is 25km/h at a minimum distance of 100m from the shore.

All lock operating hours relate to the summer months if not otherwise stated.

Since by far the greater number of German place names have no English translation, in the interests of consistency only the German versions of place names are used in Part II.

South

DONAU

The Donau, Europe's second-longest river after the Volga, rises on the eastern edge of the Schwarzwald (Black Forest) and flows northeastwards through the picturesque but little-known Schwäbische Alb (Swabian Mountains) to Ulm, the upper limit of navigation.

From Ulm to Kelheim the river flows through attractive Bavarian countryside. It is navigable only by small boats. Its 16 dams each have a lock and a hydroelectric generating plant.

Downstream from Kelheim, the Donau is an international waterway used for transport purposes by cargo vessels and passenger ships from many countries. The opening of the Main-Donau-Kanal completed the link between East and West, fulfilling a dream several centuries old. This part of the Donau valley is wide and flat, full of cornfields and livestock farms. To the north lies the Bayerischer Wald (Bavarian Forest), an area of outstanding natural beauty. Here and there along the river stand many fine examples of Bavarian Baroque abbeys. The brown waters of the Donau, although far from fulfilling the image evoked by Johann Strauss, do seem to carry you past a magical backdrop of beautiful countryside and picturesque towns like Regensburg, Straubing and Passau and on into Austria.

The river is administered by WSD-Süd from Kelheim to the Austrian border, and there are no fees for pleasure craft using this section.

1. ULM TO KELHEIM

Km 2585–Km 2411
Total distance 174km
Locks 16

Ulm, although technically in the *Land* of Baden-Württemberg, is undoubtedly Bavarian in nature. The birthplace of Einstein, Ulm's historic centre has been superbly restored. The *Fischerviertel* (fishermen's quarter), with its narrow cobbled streets and half-timbered houses, the riverside gardens, and the *Münster* (cathedral), with its 161m-high steeple, are all Bavarian in character.

Downstream from Ulm, the old fortified town of Donauwörth stands on a hill overlooking the confluence of the Wörnitz with the Donau. Ingolstadt, the home of the Audi car, also has a well

SOUTH

restored *Altstadt* (old town), with the remains of a city wall, half-timbered houses and exquisite Renaissance facades. 5km before reaching Kelheim the river runs through the spectacular Donaudurchbruch, a rocky gorge with 120m-high limestone cliffs, and passes the isolated Benedictine monastery of Weltenburg.

This part of the Donau is really only navigable by boats with a maximum height of 2m and draught of 1m, and special permission from the Burgermeister of Ingolstadt must be obtained if you wish to take your boat from Ulm to Kelheim. Liability insurance is obligatory, as is a technical inspection of the boat. When you apply for permission for the journey you are sent a list of dangers along the river, the chief of which are low bridges on the Ulm-Donauwörth stretch. As this part of the river is controlled by the *Land* of Bayern (Bavaria), and not by WSD, there is a charge. A permit costs DM 40, needs three weeks' notice and can be obtained only once a year. The address to write to is Stadt Ingolstadt, Postfach 21 09 64, Spitalstrasse 3, Ingolstadt, Germany. Boats with engines more powerful than 136hp are not allowed. There are no navigation marks and the current is very strong. The boat locks are 20x4m. Upstream passages are not permitted.

Schleuse Böfinger Halde is operated by lock-keepers. All others are self-service.

Km

ca2585	**Ulm**
2581·5	*Schleuse Böfinger Halde* Fall 6·50m
2578·8	Motor-Yacht-Club Ulm.
2575·0	*Schleuse Oberelchingen* Fall 5·75m
2568·4	*Schleuse Leipheim* Fall 5·85m
2562·8	*Schleuse Günzburg* Fall 5·40m
ca2560	**Günzburg**
2556·3	*Schleuse Offingen* Fall 4·55m
2551·9	*Schleuse Gundelfingen* Fall 4·55m
2545·5	*Schleuse Faimingen* Fall 5·60m
2539·0	*Schleuse Dillingen* Fall 4·65m
ca2537	**Dillingen**
2530·8	*Schleuse Höchstädt* Fall 5·75m
2522·3	*Schleuse Schwenningen* Fall 5·15m
2511·9	*Schleuse Donauwörth* Fall 5·15m
ca2510	**Donauwörth**
2490·1	*Schleuse Bertoldsheim* Fall 4·85m
2480·2	*Schleuse Bittenbrunn* Fall 5·15m
Ca2480	**Neuburg**
2470·0	*Schleuse Bergheim* Fall 6·00m
2459·2	*Schleuse Ingolstadt* Fall 5·10m
ca2458	**Ingolstadt.** Strong current
2444·1	*Schleuse Vohburg* Fall 6·80m
ca2438	*Schloss Wackerstein*
ca2432	**Neustadt**
2431·6	Harbour of Neustadt water authority
2422·5	Possible anchorage
ca2421	**Kloster Weltenburg**
2420–2416	**Donaudurchbruch.** Spectacular rocky gorge. Nature reserve. No anchoring. Strong current. Beware tripper boats.

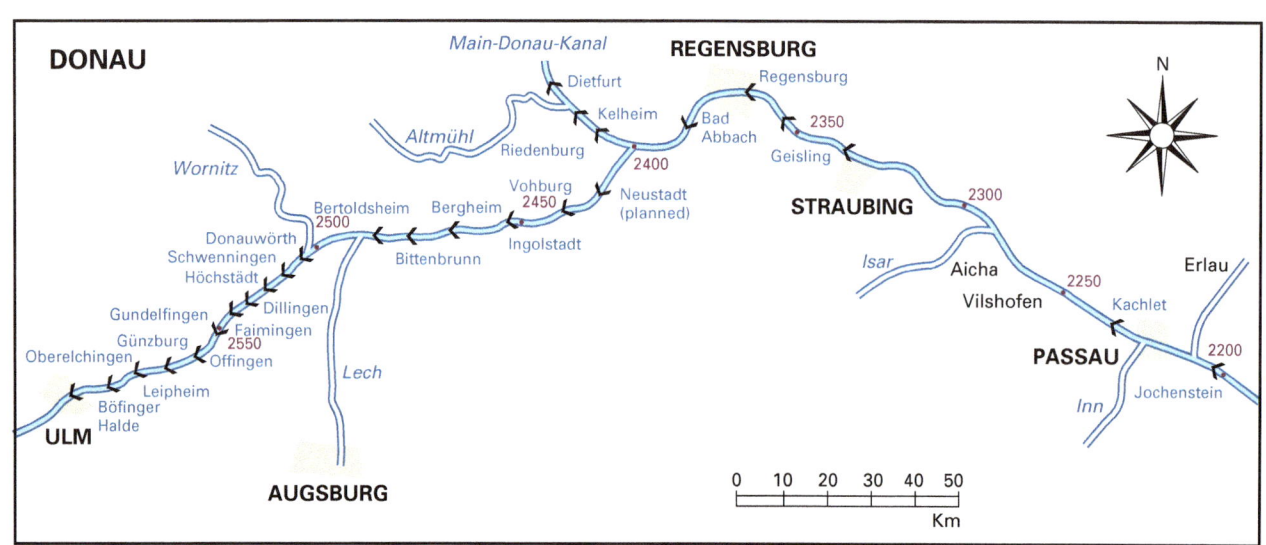

2414·7 Entrance to old Ludwig-Donau-Main-Kanal.

ca2414 **Kelheim**

2411·5 Junction with Main-Donau-Kanal.

2. KELHEIM TO AUSTRIAN BORDER

> Km 2411–Km 2202
> Total distance 209km
> Maximum draught 1·70m
> Maximum height 4·6m
> Current 4–20km/h
> Locks 6
> Hours Varied. See route description

The enchanting city of Regensburg began life as a garrison town in Roman times, and over the ages maintained a level of prosperity which can still be seen in the well preserved mediaeval buildings of the old town. It is dominated by the twin spires of St Peter's Cathedral, a superb example of Gothic architecture, and the *Steinerne Brücke* (stone bridge), built in 1146, is a masterpiece of early engineering.

Perched high on a wooded hillside overlooking the river a short distance downstream from Regensburg is the famous Walhalla, a replica of a Grecian temple built in 1842 by Ludwig I of Bavaria. Beyond Worth, with its 8-turreted castle, the river winds its way to the charming old town of Straubing, also a major centre for the thriving agricultural area surrounding the town.

Deggendorf, another attractive old Bavarian town, has colourful market stalls and a delightful promenade. Its annual *Volkfest* at the end of July and the music week in August are important events in the area.

Passing the Benedictine monastery of St Mauritius, the river flows near to Osterhofen, with the elaborate Baroque monastery church of St Margaretha, past Hilgartsberg Castle at Hofkirchen, through Vilshofen and Windorf, where there is a bird reserve on a large island, to the city of Passau, dramatically situated on a spit of land between the Donau and its broad tributary, the Inn.

With its narrow streets, elegant squares and many mediaeval buildings, Passau is a major tourist centre, but it is also a modern city with excellent facilities for sport and the arts. It hosts an annual music and drama festival, and every day at noon in summer vast crowds flock to hear a recital on the famous 17,000-pipe organ in St Stephen's Cathedral, which dominates the whole city.

At Schleuse Jochenstein, 20km below Passau, the Donau crosses the border into Austria on its long journey to the Black Sea via Vienna, Budapest and Belgrade.

The German part of the river is administered by WSD-Süd and there are no fees. Two new locks between Straubing and Kachlet (Waltendorf and Osterhofen) are planned in order to reduce the strength of the current. All locks are of a size suitable for commercial ships, but there are also boat locks at Bad Abbach and Regensburg, with a width of 4m, albeit with depth restrictions in both cases. There are fixed bollards on all locks but there is little turbulence whilst the chamber is filling, except of course near the top gates.

The river is well buoyed where appropriate, using the normal convention of reds to starboard and greens to port downstream. Kilometre signs and warning signs are also provided.

Hydrology

As with most rivers, the strength of the current and the depth of the channel vary with the rainfall in the catchment area. The river is notionally divided into four stretches, and for each stretch a depth known as the *Regulierungsniederwasserstand* (regulated lower water level), or RNW, is quoted daily. This depth corresponds to a specific depth measured at a *Pegel* (water-level gauge) situated within the stretch. The variation from this water level at the *Pegel* is then made widely available at locks, over VHF and on local radio, so that the actual depths of water along the river can easily be calculated. Unlike those along the Rhein, however, the depths thus arrived at are not guaranteed. The RNW values together with the corresponding *Pegel* readings are set out below.

> **DONAU CHANNEL DEPTHS**
> **Kelheim to Lazarettspitze-Regensburg (via Northern branch)**
> RNW 2·90m when *Pegel* Oberndorf 1·78m
> **Lazarettspitze-Regensburg to Geisling**
> RNW 2·90m when *Pegel* Regensburg-Schwabelweis 2·95m
> **Geisling to Deggendorf**
> RNW 1·70m when *Pegel* Pfelling 2·98m
> **Deggendorf to Vilshofen**
> RNW 2·00m when *Pegel* Hotkirchen 2·15m
> **Vilshofen to Kachlet**
> RNW 2·70m when *Pegel* Hotkirchen 2·15m
> **Kachlet to Jochenstein**
> RNW 2·70m when *Pegel* Passau-Donau 4·14m
> Note also:
> **Bad Abbach boat lock to end of lock cut**
> RNW 0·90m when *Pegel* Oberndorf 1·78m
> **Southern branch from Regensburg boat lock to iron bridge Regensburg**
> RNW 0·90m when *Pegel* Regensburg-Schwabelweis 2·95m

Note that in times of drought water levels can be below the RNW figures.

At RNW, the current along most of this part of the Donau is between 1km/h and 10km/h. The fastest-flowing section is in the region of Passau, Km 2230–Km 2222, where the surface water speed is around 7km/h even at low water levels. In times of flood it can run at 20km/h, and some ships may be unable to pass under several of the bridges, notably the railway bridge at Deggendorf. At such times the strength of the current can make cruising in a small boat hazardous.

From the Austrian border to the mouth of the river on the Black Sea coast the minimum depth in mid-channel is quoted as 2·30m.

SOUTH

Km

2411·5 Junction with Main-Donau-Kanal.

2411·0 Marina Saal on right bank. Depth 2·5m. Operated by Boote Rammelmeyr KG. Water, electricity, showers, fuel, repairs, crane, restaurant.

2403·5 Sportboothafen Donautal Kapfelberg on left bank. Operated by Motorsportclub Kelheim. Water, electricity, showers, fuel by arrangement, slip, shops in village.

2397·5 *Schleuse Bad Abbach*
Fall 5·7m.
VHF Ch 19
Hours 0600–2200

Boat lock on right bank. Entrance 40m above top gate of main lock. Check headroom at boat lock if water level is high.

2386·9 Sportboothafen Sinzing on left bank. Depth 1·4m. Operated by Motorboot- und-Wasserskiclub Regensburg. Water, electricity, showers, slip, crane, bar, shops and restaurant 10 minutes.

Northern branch

2379·7 *Schleuse Regensburg*
Fall 5·2m
VHF Ch 82
Hours 0600–2200

Southern branch

2381·3 *Bootschleuse Regensburg*
Fall 5·2m
Check headroom if water level is high.

2380·8 Regensburger Motorboot-und-Wassersportverein. Water, electricity, showers, repairs, crane, holding-tank emptying. Fuel from nearby filling station. Shops and restaurants in town.

ca 2380 **Regensburg**

2379·6 Steineme Brücke (stone bridge). Height 3·0–3·8m. Beware strong currents and eddies.

2377·7 Branches reunite.

2377–2372 Port of Regensburg.

2368·7 **Walhalla**. Mooring difficult because of tripper-boat traffic.

2354·3 *Schleuse Geisling*
Fall 7·3m
VHF Ch 22
Hours 24hrs

2343–2315 River narrow and with many sharp bends. Keep clear of commercial traffic.

2324·3 *Schleuse Straubing*
Fall 5·4m
VHF Ch 18
Hours 24hrs

ca2321 **Straubing**

ca2319 Entrance to weir stream, navigation permitted up to Schlossbrücke. Access to town from ferry jetty. Camp site with kiosk.

2314·0 Motorboot-und-Wasserskiclub Straubing on right bank. Water, electricity, showers, slip. Small repairs, holding-tank emptying. Shops and restaurants 2km.

2309·0 **Hermannsdorf**. Anchorage by right bank opposite entrance to Bogener Altwasser (entry forbidden) on left bank.

2305·8 **Pfelling**. Possible mooring at ferry ramp.

2297·3 **Mariaposching**. Possible anchorage near ferry by left bank.

2289·5 **Metten**. Possible anchorage at entrance to Mettener Altarm, the backwater behind Mettener island, which is a nature reserve.

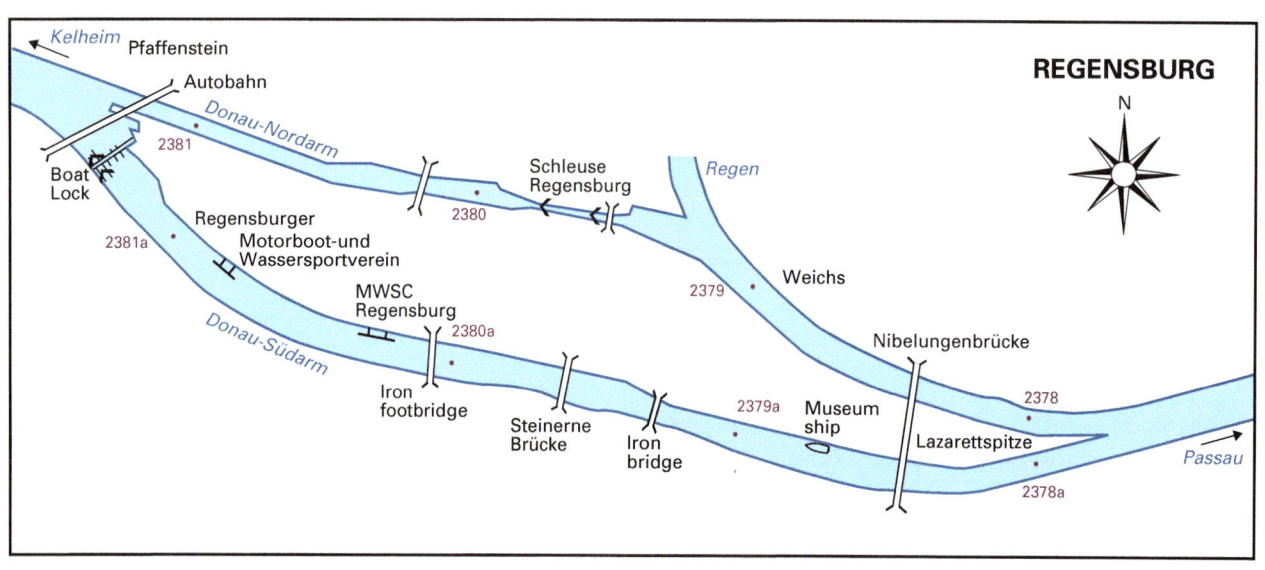

SOUTH

2288·6	Staging of Motorbootclub Deggendorf. Rudimentary facilities.
ca2285	**Deggendorf**
2284·0	Donau-Yacht-Club Deggendorf. Water, electricity, fuel 200m, restaurant.
2270·0	**Mühlham**. Small overnight mooring place for up to three boats.
2261·2	Langer Haufen. Anchor at entrance to backwater at downstream end of island on right bank. No facilities.
2257·0	**Hofkirchen**. Motorbootclub Hofkirchen. Water and electricity on the pontoon. Showers in nearby restaurant Hafenstüberl. Fuel from nearby filling station. Shops.
2249·2	**Vilshofen**. Possible mooring at commercial pontoons in river.
2237·9	Restaurant Fischerstüberl, Pontoon in river. Water. Showers in restaurant.
2232·5	**Heining**. Motor-Yacht-Club Passau on right bank. Boats up to 7m long in harbour. Larger boats moor outside. Water, electricity, showers, bar, slip, crane, small repairs.
2230·6	*Schleuse Kachlet* Fall 9·8m VHF Ch 20 Hours 0500–2300
2228·3	Hafen Passau-Racklau on right bank. Water authority harbour, but permission may be obtained for overnight mooring. No facilities.
2226·0	**Passau**. Possibility of mooring on left bank at the Luitpoldbrücke.
2225·5	Junction with River Inn. Entry forbidden.
2224·0	Restaurant Aschenberger on left bank. Staging in river.
2223–2203	Right bank Austria, left bank Germany.
2222·1	Tankschutzhafen Passau-Lindau on left bank. Possible overnight mooring with harbourmaster's permission.
2215·0	Junction with River Erlau on left bank. Possible anchorage in mouth of Erlau.
2211·4	Sportboothafen Obernzell. Two small harbours on left bank. Guest berths just inside upstream harbour. Water, electricity, showers, slip, fuel from nearby filling station.
2209·8	Customs. Austrian on right bank near ferry, German on left bank opposite.
2208·4	Sportboothafen Kasten on right bank. Water, electricity, showers, slip, crane. Fuel l50m. Shops nearby.
2205·6	Harbour of European Sea Scouts on left bank.
2203·3	*Schleuse Jochenstein* Fall 10·2m VHF Ch 22 Hours 24

Note The lock is on the border. Boats enter in Germany and exit in Austria.

MAIN-DONAU-KANAL

Total distance 171km
Maximum draught 2·50m
Maximum height 5·50m
Maximum beam 11·4m
Current Negligible
Speed limit 13km/h
Locks 16
Hours 0600–2200 weekdays, 0600–1330 Sundays

The first attempt to link the Rhein and the Donau was ordered by Charlemagne. Work started on a short canal connecting their tributaries, the Altmühl and the Rednitz, in the year 793, but the project was abandoned after a few months. Parts of the canal are still to be seen near Weissenburg.

The Bavarian king Ludwig I revived the idea, and work started in 1837 with a workforce of 6,000. The canal, linking Bamberg to Kelheim, was opened

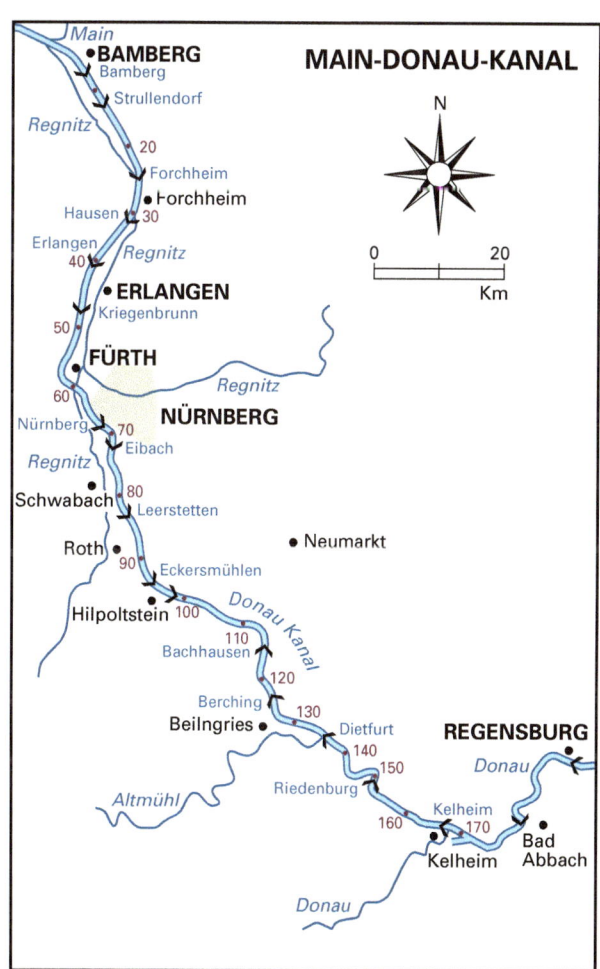

INLAND WATERWAYS OF GERMANY 25

fully in 1846. By 1850 the Ludwig-Donau-Main-Kanal was carrying almost 200,000 tonnes of freight a year. However, because the horse-drawn canal barges were not really suitable for the as yet poorly regulated Main and Donau, the canal could not compete with the booming railways. Although it remained in use until the 1940s, it is now merely an interesting relic of a bygone age.

The present Main-Donau-Kanal came into being as a result of the founding in 1892 of the Deutscher Kanal-und-Schiffahrtsverein Rhein-Main-Donau (German Rhein-Main-Donau Canal and Shipping Association). After many political attacks and uncertainties, the project finally came to fruition on 25 September 1992 with the opening of the complete link between the North Sea and the Black Sea. The diagram above demonstrates the magnitude of the engineering task which has been achieved in linking the Rhein to the Donau: 555km of waterway, 50 locks and a summit of 406m (over 1,300ft) above sea level.

The canal, which is under the control of WSD-Sld, has been built to carry both the standard 1,350 tonne *Europa* barge and the two-unit pushed train carrying up to 3,300 tonnes. Because of the shortage of water along the route, the most recent locks are of the water-saving variety, using side ponds into which 60 of the water from the lock flows when the lock empties. This means that only 40 of the water used flows into the downstream reach. The canal is also used to transport water from the Donau basin to the Regnitz-Main area, where water is less plentiful.

The traffic forecasts for the Main-Donau connection predict volumes of between 4 and 15 million tonnes per annum, and the new waterway is expected to compete strongly with existing means of transport.

The canal traverses the central part of Bayern (Bavaria), with beautiful rolling countryside and historic towns and cities, of which Bamberg and Nürnberg are the most famous.

Bamberg is a historic town of great interest, mercifully untouched by the bombs of the Second World War. Amongst its many treasures, the amazing town hall stands in the centre of the river like an anchored ship, whilst downstream from it old fishermen's houses crowd the river bank at Klein Venedig (Little Venice).

The handsome city of Nürnberg (Nuremberg), with its close associations with Adolf Hitler and the Third Reich, suffered very badly from Allied bombing in the Second World War, but has been carefully reconstructed to its former glory. Unfortunately the northern outskirts, through which the canal passes, are somewhat industrial.

Note the major restrictions on anchoring and mooring along the canal. It is necessary to plan ahead carefully to ensure safe arrival at a comfortable harbour by nightfall. It is not permitted to leave boats unmanned on the Main-Donau-Kanal.

Km

0·0	**Bamberg.** Start of canal.
2·5	Motorbootclub Regnitz-Main. In entrance to non-navigable western arm of Regnitz. Water and electricity but no sanitation.
2·6	Hafen Bamberg - *Hafenbecken* (Basin) 2. Depth 2m. 30 minutes' walk to city centre, but bus stop 2 minutes away. No facilities, but repairs can be arranged at nearby firms.
7·4	*Schleuse Bamberg* Rise 10·9m Bollards Fixed VHF Ch 20
7·4–22·2	Anchoring forbidden.
13·3	*Schleuse Strullendorf* Rise 7·4m Bollards Fixed VHF Ch 22

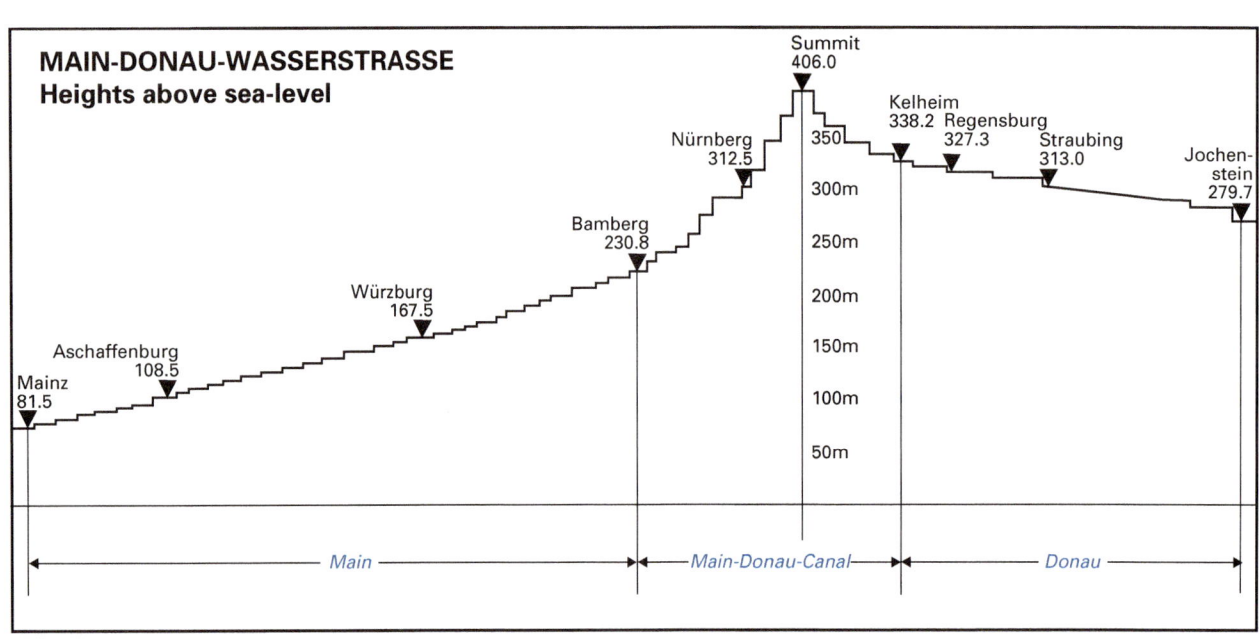

25·1	Motoryachtclub Forchheim, 0·8km into weir stream. Water, electricity, showers, slip, bar. Shops, filling station and restaurants 2·5km in Forchheim.	72·0	Hafen Nürnberg. Commercial harbour only.
25·9	*Schleuse Forchheim* Rise 5·3m Bollards Fixed VHF Ch 78	73·0	*Schleuse Eibach* Rise 19·5m Bollards Floating - east wall only. VHF Ch 20
Ca28	**Forcheim.**	84·5	*Schleuse Leerstetten* Rise 24·7m Bollards Floating - east wall only. VHF Ch 22
28·4	Yachtclub Forchheim. In entrance to old river immediately before footbridge. Water, electricity, showers, slip, bar, supermarket nearby, filling station 2km in Forchheim.	95·1	*Schleuse Eckersmühlen* Rise 24·7m Bollards Floating - east wall only. VHF Ch 78
32·9	*Schleuse Hausen* Rise 12·0m. Bollards Fixed. VHF Ch 79	Ca98	**Hilpoltstein.**
		115·6	*Schleuse Hilpoltstein* Rise 24·7m Bollards Floating - east wall only. VHF Ch 79
32·9–114·7	Anchoring forbidden.	99·1–115·6	Summit reach.
41·1	*Schleuse Erlangen* Rise 18·3m Bollards Fixed VHF Ch 81		*Schleuse Bachhausen* Fall 17·0m Bollards Floating - east wall only. VHF Ch 81
Ca45	**Erlangen**	120·0	Berchinger Yacht Club. Moor stern to buoy. Water, electricity on staging. Showers nearby. Shops and restaurants in Berching (1km). Fuel by arrangement.
47·8	Bunker boat for diesel, water and gas (propane).		
48·7	*Schleuse Kriegenbrunn* Rise 18·3m Bollards Fixed VHF Ch 82	121·0	Steganlage Berching. Staging on east bank in town. No facilities.
		122·6	*Schleuse Berching* Fall 17·0m Bollards Floating - east wall only VHF Ch 82
57·5	Sportboothafen Fürth-Unterfarrnbach. Tiny harbour on west bank. No facilities.		
Ca58	**Fürth**	128·5	Sportboothafen Beilngries. Water, electricity on staging. Showers in nearby restaurant.
65·2	Motoryachtclub Nürnberg. Finger pontoons. Water, electricity, showers, slip, bar, shops and restaurants nearby. Bus to Nürnberg, Fuel by arrangement or from filling station 10 minutes' walk away.		
		ca129	**Beilngries**
		135·4	*Schleuse Dietfurt* Fall 17·0m Bollards Floating - east wall only. VHF Ch 18
Ca66	**Nürnberg**		
69·0	Bunker boat for diesel and water.	136·6	Sportboothafen Dietfurt. Anchor in tiny basin or moor to bank. Minimal facilities.
69·1	*Schleuse Nianberg* Rise 9·4m Bollards Fixed VHF Ch 18	149·5	Sportboothafen Riedenburg. Small harbour without facilities on west bank.
		149·8–151·0	Anchoring forbidden.
72·0	Hafen Nürnberg. Commercial harbour only.		
73·0	*Schleuse Eibach* Rise 19·5m Bollards Floating - east wall only. VHF Ch 20	151·0	*Schleuse Riedenburg* Fall 8·4m Bollards Floating - west wall only. VHF Ch 20 Boat lock 20x4m on east side of main lock.
84·5	Bunker boat for diesel and water. *Schleuse Nianberg* Rise 9·4m Bollards Fixed VHF Ch 18		

SOUTH

152·6 **Riedenburg.** If not in use by passenger vessels moor to staging on west bank. Close to centre of town but no facilities.

161·5 **Essing**

161·5– Anchoring forbidden.
166·1

166·1 *Schleuse Kelheim*
Fall 8·4m
Bollards Floating - east wall only.
VHF Ch 78
Boat lock 20x4m

168·0 **Kelheim.** Staging on west bank near Altstadt (old town). Uncomfortable and no facilities. It is preferable to moor at Marina Saal in the Donau.

171·0 Junction with Donau Km 2411·5.

MAIN

Total distance 384km
Maximum draught Kostheim-Aschaffenburg 2·60m. Aschaffenburg-Bamberg 2·30m.
Maximum height 4·8m (except boat locks)
Current Negligible (can be 5km/h after prolonged heavy rain)
Speed limit None (except 8kn/h in canal at Gerlachshausen)
Locks 34
Hours Kostheim-Kleinostheim 24hrs. Obernau-Viereth 0600–2200 weekdays, 0600–1400 Sundays

The Main valley is very beautiful and very interesting. The exciting modern city of Frankfurt is the financial centre of Germany. Würzburg, 250km upstream, is one of the finest of Europe's historic cities. Most of the route, however, is amongst vine-covered slopes, attractive villages and forested hills. This is perhaps the heartland of German tradition, famous for its artists and craftsmen, but with all these riches it is off the beaten tourist track.

The waterway is controlled by WSD-Süd, and there are no fees. There were originally 37 locks between the Rhein and Bamberg, but the number was reduced to 34 by building new locks with greater lift. There is little turbulence in the locks, and all locks except two have boat locks. Some of the more modern locks have floating bollards, but in some cases whilst the channels for floating bollards exist, the bollards themselves have not been installed in them. Kleinostheim, for example, has a full set of channels, but only a few of them contain bollards.

There are many potential mooring places along the river banks, but the wash from passing ships can make many of them extremely uncomfortable. This guide does not attempt to give details of all such moorings, concentrating mainly on moorings protected from the hurly-burly of the river and thus more suitable for overnight stops.

Km

0   Junction with Rhein, Km 496·6.

1·2 Moorings at Haupt-Boot boatyard.

3·2 *Schleuse Kostheim*
Rise 3·0m
VHF Ch 20

Boat lock size 22x3·5m. Headroom 3·2m. Boat lock between main lock and the weir. Care is required when entering downstream owing to the proximity of the weir to the entrance of the lock.

SOUTH

11·5 Yacht Club Untermain. Small harbour on left bank with 2m depth. Stem to buoy. Water (not drinkable) and electricity on staging.

15·6 *Schleuse Eddersheim*
Rise 3·6m
VHF Ch 78

Boat lock size 22x3·5m. Headroom 3·2m. Boat lock on opposite side of river to main lock.

24·7 Moorings at Speck boatyard. Depth 3m. Water and electricity on staging.

28·7 *Schleuse Griesheim*
Rise 4·5m
VHF Ch 79

Boat lock size 22x3·5m. Headroom 3·2m. On opposite side of river to main lock.

29·5 **Frankfurt**. Staging provided by Speck boatyard.

31·3 Frankfurter Yachtclub. One of several stagings on left bank, with 3m depth.

33·1 Westhafen on right bank. Speck boatyard. Quiet but not very attractive. Convenient for city centre. 500m from main railway station. Water and electricity provided.

33·5 Bunker station for diesel.

38·5 *Schleuse Offenbach*
Rise 3·2m
VHF Ch 81

Boat lock size 22x3·5m. Headroom 3·2m. Between main lock and weir.

40·0 Frankfurter Osthafen on right bank. Bunker boat for diesel and chandlery.

Ca40 **Offenbach**

47·1 Sportboothafen Mainkur. 2m depth, alongside moorings in quiet harbour on right bank. Water, electricity, showers.

53·2 *Schleuse Muhlheim*
Rise 3·8m
VHF Ch 82

Boat lock size 22x4·0m. Headroom 3·7m. The newest lock on the river, built in the late eighties. It was built with only one main chamber as an economy measure. Boat lock between main lock and weir.

55·8 **Hanau**. Automobil und Motorbootclub Hanau. Staging in river. Water, electricity, showers, slip.

63·9 *Schleuse Krotzenburg*
Rise 2·7m
VHF Ch 18

Boat lock size 22x4·0m. Headroom 3·7m. Between main lock and weir.

67·0 **Kahl**. Quiet mooring on right bank. Water, electricity, showers, laundry. Engine repairs at Lassig-Motor company. Fuel by arrangement. Depth 2m.

77·9 *Schleuse Kleinostheim*
Rise 6·8m
VHF Ch 20

Boat lock size 13·8x3·5m. Headroom 3·2m.

Second newest lock on river, built in the early eighties. Some sliding bollards. Boat lock between main lock and weir.

87–88 **Aschaffenburg**. Four water-sports clubs with staging in backwater on right bank. The furthest upstream, Boots-Sport-Club Nautilus, has most facilities for visiting boats. Fuel is obtainable from a filling station close by.

92·9 *Schleuse Obernau*
Rise 4·0m.
VHF Ch 22.

Boat lock size 12x2·5m. Headroom 2·2m. Between main lock and weir.

101·2 *Schleuse Wallstadt*
Rise 4·0m.
VHF Ch 78.

Boat lock size 12x2·5m. Headroom 2·2m. Between main lock and weir.

107·0 **Erlenbach**. Erlenbacher Wassersportclub in well protected basin on right bank. Depth 2m. Water, electricity, showers. Shops and restaurants 15 minutes' walk. Filling station 1km.

113·2 *Schleuse Klingenberg*
Rise 4·0m.
VHF Ch 79.

Boat lock size 12x2·5m. Headroom 2·2m. Between main lock and weir.

122·4 *Schleuse Heubach*
Rise 4·0m.
VHF Ch 81.

Boat lock size 12·5x2·5m. Headroom 2·2m. Between main lock and weir.

Ca125 **Miltenberg**

125·1 Yacht-Club Miltenberg. Yacht harbour on right bank with 1·8m depth at entrance, reducing to 1·2m at the innermost end. Maximum length 10m. Water, electricity and showers. Town quay on left bank has 3m depth, but no protection and no facilities.

133·9 *Schleuse Freudenberg*
Rise 4·5m
VHF Ch 82

Boat lock size 12·5x2·5m. Headroom 2·2m. Between main lock and weir.

INLAND WATERWAYS OF GERMANY 29

SOUTH

144·0	Hafen Stadtprozelten. Small harbour on right bank, operated by boatyard Hock. Depth 2m. Water, electricity. Showers at boatyard. Filling station 50m.
147·1	*Schleuse Faulbach* Rise 4·5m VHF Ch 18 Boat lock size 12·1x2·5m. Headroom 2·2m. Between main lock and weir.
156·5	**Wertheim.** Motor-Yacht-Club Wertheim entrance to R. Tauber. Depth 1·5m. Water, electricity, showers.
160·5	*Schleuse Eichel* Rise 4·5m. VHF Ch 20 Boat lock size 12·5x2·5m. Headroom 2·2m. Between main lock and weir.
167·0	Yacht harbour of Wassersportverein Wertheim-Bettingen on left bank. Water, electricity, showers, laundry. Well sheltered. Shops, restaurants and filling station 1km.
174·5	*Schleuse Lengfurt* Rise 4·0m VHF Ch 22 Boat lock size 12·5x2·5m. Headroom 2·2m. Between main lock and weir.
185·9	*Schleuse Rothenfels* Rise 5·3m VHF Ch 78 Boat lock size 12·5x2·5m. Headroom 2·2m. Between main lock and weir.
198·0	**Lohr.** Town quay on right bank. Depth 2m. Filling station 300m.
200·7	*Schleuse Steinbach* Rise 5·2m VHF Ch 79 Boat lock size 12·5x2·5m. Headroom 2·2m. Between main lock and weir.
210·5	Schutzhafen Gemünden. Permission needed. No facilities.
Ca211	**Gemünden**
216·5	Wernfeld. Yachtclub Wernfeld-Main in inlet on left bank. Two basins. Visiting boats should use the upstream basin, which has a depth of 2m. Water, electricity, showers. Shops and restaurants in town on right bank (ferry).
219·5	*Schleuse Harrbach* Rise 4·9m VHF Ch 81 Boat lock size 12·5x2·5m. Headroom 2·2m. Between main lock and weir.
226·0	**Karlstadt.** Staging close to town centre.
232·3	*Schleuse Himmelstadt* Rise 4·3m VHF Ch 82 Boat lock size 12·5x2·5m. Headroom 2·2m. Between main lock and weir.
241·2	*Schleuse Erlabrunn* Rise 4·1m VHF Ch 18 Boat lock size 12·5x2·5m. Headroom 2·2m. Between main lock and weir.
248·0	Bunker boat for diesel and chandlery at entrance to commercial harbour on right bank.
252·5	*Schleuse Würzburg* Rise 2·8m VHF Ch 20 No boat lock.
252·8	**Würzburg.** Yacht-Club Würzburg immediately above lock with pontoon on right bank. Convenient for town centre. Water, electricity, showers. Shops, restaurants and filling station nearby.
253·2	Bootshaus Seubert. Entrance between posts on left bank immediately above bridge. Depth 1·5m. Water, electricity. Engine repairs.
258·9	*Schleuse Randersacker* Rise 3·3m VHF Ch 22 Boat lock size 12·5x2·5m. Headroom 2·2m. Between main lock and weir.
262·3	**Eibelstadt.** Marina Levandowski on right bank. Good shelter. Depths 1·5-1·8m. Water, electricity, showers, bar. Shops and restaurants 10 minutes away. Fuelling berth (depth 1·5m). Engine repairs.
269·0	*Schleuse Gossmannsdorf* Rise 3·4m VHF Ch 78 Boat lock size 12·5x2·5m. Headroom 2·2m. Between main lock and weir.
270·8	**Ochsenfurt.** Ochsenfurter Bootsclub at upstream end of commercial harbour. Depth 1·5-2m. Water, electricity, showers. Shops, restaurants and filling station a few minutes' walk.
275·7	*Schleuse Marktbreit* Rise 3·3m. VHF Ch 79. Boat lock size 12·5x2·5m. Headroom 2·2m. Between main lock and weir.
277·2	**Marktbreit.** Small harbour on left bank. Depth 2m. No facilities, but shops, restaurants and filling stations nearby.

284·0	*Schleuse Kitzingen* Rise 3·6m VHF Ch 81 Boat lock size 12·5x2·5m. Headroom 2·2m. Between main lock and weir.
286·5	**Kitzingen.** Convenient quay on right bank.
290·6	**Mainstockheim.** Motor-Yacht-Club Anspach in small harbour on right bank. Depth 2m. Water, electricity, showers. Showers at camping site. Shops and restaurants close by.
295·4	*Schleuse Dettelbach* Rise 5·5m VHF Ch 82 Boat lock size 12·5x2·5m. Headroom 2·2m. Between main lock and weir.
298·5	Bootshafen Mainblick. Staging and slip at camping site.
299·8	Pleasant anchorage in old river below Gerlachhausen lock. Depth uncertain.
300·5	*Schleuse Gerlachshausen* Rise 6·3m. VHF Ch 18. Lock is in 5km cut (speed limit 8km/h). No boat lock.
313·5	**Obereisenheim.** Yacht harbour of Yachtclub Frankonia on left bank.
316·3	*Schleuse Wipfeld* Rise 4·3m VHF Ch 20 Boat lock size 12·5x2·5m. Headroom 2·2m. Between main lock and weir.
316·5	Motoryachtclub Nürnberg. Immediately above weir, on opposite side of river to Wipfeld lock. Water, electricity, showers (open-air), slip. Fuel by arrangement. Shop and restaurant in village.
322·4	**Garstadt.** Schweinfurter Yacht- und Wassersportclub in harbour on right bank. Depth 1·5m. Water, showers. Shop and restaurant 10 minutes.
323·5	*Schleuse Garstadt* Rise 4·8m VHF Ch 22 Boat lock size 12·5x2·5m. Headroom 2·2m. Between main lock and weir.
330·4	Fuelling berth in commercial harbour.
332·0	*Schleuse Schweinfurt* Rise 4·6m VHF Ch 78 Boat lock size 12·5x2·5m. Headroom 2·2m. Main lock is in centre of river. Boat lock is close to right bank.
333·0	**Schweinfurt.** Town quay on right bank. Depth 2m. Quiet mooring, but no facilities.
345·3	*Schleuse Ottendorf* Rise 7·6m VHF Ch 79 Boat lock size 12·5x2·5m. Headroom 2·2m. Between main lock and weir.
350·4	Motorbootclub Obertheres on right bank. Depth 1·1m in entrance.
355·5	**Hassfurt.** Quay on right bank.
359·8	*Schleuse Knetzgau* Rise 4·3m VHF Ch 81 Boat lock size 12·5x2·5m. Headroom 2·2m. Between main lock and weir.
367·2	*Schleuse Limbach* Rise 5·3m VHF Ch 82 Boat lock size 12·5x2·5m. Headroom 2·2m. Between main lock and weir.
369·7	**Eltmann.** Yacht-Club Eltmann on left bank. Suitable for boats under 5 tonnes. Depth 2m. Water, electricity, showers, slip, crane.
380·7	*Schleuse Viereth* Rise 6·0m VHF Ch 18 No boat lock.
380·8	Motorboot-und-Wasserskiclub Bamberg. Pontoon on right bank immediately above weir. Depth 3m. Water, electricity, showers, slip.
381·9	Motorboot-und-Segelclub Coburg. Small harbour on left bank. Depth 3m. Water, electricity, showers, slip.
382·9	Sportboothafen Trosdorf. Attractive small harbour on left bank. Depth 2m. Water, electricity, showers, slip.
384·0	**Bamberg.** Junction with Main-Donau-Kanal Km 0·0.

Southwest

RHEIN

The Rhein is the third-longest waterway in Europe, after the Volga and the Donau, but by far the busiest. To cruise the full length of the Rhein, just under 900km from Rheinfelden to the sea, can take as little as seven days in a typical small cruising boat capable of travelling at a steady 5–6kn through the water. But to do it at this rate is to ignore much of the richness of interest which the river can provide. Such a journey can be a feast of history, of architecture, of art, of literature, of sociology, of food, of wine, of engineering and of transport. With so much to experience, it is a pity to hurry.

Although the source of the Rhein lies high in the Swiss Alps, the Rhein proper is generally considered to start at Konstanz on the Bodensee (Lake Constance). The Bodensee, bordered by Germany, Austria and Switzerland, is a major inland waterway, carrying a considerable amount of waterborne traffic. It has a number of major harbours and is the home of a very large number of pleasure craft. But it has no through connections to any other waterway, and therefore cannot be visited except by boats capable of being towed overland.

From Konstanz, the picturesque first 149km stretch to Rheinfelden lies partly in Switzerland and includes the dramatic Rheinfall (Rhine Falls), probably the most powerful waterfall in Europe. Until Rheinfelden the river is not navigable for anything other than small craft, and although plans for a major canalisation project to extend the navigable Rhein to the Bodensee have existed for many years, there seems little chance that they will ever come to fruition.

From Rheinfelden to the sea the river becomes a huge transport artery, carrying freighters, tankers, container ships, passenger ships, hotel ships, small seagoing ships, hydrofoils and even car-transporter ships, as well as large numbers of privately owned pleasure craft. Almost a quarter of Germany's freight travels by water, and the Rhein accounts for the biggest slice of this by far.

The Rhein flows through countryside of many types, from the meadows and windmills of the low-lying countryside near the Dutch border to the spectacular rocky crags overhanging the river in the Rhein Gorge between Wiesbaden and Koblenz; it passes through magnificent cities like Strasbourg, Koln and Bonn. It is flanked sometimes by industry and sometimes by agriculture. It traverses widely varying cultures. Its picturesque tributaries, the Neckar, the Main, the Lahn and the Mosel, are all excellent cruising grounds in their own right.

Furthermore, with its through-route connections to the French, Dutch, Polish, Czech and Austrian inland waterway systems it is also an important link in the thoroughly international waterway network which now exists in Europe.

The Rhein above Bonn is administered by WSD-Südwest, and below Bonn by WSD-West. There are no charges for leisure boats.

Hydrology

The upper sections of the Rhein have for many years been tamed by canalisation, but in the lower stretches the water levels and the currents vary widely during the year. It is therefore desirable to understand the hydrology of the river when planning a trip along it.

The primary factor in the mind of anyone involved in navigation on the Rhein is the depth of water. To enable depths to be described in a way which is useful to river users, the following system is used. For the canalised part of the river, above Iffezheim (Km 334) and below Basel (Km 179), specific minimum depths are quoted: 4·50m above Breisach (Km 227) and 3·00m between Breisach and Iffezheim. These depths are maintained throughout the year.

Below Iffezheim and above Basel the depth of water varies over a wide range during the course of the year. To demonstrate this, the variations in depth as measured at Kaub (above Köln) during 1991 are shown graphically below. The river is notionally divided into *Strecken* (stretches); for each *Strecke* there is a published *Gleichwertiger Wasserstand-Fahrrinnentiefe* (normal minimum depth), and the depth is not expected to fall below this for more than 20 days in any year. Somewhere in each stretch is a master *Pegel* (water gauge) which has a known *Pegelnullpunkt* (datum level at the *Pegel*) corresponding to the *GlW-Fahrrinnentiefe* for the stretch of river. The actual depth of water in each stretch can therefore be calculated by taking the known *GlW-Fahrrinnentiefe* and adding the difference between the current *Wasserständ* (water level) at the *Pegel* and the *Nullpunkt*. As *Wasserstände* are displayed at locks, made available over VHF radio, broadcast over local radio and even shown on local teletext services on television, it is seldom difficult to obtain the information necessary for your journey. The maximum draught quoted for

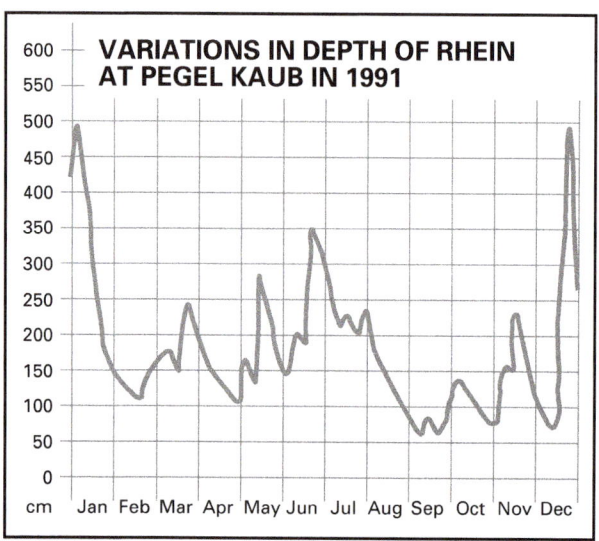

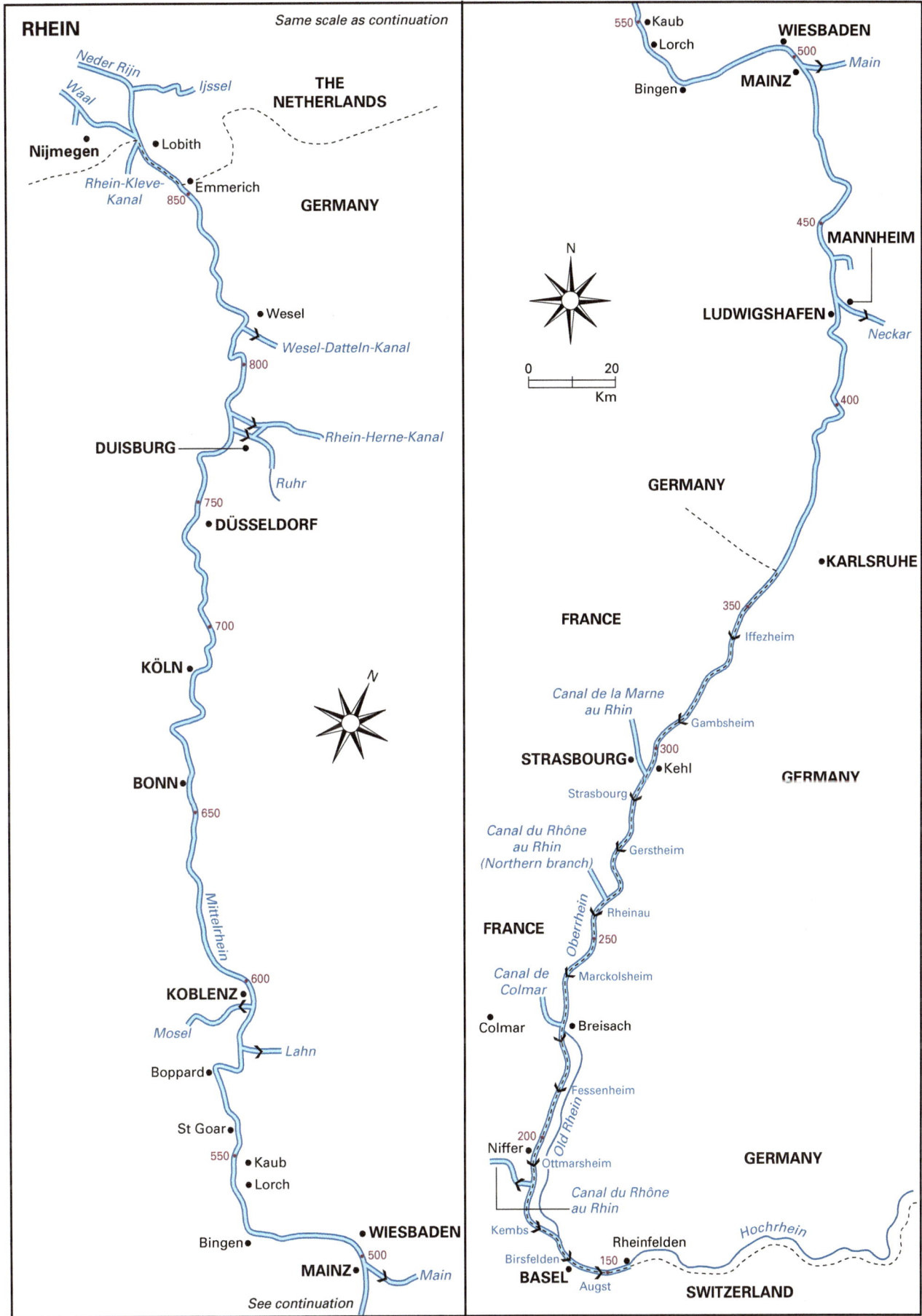

INLAND WATERWAYS OF GERMANY 33

each section of the river in the following route descriptions is based on the published *GlW-Fahrrinnentiefe* for that stretch. The *Pegels*, together with the corresponding *Nullpunkt* for each, are listed in the following table.

RHEIN *PEGELS* AND CHANNEL DEPTHS

Strecke	Pegel	Nullpunkt	GlW-F
Km 166–179	Rheinfelden	1·70m	2·50m
Km 179–334	Guaranteed minimum depth 2·50m		
Km 334–384	Maxau	3·50m	2·10m
Km 384–412	Speyer	2·15m	2·10m
Km 412–431	Mannheim	1·60m	2·10m
Km 431–462	Worms	0·70m	2·10m
Km 462–511	Mainz	1·70m	1·90m
Km 511–540	Bingen	0·60m	1·90m
Km 540–566	Kaub	0·85m	1·90m
Km 566–601	Koblenz	0·95m	2·10m
Km 601–624	Andernach	1·05m	2·10m
Km 624–660	Bonn	1·55m	2·10m
Km 660–716	Köln	1·50m	2·50m
Km 716–763	Düsseldorf	1·25m	2·50m
Km 763–794	Ruhrort	1·95m	2·50m
Km 794–837	Wesel	1·70m	2·50m
Km 837–857	Emmerich	1·10m	2·50m

At times of flood (most likely late spring), if the *Wasserstand* for each stretch reaches a predetermined level, *Marke I* (high-water mark 1), vessels are required to announce their movements on VHF. Vessels without VHF are not allowed to move. If the *Wasserstand* reaches a second predetermined level, *Marke II* (high-water mark 2), all traffic in the stretch is prohibited from moving. In the unlikely event of either situation arising during a cruise, appropriate warnings will be issued by WSP patrol vessels and displayed at relevant locks.

During exceptionally dry periods, most likely September or October, the water level may fall below the *GlW-Fahrrinnentiefe*. If this occurs barges may be forced to operate at half load, and it may become difficult for some vessels to enter many of the smaller harbours.

If the strength of the current is crucial, it is possible to find out from the appropriate WSD office the strength of the stream likely to be experienced for various water levels at the *Pegel* for each stretch. From these the current likely to be found in other stretches can be deduced.

Navigational marks

The Rhein is well buoyed wherever appropriate, using the normal convention of green to port and red to starboard when travelling downstream. It is also sufficiently well lit to enable commercial traffic (in most parts of the river) to keep going all through the night, but it is extremely dangerous for a small vessel to travel after dark. Experience of night passages at sea is not relevant to night operations on the Rhein, and skippers of leisure craft are warned against attempting night passages.

The river is also amply provided with kilometre marks and conventional navigation marks on banks and bridges (see Appendix IV).

VHF radio

The main channel allocations on UKW (VHF) are listed below. Ship-to-lock channels are given for each lock in the route descriptions.

Channel	Purpose
10	Safety and calling channel
13	Ship-to-ship and harbourmasters
15, 17	On-board communications, closed for small craft
73, 77	Ship-to-ship
18, 20, 22, 78, 79, 80, 81, 82	Nautical information (WSDIWSA)

Stopping places

As set out in the descriptions of the individual segments of the river, there is an abundance of harbours, yacht clubs and other places to tie up for the night (or a few days or weeks - or even for wintering). It is essential, however, to plan ahead carefully because of the strength of the current. It is easy to overshoot a harbour, and getting back upstream to it can be extremely hard going.

Along the canalised section of the river, in addition to normal harbours and yacht clubs, there are many places where access can be obtained to the Altrhein (Old Rhein). Although frequently shallow and perhaps unbuoyed, some of these stretches of the old river often provide attractive anchorages. Some of them too have become the homes of yacht clubs. Where possible, such places are indicated in the route descriptions which follow.

1. RHEINFELDEN TO BASEL

Km 149–Km 170
Total distance 21km
Maximum draught 3·20m
Maximum height 4·80m
Current 4–6km/h
Locks 2
Hours 0500–2100

This short stretch is the highest navigable part of the river. It runs westwards between the Black Forest in Germany and the mountains of Switzerland into the urban surroundings of Basel.

The left bank is Switzerland and the right bank is Germany, and the river is administered jointly by the Swiss authorities and WSD-Südwest.

Km

149·8 **Rheinfelden**. Hafen Rheinfelden. For commercial shipping.

152·4 Possible mooring.

155·6	*Schleuse Augst* Fall 4·6–6·6m VHF Ch 79	193·6	*Schleuse Ottmarsheim* Fall 14·7m VHF Ch 22
163·4	*Schleuse Birsfelden* Fall 5·9–9·3m VHF Ch 22	210·5	*Schleuse Fessenheim* Fall 15·1m VHF Ch 20
ca167	**Basel**	224·5	*Schleuse Vogelgrün* Fall 11·8m VHF Ch 22
170·0	Hafen Kleinhüningen. Mooring may be possible by negotiation with harbourmaster. Bunker station for diesel.		

155·6 *Schleuse Augst* Fall 4·6–6·6m VHF Ch 79

163·4 *Schleuse Birsfelden* Fall 5·9–9·3m VHF Ch 22

ca167 **Basel**

170·0 Hafen Kleinhüningen. Mooring may be possible by negotiation with harbourmaster. Bunker station for diesel.

2. BASEL TO BREISACH

Km 170–Km 227
Total distance 57km
Maximum draught 4·50m
Maximum height 6·70m
Current 4–6km/h
Locks 4
Hours 24 hour (after-dark use not recommended)

Between Basel and Iffezheim, 40km below Strasbourg, the Rhein is canalised. The stretch from Basel to Breisach is one continuous canal, with the old river running a parallel course immediately to the east. To the French this section is known as the Grand Canal d'Alsace. To the Germans it is known as the Rhein-Seitenkanal. It is wide and somewhat featureless, but the moderate current makes a downstream passage relatively fast. It is possible, for example, to complete the passage from the junction with the Canal du Rhone au Rhin at Niffer to Strasbourg well within one day.

The locks operate 24 hours a day for the benefit of commercial shipping, but it is strongly recommended that pleasure craft should not travel after dark. All locks are equipped with sliding bollards, although the amount of turbulence while the lock is filling is not serious (except of course close to the upper gates). Note that the Niffer lock, in the entrance to the Canal du Rhone au Rhin, has a lift of around 5m, and has neither sliding nor stepped bollards. It is necessary to make fast to the top of the lock.

Km

172·4 Motor- und Yacht-Club Weil. Landing stage in river.

173·7 Start of Grand Canal d' Alsace.

179·1 *Schleuse Kembs* Fall 13·2m. VHF Ch 20.

185·4 **Niffer.** Entrance to Canal du Rhone au Rhin via Niffer lock (VHF Ch 22). Port de Plaisance Kembs in Canal de Huningue through Niffer lock. Depth 2m. Water, electricity, showers, fuel, shops and restaurants 1·5km.

193·6 *Schleuse Ottmarsheim* Fall 14·7m VHF Ch 22

210·5 *Schleuse Fessenheim* Fall 15·1m VHF Ch 20

224·5 *Schleuse Vogelgrün* Fall 11·8m VHF Ch 22

225·7 Motorboot-und-Yachtclub Breisach in old river below weir on right bank. Depth 2m. Good shelter. Water, electricity, showers, slip. Shops and restaurants nearby.

226·0 **Hafen Breisach.** On right bank at entrance to old river below weir. Commercial harbour.

226·3 End of Grand Canal d'Alsace. On left bank, entrance to Canal de Colmar (23km long, depth 1·5m, 3 locks).

3. BREISACH TO IFFEZHEIM

Km 227–Km 334
Total distance 107km
Maximum draught 3·00m
Maximum height 6·70m
Current 5–6km/h
Locks 6
Hours 24 hour

Still canalised along this stretch, until Strasbourg the river continues to be somewhat featureless, but not far away to the west lies the beautiful wine-growing area of Alsace, centred on Colmar, with its own canal connecting it to the Rhein at Breisach.

It is as if the undramatic nature of the countryside along the canalised river is specially planned to enhance the drama of arriving at Strasbourg. This city must surely be one of the most attractive places to visit in Europe. Not only the cultural and economic centre of its own region, it has become the home of both the European Parliament and the Council of Europe. It has the atmosphere of a thoroughly modern cosmopolitan city, whilst successfully preserving the charm of its long history. No cruise down the Rhein should omit a leisurely stay here.

The huge locks are all equipped with floating bollards and operate 24hrs a day for the benefit of commercial shipping.

Km

227·6 Marina Schumacher on right bank. Depth 2·5m. Water, electricity, showers, restaurant. Shops 2·5km. Small repairs.

234·4 Associated watersports clubs of Burkheim on right bank above weir at Marckolsheim. Staging in river. Depth 2m. Electricity. Shops 1·5km.

SOUTHWEST

239·9 *Schleuse Marckolsheim*
Fall 13·8m
VHF Ch 20

249·0 Associated water-sports clubs of Weisweil on right bank above weir at Rhinau. Staging in river.
Depth 2m. Water, electricity. Shops and restaurants 2km, but kiosk nearby.

256·1 *Schleuse Rhinau*
Fall 12·3m
VHF Ch 22

257·9 Entrance on left bank to northern branch of the Canal du Rhone au Rhin, which has a depth of 1·8m and runs parallel to the Rhein to join the Canal de la Marne au Rhin in Strasbourg. It has 12 manually operated locks.

268·4 Yachtclub Lahr on right bank. Staging in river above Nonnenweier weir. Depth 2m. Water, electricity. Shops 3km.

272·2 *Schleuse Gerstheim*
Fall 11·0m
VHF Ch 20

287·4 *Schleuse Strasbourg*
Fall 10·8m
VHF Ch 22

289·8 Club du Port de Plaisance de Strasbourg in Bassin Adrien Haelling on left bank. Depth 2m. Water, electricity, showers, restaurant. Shops 2km.

291·3 Southern entrance to port of Strasbourg, with connection to Canal de la Marne au Rhin and northern branch of Canal du Rhone au Rhin, leading to Rhinau.

291·3 Grand Garage Ruhlmann - Base Nautique adjacent to southern entrance to port of Strasbourg. Water, electricity, repairs. Shops 2km.

293·8 Harbour of Nautic-Club Kehl on right bank. Depth 2m. Water, electricity, showers, restaurant, fuel, repairs. Shops and restaurants 1km.

295·6 Northern entrance to Strasbourg commercial harbour and to Canal de la Marne au Rhin. Mooring possible in port area.

308·2 Karcher boat yard in Altrheinarm Grossenwasser on right bank above Gambsheim weir. Depth 2m. Water, electricity, showers, repairs, slip, crane. Shops and restaurants 2km.

308·8 *Schleuse Gambsheim*
Fall 10·4m
VHF Ch 20

312·4 Entrance to Petersee (Baggersee Freistett) on right bank. Narrow channel leads to deep tree-lined lake, once a gravel pit, with a sandy beach. There are two yacht clubs, a sailing school and a boatyard. Most facilities, but shops and restaurants are 2km away.

313·7 Entrance to Baggersee Offendorf, once a gravel pit, on left bank. Ignore sign 'Wassersport Verboten'. Good overnight mooring at Marina Offendorf at far end of basin. Water, electricity, showers, restaurant (weekends only), repairs. Shops and restaurants 2·5km.

321·3 Hafen Greffern on right bank. Motor-Yacht-Club Greffern staging on port hand. Water, electricity, bar. Shops and restaurants 1km.

334·0 *Schleuse Iffezheim*
Fall 10·3m
VHF Ch 18

4. IFFEZHEIM TO KARLSRUHE

Km 334–Km 360
Total distance 26km
Maximum draught 2·10m (at normal minimum water level)
Maximum height 9·00m (at normal minimum water level)
Current 6-5km/h (at normal minimum water level)
Locks 0

The canalisation of the Rhein stops at Iffezheim, and from here downstream navigation requires more care, but the river becomes more interesting. Its banks are at once more mature, with woods, seemingly well established communities and interesting buildings. The countryside is mostly green and rural; the land, relatively low-lying and fertile, is increasingly devoted to intensive farming. Leaving behind the canalised part of the river, immediately the channel width reduces from around 200m to 90m, and the depth (at normal minimum water level - normally exceeded for most of the year) drops from 3·00m to 2·10m. Consequently the current increases dramatically. From Km 336 to Km 420 the rush of water over the uneven gravel bottom creates turbulence, with boiling eddies and whirlpools clearly visible; buoys and bridge supports all have vigorous bow waves, but in practice the speed of the current has little effect on small-boat navigation downstream.

The strength of the current does, however, vary considerably with the water level, reaching as much as 15-18km/h in times of flood. Hand-in-hand with the variations in current, the height of water too varies by several metres according to the volume of water in the river. During times of drought the depth can reduce to below the normal minimum depth of

SOUTHWEST

2·10m. In bad years barges are even forced to operate at half load because of the lack of water. Deep-draught boats, for which these reduced depths might constitute a danger, are advised to plan their journeys so as to complete this stretch of the river before mid-August, the time at which in a dry summer water levels may become exceptionally low.

There are numerous flooded gravel pits along this stretch of river, usually connected to the river by a narrow channel. Some of these have been developed for water sports and now have yacht clubs based in them, and others may be suitable as emergency overnight stops, although there is often an element of uncertainty about the depth of water. Nevertheless, as far as possible the entrances have been noted in the route description.

Km

335·4	**Hafen Beinheim.** Leaving Iffezheim lock downstream, pass under the railway bridge, then turn to port and go back upstream under the bridge into the river below the weir. The entrance to Hafen Beinheim is immediately to starboard. There are two yacht clubs, with good facilities. Restaurant in club-ship of MYC Baden-Baden. Other restaurants and shops in Beinheim (2km).
339·0	Entrance to gravel pit on left bank.
339·7	Entrance to gravel pit on left bank.
341·1	Entrance to gravel pit on right bank.
341·6	Entrance to gravel pit on left bank.
347·1	Entrance to Goldkanal on right bank. Leads into gravel pit with rowing club.
349·2	Hafen Lauterbourg on left bank. Restaurant.
354·1	Customs post in entrance to Neuburger Altrhein on right bank. All boats should still report here when entering or leaving Germany, but formalities are minimal. Care needed, as entrance not obvious. Overnight mooring possible at Yachtclub Oberrhein, immediately beyond the Customs post. Depth 1·8m. Water, electricity, shops 2km.
355·2	Entrance to Neue Lauter river. Entrance difficult due to current and underwater obstruction. Two yacht clubs. Water, electricity, cold showers, restaurant. Shops and filling station 2km.
359·9	Hafen **Karlsruhe** on right bank. Mooring prohibited.

5. KARLSRUHE TO BUDENHEIM

Km 360–Km 508
Total distance 148km
Maximum draught 2·10m (at normal minimum water level)
Maximum height 9·00m (at normal minimum water level)
Current 5–10km/h (at normal minimum water level)
Locks 0

Becoming more beautiful and more interesting with every kilometre, the Rhein now enters wine country. The two largest German wine-producing areas, the Rheinpfalz and Rheinhessen, lie near the left bank, and from the historic city of Worms northwards village names - like Nierstein and Oppenheim – take on the character of a wine merchant's list as vineyards begin to line the steepening slopes along the river.

Km

362·6	Hafen Maximiliansau on left bank. Commercial harbour. Mooring possible in northern part of harbour. Bunker boat for diesel.
362·6	Hafen Maxau on right bank. Round tower at downstream side of entrance. Depth 2m. Motorboot-Club Karlsruhe. Water, electricity, showers, restaurant in clubhouse on barge, fuel. Shops 2km.
365·8	**Karlsruhe.** Hafen Worth on left bank. Commercial harbour. Mooring possible.
373·1	Hafen Leimersheim on left bank. Depth 1·0–1·2m. Club Nautico Karlsruhe. Water, electricity. Shops 2km.
376·7	Hochstetter Altrhein on right bank. Mooring possible. Two restaurants nearby.
385·3	Hafen Germersheim on left bank. Depth 1·5m. 3 yacht clubs. Water, electricity, showers, restaurant. Shops 3km.
386·6	Entrance to gravel pit on left bank.
389·2	Entrance to gravel pit on right bank. Small canoe and rowing club near a nuclear power station.
391·8	Entrance to Oberhauser Altrhein on right bank. Large shallow lagoon.
393·5	Berghauser Altrhein on left bank. Lagoon suitable for shallow-draught boats.
399·5	Neuer Hafen **Speyer** on left bank above bridge. Marina Braun. Water, electricity, showers, fuel, slip, crane, repairs, winter storage.
400·6	Alter Hafen Speyer on left bank below bridge. Mooring possible, but subject to wash from passing ships.
405·1	Entrance to gravel pit on left bank.

INLAND WATERWAYS OF GERMANY

SOUTHWEST

406·3	Reffenthaler (Angelhofer) Altrhein on left bank. 1km inside, 4 yacht clubs with good facilities, including travel-lift. No fuel.
411·0	Otterstätter Altrhein on left bank. Depth 3m. Anchorage and marina. Water, electricity, showers, restaurant. Shops 3km.
412·4	Harbour of Motoryacht-Club Kurpfalz Mannheim on right bank. Water, electricity, showers, restaurant, fuel, repairs, shops 1km.
ca415	Hafen **Mannheim**. Commercial harbour.
416·9	Motorboot-Club Altrip on left bank in Altriper Arm. Water, showers. Shops 1km.
418·9	Entrance to Kiefweiher on left bank. 4 yacht clubs. Water, electricity, showers, repairs.
420–430	**Ludwigshafen**
421·4	Kaiserworthhafen on left bank. Commercial harbour. Emergency mooring possible.
423·8	Luitpoldhafen on left bank. Emergency mooring possible.
424–428	Several bunker boats for diesel.
427·3	Mühlauhafen on right bank. Commercial harbour.
427·6	Bunker boat for diesel on right bank.
428·0	Bunker boat for diesel and provisions on right bank.
428·1	Junction with Neckar on right bank.
431·4	Entrance to Sandhofer Altrhein on right bank. Xylon-Werft boatyard. Repairs, travel-lift.
431·7	Nordhafen on left bank. Commercial harbour.
440·3	Lampertheimer Altrhein on right bank. Entrance to 4 yacht clubs. Water, electricity, slip, showers, crane. Shops 3km.
442·1	Entrance to Motor-Yacht-Club Worms on left bank. Depth 1·8m. Water, electricity, showers, restaurant, fuel, repairs. Shops 2km.
ca445	**Worms**
462·1	Entrance to Hafen Gernsheim on right bank. Marina of Gernsheim harbour company. Water, electricity, showers, restaurant, fuel, repairs. Shops 2km.
466·0	Entrance to Eicher See on left bank. Flooded gravel pit with two sailing clubs and a restaurant. Ignore 'no entry' sign at entrance.
473·9	Entrance to Erfelder Altrhein on right bank. Navigable for 9km. Depths uncertain. Entrance needs care. Two yacht clubs.
480·4	**Oppenheim**. Hafen Oppenheim on left bank. Two small yacht clubs. Fuelling berth in harbour.
ca481	**Nierstein**
484·8–488·4	Nackenheimer Mühlarm on left bank. Backwater behind two islands. Automobil- und Wassersport-Club Oppenheim-Nierstein.
484·8	Upstream entrance to Nackenheimer Mühlarm. Closed.
486·3	Middle entrance to Nackenheimer Mühlarm.
488·4	Downstream entrance to Nackenheimer Mühlarm.
492·9	Entrance to Ginsheimer Altrhein on right bank. Bootshaus Haupt, near centre of Ginsheim. Restaurant opposite.
495·9	Hafen Gustavsburg on right bank above bridge. Commercial harbour.
496·6	Junction with Main on right bank.
497·0	Bunker station for diesel on right bank just below entrance to Main.
497·2	**Mainz**. Winterhafen Mainz on left bank. 3 yacht clubs. Water, electricity, showers, fuel, repairs, slip.
497·8	Bunker station for diesel on right bank.
498·1	Entrance to Flosshafen Mainz-Kastel on right bank. Bootsclub Maaraue. Water, electricity, showers. Shops and restaurants 1km.
501·8	Leave island to port.
502·0	Downstream entrance to Kasteler Arm on right bank in backwater behind island. Note that upstream entrance is very shallow. Two small yacht harbours. Water and electricity. Shops and restaurants 1km.
505·8	**Wiesbaden**. Hafen Schierstein. 4 yacht clubs. Water, electricity, showers, restaurant, fuel, shops nearby.
506·7	Fuelling station on left bank.
507·9	Niederwalluf. Segelclub Rheingau in small harbour on right bank. Water, electricity, showers, slip, repairs. Shops and restaurants nearby.

SOUTHWEST

6. BUDENHEIM TO ST GOAR

Km 508–Km 557
Total distance 51km
Maximum draught 1·90m (at normal min. water level)
Maximum height No bridges
Current 5–7km/h (at normal minimum water level)
Locks 0

This is the climax of any Rhein journey. The Rhein Gorge is the picture-book Rhein. On both banks high craggy hills tower over the river. Vineyards with names direct from wine merchants' shelves stream past as the current once again gathers pace. Buoys and rocks, often apparently in mid-stream, tear their way through the water; those barges and passenger boats heading upstream struggle with wide-open throttles to make headway against the current, whilst others dance their way downstream, as if almost out of control. Picture-book castles appear round every corner, perched on hill tops high above the river. The 'Mouse Tower' at Bingen, the Pfalz, the Loreley rocks - these are the images of the Rhein which we all know.

Soon after Wiesbaden the river seems to go wild. For most of the year the river is normally above normal minimum level, and so the current is generally stronger than quoted, often running at around 10–12km/h. In a small boat there is now no turning back; it feels like shooting rapids. But in fact there are no great problems so long as the helmsman looks well ahead to see the line of the channel markers and to anticipate the movements of upstream ships, many of which will be blue-flagging to avoid the strongest current as they toil upriver.

The excitement reaches its peak at Binger Loch (Bingen Hole), the 1km stretch between Km 530 and Km 531, where the current is faster than anywhere else on the whole of the navigable part of the river. After this the force diminishes, and the helmsman can relax and settle down to enjoying the drama of the terrain.

There is a long-term project in hand to dredge the Budenheim to St Goar section to a uniform 2·10m at normal minimum water level. When the work is complete the whole length from Iffezheim to Köln will have a normal depth of 2·10m. In the meantime, travellers along this stretch of the river should take care to note the relevant Pegelstand information, displayed at locks and broadcast on local radio stations as explained earlier.

Km

510·8   Burg Crass on right bank.
512·0   Leave island to port.
512–527   Nature reserves on islands.
513·3   Schloss Reinhartshausen on right bank.
516·7   Schloss Reichardshausen on right bank.
519·5   Hafen **Ingelheim**. Emergency mooring possible.
520·7   Entrance to backwater behind island at Winkel on right bank. Two yacht clubs. Possible mooring
524·5   Leave island to port.
525·3   Hafen Rüdesheim. Marina and yacht club. Water, electricity, showers, restaurant, repairs. Shops 1km.
526·6   **Rüdesheim**. Brömser Burg. Bunker boat for diesel on right bank.
527·4   Hafen Bingen on left bank just below island. Motor-Yacht-Club Bingen. Water, electricity, showers, restaurant. Shops 3km. Beware ferries.
528·4   **Bingen**
529·1   Junction with Nahe on left bank. Not navigable.
530–531   Binger Loch. The fastest current in the whole of the navigable part of the river. Current 8km/h at normal minimum water level - but often 10–12km/h and can be 20km/h at times of peak flood.
530·1   Mäuseturm (Mouse Tower) on upstream end of island near left bank.
530·5   Burg Ehrenfels on right bank.
533·0   Burg Rheinstein on left bank.
534·4   Burg Reichenstein on left bank.
537·1   Burg Sooneck on left bank.
539·0   Burg Hohneck on left bank.
539·7   **Lorch**. Small yacht club on right bank just below island. Entry difficult, but suitable for small boats.
540·8   Burg Nollig on right bank.
541·2   Burg Fürstenberg on left bank.
543·0   Burg Stahleck on left bank.
544·5   Leave island to starboard.
546·0   The Pfalz (Pfalzgrafenstein Castle) on downstream end of island.
546·5   **Kaub**. Burg Gutenfels on right bank.
548·8   Burg Schonburg on left bank.
549·7   Entrance to Hafen **Oberwesel** on left bank. Overnight mooring if space available.
550·6   Signal station A on left bank (traffic signal for commercial shipping).
552·8   Signal station B on left bank (traffic signal for commercial shipping).
553·6   Signal station C on left bank (traffic signal for commercial shipping).
554·3   Signal station D on left bank (traffic signal for commercial shipping).

SOUTHWEST

554·3 Loreley rock on right bank.

554·3 Loreleyhafen on right bank. Mooring possible but difficult.

555·4 Signal station E on left bank (traffic signal for commercial shipping).

555·9 Burg Katz on right bank. Pilot station on left bank.

556·1 **St Goar**

557·0 Hafen St Goar on left bank. New marina.

7. ST GOAR TO KÖLN

Km 557 – Km 686
Total distance 129km
Maximum draught 2·10m (at normal min. water levels)
Maximum height 9·0m (at normal min. water levels)
Current 3–7km/h (at normal min. water levels)
Locks 0

After the high drama of Binger Lock and the Lorely, the mountains become more rounded and less craggy. The steep hillsides are now covered with pine trees and terraced vineyards, but castles still cast their spells over the river. Below Koblenz, the river still flows amid steep wooded hillsides, pretty villages and attractive towns.

The current remains strong, still running at 7–9km/h, not much less than in the more dramatic stretches a little higher upstream, with much less turbulence.

Km

558·9 Burg Maus on right bank.

559–578 VHF Ch 18

559·0 Hafen 'Am Hunt' on left bank. Boats with draught greater than 1.50m should keep to upstream side of entrance. Harbour not recommended when water levels are low.

559·8 Leave promontory to port side.

565·9 Ferry crossing diagonally, arriving at Km566.9

566·2 Burg Liebenstein on right bank.

566·5 Burg Sterrenberg on right bank.

570·5 Ferry

ca571 **Boppard**

578–617 VHF Ch 22

579·3–580·4 Follow navigation buoys to avoid 'Braubacker Grund', a shoal of shallow water in centre of river.

579·9 Burg Marksburg on right bank.

584·5 Ferry crossing from right bank diagonally to left bank at Km585.4 then back to right bank at Km585.9

Schloss Stolzenfels Km 585.2

585·2 Burg Stolzenfels on left bank.

585·7 Junction with Lahn Km137.3 on right bank. Hafen Oberlahnstein at junction not for sport boats.

Bootshaus Radermacher at 0.5km into Lahn on Starboard side between the two bridges. Water, electricity, restaurant. Shops and railway station nearby.

589-594 **Koblenz**

590·0 Hafen Rheinlache on left bank. Wassersportfreunde Oberworth. Guest moorings, water, electricity, repairs.

591·3 Hafen Ehrenbreitstein on right bank, not for sports boats.

591·4 Rhein-Marina on right bank. Limited guest moorings, water, electricity ✆ 0261 71275.

591·5 Ferry crossing.

592·3 Junction with Mosel Km 0·0 on left bank.

594·0 Keep left, leaving island to starboard.

Junction with the Lahn Km 585.7

SOUTHWEST

Rhein at Km 615

605·7 Yacht club staging on right bank. Subject to current. MYC Neuwied, guest moorings max length 20m, water, electricity, shower, WC, club house, service and repairs, fuel.

606·0 Passage either side of island.

ca608 **Neuwied**

611·8 Hafen Andernach, left bank, not for sports boats.

ca612 **Andernach**

613·0 Ferry crossing.

615·7 Burg Namedy.

617-624 VHF Ch 18

617-618 Island near right bank. Shallow waters on south side. Enter at Km 618 via North Side only, for mooring between island and right bank possible at two small yacht clubs. No facilities. Nature reserve.

617·8 Burg Hammerstein on right bank.

621·6 Hafen Brohl on left bank. Not for sports boats.

622·8 Ferry crossing.

623·8 Ferry crossing.

624-632 VHF Ch 22

624·8 Schloss Arenfels on right bank.

628·8 Schloss Dattenberg on right bank.

629·9 **Linz**. Ferry crossing.

630·7 Burg Ockenfels on right bank.

632-640 VHF Ch 18

632·9 Brück von Remagen Museum – destroyed during the Second World War.

Cars waiting for the ferry at Linz Km 629.9

Ruins of 'Brucke von Remagen' Km 632

INLAND WATERWAYS OF GERMANY **41**

SOUTHWEST

634·2 Ferry crossing.
634·4 Kloster Apollinarisberg on left bank.
635·6 Schloss Marienfels on left bank.
636·5 Ferry crossing.
639·1 Hafen Oberwinter on left bank. Yacht-Club Mittelrhein and Bonner Yacht-Club ☏ 02228 910177. Guest moorings, water, electricity, showers, WC, restaurant, repairs, fuel, shops, slip, crane, shops nearby. Internet in the restaurant.
639·4 Repairs service on left bank. ☏ 02228 8077
640-702 VHF Ch 22
640·2 Ferry crossing.
641·5 Ferry crossing.
642·0 Yacht club behind island near right bank. Entrance below island. Water, electricity, showers, WC, restaurant, slip. Shops 1km. Small repairs.
643·8 Castle ruin Drachenfels, right bank.
644·2 Drachenburg, right bank.
647·8 Ferry crossing.
655·1 Ferry crossing.
650-660 **Bonn**
659·7 Hafen Mondorf on right bank. Two yacht clubs. Water, electricity, shops, restaurant, slip, repairs.
661·0 Upstream entrance to channel behind Herseler Werth Island on left bank. Depth can be problematic. Water, electricity, shops 1km.
662·4 Downstream entrance to channel behind Herseler Werth. Anchoring may be possible.
668–669·5 Ferry crossing.
672·0 Hafen Godorf-Wesselig on left bank not for sports boats.
675·1 Sürther Boothaus on left bank, guest moorings max 9m length.
676·4 Ferry crossing.
677·3 Hafen Porz-Zündorf on right bank. Guest moorings, water, electricity, showers, WC, clubhouse. ☏ 02203-9810170. Shops 1km.
680-700 **Köln**
702-745 VHF Ch 23

8. KÖLN TO DUISBURG

Km 686 – Km 780
Total distance 94km
Maximum draught 2·50m (at normal min. water levels)
Maximum height 9·0m (at normal min. water levels)
Current 3–7km/h (at normal min. water levels)
Locks 0

The route now passes through the industrial heartland of Germany; but there is little ugliness. From the river, the view remains remarkably rural until Düsseldorf, and even amidst the steelworks, power stations, petrochemical plants and chemical factories of the area around Düsseldorf and Duisburg, the impression one gets, is of modern, well planned industrial complexes and often exciting architecture.

Km

700 **Köln**
702-745 VHF Ch 23
687·3 Deutzer Hafen on right bank. Not for sports boats.
687·5 *Pegel* Köln ☏ 0221-19429, left bank.

Köln

Entrance to KAMC Köln, Km 687.5

42 INLAND WATERWAYS OF GERMANY

SOUTHWEST

MYC Hilde at Hitdorf Km 706.8

687·5 Rheinauhafen on left bank. Bridge at entrance opens on three long blasts, between 0700–2300 ① 0221 3900/3900 or 0172 225226320.

Yachthafen KAMC ① 0221 9320585 Guest moorings, water, electricity, showers, WC, fuel, slip. Shops and restaurants.

Fa. Marine Olbermann for repairs and services. ① 0221 9318180.

691·5 Hafen Mülheim. Not for sports boats.

695·7 Köln-Diehl commercial port. Not for sports boats.

699·0 Ölhafen Köln-Niehl, left bank. Not for sports boats.

701·2 Yachthafen des Leverkusener, right bank. Water, electricity, pump-out ① 0214 66881.

707·0 Hafen Hitdorf on right bank. Four Yacht Clubs. Water, electricity, showers, WC, 12-tonne crane, services. Baker, shops and restaurants nearby.

709·6 Hafen Worringen on left bank. Commercial harbour, not for sports boats.

705·4 Ferry crossing.

730–730 **Düsseldorf.**

735·2 Yacht harbour on right bank. Small yachts only.

735·5 Neusser Sporthafen (napoleonshafen) on left bank. Three yacht clubs. Water, electricity, slip, repairs. Shops and restaurants. ① 02131 177576.

740·5 Entrance to Erftkanal on left bank. Not for sports boats.

743·1 Entrance to Hafen Düsseldorf on right bank near television tower. Yacht club in Becken (Basin) A and C. Guest moorings max length 20m. Water, electricity. Bunker boat for diesel.

Marina in Zollhafen at entrance to industrial harbour. Water, electricity, showers, WC, crane, repairs. Shops and restaurants nearby.

Convenient for centre of Düsseldorf.

745–754 VHF Ch 18

746·3 Düsseldorfer Sporthafen on right bank. Small boats max length 6m.

747·2 Yachthafen Düsseldorf on right bank. Three yacht clubs. Water, electricity, showers, WC, slip, repairs, shops, restaurants.

748·9 *Pegel* Düsseldorf ① 0211-19249

748·9 Wassersporthafen Düsseldorf-Lörick (Paradieshafen) on left bank. 4 yacht clubs. Limited guest moorings, ① 0163 4350377. Water, electricity, showers, WC. Shops, restaurants 1km.

754–762 VHF Ch 23

761·8 Entrance to yacht harbour of Crefelder Yacht-Club on left bank. Depth 2m. Guest moorings, sheltered harbour, water, electricity, showers, WC, clubhouse, restaurant, repairs. Shops 1km.

762–810 VHF Ch 18

763·9 Entrance to Hafen Krefeld-Uerdingen on left bank. Entry only from below bridge. Yacht club 2km into harbour. Water, electricity.

770–790 **Duisburg**

Yachthafen des Crefelder Km 761.8

Duisburg

INLAND WATERWAYS OF GERMANY 43

SOUTHWEST

9. DUISBURG TO LOBITH

Km 780 – Km 863
Total distance 83km
Maximum draught 2·50m (at normal min. water levels)
Maximum height 9·0m (at normal min. water levels)
Current 3–7km/h (at normal min. water levels)
Locks 0

The heavy industry of Duisburg is soon left behind, and the countryside becomes once more rural; but it now begins to take on an increasingly Dutch character, low-lying, verdant with cattle grazing on the river banks. The architecture too, demonstrates the same shift in style as the Dutch border approaches.

Km

773·5	Entrance to Hafen Reinhausen, left bank. Not for sport boats.
776·6	Right bank, entrance to Aussenhafen – Marina Duisburg in Innenhafen, a modern marina with guest moorings, WC, shower, water, electricity, fuel, service repairs. ☎ 0203 2895697.
780·1	Junction with Ruhr.
780·4	Junction with Rhein-Herne-Kanal.
780·5	Bunker boat for diesel on left bank just before bridge.
780·6	Entrance to Duisburg Hafenmund and Kaiserhafen on right bank under bridge.
781·0	Entrance to Eisenbahnhafen on right bank below bridge. Ruhrorter Yacht-Club. Guest moorings, water, electricity, showers, restaurant, clubhouse ☎ 0203 82409.
790·2	Hafen Schwelgern on right bank.
791·2	Südhafen Walsum on right bank.
792·5	Car ferry crossing.
793·0	Nordhafen Walsum on right bank. WSV Walsum small landing stage.

Bunker Barge Km 780.5 Duisburg

Pegel Wesel Km 814.1

Yachthafen Wesel Km 816.5

810-835	VHF Ch 22
813·2	Junction with Wesel-Datteln-Kanal on right bank.
814·0	*Pegel* **Wesel** ☎ 0281 19429.
814·6	Hafen Wesel on right bank.
816·5	Entrance to Yachthafen Wesel on right bank. Two yacht clubs. Guest moorings, water, electricity, showers, slip, crane, repairs. ☎ 0281 21885 and 0281 22073. Shops 2km.
820·8	Entrance to Flurener Altreheim, anchoring permitted.
823·5	Car Ferry crossing.
835-865	VHF Ch 18
837·2	*Pegel* Rees on right bank.
838·0	Entrance to gravel pit on left bank. Wassersportverein Xanten. ☎ 0171 7674059. Water, electricity. Shops 1km.
842·7	Entrance to gravel pit on right bank. Three yacht clubs. Water, electricity. Clubhouse. ☎ 02851 1867 or 0172 9401793. Shops 5km.
845·1	Passenger ferry
851·7	Hafen Emmerich and Container Port on right bank. Not for sport boats.

SOUTHWEST

Pegel at Rees Km 837.3

Entrance to Bijland-Plas anchorage, Jachthaven De Bijland and fuel station for leisure craft, Km 864.2

Pegel at Emmerich Km 852

851·8	**Emmerich**. Zollhafen (Customs Harbour for non EU vessels) adjacent to Container Port, on right bank.
852·0	*Pegel* Emmerich ☎ 02822 19429.
853·7	Entrance to Sporthafen Emmerich on right bank. Yacht club and marina. ☎ 02822 538150. Guest moorings, water, electricity, showers, restaurant, slip, repairs, 29 tonne-crane. Shops 2km.
857·7	Dutch-German border on right bank.
862·0	Fuel Bunkers on right bank.
862·4	**Lobith Tolkamer** right bank.
863·3	Vluchthafen Lobith-Tolkamer for commercial vessels on right bank.
863·9	Junction with Rhein-Kleve-Kanal (Schiffahrtsweg Kleve) on left bank.
864·3	Entrance to gravel pit De Bijland on right bank.
	Depth 1·7m at entrance even at lowest water levels. Keep close to stone groyne on upstream side of entrance side of entrance to avoid shallow patch marked by buoy. Fuel bunker boat for leisure craft immediately inside after bridge. Major yacht harbour 1km to starboard. Quiet mooring. Depth 3–4m.
865·5	Dutch-German border on left bank.
866·0	Bunkerstation Millingen fuel and provisions for commercial vessels on left bank.

NECKAR

Length 201km
Maximum draught Feudenheim-Lauffen 2·50m
Lauffen-Plochingen 2·30m
Maximum height 5·50m
Current Negligible except during flood conditions.
Locks 27. None equipped with floating bollards
Hours From Feudenheim to Heilbronn inclusive the locks operate 0600–2200 Mon–Sat and 0800–1600 Sundays. From Horkheim to Deizisau inclusive they operate Mon–Sat 0600– 2100 and Sunday 0800–1600
Speed limits 18km/h in river, 14km/h in canalised sections

From its source, close to that of the Donau, in Baden-Württemberg to the east of the Schwarzwald (Black Forest), the Neckar makes its way through Stuttgart, a modern city built almost from scratch after being destroyed by Allied bombing, and famous as the home of Mercedes and a centre of the arts. Navigable from Plochingen, a little way above Stuttgart, the river meanders northwards to Heilbronn and then winds majestically through the rolling wooded hills of the Odenwald (Oden Forest), between steep hillsides covered with pine trees and vines and with castles sitting on hill tops. Finally, it runs through the legendary university city of Heidelberg to join the Rhein.

Heading upstream from the Rhein, Heidelberg is the first of the many essential stopping places on the Neckar. Although somewhat overrun by tourists, Heidelberg is a wonder of preservation. It is difficult to believe that the historic gabled buildings and cobblestone streets of the Altstadt are real and not a film set.

Continuing upstream towards Stuttgart, with huge sweeping bends and spectacular tree-covered hillsides, it is sheer joy to travel up the river:

SOUTHWEST

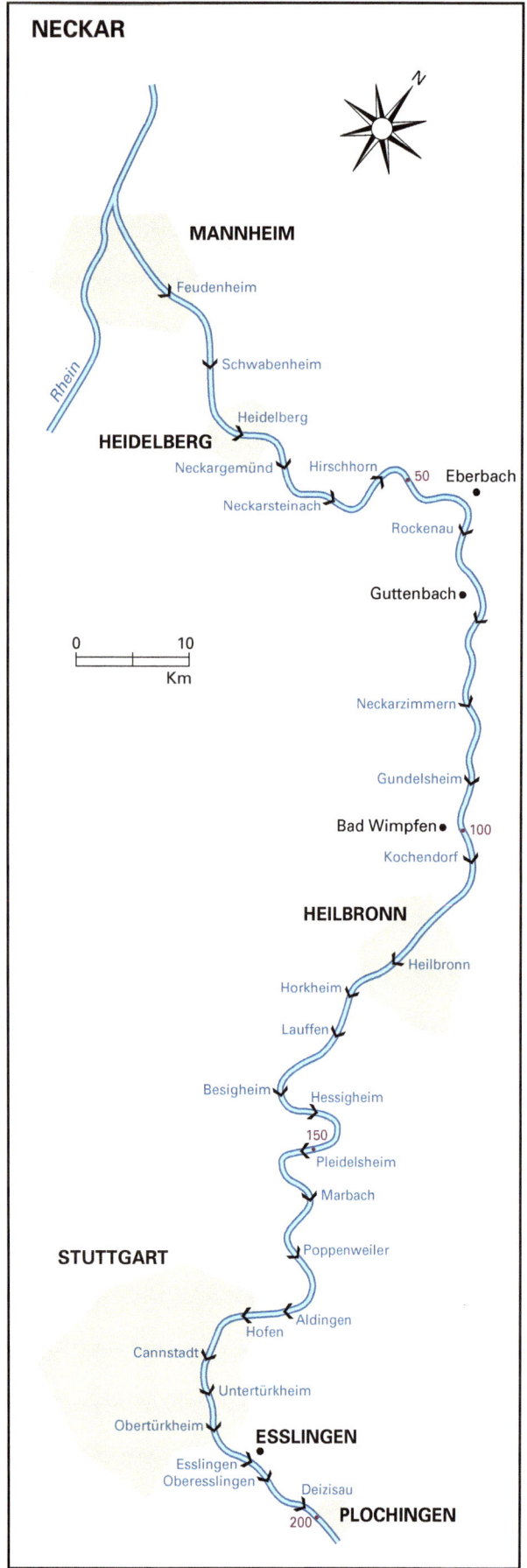

Neckarsteinach, with its four hill-top castles, Hirschhom, Burg Guttenberg, Bad Wimpfen: each one a delight to the eye.

Since the river is entirely canalised along its navigable length, its depth is closely controlled. The current too is normally slight, although heavy rainstorms can cause a sudden swelling of the stream and a strong current can be generated, taking the unwary by surprise.

The Neckar is administered by WSD-Südwest. There are no charges.

Km

0·0	Junction with Rhein Km 428·2.
6·2	*Schleuse Feudenheim* Rise 5·6–10m (depends on level in Rhein) VHF Ch 20
17·7	*Schleuse Schwabenheim* Rise 8·7m VHF Ch 78
23–27	**Heidelberg**
ca24	Three yacht clubs on left bank. Pontoons in river. Water, electricity, showers, clubhouse, crane, repairs. Shops and restaurants nearby in city centre.
26·1	*Schleuse Heidelberg* Rise 2·6m VHF Ch 79
28·7	Motor-Boot-Club Heidelberg. Staging in river on left bank. Depth 2m. Water, electricity, showers. Bus stop to city centre.
30·9	*Schleuse Neckargemund* Rise 3·9m VHF Ch 81
34·2	**Neckargemünd**. Junction with Elsenz on left bank. Bank mooring 2m.
ca38·5	**Neckarsteinach**. Possible but uncomfortable mooring at pleasure-boat landing on right bank if a vacant space can be found.
39·3	*Schleuse Neckarsteinach* Rise 4·7m VHF Ch 82
39·4	Good mooring at Dilsberg, immediately above lock on left bank.
40·1	Boatyard on right bank. Repairs.
Ca47	**Hirschhorn**. Town quay on right bank below lock. Depth 2m. Beware strong currents from weir following heavy rain. No facilities.
47·7	*Schleuse Hirschhorn* Rise 5·3m VHF Ch 18

SOUTHWEST

Ca57·5 **Eberbach**. Small landing stage at camp site on left bank. Also possibility of mooring at downstream end of town quay on right bank, out of the way of passenger ships.

61·4 *Schleuse Rockenau*
Rise 6·0m
VHF Ch 20

Supermarket near lock.

63·1 Krösselbach, Mooring possible at private quay on left bank. Depth 2m. No facilities, but repairs possible at Neckarsport.

63·2 Possibility of mooring at Lindach on right bank close to ferry. No facilities.

66·2 Motor-Yachtclub Neckar. Staging on left bank. Deepest water 1·60m near ferry. Water, electricity, showers, clubhouse. Shops and restaurants nearby.

69·6 **Neckargerach**. Quay on right bank. Depth 2·50m. No facilities, but shops and restaurants nearby.

72·2 *Schleuse Gütenbach*
Rise 5·3m.
VHF Ch 22

75·8 **Binau**. Staging at camp site on right bank. Water, electricity, showers, restaurant, swimming pool.

80·8 **Obrigheim**. Motor-Boot-Club Obrigheim on left bank. Depth 1·20m. Water, electricity, showers. Shops and restaurants nearby.

86·0 *Schleuse Neckarzimmern*
Rise 5·6m
VHF Ch 78

Good mooring place above lock on left bank. Shops, including chandlery.

86·2 Boatyard on right bank. Depth 1·20m.

86·5 Burg Hornberg on right bank.

87·3 Possibility of using river authority harbour on left bank. Depth 1·20m. No facilities.

88·2 **Hassmersheim**. Possibility of mooring close to ferry.

88·6 Bunker boat for diesel on left bank.

91·2 **Neckarmühlbach**. Possibility of mooring in 2·5m at new quay on left bank. No facilities.

93·0 **Gundelsheim**. Quay on right bank. Depth 2·50m. No facilities, but shops and restaurants in village.

93·9 *Schleuse Gundelsheim*
Rise 4·2m
VHF Ch 79

Long stretch of left bank with bollards above lock. Suitable for overnight mooring after barges stop for the night. Depth 2·5m. No facilities.

98·3 **Offenau**. Motorboot-Club Mittlerer Neckar. Staging on right bank.

Ca100 **Bad Wimpfen**. Picture-book mediaeval town high above left bank. Possibility of mooring at end of passenger landing stage.

103·0 Yacht club in backwater on left bank. Depth 1·30m. No facilities.

103·9 *Schleuse Kochendorf*
Rise 8·0m
VHF Ch 81

108·0 Osthafen Heilbronn. Possibility of mooring if a space is vacant. Depth 2·00m. Water, electricity, repairs.

110·6 Old branch of river, leading to the 1521-built, self-operated Wilhelmschleuse, bypassing main lock (Schleuse Heilbronn). Suitable for boats of up to 1·20m draught.

112·0 **Heilbronn**. Bunker boat in old river on left bank below lock.

113·6 *Schleuse Heilbronn*
Rise 3·2m
VHF Ch 82

Situated in new branch of river.

114·0 Württembergischen Motor-Boot-Club Heilbronn in old branch of river above Wilhelmschleuse. Depth 2·00m. Water, electricity, showers, clubhouse, repairs. Shops and restaurants nearby. The largest yacht club on the Neckar.

117·0 Entrance to old branch of Neckar on left bank below Schleuse Horkheim. Depth 2·00m. Mooring to bank.

117·5 *Schleuse Horkheim*
Rise 7·3m
VHF Ch 18

124·2 Entrance to old Neckar on left bank at entrance to lock cut. Depth 2·00m. Mooring to bank.

125·2 *Schleuse Lauffen*
Rise 8·4m
VHF Ch 20

Overnight mooring possible on left bank below lock.

136·3 *Schleuse Besigheim*
Rise 6·3m
VHF Ch 22

137·5 Bootshafen Waiter on left bank. Cramped, but possibility of overnight stay. Water, electricity, showers. Shops and restaurants nearby.

143·0 *Schleuse Hessigheim*
Rise 6·2m
VHF Ch 78

150·1 *Schleuse Pleidelsheim*
Rise 8·0m
VHF Ch 79

SOUTHWEST

155·5 Motor-Boot-Club Binningen on left bank. Depth 1·30m. Water, electricity, showers, clubhouse.

157·6 *Schleuse Marbach*
Rise 6·0m
VHF Ch 81

165·0 *Schleuse Poppenweiler*
Rise 7·0m
VHF Ch 82

Mooring possible on right bank for 1 km above lock.

166·5 Motor-Boot-Club Poppenweiler on right bank. Wash from passing vessels can be severe. Water, electricity, showers, clubhouse.

168·8 Boatyard on right bank. Depth 2·5m. Repairs. Wintering possible.

170·1 Small yacht club behind island near right bank. No facilities. Depth 2·00m.

170·5 Junction with Rems. Mooring to bank possible inside entrance. Shops and restaurants nearby.

172·0 *Schleuse Aldingen*
Rise 3·6m
VHF Ch 18

176·3 *Schleuse Hofen*
Rise 6·8m
VHF Ch 20

176·5 Bootshaus Sonder on right bank. Water, electricity, showers. Tram to Stuttgart centre.

178·5 Signal station for upstream and downstream traffic. Observe red and green lights.

180-190 **Stuttgart**

182·7 *Schleuse Cannstadt*
Rise 5·4m
VHF Ch 22

Boat lock size 11·4x2·4m. Headroom 2·7m. Self-service.

186·5 *Schleuse Untertürkheim*
Rise 3·7m
VHF Ch 78

Ca188 Hafen Stuttgart. Very large commercial harbour.

189·5 *Schleuse Obertürkheim*
Rise 8·4m
VHF Ch 79

194·0 *Schleuse Esslingen*
Rise 5·2m
VHF Ch 81

194·8 *Schleuse Oberesslingen*
Rise 5·9m
VHF Ch 82

196·8 Harbour of Motor-Yacht-Club Esslingen. Behind island. Depth 2·00m. Water, electricity, showers, clubhouse. Tram to Esslingen and then S-Bahn train to Stuttgart centre.

199·6 *Schleuse Deizisau*
Rise 5·1m
VHF Ch 18

200·1 **Plochingen**. Yachtclub Plochinger Wassersportfreunde on right bank. Quay, water, electricity, showers, clubhouse. Shops and restaurants 1·5km.

201·5 End of navigation.

LAHN

Navigable distance 67·3km
Maximum draught 1·5m
Maximum height 3·2m (when river at its highest for navigation)
Maximum beam 5·25m
Current Negligible except in times of flood
Locks 12
Hours 1 April to 31 October, Mon–Sun 1000–1200 & 1230–1830. 1 November to 31 March closed
Speed limit 12km/h

The Lahn must be one of the most attractive waterways in Europe for cruising, with no commercial traffic (apart from three passenger vessels), the river winds its way along a beautiful valley amongst steep wooded hills. Postcard villages nestle at every bridge and castles tower over the valley from their hill-top vantage points and several nature reserves in the vicinity of Nassau. It is being mooted that this river may be closed for navigation during the next few years; so if you have the opportunity, use it now.

There are 12 locks on the 67km river and with a minimum depth of 1·60m it is perfectly practicable for boats drawing 1·50m to navigate its waters. Boats drawing more than 1·20m are advised to keep to the centre of the channel as far as possible. A very popular river with canoeists and leisure craft. Boats with shallower draughts are expected to give way. There are plenty of excellent places for overnight mooring.

In summer there is normally very little current, but the river does swell rapidly after heavy rain. When *Pegel* Kalkofen reaches 3·60m all navigation is temporarily stopped. The locks are not equipped with VHF radio.

Kilometering starts at Giessen, 70km above the practical navigable limit at Dehrn near Limburg. Although the locks on the river above Dehrn are maintained in good working order, the river is navigable only by canoes and small boats. There is also a staircase lock and tunnel (the only one in Germany) at Weilburg.

SOUTHWEST

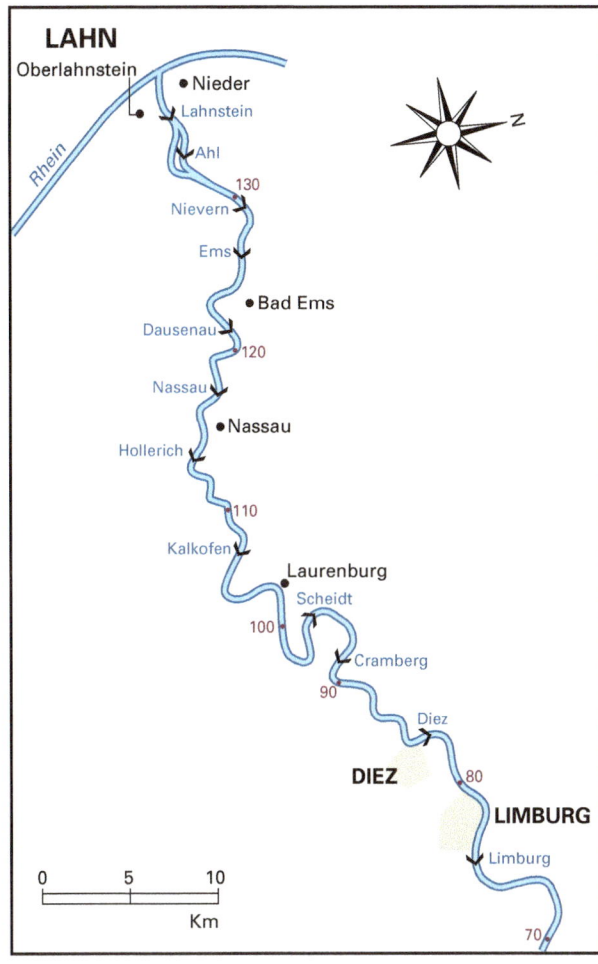

Schleuse Ahl Km 133.1

Km

137·3 Junction with Rhein Km 585.7. VHF Ch 10

136·6 **Lahnstein**. Bootshaus Radermacher on left bank above railway bridge. Guest moorings. Water, electricity, repairs, restaurant. Shops nearby. Railway stations close by; Oberlahnstein on left bank and Niederlahnstein on north side.

136·0 *Schleuse Lahnstein*
Rise 6·0m
Length 42·0m
Breadth 5·34m
☏ 02621 62558

Mooring for pleasure craft permitted above lock, only between 1800–1000.

135·1 Boatyard on right bank. Water, electricity.

134·3 Yacht-Club Lahn on right bank. Guest moorings. Water, electricity, WC, shower.

133·1 *Schleuse Ahl*
Rise 3·0m
Length 34·0m
Breadth 5·35m
☏ 02621 8563

Beware narrow exit/entry channel above lock.

132·4 Boatyard on left bank above weir. Repairs, service, 25-tonne crane, slip.
☏ 02621 40550.

129·4 *Schleuse Nievern*
Rise 3·4m
Length 45·0m
Breadth 6·30m
☏ 02603 14527

Bootshaus an der Lahn Km 136.6

INLAND WATERWAYS OF GERMANY **49**

SOUTHWEST

128·8 Narrow channel, take care on exiting, strong weir on left side.

127·0 *Schleuse Ems*
Rise 3·1m
Length 47·0m
Breadth 5·35m
☎ 02603-70540

126·8 Yachthafen Bad Ems, tight right angled entry on left bank. Max 15m length, max 1·3m depth. Guest moorings, water, electricity, shower, toilet. ☎ 02603 4297. Shops nearby.

126·5 Boat Service Kutscher on left bank. Fuel, repairs, 6·6-tonne crane and 90-tonne mobile crane.

ca.125 **Bad Ems**. Guest bank side short jetty mooring points through town. Shops, restaurants nearby.

125·0 Fountain in middle of river.

124·6 Double bridge beware of sloping bridge, max height 3·20m when river at its highest for navigation. Height can be 3·9m under normal conditions.

124·0 Mototboot-Club Bad Ems on right bank. Guest moorings max 14m length, water, electricity. ☎ 0163 6604093. Shops, restaurants nearby.

122·4 *Schleuse Dausenau*
Rise 3·5m
Length 34·0m
Breadth 6·0m
☎ 02603-3609

120·7 **Dausenau**. Motor-Yacht-Club Siegerland on right bank. Guest moorings, water, electricity. Shops and restaurants nearby.

117·6 *Schleuse Nassau*
Rise 3·8m
Length 34·0m
Breadth 6·0m
☎ 02604 5557

Sloping bridge arch at Bad Ems Km 124.6

ca.117 **Nassau**

116·8 Burg Nassau, left bank.

113·1 *Schleuse Hollerich*
Rise 5·2m
Length 34·0m
Breadth 5·34m
☎ 02604 5444
Drinking water available at lock house by request only.

113·0 Attractive rural yacht harbour above weir. Guest moorings, non-drinking water, electricity. No other facilities. Max depth 1·5m on outside guest quayside.

106·5 *Pegel* Kalkofen on right bank.
☎ 06439-19429

105·8 *Schleuse Kalkofen*
Rise 5·5m
Length 46·0m
Breadth 5·8m
☎ 06439 57111

104·8– Water-skiing area.
103·6

102·5 **Laurenburg**. Fuel available from filling station close to right bank. Guest mooring bank side on short jetty, mooring points above bridge.

Tight entrance to Yachthafen Bad Ems Km126.8

Rural mooring Km 113

SOUTHWEST

Canoeists emerging from Schleuse Kalkofen Km 105.8

Limburg Km 76

98·6 Beware outflow from power station from left bank.

96·8 *Schleuse Scheidt*
Rise 3·8m
Length 34·0m
Breadth 6·0m
☏ 06439 6946

91·8 *Schleuse Cramberg*
Rise 4·7m
Length 34·0m
Breadth 6·0m
☏ 06439 6431

91·0 Mooring possible on right bank above lock. No facilities.

90·8 **Balduinstein**. Motor-Yacht-Club Schaumburg on right bank. Guest moorings for boats under 14m x 4m. Water, electricity, showers, WC, clubhouse.

85·6 Staging on right bank. No facilities.

ca.84 **Diez**

83·8 Pontoon for guests on left bank. Water and electricity.

83·7 Schloss Diez, left bank.

83·6 WSA-Hafen. Pleasure craft forbidden.

83·2 *Schleuse Diez*
Rise 3·4m
Length 34·0m
Breadth 6·0m
☏ 06432 3814

81·6 Staging on left bank. Diez town 1·5km.

76·6 *Schleuse Limburg*
Rise 3·6m
Length 34·0m
Breadth 5·30m
☏ 06431 24166

76·4 Mooring for leisure craft permitted above lock alongside 80m-long quayside, only between the hours of 1800 and 1000.

ca.76 **Limburg**

Diez Km 84

Waiting for Schleuse Limburg to open Km 76.6

75·8 Nautic-Club Mittellahn. Guest moorings, 60m staging on left bank. ☏ 06475 447. Drinking water and electricity. Convenient for town centre.

73·0 Dietkirchen. Yachthafen Dietkirchen on right bank. Precarious moorings, max 15m long, water, electricity. Shops and restaurant nearby.

INLAND WATERWAYS OF GERMANY **51**

SOUTHWEST

Moorings at Nautic-Club Mittellahn, Limburg Km 75.8

71·7   **Dehrn.** Bootsclub Limburg on right bank. Guest moorings, water, electricity, showers, repairs, clubhouse. Shops and restaurants nearby.

Current and depth can be problematic at head of navigation, take care when turning round.

70·0   End of navigation.

Bootsclub Limburg at Dehrn Km 71·7

Dietkirchen Km 73

MOSEL

Navigable distance 242km
Maximum draught 2·5m
Maximum height 3·10–5·20m
Current 0·5–1·0km/h
Locks 13
Hours 24 hour
Speed limit 30km/h except where indicated

From the French border, and on to the Luxembourg and German borders, all the way through to the Rhein, the Mosel valley is gorgeous. The breathtaking scenery is very dramatic with hillsides rising steeply from the water's edge, covered with vineyards or pine forests, picturesque villages, towns and castles. This excellent white wine producing region of Germany has redeemed its chequered former past of the 1960/70s and one should not pass through the notable towns and villages without sampling the delights of the fruity locally produced golden white wines.

The river is fully canalised and has a minimum depth of 2·70m when the Cochem 'Pegel' reads 2·20m. At normal times it flows at only 0·5–1·0km/h. When the river is in flood the speed of the current will increase significantly. If the Cochem *Pegel* reaches 6·00m then all navigation must stop. The lowest bridge is just downstream of Schleuse Koblenz, with a height of 5·20m at the highest water on the Rhein.

The meandering waterway is shared with myriad vessels including large commercial barges, hotel barges, tripper boats and pleasure craft. There are several marinas adjacent to the River Mosel, but quayside moorings for pleasure craft along the River Mosel are few and far between, with priority for hotel barges and tripper boats. However, along the Luxembourg river bank, quayside moorings can be shared with the hotel barges and tripper boats on certain days and during specified times, as displayed on a well advertised board. Under no circumstances should one moor during the prohibited hours reserved for hotel barges and tripper boats. Nonetheless, all trips should be well planned and moorings identified before hand, with reservations for moorings during the peak season strongly recommended.

There are 13 locks on this river which operate 24 hours a day, all of which have fixed bars or bollards, and none with floating bollards. You should expect to share the locks with several commercial and passenger boats, some of which will be very large and heavily laden; often only being invited to enter the lock at the last minute when no more space is available for any more large vessels. At each lock there are small self-operating locks specifically for small pleasure craft less than 3·20m wide.

SOUTHWEST

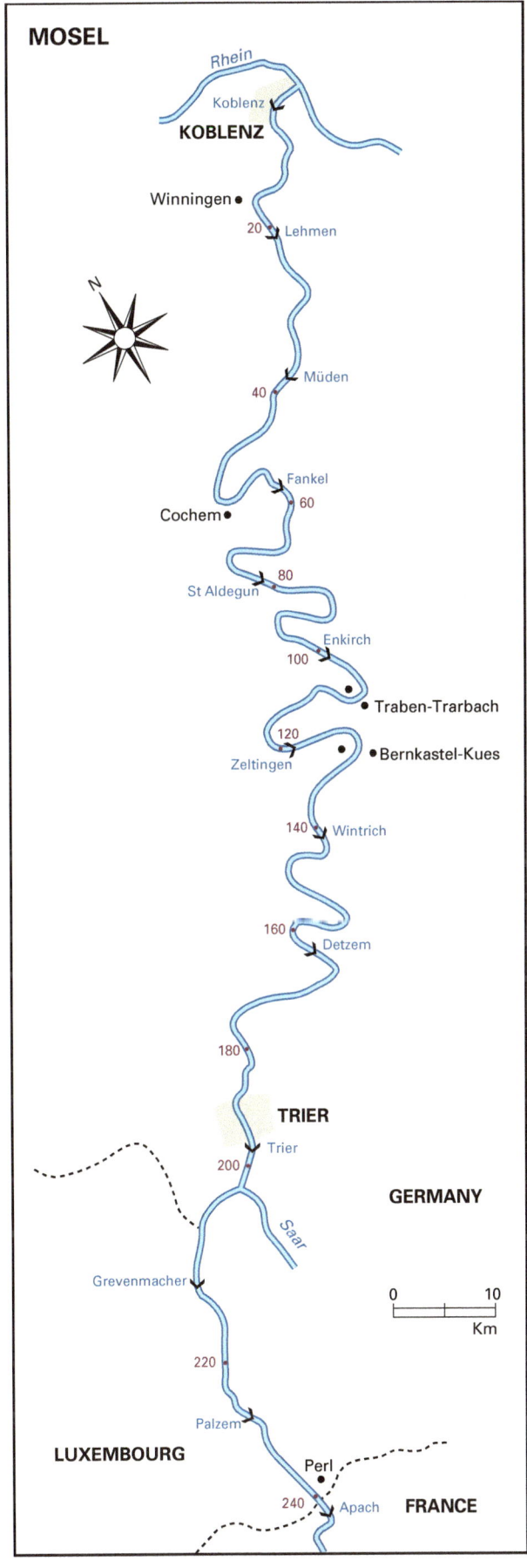

Kaiser Wilhelm I overlooking the junction of the Rhein and the Mosel at Koblenz

Km

0·0	Junction with Rhein Km 592·3
0·4–1·0	Waiting quays for barges and passenger ships. Small boats not welcome.
	Koblenz
1·8	*Schleuse Koblenz* Rise 6·0–4·9m Chamber 122.0m x 12·0m Small Chamber 18m x 3·29m VHF Ch 20 ☏ 0261 98193850.
2·5–6·0	Speed limit 8km/h.
3·0	Left bank, Service – Steiger der fa. Litzke. ☏ 0261 23044. Service and repairs.
3·7	Segel and Motor-Yacht-Club on left bank. Guest moorings max 20m. Water, electricity, showers, clubhouse, 4-tonne crane, slipway. Shops and restaurants nearby.
3·8	Motorboot-und-Wasserski-Club Koblenz on left bank. Guest moorings max 12m. Water, electricity, showers, clubhouse. Shops and restaurants nearby.
3·9	Yachtclub Rhein-Mosel-Koblenz on left bank. ☏ 0261 21985. Guest moorings max 12m. Water, electricity, showers, 4-tonne crane, slipway.
4·5	Bootshafen Grühn on left bank. ☏ 0261 22843 Repairs.
7·0	Yachthafen Güls on left bank. ☏ 0261 401672. Max bridge height 2·8m. guest moorings, water, electricity, repairs, wintering, restaurant, hotel.
11·3	**Winningen**. Guest moorings max 10m. Fuel berth and railway station on left bank.
12·4	Marina Winningen on left bank. ☏ 02606 2296 Guest moorings. Water, electricity, showers, restaurant, fuel, WiFi, crane, repairs.

INLAND WATERWAYS OF GERMANY

SOUTHWEST

13·5	Spectacular Autobahn-Hochbrücke. Height 113m.
18·2	The Wasserburg on left bank at southern end of Kobern-Gondorf.
20·8	*Schleuse Lehmen* Rise 7·5m Chamber 170·0m x 12·0m Small Chamber 18m x 3·40m VHF Ch 78
24·2	**Alken**. Burg Thurant. Staging on right bank for leisure craft max 25m.
25·4	Yacht-Club Löf with staging on left bank. Water, electricity, clubhouse with shower and WC. ☏ 02605 1588.
26·7	**Brodenbach**. Yacht harbour on right bank. ☏ 0171 3161598. Depth 3m. Convenient for town centre. Water, electricity, showers, washing machine, drier, slipway. Shops and restaurants nearby.
29·0	**Hatzenport**. Pretty village.
31·2	Ruin remains of 12th century castle, restored in 1689, Bischofsteine, left bank.
32·0	Small yacht harbour at Burgen on right bank. Water, electricity, showers, restaurant.
37·1	*Schleuse Müden* Rise 6·5m. Chamber 170·0m x 12·0m Small Chamber 18m x 3·20m VHF Ch 79
40·5	Large Yachthafen Mosel-Boating-Centre Treis-Karden on right bank. All main facilities including restaurant. Burg Tries and Wilburg castles, shops and restaurants nearby.
46·8	**Klotten**. Ruin castle remains, Coraidelstein, left bank.
47·5	Ferry.
50–53	**Cochem**. Left bank. A beautiful old roman town with its imposing Reichsburg castle overlooking the River Mosel.
51·3	Cochem municipal Sportboothafen on right bank just above the bridge. ☏ 02671 4528. Electricity and water. Restaurants, wine tasting and shops nearby. Whether approaching the marina from upstream or downstream, this is a tricky entrance. Do not use the right bank shore side bridge arch, as the water is very shallow under the arch.
51·5	Mooring for larger vessels along 250m concrete quayside with vertical wood posts. Large mooring rings 20m apart, some cleats 5m apart. Electricity available on request, speak to ferry master who acts as harbourmaster.

Early morning mist at Sportboothafen Cochem, Mosel Km 51.3

59·4	*Schleuse Fankel* Rise 7·0m Chamber 170·0m x 12·0m Small Chamber 18m x 3·20m VHF Ch 81
61·0	**Beilstein**. Pretty village on right bank. Ruin remains of Metternich castle.
61·2	Ferry.
67·9	Senheim Yachthafen on right bank. ☏ 02673 4660. Guest moorings in an attractive setting. Pontoons. Good facilities. 16A Electricity.
73·1	Ferry.
75·5	Right bank. Kloster ruins.
78·3	*Schleuse St Aldegubd* Rise 7·0m. Chamber 170·0m x 12·0m Small Chamber 18m x 3·4m VHF Ch 82
81·4	**Bullay**. Steel H Pontoon right bank. Moorings on 6m fingers parallel to shore. Max 15m using end fingers.
81·3	Ferry.
82·1	**Alf**. WSA-hafen, river authority harbour on left bank. Possible mooring on quay wall.
87·2	**Zell**. Town quay moorings. Steel H Pontoon right bank. Moorings on 6m fingers parallel to shore. Max 15m using end fingers.
93·7	**Pünderich**. Close to the Marienburg restaurant.
93·9	Ferry.
101·9	Ferry.

SOUTHWEST

103·0	*Schleuse Enkirch* Rise 7·5m Chamber 170·0m x 12·0m Small Chamber 18m x 3·4m VHF Ch 18
104·2	Yachthafen Boot-Polch left bank at Traben-Trarbach. ☎ 06541 2010. Guestmoorings with water, electricity 16A, WC, shower, WiFi, repairs. Restaurants, wine tasting and shops nearby.
105·9	Fuel berth and river mooring place on right bank at Trarbach.
107·0	**Traben**. Small public mooring on left bank, close to railway. Impressive bridge between the two towns.
107·0	**Trarbach**. On right bank. Castle ruin, Grevenburg.
107·5	Public mooring for leisure craft max 25m.
112·8	**Kröv**. Very attractive village on left bank, but no mooring place.
123·9	*Schleuse Zeltingen* Rise 6·0m Chamber 170·0m x 12·0m Small chamber 18m x 3·4m VHF Ch 20
124·0	Guest mooring above lock at Hotel Zeltinger Hof ☎ 06532 93820.
128–132	**Bernkastel-Kues**
130·2	Café Rose, left bank, guest mooring for diners, no facilities ☎ 06531 6433.
130·8	Yachthafen des BC Bernkastel on left bank at Kues. Beautiful view of the Landshut castle ruin. Guest moorings max 15m. Water, electricity, showers, clubhouse. Shops, wine tasting and restaurants nearby.

Bernkastel on the River Mosel

Yachthafen BC Bernkastel Km 130

Bridge at Traben-Trarbach

SOUTHWEST

Horseshoe bend near Leiwen Km 157

River Mosel Km 152.5 Neumagen-Dhron Yachthafen

141·4	*Schleuse Wintrich* Rise 7·5m Chamber 170·0m x 12·0m Small chamber 18m x 3·4m VHF Ch 22
145·0	Hotel-Café Moselblick, right bank, guest moorings for diners.
Ca 148	**Piesport**. Picturesque, but no moorings.
152·4	**Neumagen-Dhron**. Yachthafen on right bank. ☏ 06507 701670. Guest moorings, max depth 2.2m. Electricity 16A, water, fuel, showers, WC, restaurant, slipway. Shops, wine tasting and restaurants nearby.
156·0	**Trittenheim**. Left bank but no moorings.
158·5	**Leiwen**. Right bank. Hotel-restaurant, guest mooring for dinners.
166·8	*Schleuse Detzem* Rise 9·0m Chamber 170·0m x 12·0m Small chamber 18m x 3·4m VHF Ch 78
169·1	**Pölich**. Yachthafen Moselherz left bank. Guest moorings, water, electricity, showers, WC.
170·0	WSC Mehring, right bank, guest moorings on staging pontoon, max 10m. Water, electricity, WC, slipway.
178·4	Sport-boothafen Schweich, left bank. ☏ 06502 91300. Depth 1·8m. Electricity, water, showers, WC, Restaurant, Campsite. WiFi in restaurant. Pontoon in river subject to severe wash. Water, electricity, showers, clubhouse, fuel, chandlery. Restaurant. Shops and restaurants nearby.
184·1	Hafen Trier. Commercial vessels only.
188–197	**Trier**. Interesting Roman town.
195·8	*Schleuse Trier* Rise 7·3m Chamber 170·0m x 12·0m Small Chamber 18m x 3·4m VHF Ch 79
196·3	Yacht club pontoons on right bank.
196·4	WSA Bauhafen des Trier, left bank.
197·5	Sporthafen Trier-Monaise, left bank. Guest moorings for leisure boats, water, electricity, WC, shower, slipway.
200·0	**Konz**. Municipal harbour. Marina and pontoons in river. Water, electricity, showers, clubhouse. Shops, supermarket and restaurants nearby. Train station.
200·8	Junction with Saar.
205·9	Junction with Sauer. Left bank now Luxembourg.
206·0	**Wasserbillig**. Ferry.
206·0	Quay on left bank 100m long. Used by Passenger Boats check timetable for authorised times for pleasure craft moorings. Shops, restaurant and border railway station, trains to Luxembourg, Germany and France.
206·3	Cercle Nautique Wasserbillig, guest moorings, electricity, water, WC, security gate.

SOUTHWEST

208·4 Hafen Mertert on left bank. Commercial harbour.

212·6 **Grevenmacher.** Quay on left bank 70m long. Used by Passenger Boats check timetable for authorised times for pleasure craft moorings. Bollards variable 20/30m spacing. 2·2m deep

212·9 *Schleuse Grevenmacher*
Rise 6·3m
Chamber 170·0m x 12·0m
Small chamber 18m x 3·3m
VHF Ch 18

222·0 **Wormeldange.** Quay on left bank 100m long. Used by Passenger Boats check authorised times for pleasure craft moorings. Close to wine cellars. Wine tasting, shops and restaurants nearby.

229·8 *Schleuse Stadtbredimus* (Palzem)
Rise 3·8m
Chamber 170·0m x 12·0m
Small Chamber 18m x 3·3m
VHF Ch 20

233·4 **Remich.** 70m Quay on left bank, used by Passenger Boats check timetable for authorised times for pleasure craft moorings. No facilities. Shops and restaurants nearby. Bus station, buses to Luxembourg.

235·1 **Bech-Kleinmacher.** 60m quay on left bank, used by passenger boats check timetable for authorised times for leisure craft moorings.

236·9 High pile 70m wall right bank. Possible mooring.

237·5 **Schwebsange.** Large marina / campsite on left bank (Luxembourg side). Excellent facilities. Water, electricity, showers, restaurant, shop, chandlery. Fuel cheaper than France and Germany. Internet available by harbourmaster's office.

238·4 **Besch.** Mooring on right bank. No facilities. Baker.

242·0 **Schengen.** Where the signing of the Schengen Agreement took place on 14 June 1985.

Quay on left bank 100m long. Used by Passenger Boats check timetable for authorised times for pleasure craft moorings.

242·2 French/German border on right bank.

242·4 *Schleuse Apach*
Rise 4·4m
Chamber 170m x 120m
VHF Ch 20.

242·6 Enter France, continue on the River Moselle.

Schengen at Km 242, Luxembourg

Sunset at Schwebsange Yachthafen, Luxembourg

SAAR

Navigable distance 94·6km
Maximum draught 2·5m
Maximum height 5·25m
Maximum beam 12·0m
Current Negligible except in times of flood
Locks 8
Hours Open 24hrs/7days a week
Speed limit 16km/h

The Saar is a beautiful meandering river bordered by steep wooded hillsides and spectacular vineyards. Many of the slopes are reminiscent to the Mosel, apart from the industrial areas heading towards Saarbrücken. It has taken many years for this canalised river to be connected straight through from the Mosel to the French water way network via the German/French border, just south of

SOUTHWEST

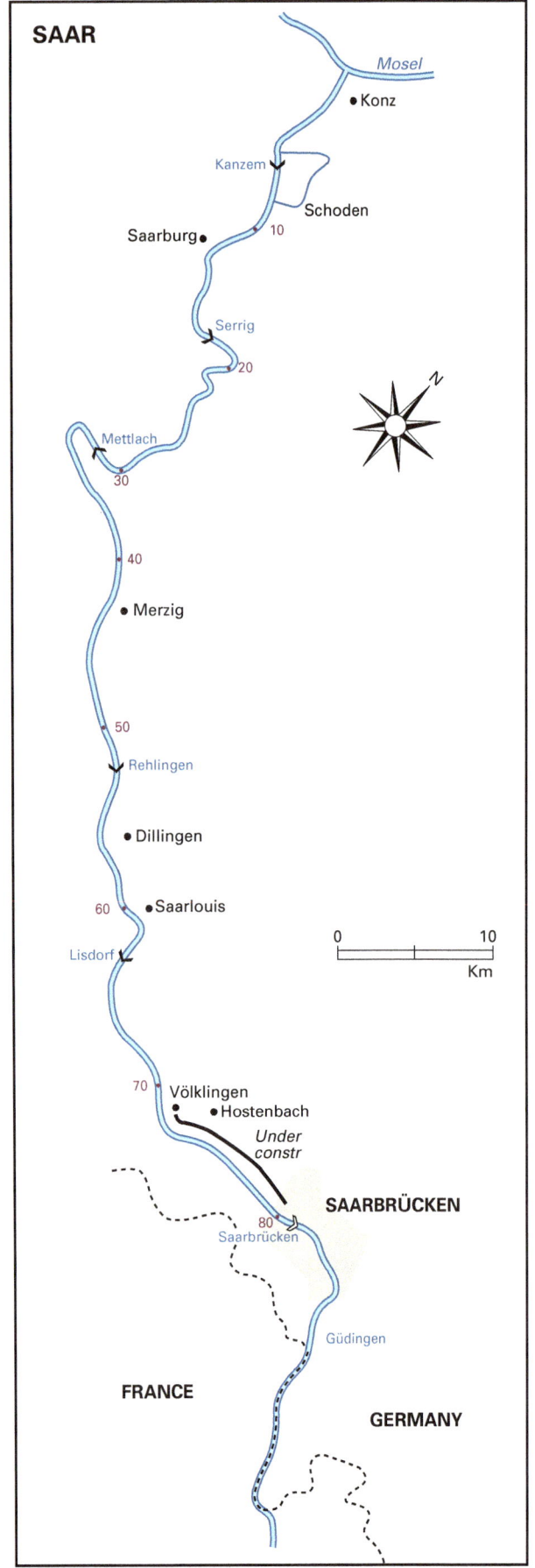

Saarbrücken and onwards to the Canal de la Marne au Rhein. Rather belatedly for the intended heavy commercial traffic that would have transported heavy industry material and coal from the Saar region. Nonetheless, there is still a reasonable number of commercial vessels using this route to and from Saarbrücken, intermingled with passenger tripper boats, hotel barges, leisure boats and canoeists.

This scenic waterway provides a wonderful route for pleasure craft users to traverse from Germany to France and back again, whilst enjoying the rich delights of the region.

Km

0·0   Junction with Mosel Km 200·8.

5·1   *Schleuse Kanzem*

Chamber 1	**Chamber 2**
(larger than 40·0m)	(less than 40·0m)
Floating Bollards	Cruciforms
Rise 11·75m	Rise 11·75m
Length 190·0m	Length 40·0m
Breadth 12·0m	Breadth 6·75m

VHF Ch 78

7·5   Short Quay with two bollards 30m apart on left side

7·9   Small pontoon at Wassersportzentrum Schode on right bank.

10·2   Bauhafen des WSA on left bank. Possibility of mooring in emergency.

10·5   Yachthafen Beurig, WSC Saarburg, guest moorings on finger pontoons with water and electricity, WC, showers, washing machine, tumble dryer, slip, BBQ, Clubhouse. Depth 1·5m

11·4   **Saarburg.** Pretty town with vineyard slopes, and castle restaurant on top of hill. There is a cable car up to a theme park and café, with spectacular panoramic views of the river and countryside.

Entrance to small chamber Schleuse Kanzem Km 5.1

58 INLAND WATERWAYS OF GERMANY

SOUTHWEST

Entrance to Saarburg Sportboofhafen Km 10.4

Yachthafen Beurig des WSC Saarburg Km 10.5

Floating pontoon at Saarburg

Schleuse Serrig Km 18.4

Saarburg

Guest mooring pontoon 30m long, €10/night. No facilities.

Do not moor on quay or on passenger landing points to avoid fines. All shops and facilities, restaurants, wine tastings and wine cellars. Railway station.

11·8	Burgruine Saarburg, left bank.
14·8	Schloss Saarstein, right bank.
15·2	Schloss Saarfels, right bank.
18·4	*Schleuse Serrig*

Chamber 1	Chamber 2
(larger than 40·0m)	(less than 40·0m)
Floating bollards	Cruciforms
Rise 11·4m	Rise 11·4m
Length 190·0m	Length 40·5m
Breadth 12·0m	Breadth 6·75m
VHF Ch 82	

19·4	**Hamm.** Possible mooring on left bank.
30·4	**Mettlach.** 60m mooring place before Schleuse Mettbach.
31·4	*Schleuse Mettlach*

Chamber 1	Chamber 2
(larger than 40·0m)	(less than 40·0m)
Rise 11·0m	Rise 11·0m
Length 190·0m	Length 40·0m
Breadth 12·0m	Breadth 6·75m
VHF Ch 18	

35·5	Ferry crossing.
36·7	Restaurant with landing stage.
38·4–38·6	Landing stage for pleasure craft. Depth 1·6m, max seven days.

SOUTHWEST

Mettlach

Quarry Works Km 26

Yachthafen Merzig

43·6–44·0	Moorings, maximum seven days.
44·2	Yachthafen Merzig with guest moorings with water, electricity, restaurant, beer garden, BBQ, repairs, 10t-crane, WC, showers. Depth 2·0m.
ca.44	**Merzig**
54·1	*Schleuse Rehlingen*

Chamber 1	Chamber 2
(larger than 40m)	(less than 40·0m)
Floating Bollards	Cruciforms
Rise 8·0m	Rise 8·0m
Length 190·0m	Length 40·0m
Breadth 12·0m	Breadth 6·75m
VHF Ch 20	

56·4	Yachthafen des YWSC Dillingen e.V. VHF Ch 77. Guest moorings, water, electricity, restaurant, WC, shower, slip, repairs. 35 minutes walk to town.
58·8	**Dillingen.** Commercial harbour.
61·3	**Saarlouis.** 50m long landing stage for pleasure craft on left bank. Water and electricity. 20 minutes to town centre.
64·9	Yachthafen for 80 boats
66·1	*Scleuse Lisdorf* With floating Bollards Rise 3·80m Length 190·0m Breadth 12·0m VHF Ch 22
73·3	**Hostenbach.**
75·0	Leisure craft mooring for two boats max three days through the old lock Mon–Fri 0900–1630. ☎ 06808-1328
ca.75	**Völklinger.** Heavy industrial area.
82·5	*Schleuse Saarbrücken* Rise 5·95m Length 190·0m Breadth 12·0m VHF Ch 78
83·3	**Saarbrücken.** Leisure craft moorings. Shops, restaurants, mainline railway Station.
88·0–88·1	Landing stage for small boats on right bank. Electricity.
89·8	Yachthafen des MBC Saar, moorings for pleasure craft max 15m long, water, electricity, WC, shower, Clubhouse, slip. Depth 2m.
ca.92	**Güdingen.** French/German border on left bank.
92·8	*Schleuse Güdingen* Standard Freycinet Lock Rise 2·30m Length 38·5m Breadth 5·05m VHF Ch 78
94·06	The joining point of the end of the Saar kilometering and Km 75·62 end of the Saar-kanal kilometering. The German/French border being at Km 64·795 on the Saar-kanal at Sarreguemines.

West

RUHR

The Ruhr: the very name conjures up an image of industrial wastelands and ugliness. Maybe this was once an accurate picture of the area, but there are few such sights still existing. From the Rhein the first 12km stretch of the river Ruhr is indeed still industrial, but by no means ugly. Beyond Mülheim the river becomes pleasantly rural, used mostly for leisure purposes.

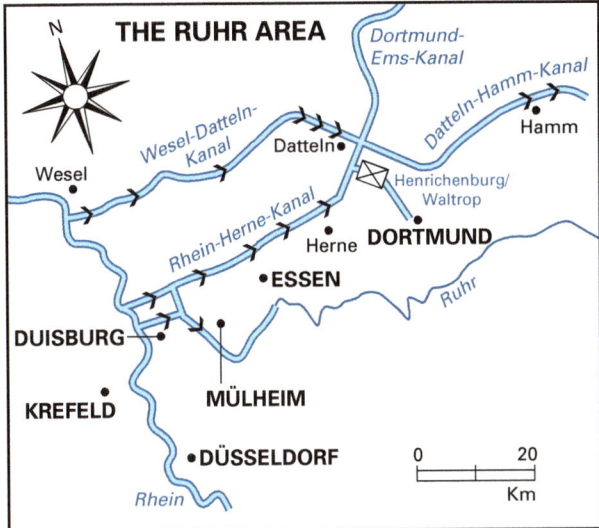

1. RHEIN TO MÜLHEIM

Km 0·0–Km 12·2
Navigable distance 12·2km
Maximum draught 2·60m
Maximum height 6·50m
Current Negligible
Locks 2
Hours 0500–2100 weekdays; 0500–1300 Sundays
Speed limit 12km/h

This stretch of the river is administered by WSD-West, and there are no charges.

Km

0·0 Junction with Rhein Km 780·1.

2·5 *Schleuse Duisburg*
Rise 5m but varies with level in Rhein.
VHF Ch 20

4·3 Connecting link to Rhein-Herne-Kanal.

7·9 *Schleuse Midheim-Raffelberg*
Rise 6·9m
VHF Ch 78

ca9 Hafen **Mülheim** on left bank. Large commercial port.

8·6 Harbour of Yacht club Mülheim Ruhr on left bank. Water, electricity, clubhouse. Shops and restaurants nearby.

12·2 End of WSD-West jurisdiction.

2. MÜLHEIM TO ESSEN-RELLINGHAUSEN

Km 12·2–Km 41·4
Navigable distance 29·2km
Maximum draught 1·70m
Maximum height 3·2m (4·75m in centre of arches)
Current Negligible
Locks 3
Hours Varied. See route description
Speed limit 12km/h (6km/h in narrow parts)

The river passes through some very interesting and attractive countryside. Between Baldeney-See and Rote-Mühle motorboats must stay in the marked channel. Mooring is not permitted in the Baldeney-See, above Schleuse Baldeney.

This part of the Ruhr is not operated by WSD: it is owned by the Land of Nordrhein-Westfalen, and a fee is charged for using it. The locks are not equipped with VHF radio.

Km

12·5 *Schleuse Mülheim*
Rise 5·5m
Hours Monday–Friday 0700–1630,
Saturday/Sunday 0730–2000.

ca13 Possible mooring place on right bank.

21·5 *Schleuse Kettwig*
Rise 5·5m
Hours Mon–Fri 0730-1630, Sat/Sun 0900–1200 & 1500–2000.

22·1 Motorbootclub Kettwig on right bank. Water, electricity. Shops and restaurants nearby.

22·7 Campsite on left bank with moorings.

25·7 Essener Outboard-Club on left bank. Water, electricity.

26·1 Werdener-Yacht-Club on right bank.

29·3 *Schleuse Baldeney*
Rise 9·2m
Hours as per Schleuse Kettwig (Km 21·5)

Note that in Baldeney-See it is not permitted to leave the marked channel or to land on the shore.

33·5 Private harbour on left bank.

38·4 Schleuse Rote-Mühle. Permanently open: no longer in operation. Restaurant and landing stage.

41·4 Essen-Rellinghausen. End of navigation.

INLAND WATERWAYS OF GERMANY 61

RHEIN-HERNE-KANAL

Navigable distance 49·2km
Maximum draught 2·50m
Maximum height 4·50m
Current Nil
Locks 5
Hours 24 hours a day from 0500 Monday to 2100 Saturday; Sunday 0500–1300
Speed limit 12km/h

At one time this canal was heavily industrial, but it has been transformed into a waterway which is now largely rural. There are still a few industrial plants in evidence, but they are mostly modern and clean. The canal itself is bordered for most of its length by trees; there is copious wildlife, and it is popular with anglers. In warm weather it is likely that swimmers too will be enjoying water which is presumably therefore not significantly polluted.

The first 3·6km of the canal is technically the Hafenkanal Duisburg, and Km 0·0 of the RHK is at the end of this stretch, just before the first lock. There is a fairly busy traffic of barges in the canal, but passage through the locks is quick and easy. The full length of the canal is likely to take some nine hours to traverse.

The Rhein-Herne-Kanal is a Bundeswasserstrasse operated by WSD-West, and passage is free.

Km

0·0	Start of Hafenkanal Duisburg. Junction with Rhein Km 780·4.
3·6/0·0	End of Hafenkanal Duisburg. Start of Rhein-Herne-Kanal.
0·7	*Schleuse Duisburg-Meiderich* Rise 5m (depends on water level in Rhein). VHF Ch 82
1·8	Connecting link to Ruhr river.
5·5	*Schleuse Oberhausen* Rise 4·1m VHF Ch 81
13–20	**Essen**
23·0	*Schleuse Gelsenkirchen* Rise 6·5m VHF Ch 79
	Floating bollards on south side.
30·1	*Schleuse Wanne-Eickel* Rise 8·1m VHF Ch 78
37·0	*Schleuse Herne-Ost* Rise 12·6m VHF Ch 22
	Floating bollards on north side.
37·8	Yacht harbour on south bank.
38·2	Yacht harbour on north bank. Water, electricity, clubhouse.
45·6	Junction with Dortmund-Ems-Kanal Km 15·5.

WESEL-DATTELN-KANAL

Navigable distance 60·3km
Maximum draught 2·50m
Maximum height 4·50m
Current Nil
Locks 6
Hours 24 hours a day from 0500 Monday to 2100 Saturday; Sunday 0500–1300
Speed limit 12km/h

Like the RHK, this canal carries a considerable traffic of barges, but it runs entirely through pleasant rural countryside. The locks are all easy to deal with and for planning purposes it is likely to take about eight hours to travel from one end to the other. It is possible to tie up for the night above or below all the locks except Friedrichsfeld, but if entering from the Rhein it may be useful to note that the yacht harbour at Wesel, close to the entrance to the canal, is well equipped for an overnight stop.

The WDK is administered by WSD-West and there are no charges. None of the locks have floating

WEST

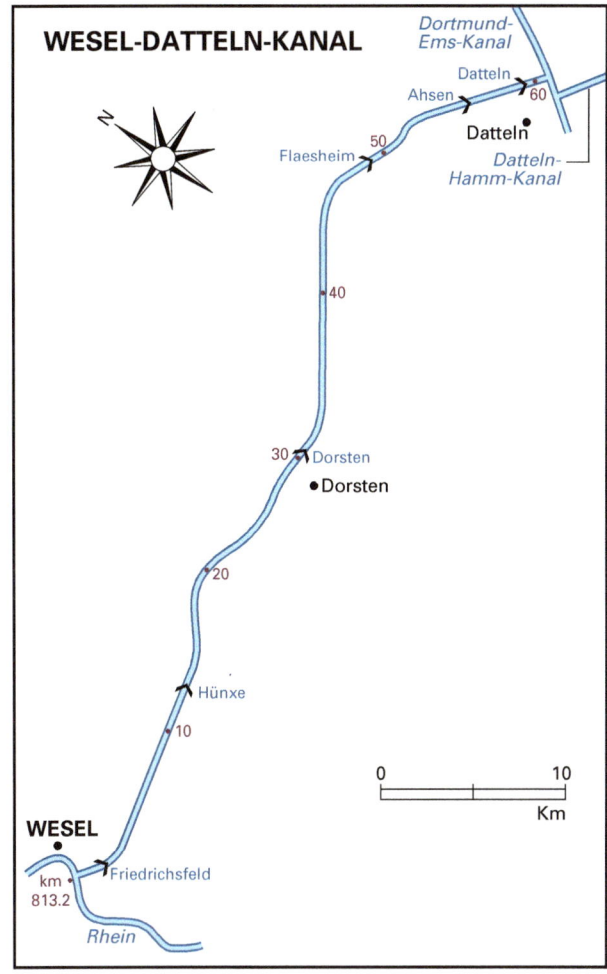

bollards. Although the locks operate round the clock for much of the week, barge traffic in practice ceases at night.

Km

0·0 Junction with Rhein Km 813·2.

1·8 *Schleuse Friedrichsfeld*
Rise 8m (depends on water level in Rhein)
VHF Ch 20

2·0 Work harbour on south bank. Mooring possible by negotiation.

13·2 *Schleuse Hünxe*
Rise 5·5m
VHF Ch 78

28·5 Yacht harbour on north bank. Water, electricity, showers, clubhouse.

30·5 *Schleuse Dorsten*
Rise 9·0m
VHF Ch 79

37·7 Commercial harbour on south bank. Possibility of mooring, with permission.

49·4 *Schleuse Flaesheim*
Rise 4·0m
VHF Ch 81

55·8 *Schleuse Ahsen*
Rise 7·5m
VHF Ch 82

59·3 Water authority harbour on south bank. Possibility of mooring, with permission.

59·5 *Schleuse Datteln*
Rise 7·5m
VHF Ch 78

60·3 Junction with Dortmund-Ems-Kanal Km 21·3. Bunker boats for diesel in DEK at Datteln.

DATTELN-HAMM-KANAL

Navigable distance 47·2km
Maximum draught 2·50m
Maximum height 4·0m
Current Nil
Locks 2
Hours 0500–2100 weekdays only
Speed limit 12km/h

The modernisation of German industry has improved the ambience of this canal, but it is not one of the most interesting of waterways. Its traffic is mostly commercial.

Km

0·0 Junction with Dortmund-Ems-Kanal Km 19·5.

1·9 Yacht harbour on south bank. Water, electricity, shops.

23·3 Yacht harbour on south bank.

27·0 Yacht club on south bank.

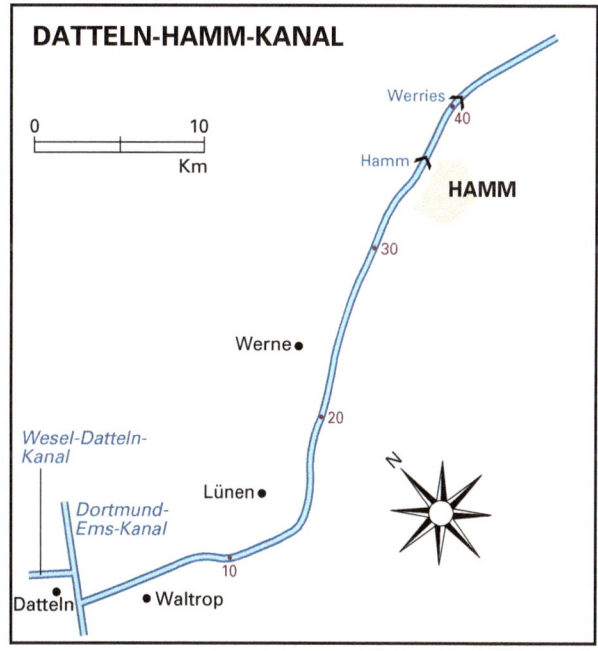

INLAND WATERWAYS OF GERMANY 63

WEST

ca30	Hamm
36·9	*Schleuse Hamm* Rise 1·7m VHF Ch 18
40·3	*Schleuse Werries* Rise 5·1m VHF Ch 22
47·2	End of canal.

DORTMUND-EMS-KANAL

Navigable distance 225·8km (see note below)
Maximum draught 2·50m
Maximum height 4·25m
Current Nil
Locks 16
Hours 0500–2100 Mon–Sat and 0900–1200 Sunday
Speed limit 12km/h

The first 15km, from Dortmund to Henrichenburg/Waltrop, was once through an area of heavy industry, but most of the industrial debris has now been cleared away and the countryside is gradually becoming rural.

For those interested in canal engineering it is mandatory to stop for a few hours at Henrichenburg/Waltrop, at the junction of the Rhein-Herne Kanal with the Dortmund-Ems-Kanal, to see the old *Schijfshebewerk* (ship lift), opened in 1899 and with a vertical lift of 13·5m. Alongside it is the original *Schachtschleuse* (shaft lock), built in 1914 to provide extra capacity. The two now form the basis of a very interesting canal museum; they have been replaced by the present ship lift, opened in 1962, and next to it the 1989 shaft lock. All are fascinating examples of canal engineering.

From the ship lifts, the DEK passes through Datteln, an important canal crossroads, and then northwards through Münster to join the Ems and pass into the North Sea. More importantly from the point of view of inland waterway navigation, it provides links to the Mittellandkanal, which traverses northern Germany from east to west, and to the Kustenkanal, which is a fast barge route to the lower Weser.

From Datteln northwards the route is almost entirely rural, passing through fertile farmlands and interesting small towns. Not surprisingly, being so close to the Dutch border, the more northerly stretches of the canal have a distinctly Dutch atmosphere, with fewer trees, grassy dykes, cattle grazing, herons fishing and a general air of neatness.

The university city of Münster, capital of the old kingdom of Westphalia, played an important part in the early history of Germany. Badly bombed in World War II, its rebuilt cathedral has at its entrance a stone from the equally badly damaged Coventry Cathedral as a symbol of mutual forgiveness.

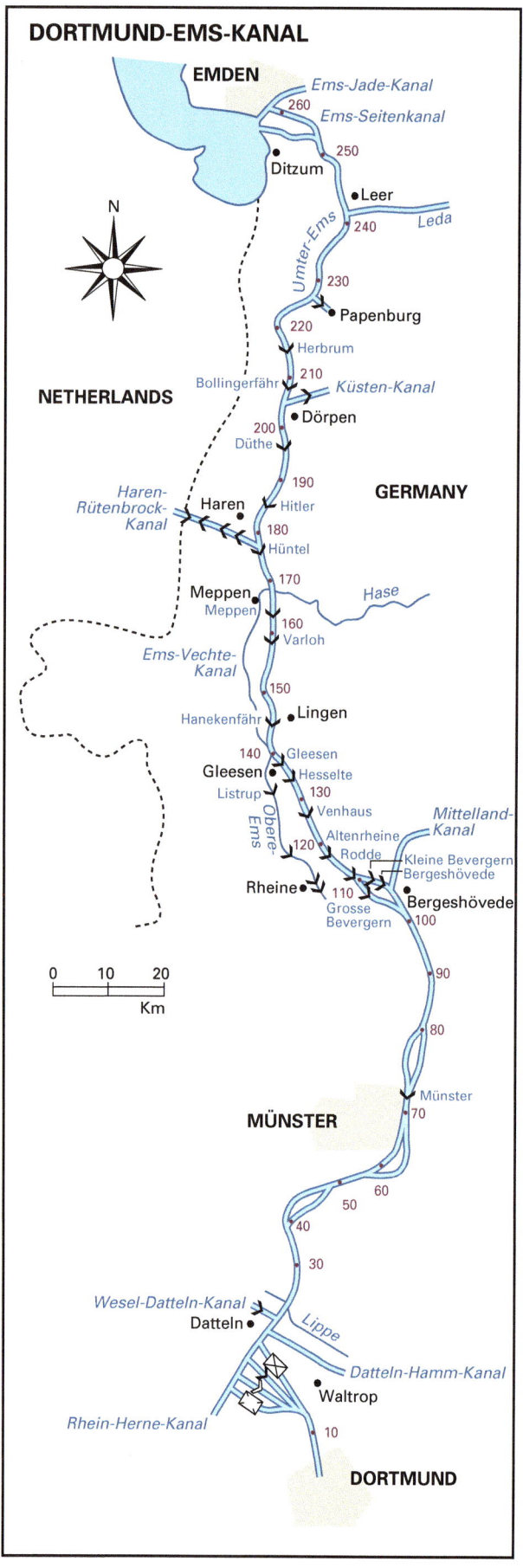

WEST

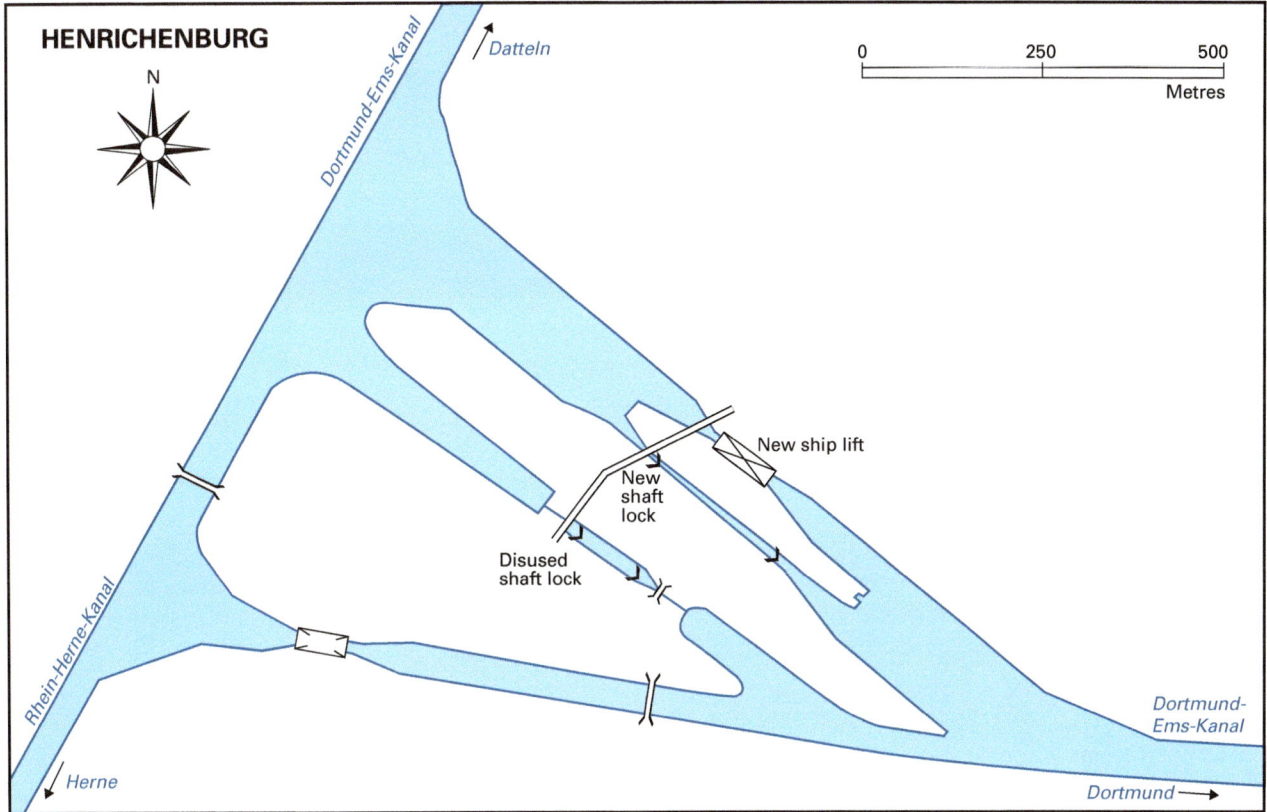

There are numerous yacht clubs along the canal. In addition there are long stretches of canal bank with mooring bollards or rings where a pleasant overnight stay amongst pleasant rural scenery can be had after the barge traffic stops, around 2100 on weekdays.

The canal is controlled by WSD-West. There are no fees. All the locks are equipped with VHF radio and have fixed bollards, except the new Henrichenburg shaft lock, which has floating bollards.

Technically, the DEK continues along the tidal Unter Ems beyond Km 225·8 and includes the Ems-Seitenkanal, terminating in Emden. North of Km 225·8 the waterway is administered by WSD Nordwest. For the sake of simplicity, this book deals with the Unter Ems and the Ems-Seitenkanal as separate entities.

Km

0·0   Dortmund south harbour

15·0 *Schachtschleuse Henrichenburg*
      Fall 13·5m
      VHF Ch 20

      Schiffshebewerk Henrichenburg
      Fall 13·5m
      VHF Ch 20

15·3 Motorboot-Club Lüdenscheid below old shaft lock. Water, electricity, showers, shops, restaurants. Fuel nearby.

      Yachtclub Hebewerk Henrichenburg below old ship lift. Water, electricity, showers, shops, restaurants. Fuel nearby.

15·5 Junction with Rhein-Herne-Kanal Km 45·6.

19·5 Junction with Datteln-Hamm-Kanal Km 0·0.

20·5 Hafen Datteln on east bank. Commercial harbour, but possibility of overnight mooring if space allows.

21·2 Bunker boat for diesel on west side. Also repairs and supplies nearby.

21·3 Junction with Wesel-Datteln-Kanal Km 60·3.

30·0 Yachtclub Dortmund-Ems in old river on west bank. Water, electricity. Depth 2m.

34·6 Hafen Ludinghausen on west bank. Water authority harbour, but overnight mooring a possibility.

39·6 Motoryachtclub Kanalstadt Datteln in southern entrance to old river on east bank. Water, electricity, showers, clubhouse. Depth 1·5–2·5m.

46·6 Yachtclub Kranecamp Senden in northern entrance to old river on east bank. Depth 2m. Water, electricity. Supermarket nearby.

50·3 Yachtclub Tomberge on east bank. Depth 1m. Water, electricity.

55·7 Yachtclub Münsterland in inlet on east bank. Depth 2m. Water, electricity, showers. Shops and restaurants 2km.

67–68 Commercial harbour on west bank. Mooring possible. No facilities.

INLAND WATERWAYS OF GERMANY 65

WEST

Km	
70·5	Bunker station for diesel.
70·7	**Münster.** Monasteria Yachtclub Münster in inlet on west bank. Depth 2m. Water, electricity, showers, slip. Supermarket nearby. Good base for exploring Münster.
71·5	*Schleuse Münster* Fall·6·2m VHF Ch 22
77·6	Boots-Center Münster on east bank. Depth 2m. Water, electricity, showers, slip, crane, repairs, fuel. Shops nearby, restaurants 10 mins.
79·7	Marina Alte-Fahrt Fuestrup in old canal on east side. Depth 2m. Water, electricity, showers, restaurant, slip, crane.
107·6	Bunker boat (for diesel), grocery shop and chandlery on west bank. Restaurant nearby. Bunker boat for diesel on east bank. Extensive bank-side mooring places.
108·3	Junction with Mittellandkanal Km 0·0.
108·4	Channel divides. Eastern channel leads through two locks, Schleuse Bergeshovede and Kleine Schleuse Bevergern, whilst the western channel leads through a single lock, Grosse Schleuse Bevergern, before the two branches rejoin each other ca. Km 110. Pleasure craft normally lock through the two smaller locks.

Eastern branch

108·6	*Schleuse Bergeshövede* Fall 4·1m VHF Ch 20
109·7	*Kleine Schleuse Bevergern* Fall 4·0m VHF Ch 20

Western branch

Km	
0·0	The Mittellandkanal joins the Dortmund-Ems-Kanal just before Schleuse Bevergern.
109·0	*Schleuse Bevergern* Fall 8·1m VHF Ch 20
110·2	Public overnight mooring along east side of canal, no facilities.
112·4	Public overnight mooring for leisure craft adjacent to southwest side of Schleuse Rodde
112·5	*Schleuse Rodde* Fall 3·8 VHF Ch 18
117·8	Public overnight mooring for leisure craft adjacent to southwest side of Schleuse Altenrheine.
117·9	*Schleuse Altenrheine* Fall 3·6m VHF Ch 82
123·1	Hafen Spelle-Venhaus. Small commercial harbour without facilities, but suitable for overnight mooring if space can be found. Depth 3m.
126·64	*Schleuse Venhaus* Fall 3·5m bottom fill VHF Ch 81
134·47	*Schleuse Hesselte* Fall 3·4m bottom fill VHF Ch 79 Restaurant by lock.
137·9	*Schleuse Gleesen* Fall 6·4m bottom fill VHF Ch 78
138·3	Entrance to Obere Ems on west side. Navigable for 7–8km to Schleuse Listrup for vessels drawing up to 1m.
139·8	Entrance to Ems-Vechte-Kanal on west side. Speed limit 6km/h. Navigable to Nordhorn at 16·0km, max 5m long and 1·50m beam.

Schleuse Altenrheine and adjacent public moorings, Km 117.9

WEST

Flood lock Hanekenfähr

Commercial barge emerging from Schleuse Varloh

140·0 Hotel am Wasserfall at **Lingen-**Hanekenfähr: Hafen with one guest mooring.

141·0 Flood Lock Hanekenfähr

141·57 EYC Rheine at Lingen: two guest moorings, water, electricity, showers, toilets.

141·57 Ems-Yacht Club Lingen at Lingen: five guest moorings, water, electricity, showers, toilets, telephone

141·57 Yacht Club Lingen at Lingen: two guest moorings, water, electricity, showers, toilets, slip, fuel.

145·9 Lingen Old Harbour, Public Mooring close to shops. No facilities.

148·6 Short restaurant quay for guests and overnight mooring.

158·2 *Schleuse Varloh*
Fall 3·7m
VHF Ch 20
Leisure craft usually use small lock.

163·89 *Schleuse Meppen*
Fall 7·5m
VHF Ch 18

166·9 Hafen Meppen Public Mooring on canal, no facilities, uncomfortable.

169·1 Yachtclub Hase-Ems e.V. Meppen at Meppen: 15 guest moorings, water, electricity, showers, toilets, telephone, slip, fuel, pumpout.

174·24 *Schleuse Hüntel*
Fall 2·9m
VHF Ch 82

Entrance to Lingen harbour

INLAND WATERWAYS OF GERMANY **67**

WEST

Schleuse Meppen 7.5m

177·0 Jachthafen Emspark at Haren: 10 guest moorings, water, electricity, showers, toilets, washing machine, fuel, slip, pumpout. 1·5km from shops.

178·1 Junction with Haren-Rütenbrock-Kanal

178·6 Alter Hafen at **Haren**: five guest moorings, water, electricity, showers, toilets, washing machine, fuel, slip. Convenient for Haren town centre and shops.

185·89 *Schleuse Hilter*
Fall 1·5m
VHF Ch 81

190·15 WSC Lathen at Lathen: seven guest moorings with water, electricity, showers, toilets, slip, pumpout.

195·07 *Schleuse Düthe*
Fall 2·2m
VHF Ch 79

197·0 Old river entrance. Navigable for 7km by vessels drawing up to 1m. Possible overnight stop.

199·0 Marinapark Emstal at Walchum: 15 guest moorings with water, electricity, showers, toilets, washing machine, fuel, slip.

202·6 Junction with Küstenkanal Km 69·6

205·8 *Schleuse Bollingerfähr*
Fall 1·8m
VHF Ch 78

211 Hotel Emsblick at Herbrum: moorings with showers, toilets, restaurant.

211·15 Ems-Yacht Club Lingen at Herbrum: moorings with electricity, water, fuel.

212·3 *Schleuse Herbrum*
Fall 0·2–1·8m (depends on tide).
VHF Ch 22
River below lock is tidal. Minimum depth at LW ca. 1·5m. Soft bottom. Channel well marked with red/green and cardinal buoys.

217·5 WSC Rhede: 20 guest moorings in inner harbour, water, electricity, showers, toilets, telephone, fuel, slip.

225·8 Entrance to basin below Seeschleuse Papenburg (VHF Ch 131·6) on east side. Possible overnight mooring. Yachtclub Papenburg: water, electricity, showers, toilets, telephone, slip.

226 Yacht Club Turmkanal zu Papenburg e.V: 10 guest moorings, water, electricity, showers, toilets, fuel, slip, pumpout.

UNTER EMS

Navigable distance 40·7 km
Maximum draught 1·5m at LW
Maximum height Unlimited (two opening bridges)
Current 5–10km/h
Locks 0

The Unter Ems north of Km 225·8 and the Ems-Seintenkanal are administratively considered to be a continuation of the DEK to Emden. The situation is slightly confused by the fact that the DEK kilometering continues beyond Km 225·8, but then changes to the Unter Ems markings. For the sake of simplicity this book treats the DEK, the Unter Ems and the Ems-Seitenkanal as separate entities.

The tidal Ems winds its way northwards through mudflats, saltmarsh and sea banks. Redshanks, oystercatchers and other waders wheel around, fishermen manipulate drop nets and fishing boats ply to and fro. Estuary life has not changed much over the years apart from the presence of several quite large suction dredgers.

The channel is well marked with red, green and cardinal marks, to such an extent that a detailed chart is not essential. However, there are various

Schleuse Herbrum - Sea lock

Positive tide on the Unter Ems

Tidal barrier Ems-Sperrwerk Oldersum Km 32

uncharted dredging obstructions at various places along the river, most are on the edge of the deep water channel. The tide, however, runs strongly and whether entering or leaving requires great care with important and accurate timing. The Ems Estuary provides a good link between Emden in Germany to Delfzjil in Holland, when the combined conditions of tide, weather, visibility, wind and wave heights are right. There are several websites for checking the last minute tidal and weather information, such as www.tide-forecast.com; www.windfinder.com. Both the ports of Emden and Delfzjil provide good moorings when waiting for a good weather window for crossing the Ems Estuary.

The city of Emden, the small fishing village of Ditzum opposite and the attractive small town of Leer, all make interesting overnight stops. It is also from this stretch that access is gained to the fascinating small northern waterways: the Leda, the Jümme and the Ems-Jade-Kanal.

Km

0·0	Junction with Dortmund-Ems-Kanal Km 225·8 Entrance to lock basin at **Papenburg**. Possible overnight stop.
6·9	Opening bridge. VHF Ch 15.
7·6	**Weener.** Yacht harbour on left bank. Fuel, restaurant.
14·3	Junction with Leda. Town moorings in **Leer** through sea lock. 1·7km upstream from mouth of Leda. Passage is free if with commercial ships or at 1730 on Fridays and 0800, 1400 and 1730 on Saturdays and Sundays. Otherwise, there is a fee. VHF Ch 13.
15·1	Opening bridge. VHF Ch 15.
16·9	Marina Bingum on left bank. Fuel, shops.
21·3	Hafen Jemgun. Dries at LW.
30·3	**Oldersum.** Junction with Ems-Seitenkanal. (DEK Km 256·4).
32·0	New sea barrier. Call VHF Ch 15 to request passage through.
32·2	Flood barrier. No lock
33·8	**Ditzum.** Small fishing harbour on left bank. Dries at LW but very soft mud. Major boatyard.
40·7	**Emden.** Sea lock on right bank. *Grosse Seeschleuse* VHF Ch 13 Hours 0800–1730. For entry outside of these hours leisure boats should call ☎ 04921 89 72 65.

Leaving the Emden Grosse Sealock into the Ems estuary at dawn

Schleuse Weener - entrance to the yacht harbour Km 7.6

Waiting to enter the Emden Grosse Seeschleuse at dawn

WEST

It is always best to call and register your presence with the lock master and wait for entry advice. Expect to share the lock with large commercial ships. There are specific floating pontoons for pleasure craft on both sides and at both ends of the lock.

Access to Neuer Binnen Hafen, Commercial Port, Yacht Harbour, Ems-Jade-Kanal and outer end of Ems-Seitenkanal. Bunker boat for diesel in Emden outer harbour.

EMS-SEITENKANAL

Navigable distance 9·1km
Maximum draught 1·10m to 2·00m (varies)
Maximum height 2·80m to 3·20m (varies)
Current Negligible
Locks 2
Hours Varied. See route description
Speed limit 7km/h if draught is less than 1·30m, 5km/h if draught is more than 1·30m.

Technically considered an extension of the Dortmund-Ems-Kanal, the Ems-Seitenkanal provides access for inland shipping to the port of Emden, minimising the amount of tidal navigation necessary. It also provides a link to the Ems-Jade-Kanal.

Km

256·4 Start of canal. Junction with Unter Ems Km 30·3

256·5 Yachtclub Unterems at entrance to channel before Schleuse Oldersum – tidal.

256·6 *Schleuse Oldersum*
Rise 0·5–3·0m (depends on tide).
Chamber 80m x 9·8m
VHF Ch 13
Hours 0800–1100 & 1500–1800 daily (depends on tide) Closed in winter. Check opening times on ☎ 04924 2022

Floating pontoon.

Schleuse Oldersum at the start of the Ems-Seitenkanal and after the junction with the Unter Ems

Schleuse Borsum at Emden at the entrance to the Ems-Seitenkanal

256·8 Lock waiting platform 1·10m depth.

256·9 Yachtclub Unterems e.V., Oldersum. Clubhouse, Guest places, WC, Shower, water, electricity. 1·0m depth. Small boxes.

259·1 Nordufer, BSC Gandersum. Guest places, Water, Electricity, Clubhouse.

262·0 Clubhafen des WSV Petkum. Guest places, WC, Showers, Water, Electricity, Clubhouse, 8-tonne. Crane. 1·40m depth

265·1 Junction with connecting canal to Ems-Jade-Kanal.

265·4 *Schleuse Borsum*
Rise 2·1m
Chamber 56m x 10m
VHF Ch 13
Hours Weekdays 0800–1200 & 1400–1630. Phone for weekend opening hours ☎ (0)4921 897273. Closed in winter.

265·5 End of canal in Emden port. Also connects to EJK.

Entrance to Schleuse Oldersum from the Unter Ems

HAREN-RÜTENBROCK-KANAL

Navigable distance 13·5km
Maximum draught 1·50m
Maximum height 3·70m
Maximum beam 6·00m
Maximum length 33·00m
Locks 4
Hours See introduction below
Speed limit 5km/h
℡ 05932 4376 Mobile 0171 4772 783

Passing through flat attractive rural countryside, the Haren-Rütenbrock-Kanal is a useful waterway link between Holland and Germany for pleasure boats up to 6m beam. There are several 'Hafens' with good facilities at Haren accessed via the Dortmund-Ems-Kanal. The pretty town of Haren has excellent shops. The 12 opening bridges and four locks are all centrally controlled at Haren and automatically opened at given times depending upon the day of the week, high or low season. All passages are organised in convoy and take two and a half hours, no stopping en-route.

Low Season 1 April to 30 April and 1 October to 31 October 0800–1200 and 1230–1800.

Recommend you telephone ahead to book your passage. There are landing platforms at both ends of the canal to wait for your agreed passage time.
Monday, Tuesday, Friday and Saturday the passage fee is €20.

Wednesday and Thursday the passage fee is €2
Closed on Sundays and Bank Holidays

High Season 1 May to 30 September. Operates Mon–Sat 0800–1200 & 1230–1800

Closed on Sundays and Bank Holidays.

The passage fee is €2 and you may need to book your time slot.

Schleuse 1 at Haren

Rütenbrock Schleuse 4 on the Haren-Rütenbrock-Kanal border crossing from Holland to Germany

Km	
0·0	Junction with Dortmund-Ems-Kanal KM 178·1
1·0	*Schleuse 1 – Haren* Rise 1·00m
6·8	*Schleuse 2* Rise 1·85m
10·9	*Schleuse 3* Fall 0·82m
13·5	*Schleuse 4 – Rütenbrock.* Fall 0·12m

Junction with the Dutch Ter Apelkanaal at the German/Dutch border leading to the small town of Ter Apel, where there is the marina JH de Runde.

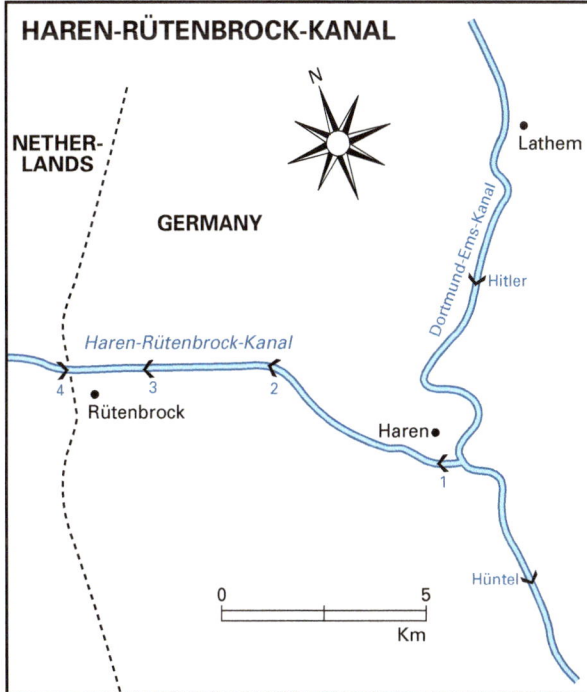

INLAND WATERWAYS OF GERMANY

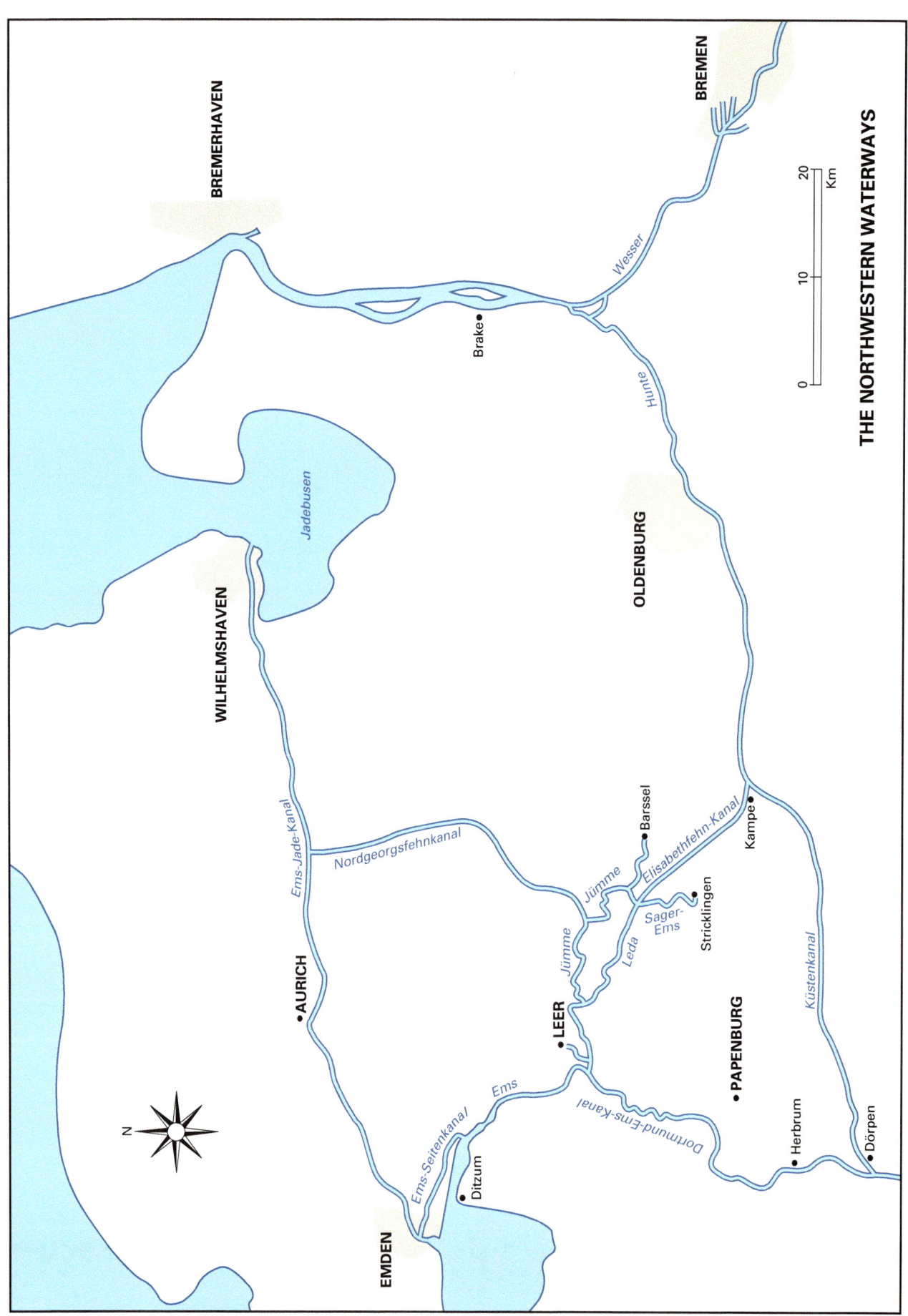

Northwest

EMS-JADE-KANAL

Navigable distance 72·23 km
Maximum draught 1·70m
Maximum height 3·75m
Current Negligible
Locks 7
Hours In summer, the locks work daily 0800–1700, although the opening times may vary slightly from lock to lock. All locks close for 1 hour at lunch time.
Speed limit 8km

This canal is not particularly scenic, but it passes through pleasant rural countryside with much wildlife in evidence. The town centre of Emden is well worth a visit with its many museums including the Museumsfeuerschiff *Deutsche Bucht*.

In dry summers the minimum depth in the summit reach can be less than the amount indicated and it is best to make enquiries about the situation when entering the canal. There are many opening bridges, including two railway bridges which operate by a timetable, and it is necessary to give advance warning of one's arrival by sounding a foghorn using the 'M' signal. (- -).

The Kesselschleuse at Emden is a very interesting example of canal engineering: it is a 'crossroads' with four gates, built in 1886. The Ems-Jade-Kanal route is the one normally kept open.

The Nesserland Schleuse is currently closed and scheduled to reopen in 2017, so access to the Ems Jade Kanal is via the Grosse Seeschleuse and the Binnenhafen

Km

0·0   **Emden**
      No suitable moorings for pleasure craft outside Sea Lock.

0·0   *Grosse Seeschleuse* (Sea Lock Emden leading to the Neuerhafen)
      Rise 3·0m to 1·7m depending upon tide
      VHF Ch 13

Grosse Seeschleuse, Emden entrance to Ems-Jade-Kanal

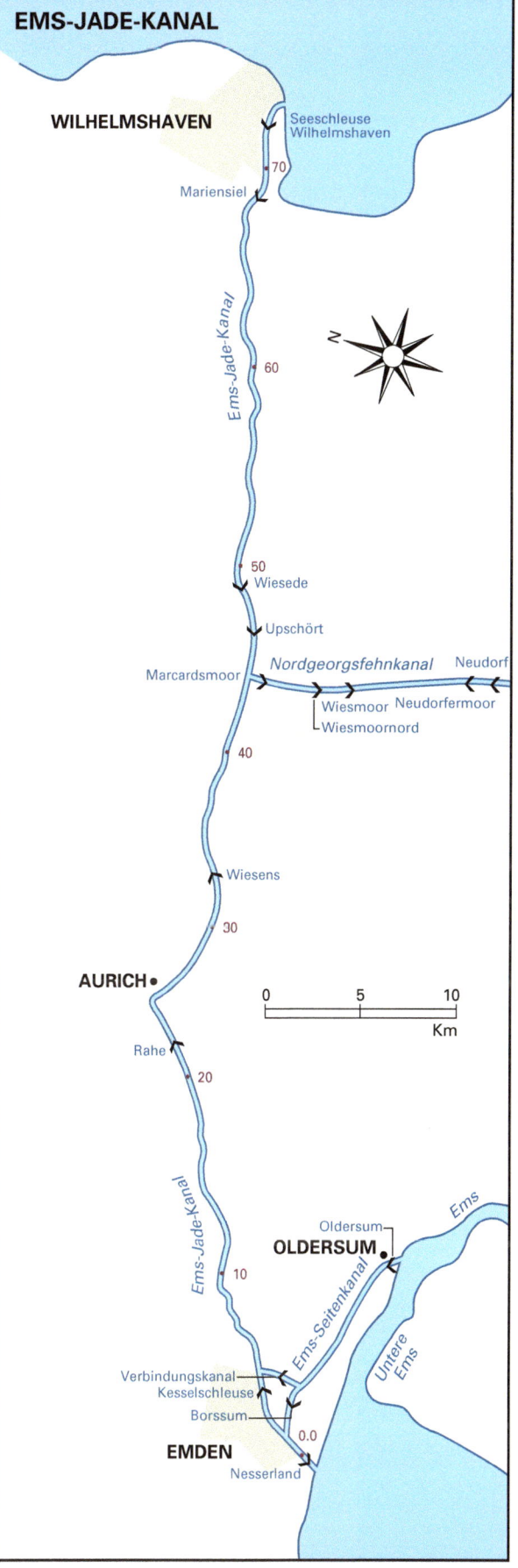

INLAND WATERWAYS OF GERMANY 73

NORTHWEST

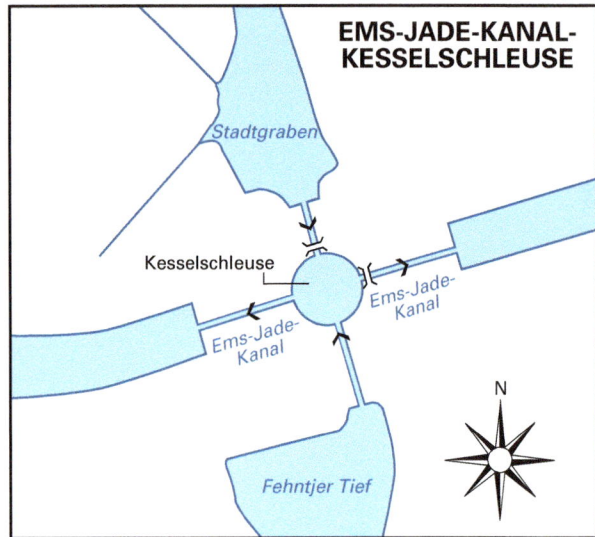

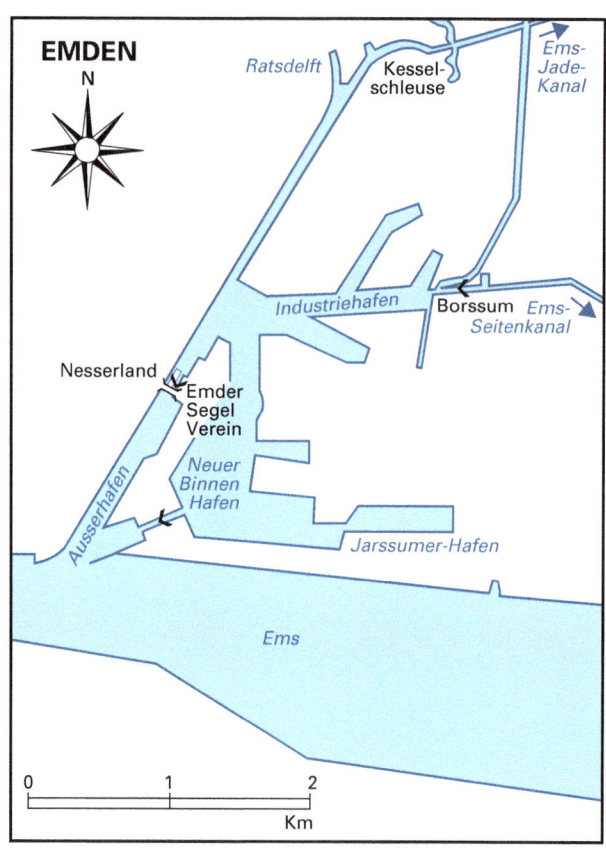

Eisenbahnbrücke - Emden

Ratsdelft Emden, Km2.5

Kesselschleuse Km3.3

Opening times for pleasure craft 0800–1730.

Expect to share the lock with large commercial ships. Pleasure craft must tie up at north end of lock, alongside designated floating platform area.

Use of lock outside of hours on request VHF Ch 13 or ☎ 04921 897265.

Bear left and northwards when exiting lock passing through west side of Industrialhafen.

0·9 *Nesserlander Schleuse* (No through passage at present)
Currently closed, due to re-open in 2017. Use Grosse Seeschleuse instead.

2·0 Private moorings for pleasure craft, possible limited mooring with permission.

2·3 *Eisenbahnbrücke Emden*
The three-bridge rail and road bridge opens on request Monday–Sunday 0650, 0855, 0955, 1140, 1335, 1555, 1735, 1820, 2140

Sound 'M' (--) for opening.
☎ 04921 950155

No holding area.

2·9 **Ratsdelft.** Attractive town centre. City Marina with three berthing areas managed by the Reederei AG Ems. Good public moorings. Electricity and water (50 cent meters). Public shower and toilet. Pump

74 INLAND WATERWAYS OF GERMANY

NORTHWEST

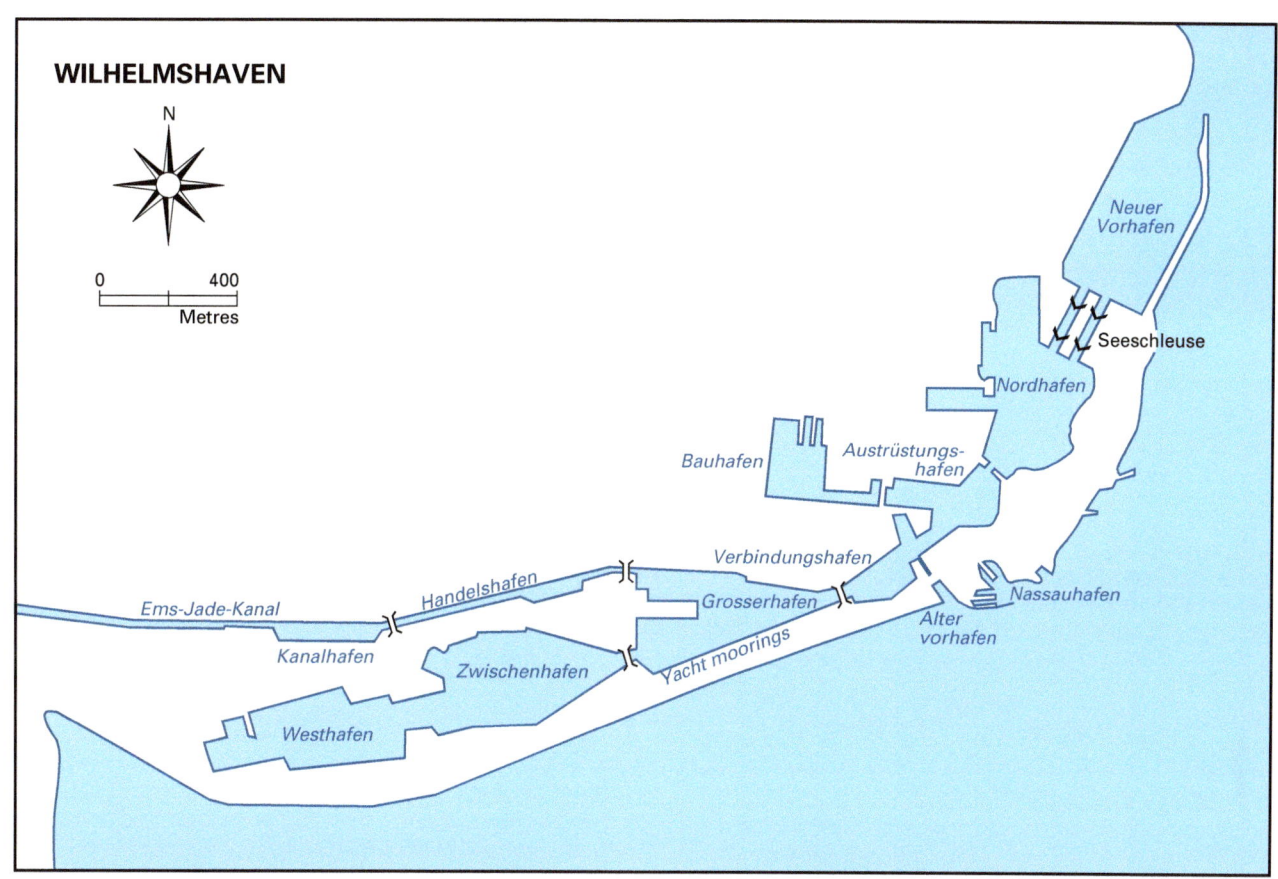

	out. Numerous restaurants and shops. Tourist information.
3·4	*Kesselschleuse Emden* Straight through chamber on EJK waiting platform both sides of lock. VHF Ch 72 The four-gate lock operates weekdays 0800–1230 & 1330–1700. Saturdays 0800–1300 ☏ 0160 90 74 18 70 Mooring at Bootssteg at lock entrance via FehntjerTief (2·4m rise in lock). Mooring at Liegeplätz at lock entrance in Ember Stadtgraben (2·4m fall in lock). Toilet, shower, water, electricity, slip, crane, clubhouse.
4·2	2·1km connecting canal Verbindungskanal to Ems-Seitenkanal (DEK).
20·0	Yachthafen Westerende-Kirchloog. Mooring, water, electricity, slip, repairs.
22·8	*Schleuse Rahe* Rise 1·90m Chamber 55m x 8·20m Waiting platform both sides of lock.
25·0	**Aurich**. Yacthafen WSA-Hafen Aurich, toilet, showers, water, electricity. Slip and 10-t crane. Public moorings in Sportboothafen in town centre. Shops, restaurants. Historic market town.
32·6	*Schleuse Wiesens* Rise 2·60m VHF Ch 13 ☏ 0170 8512382
32·8	Yachthafen WSAWiesens with guest mooring.
42·0	Yachthafen. WSV Marcardsmoor. Guest moorings toilet, showers, water, electricity. Shops.
42·4	Junction with Nordgeorgsfehnkanal.
44·0	*Schleuse Upschört* Fall 2·90m VHF Ch 13 ☏ 0170 8512390
45·9	*Schleuse Wiesede* Fall 1·40m VHF Ch 13 ☏ 0170 2291417
49·5	Mooring place.
60·0	Yachthafen WSV Dykhausen. Guest mooring place, water, electricity, toilet, shower. Shop in village.
62·8	Mooring for leisure craft north side.
63·6	Mooring for leisure craft north side.
65·8	*Eisenbahnbrücke Mariensiel* Railway bridge opens on request Monday to Sunday; check opening times. Sound 'M' (--) for opening. ☏ 0170 8512396 No holding area.

NORTHWEST

67·3	*Schleuse Mariensiel* Fall 0·30m VHF Ch 13 ☎ 0170 8512396
69·5	*Rüstringer Klappbrücke* Bridge opens on request VHF Ch 11
70·5	*Rüstringer Deichbrücke* Bridge opens on request VHF Ch 11
71·5	**Wilhelmshaven.** HYC Germania Clubhaus. Toilet, shower, slip, crane. Bus to town.
71·9	*Kaiser-Wilhelm-Brücke* Height 9m. Bridge opens on request VHF Ch 11 Monday to Saturday 0600–1800, Sunday 0800–1900
72·3	*Seeschleusen Wilhelmshaven* Fall Depends on tide level. VHF Ch 13 ☎ 04421 755760 Check operating times for leisure craft. Position of Jade Traffic VHF Ch 20 broadcast hourly +10 minutes

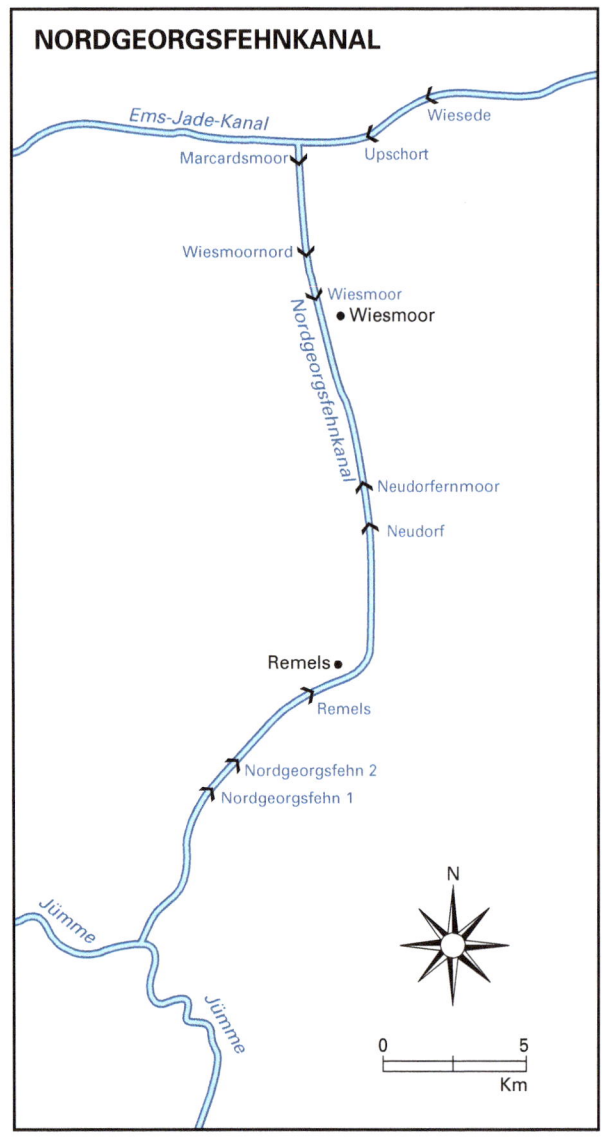

NORDGEORGSFEHNKANAL

Navigable distance 31·8km
Maximum draught 1·40m
Maximum height 1·50m (soon to be 3·50m)
Current Nil
Locks 8
Speed limit 6km/h

A quiet, little-used canal linking the Ems-Jade to the Jümme, and running through low-lying agricultural land. Administered by the Land of Niedersachsen, it is open only by arrangement. It is necessary to contact Staatliches Amt für Wasser und Abfall, in Aurich ☎ 04948 219, 04956 3339 or 04941 2392. A small fee is payable. It is also possible to go from the EJK at Marcardsmoor southwards to Wiesmoor and back by hiring a key which allows the Marcardsmoor Cif not standing open, Wiesmoor Nord and Wiesmoor locks to be operated by the boat crew. A fee is payable for this, together with a deposit.

The depth can reduce to below 1·40m during especially dry summers. There is a fixed bridge between Wiesmoor and Neudorfermoor locks, with a clearance of only 1·50. One more fixed bridge, further south, with headroom of 1·70m.

Km

0·0	Junction with Jümme Km 9·8.
5·7	*Schleuse Nordgeorgsfehn I* Rise 2·20m.
9·5	*Schleuse Nordgeorgsfehn II* Rise 1·70m.
12·0	*Schleuse Remels III* Rise 1·10m.
18·5	*Schleuse Neudorf IV* Rise 2·20m.
19·9	*Schleuse Neudorfermoor V* Rise 1·50m.
27·1	*Schleuse Wiesmoor VI* Fall 1·70m.
28·1	*Schleuse Wiesmoor-Nord VII* Fall 1·40m.
31· 5	*Schleuse Marcardsmoor VIII* Fall Nil (normally stands open).
31·8	Junction with Ems-Jade-Kanal Km 42·4.

LEDA AND SAGTER EMS

The tidal Leda forms a link from the Unter Ems to the Jümme, the Sagter Ems and the Elisabethfehnkanal. The surrounding terrain is flat, fertile and agricultural, but not without charm. The area abounds in wildlife and is especially good for the bird-watcher.

NORTHWEST

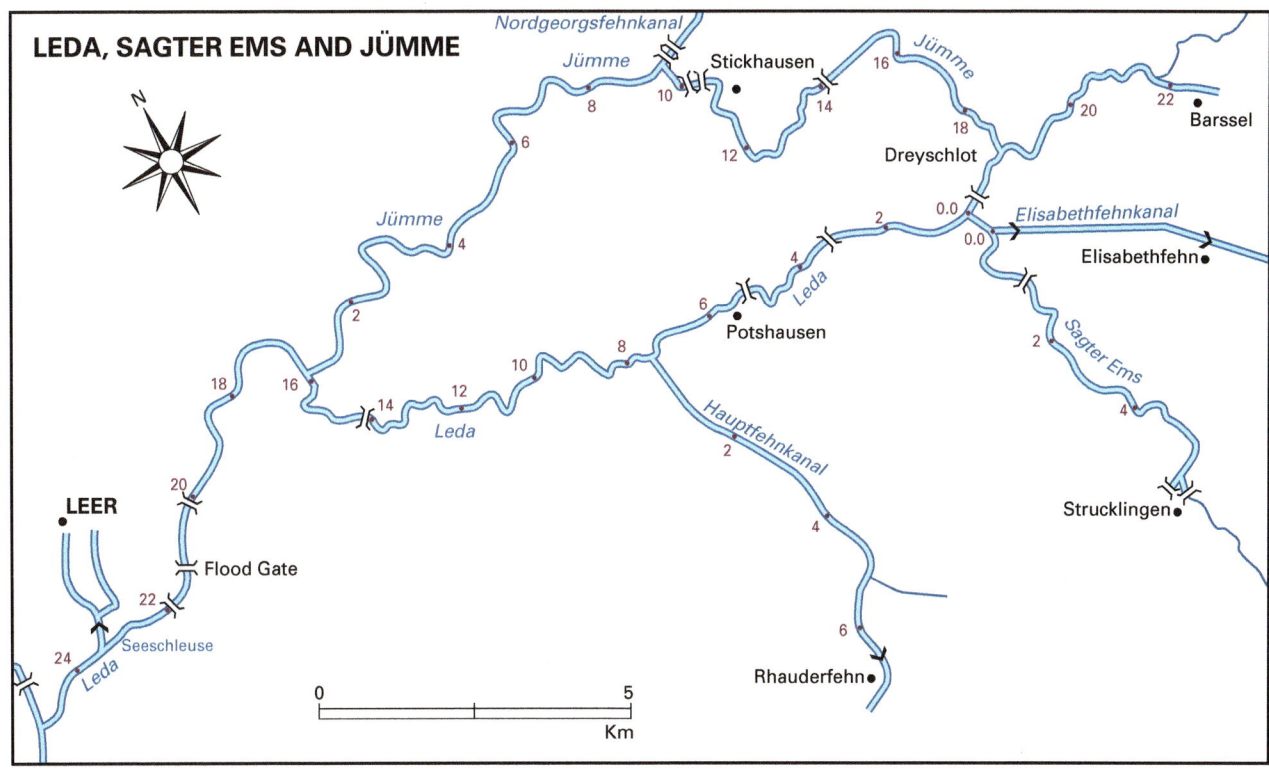

The Sagter Ems is the continuation of the Leda to Strücklingen. It is a quiet backwater which meanders gently through agricultural land and is the home of two sailing clubs. Towards Strücklingen the depth dwindles to 0·6m.

1. LEDA

Navigable distance 24·7km
Maximum draught 1·20m at LW, 2·50m at HW
Maximum height 6·10m at LW, 4·80m at HW
Current Tidal. Strong at times
Locks 0
Speed limit 7km/h against the tide, 10km/h with the tide

Km

24·7 Junction with Unter Ems Km 14·3.

23·0 Seeschleuse Leer, leading into Leer town harbour.

Passage through the sea lock is free if with commercial ships or at 1730 on Fridays, 0800, 1400 and 1730 on Saturdays and Sundays. Otherwise there is a fee.
VHF Ch 13.

22·6 Sailing club with staging on right bank.

21·1 Flood barrier. 5 openings, each 14m wide. Use centre opening.

18·4 Sailing club on right bank. Water, electricity available.

16·9 Sailing club on left bank. Water, electricity available.

16·0 Junction with Jümme Km 0·0.

7·5 Junction with Hauptfehnkanal on left bank.

5·3 Potshausen. Lift bridge. Open 0830–1000, 1300–1400 & 1700–2000 in summer.

0·0 Entrance to Dreyschlot on right bank, giving second connection with Jümme (and access to Barssel). Length 1·1km. Depth 1·40m at LW.

River continues upstream as Sagter Ems.

2. SAGTER EMS

Navigable distance 5·9km
Maximum draught 1·40m
Current Tidal
Locks 0

Km

0·0 Junction with Leda Km 0·0.

0·3 Junction with Elisabethfehnkanal on right bank.

1·2 Lift bridge. Advance notice required.

1·9 Sailing club on right bank.

5·9 **Strücklingen**. Sailing club. End of navigation.

NORTHWEST

JÜMME

Navigable distance 22·3km
Maximum draught 1·40m at LW, 2·90m at HW
Maximum height 1·30m at HW, 2·80m at LW
Current Tidal
Locks 0
Speed limit 6km/h

The Jümme is a tributary of the Leda, joining it at Km 16. It is also connected to the Leda further upstream at the point where it becomes the Sagter Ems. The lkm linking canal is known as the Dreyschlot. There is a low fixed bridge at Km 14·8 and vessels heading for Barssel should proceed via the Leda and the Dreyschlot.

Km

0·0	Junction with Leda Km 16.
0·1	Sailing club on right bank. Water, electricity available.
9·5	Small yacht harbour at junction with Nordgeorgsfehnkanal on right bank.
10·8	Lift bridge. When closed height 1·75m.
14·8	Fixed bridge 1·95m. Restaurant and moorings.
20·3	Junction with Dreyschlot on left bank. Connects to Leda Km 0·0.
25·8	Bootshafen Barssel. Large yacht harbour with good facilities in centre of village.

ELISABETHFEHNKANAL

Navigable distance 14·9km
Maximum draught 0·90m
Maximum height 4·00m
Maximum beam 4·5m
Current None
Locks 4
Speed limit 7km/h if draught is less than 1·30m, 5km/h if draught is more than 1·30m

The Elisabethfehnkanal provides a link for shallow-draught boats from Kampe on the Küstenkanal to the Leda. It is fairly straight, passing through low-lying agricultural land, but is very peaceful and pleasant.

It is administered by WSD. Passage through the canal, which takes 3–4 hours, can be made only between May and September inclusive, and is organised in convoys. The collecting points are at the first bridge (Kamperfehn) when coming from the Küstenkanal and downstream of Osterhausen lock when coming from the Leda. There is only one lock-master, who travels from lock to lock by bicycle, operating the locks and the eight opening bridges.

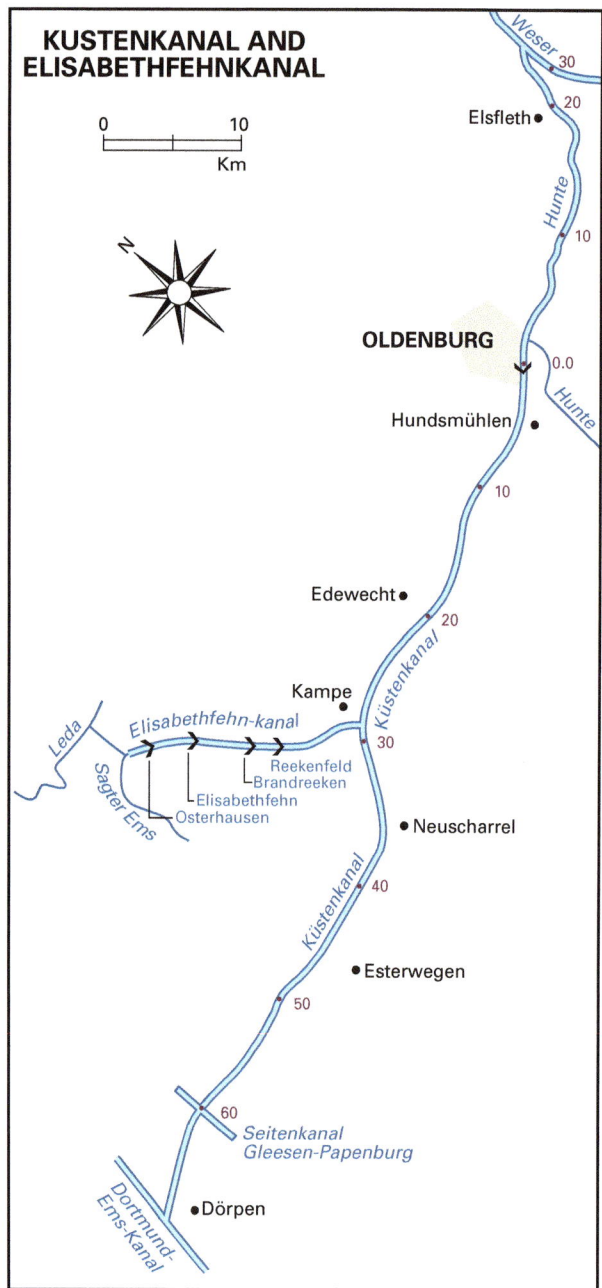

It is necessary to give advance notice of an intention to use the canal. This must be done by 1500 the day before the passage (Fridays for Sundays and Mondays), by informing the lock master (① 04405 49852 or 04405 7437). Alternatively, notice can be given to the lock-masters at either Oldenburg or Dorpen on the Küstenkanal.

Km

0·0	Junction with Kustenkanal Km 29·3.
5·3	*Schleuse Reekenfeld* Fall 1·40m
7·7	*Schleuse Brandreeken* Fall 1·00m
11·3	*Schleuse Elisabethfehn* Fall 1·35m

11·5	**Elisabethfehn.** Attractive mooring in village. Fuel available.	47·8	Esterwegen. Barge overnight stopping place.
14·4	*Schleuse Osterhausen* Fall 0·3–0·8m	38·4	Neuscharrel. Barge turning place. Possible mooring.
14·8	Junction with Sagter Ems Km 0·3.	29·3	Junction with Elisabethfehnkanal Km 0·0.

KÜSTENKANAL AND UNTERE HUNTE

The Küstenkanal is straight, fairly heavily used by commercial shipping and not particularly interesting from the scenic point of view, but it is nevertheless a quick and convenient through route between the Dortmund-Ems-Kanal and the Weser. After the lock at Oldenburg the Küstenkanal becomes the tidal Untere Hunte, which flows into the Unter-weser at Elsfleth.

There are no real overnight stopping places, but it is usually possible to find an out-of-the-way spot at one of the barge overnight moorings if need be.

To the west of Km 8·1 the canal is administered by WSD-West. To the east it is under the control of WSD-Nordwest. The Untere Hunte is operated by WSD-Nordwest. There are no charges in any section, but there is strict enforcement of the 10km/h speed limit on the Untere Hunte.

The Untere Hunte, from Oldenburg to the Weser, is a wide tidal river, bordered by sea walls and mudflats. It is an excellent area for sea birds and waders, but is otherwise somewhat featureless. However, if the tide is judged correctly the 25km will be covered in a very short time. Navigation at night is forbidden in the direction from Oldenburg to Elsfleth.

1. KUSTENKANAL

Navigable length 69·6km
Maximum draught 2·50m
Maximum height 4·50m
Current None
Locks 2
Hours 0500–2100 Mon–Sat and 0900–1200 Sunday
Speed limit 12km/h

Km

69·6	Junction with Dortmund-Ems-Kanal Km 202·6.
64·8	*Schleuse Dürpen* Rise 1·2m VHF Ch 82
64·0	Junction with Seitenkanal Gleesen-Papenburg. Watersports club with deep-water moorings. Water, electricity, showers.
55·0	Yachtclub Surwold on north bank. Water, electricity, showers, fuel, repairs.
47·8	Esterwegen. Barge overnight stopping place.
38·4	Neuscharrel. Barge turning place. Possible mooring.
29·3	Junction with Elisabethfehnkanal Km 0·0.
28·8	Kampe. Barge overnight stop.
19·7	Edewechterdamm. Possible overnight stop.
5·5	Hundsmühlen. Possible overnight stop.
5·2	Flood barrier. Open at all normal times.
2·6	Bunker boat for diesel. Repairs.
1·9	*Schleuse Oldenburg* Fall 2·8–5·6m VHF Ch 20
0·8	Lift bridge. Make sound signal to open.
0·0	**Oldenburg** town harbour. North side no facilities. South side Yacht-Club Oldenburg. Water, electricity, showers, repairs, shops.
	Junction with Untere Hunte Km 0·0.

2. UNTERE HUNTE

Navigable length 25·1km
Maximum draught 2·30m at LW (tidal range approx 3m)
Maximum height 4·50m at mean HW
Current Strong tide
Locks 0
Speed limit 10km/h

Km

0·0	Junction with Küstenkanal Km 0·0. Hafen Oldenburg. Commercial harbour.
0·5	Opening railway bridge. Call on Ch 73.
18·4	Huntebrücke. Call *Hunte Bridge* on Ch 73.
20·7	Opening railway bridge Elsfleth-Ohrt. Call *Elsjleth Bridge* on Ch 73.
21·7	Old branch of river (Westergate) on right bank. Shallow.
22·6	Hafen Elsfleth. Possibility of mooring. Bunker boat.
24·1	Flood barrier. Normally open.
25·1	Junction with Unterweser Km 32·0.

Middle

FULDA

Navigable distance 29·0km
Maximum draught 1·20m
Maximum height 3·40m
Current Slight
Locks 5
Hours 0800–2000 daily during the summer months
Speed limit 12km/h upstream, 18km/h downstream

Once the industrial surroundings of Kassel are left behind, the Fulda flows through attractive hilly countryside to its confluence with the Werra, which, like the Fulda upstream of Kassel, is unnavigable except by very shallow-draught boats.

With no commercial traffic, this is an extremely pleasant area in which to cruise, but it should be done in the earlier part of the summer, when water levels are less likely to be depleted. The beautiful old town of Hannoversch-Münden, standing at the junction of the Fulda and the Werra, should not be missed.

The river is controlled by WSD-Mitte, and no fees are payable. The locks are not equipped with VHF. The new Wahnhausen lock, with a rise of 8'5m, replaces four older locks.

Km

79·8	Motor-Yacht-Club **Kassel**. Water, electricity, showers, clubhouse, repairs, slip. Shops and restaurants nearby.
81·1	Nautic-Club Kassel. Water, electricity, showers, clubhouse, repairs, slip. Shops and restaurants nearby.
81·3	*Schleuse Kassel* *Fall 2·8m*
82·2	Hafen Kassel. Yacht harbour with water, electricity, clubhouse. Shops and restaurants nearby.
85·4	Motor-Yacht-Club Sandershausen.
90·4	Yacht harbour on left bank.
93·5	*Schleuse Wahnhausen* *Fall 8·5m*
101·0	Motor-Yacht-Club Wilhelrnshausen.
101·4	*Schleuse Wilhelmshausen* *Fall 2·4m*
105·3	*Schleuse Bonaforth* *Fall 2·4m*
108·3	*Schleuse Hannouersch-Münden* *Fall 2·9m*
108·8	Junction with Werra and Weser Km 0·0.

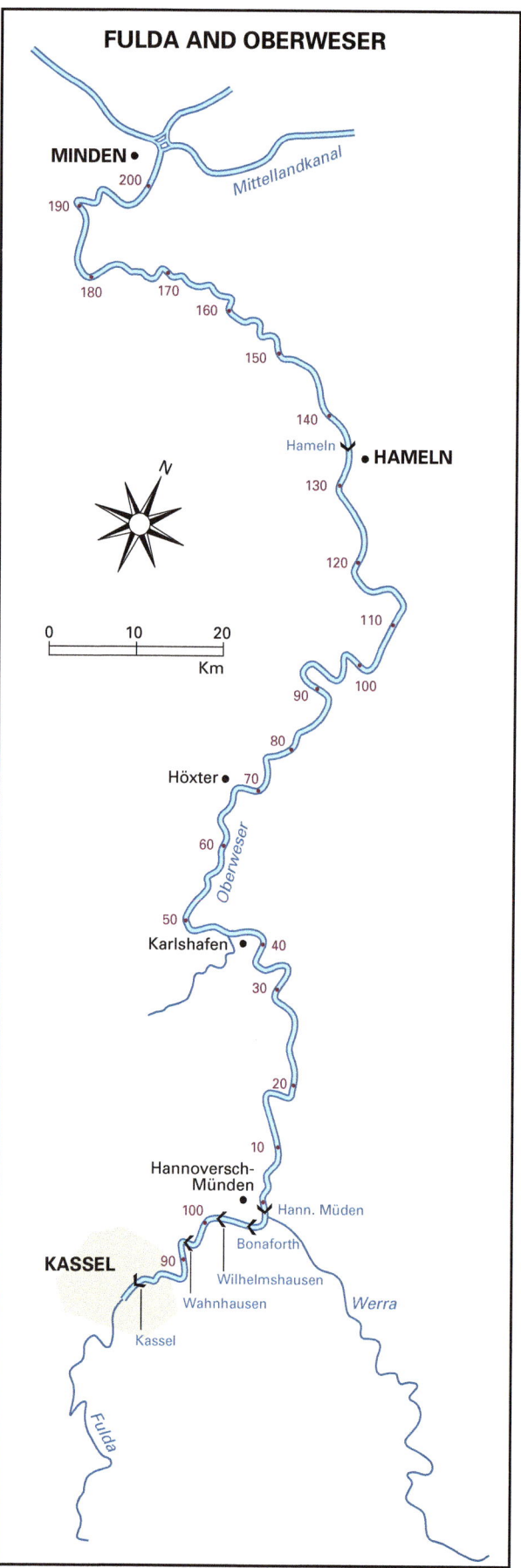

FULDA AND OBERWESER

WESER

The Weser is formed by the Fulda joining forces with the Werra at Hannoversch-Münden. From here to Minden, where it crosses underneath the Mittellandkanal, it is known as the Oberweser. From Minden to Bremen it is the Mittelweser, and the tidal part below Bremen is the Unterweser.

The Oberweser is very attractive and there is no commercial shipping above Hameln, but it suffers from a shortage of water in the middle-to-late summer in most years. The Mittelweser is a commercial shipping route and flows through pleasant rolling farmland. The tidal section below Bremen unfolds to become a typical low-lying estuary with salt-marsh, mudflats and sea walls.

Hannoversch-Münden, Hameln (of Pied Piper fame) and Minden are interesting historic towns, as is the old part of Bremen. However, away from the Altstadt, Bremen suffers somewhat from the same problems which beset most large industrial cities in our present age.

1. OBERWESER: HANNOVERSCH-MÜNDEN TO MINDEN

Km 0·0–Km 204·9
Navigable distance 204·9km
Maximum draught See table below
Maximum height 4·30m
Current 2–5km/h at normal water levels
Locks 1
Hours 0630–1800 Mon–Sat, 0800–1100 Sunday
Speed limit 12km/h upstream, 12km/h downstream

The depth of the Oberweser varies between 0·8m and 4·2m according to the volume of water in the river, and the current can attain speeds of 10kn in places in times of flood. It is necessary to check the level of water at the appropriate Pegel to establish the depth of water at any specific time. The highest and lowest levels shown in the table below demonstrate the variation in water levels.

Depths

Pegel	☏	Min	Mid	Max
Hann. Münden	05541 19429	1·00	1·90	5·10
Karlshafen	05672 19429	0·90	1·90	4·20
Hameln Wehrbergen	05151 19429	0·80	1·90	5·70

Km	
0·0	Junction with Fulda and Werra.
44·0	Motorsportclub Weser-Diemel, left bank. Water, electricity, showers, clubhouse, slip. Shops and restaurants nearby.
50·5	Yacht club. Difficult to enter when water level is low.
69·9	Höxter. Water authority harbour which also houses a yacht club.
80·2	Holzminden. Yacht harbour on right bank. Depth uncertain.
111·9	Hafen Kemnade. Motorbootclub Bodenwerder. Water, electricity, clubhouse, crane.
132·3	Yacht harbour on right bank. Motorboot-Club Hameln. Water, electricity, showers, clubhouse, slip, restaurant.
134·5	Hafen **Hameln**. Less than ideal for leisure boats, but repairs available at boatyard.
134·8	*Schleuse Hameln* Fall 2·60m VHF Ch 20
134·9	Yacht moorings near centre of town.
163·6	**Rinteln**. Tripper-boat quay near centre of town.
166·4	Entrance to Doktorsee on left bank. Entrance marked by red and green buoys. Water, electricity, showers, clubhouse, slip, crane. Shops and restaurants nearby.
173·1	Entrance to yacht harbour on left bank. Water, electricity, clubhouse.
175·6	Yacht harbour on left bank. Westfalischer Motor-yachtclub. Water, electricity, clubhouse, slip. Depth uncertain.
177·7	Yacht harbour on right bank. Water, electricity, clubhouse, slip, crane. Shops and restaurants nearby.
204·5	Junction with Verbindungskanal Sud, Minden. Two locks to Mittellandkanal. VHF Ch 22.
204·6	Motorboot-Club Minden on left bank. Water, electricity. Shops and restaurants nearby.
204·9	Mittellandkanal viaduct. Bunker boats in Mittellandkanal near entrance to Schachtschleuse.

MIDDLE

2. MITTELWESER: MINDEN TO BREMEN

Km 204·9–Km 366·7
Navigable distance 140·0km
Maximum draught 2·30m
Maximum height 4·50m
Current Slight
Locks 7
Hours All except the Weserschleuse at Bremen (see route description) operate 0600–2200 Mon–Sat and 0800–1100 Sunday. Langwedel also operates 1700–1800 on Sundays during the summer
Speed limit 35km/h in river, 12km/h in lock canals

Water levels in the Mittelweser are closely controlled and the waterway has a least depth of 2·50m. It is used by commercial shipping, but it is a fine river set in a very pleasant landscape.

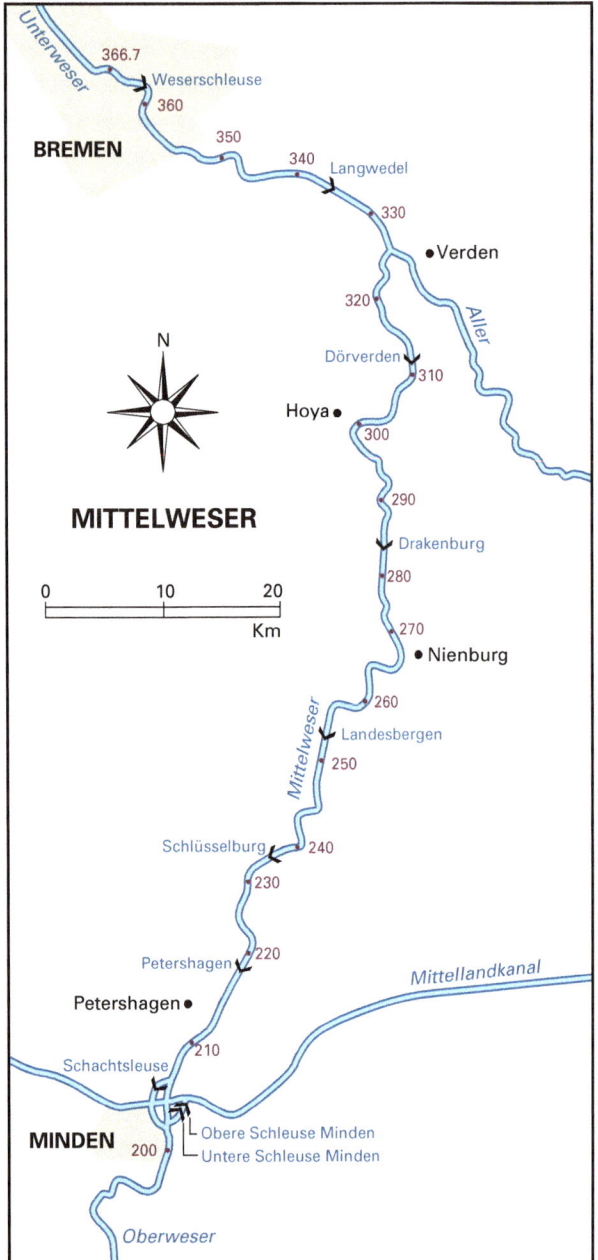

The locks are all fitted with VHF, but not with floating bollards.

Km

204·9 Mittellandkanal viaduct.

206·2 Junction with Verbindungskanal Nord. Schachtschleuse Minden

        VHF Ch 22.

213·5 Junction with Schleusenkanal Petershagen Km 0·0.

213·6 Motor-Yacht-Club Lahde. Water, electricity, clubhouse, slip.

214·0 Weir.

Schleusenkanal Petershagen

0·0 Junction with Weser Km 213·5.

6·7 Possible mooring place on left bank.

7·0 *Schleuse Petershagen*
     Fall 6·0m
     VHF Ch 20

7·3 Possible mooring place on left bank.

8·3 Junction with Weser Km 224·1

Mittelweser (continued)

224·1 Junction with Schleusenkanal Petershagen.

231·4 Junction with Schleusenkanal Schlusselburg.

236·6 Weir.

Schleusenkanal Schlüsselburg

0·0 Junction with Weser Km 231·4.

2·5 Possible mooring place on left bank.

2·8 *Schleuse Schlüsselburg*
     Fall 4·5m
     VHF Ch 18

3·1 Possible mooring place on left bank.

3·6 Junction with Weser Km 238·8.

Mittelweser (continued)

238·8 Junction with Schleusenkanal Schlüsselburg,

243·5 Hafen Stolzenau on left bank. No facilities, but overnight mooring permitted.

250·9 Junction with Schleusenkanal Landesbergen.

252·0 Weir.

Schleusenkanal Landesbergen

0·0 Junction with Weser Km 250·9.

1·3 Possible mooring place on left bank.

1·5 *Schleuse Landesbergen*
     Fall 5·5m
     VHF Ch 22

1·8   Possible mooring place on left bank.
2·2   Junction with Weser Km 252·5.

Mittelweser (continued)

268·5   **Nienburg.** Water authority harbour and yacht harbour on right bank. Close to town centre.
269·4   Boatyard. Repairs.
274·2   Marina Mehlbergen on left bank. Water, electricity, repairs, slip.
275·6   Junction with Schleusenkanal Drakenburg.
277·7   Weir.

Schleusenkanal Drakenburg

0·0   Junction with Weser Km 275·6.
2·9   Possible mooring place on left bank.
3·2   *Schleuse Drakenburg*
      Fall 6·4m
      VHF Ch 20
3·5   Possible mooring place on left bank.
4·4   Junction with Weser Km 286·3.

Mittelweser (continued)

286·3   Junction with Schleusenkanal Drakenburg.
298·3   Yacht harbour on left bank. Water, electricity, showers, clubhouse, repairs. Shops and restaurants nearby.
308·4   Junction with Schleusenkanal Dörverden.
308·8   Weir.

Schleusenkanal Dörverden

0·0   Junction with Weser Km 308·4.
1·7   Possible mooring place on left bank.
2·0   *Schleuse Döruerden*
      Fall 4·6m
      VHF Ch 18
2·2   Possible mooring place on left bank.
2·7   Junction with Weser Km 314·4.

Mittelweser (continued)

314·4   Junction with Schleusenkanal Dörverden.
323·2   Bunker boat and shipyard.
326·4   Junction with Aller Km 117·2.
327·7   Junction with Schleusenkanal Langwedel.
329·4   Weir.

Schleusenkanal Langwedel

0·0   Junction with Weser Km 327·7.
5·3   Possible mooring place on left bank.
5·6   *Schleuse Langwedel*
      Fall 5·50m
      VHF Ch 22
5·8   Possible mooring place on left bank.
8·5   Junction with Weser Km 338·9.

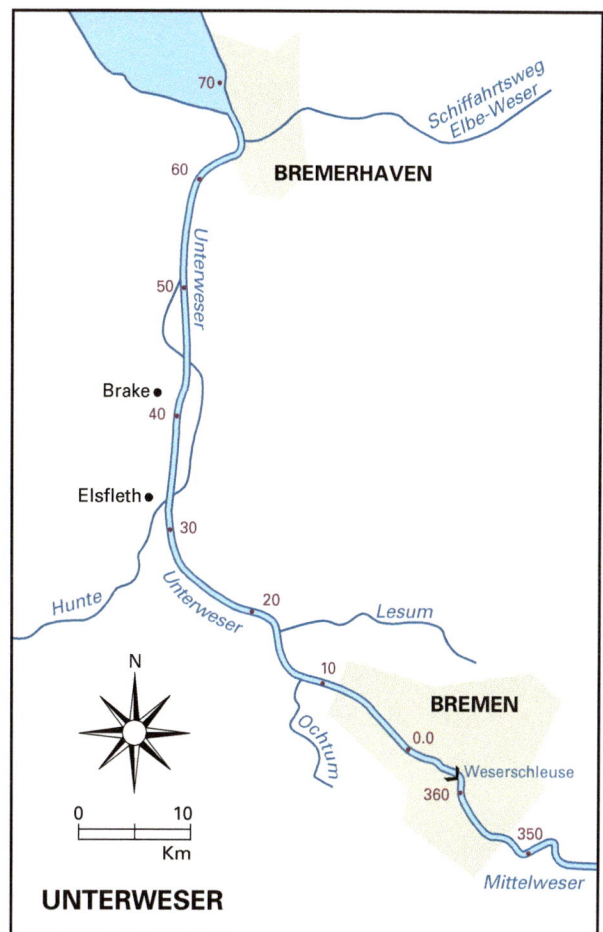

UNTERWESER

Mittelweser (continued)

338·9   Junction with Schleusenkanal Langwedel.
340·9   Mooring place at ferry on left bank.
341·0   Entrance to gravel pit on right bank. Overnight mooring with permission.
350–
366·7   **Bremen**
355·2   Marina Wieltsee on left bank. Water, diesel.
359·1   Marina Oberweser on right bank. Bremer Motor-Yacht-Club. Water, electricity, showers, fuel, repairs, slip, crane. Shops and restaurants nearby.
359·5   Yacht harbour on left bank. Water, electricity, slip.
360·4   Yacht harbour on right bank. Water, electricity, clubhouse, slip, crane.
360·8   Yacht harbour on left bank. Water, electricity, clubhouse.
362·0   *Bremer Weserschleuse* (Hemelingen)
        Fall 2·00–6·00m according to tide.
        VHF Ch 20.
        Hours Mon–Sat 0500–2100. Sundays in summer 0800–1400 & 1730–1930.

MIDDLE

Km	
363·0	Waiting place for leisure craft on right bank.
364·6	Yacht harbour on right bank. Bremer Yacht Club. Dries at LW.
366·7	Wilhelm-Kaisen-Brücke. End of Mittelweser and start of Unterweser.

3. UNTERWESER: BREMEN TO BREMERHAVEN

> **Km 0·0–Km 66·0**
> **Navigable distance** 66·0km
> **Maximum draught** No practical limit
> **Maximum height** 5·20 above MHW
> **Current** Tidal
> **Locks** 0

The tidal part of the Weser carries a considerable amount of traffic, and both Bremen and Bremerhaven are major ports. There are numerous commercial docks and port facilities along the Unterweser, but no attempt has been made to give details of them, as it is unlikely that they will be relevant to leisure craft.

Km

0·0	Junction with Mittelweser Km 366·7.
0·0–10·0	**Bremen**
11·5	Sporthafen Hasenburen on left bank.
12·8	Junction with Ochtum on left bank.
17·2	Yacht harbour of Weser-Yacht-Club on left bank.
17·5	Junction with Lesum on right bank. Fuelling berth inside. Several yacht clubs and boatyards.
25·6	Yachthafen Juliusplate on left bank.
32·6	Junction with Untere Hunte. Entrance to Hunte and Küstenkanal.
32·8	Yacht harbour with lock in the old mouth of the Hunte.
40·6	Brake. Sea lock into commercial harbour. Good mooring place inside.
49·9	Yacht-Club Absen on left bank. Available 2 hours either side of HW.
50·4	Yacht harbour Strohausersiel on left bank. Available 3 hours either side of HW.
51·6	Entrance to Marina Rodenkirchen on right bank.
56·0	Grossensiel. Yacht harbour on left bank.
65·6	Junction with Geeste. Entrance to Hadelner Kanal (Schiffahrtsweg Elbe-Weser) and via lock into fishing harbour on right bank.
66·0	**Bremerhaven.** Four mooring places for yachts inside main harbour. Perhaps the most convenient in the Haupt-Kanal (immediately to port after the Fischereihafenschleuse).

ALLER

> **Navigable distance** 117·1km
> **Maximum draught** 2·20m (water level varies)
> **Maximum height** 2·30m (water level varies)
> **Current** 3–5km/h
> **Locks** 4
> **Hours** In the summer the locks operate 0900–1200 & 1400–1600 weekdays and 0800–1200 & 1300–1700 weekends. Oldau in addition works 1600–1800 on Tuesday, Thursday, Saturday and Sunday
> **Speed limit** 12km/h upstream, 18km/h downstream

The Aller attracts many leisure craft in summer. It carries no commercial traffic and flows through very pleasant farmland and woods. There are attractive overnight stopping places. Celle, the town at the head of navigation, has 700 years of history on display, with numerous beautiful old buildings in the Altstadt.

Possible problems are that the depth can reduce to as little as 1m during the latter half of a dry summer and that there is one bridge, at Km 50·6, with a clearance of only 2·3m at HW. However, as the water level varies by about 3m, by careful judgement it may be possible to pass. It is possible to assess the current state of the water levels by telephoning *Pegel Celle* ① 05141 19429.

The river is administered by WSD-Mitte and there are no charges.

Km

0·0	Head of navigation.
0·9	Hafen Celle. Yacht Club Celle. Water, electricity, showers, clubhouse, repairs, slip, crane. Shops and restaurants nearby.
Ca2	**Celle**
14·4	Oldauer Bootsclub. Restaurants and shops nearby.
14·6	Overnight mooring possible (with permission) above lock.
14·7	*Schleuse Oldau* Fall 3·4m
14·8	**Oldau**
16·8	Good overnight mooring on right bank.
21·0	Restaurant with mooring place on left bank.
26·7	*Schleuse Bannetze* Fall 2·2m
38·3	*Schleuse Marklendorf* Fall 3·2m

MIDDLE

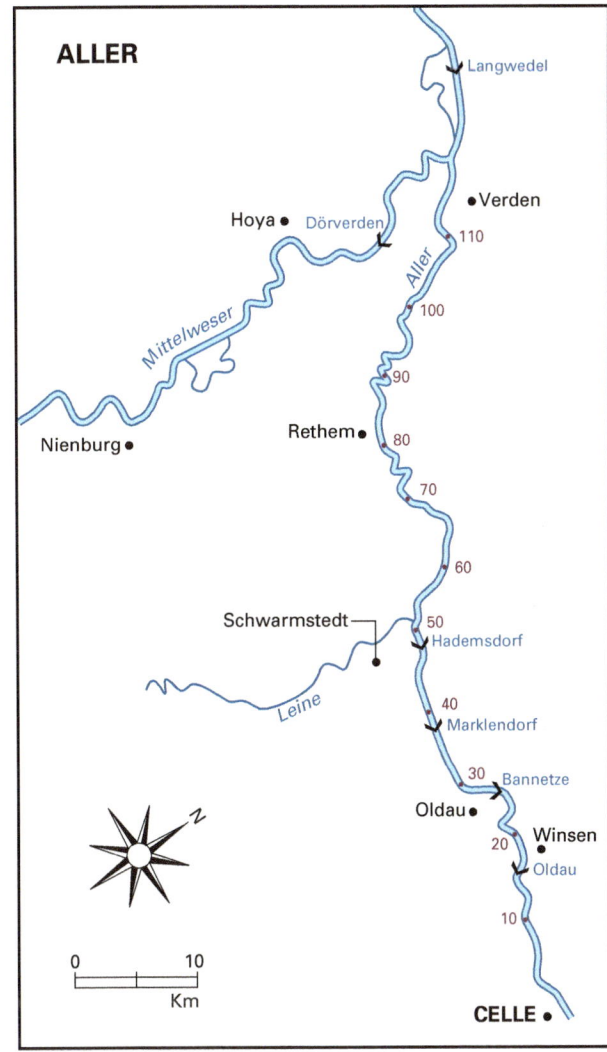

MITTELLANDKANAL

Navigable distance 325·1km
Maximum draught 3·5m
Maximum height 4·00m
Current Nil
Locks 2
Speed limit 12km

This long relatively straight canal is a major axis of the German waterways system; it is the main east-west trunk route. Through the Mittellandkanal it is possible to travel from Holland, France, or Switzerland to eastern Germany, the Czech Republic, Poland and the eastern Baltic.

It is not unattractive, but the scenery does not vary very much as it traverses the predominantly flat agricultural and wooded terrain. The canal and its surroundings do, however, create a good habitat for a wide range of wildlife including otters, kites, herons, ducks, myriad geese and swans. This main waterway's chief asset for both cruising and commercial traffic is that it is a fast and easy route from, and to, various interesting cruising parts of Germany; linking the European waterways from east to west.

It has two locks with a variety of overnight stopping places both at established Yacht Clubs and in inlets specifically reserved for leisure boats. Whilst the journey from end to end of the canal can take two and a half days it is best to allow several days from the Dortmund-Ems-Kanal (DEK) to the Elbe-Havel-Kanal (EHK), or vice versa, in order to explore some of the interesting historical places en route, such as Osnabrück, Minden, Hannover, Hildesheim and Braunschweig.

49·8	*Schleuse Hademsdorf* Fall 1·2m
50·0	Junction with Leine.
66·4	Restaurant with mooring place on left bank.
78·0	Overnight mooring at camp site on left bank.
112·7	**Verden**
113·4	Water authority harbour on right bank. Mooring possible with permission.
114·9	Yacht harbour on right bank. Water, electricity, showers, slip.
117·1	Junction with Mittelweser Km 326·4.

The Mittellandkanal in spring

INLAND WATERWAYS OF GERMANY **85**

MIDDLE

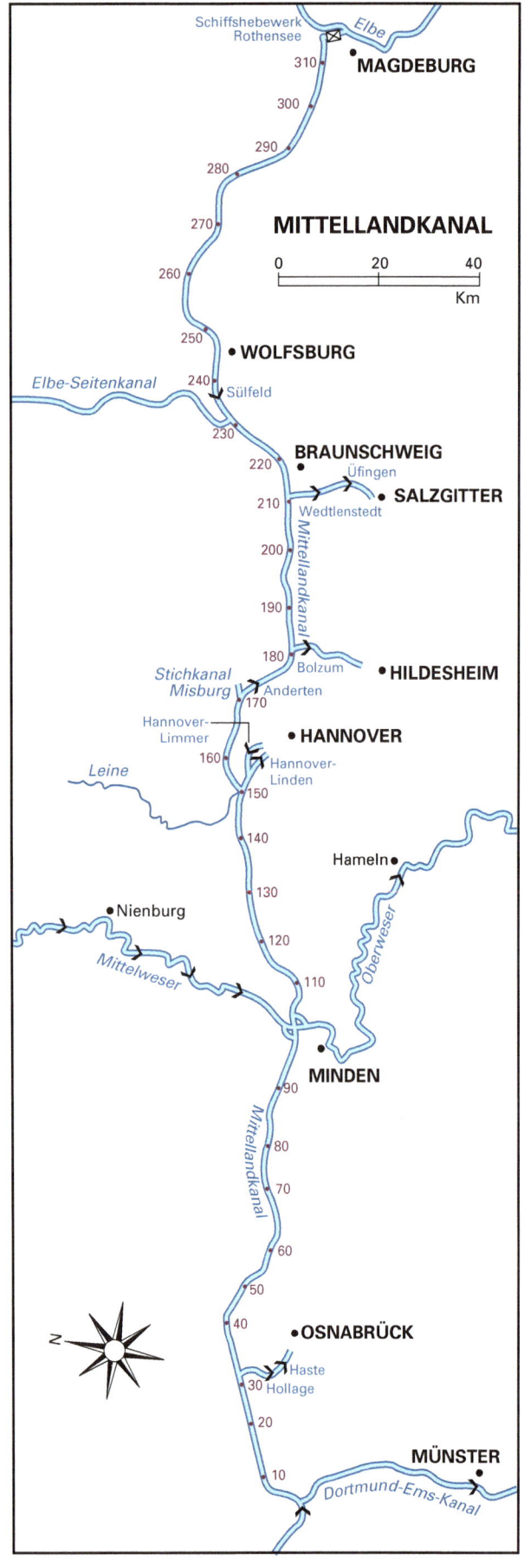

For canal engineering enthusiasts, there are several installations worthy of inspection. Adjoining the new Minden Aqueduct built in 1993, which in itself is impressive, is the old 375m-long eight-arch Minden viaduct, constructed in 1914 in ferroconcrete, which was a major achievement at the time. Nearby, the Minden Schachtschleuse, completed in 1912 and linking the MLK with the Weser, was an important example of sophisticated lock technology. The 1939-built Rothensee ship-lift at Magdeburg is yet another interesting piece of canal engineering history. The future of the lift is uncertain, as it has been replaced by the new Schleuse Rothensee and the long awaited impressive Magdeburg Aqueduct which now joins the Mittellandkanal with the EHK, providing a swift, unimpaired passage across the River Elbe with panoramic views extending across the valley. It was opened for navigation in July 2004, but the idea was first conceived in 1919; its construction having been hampered by World War and various economic problems.

There is a steady flow of European commercial barges and large pusher tows with various leisure boats amongst them, navigating their way across Germany. It is wise to listen out on VHF Ch 10 for local barge to barge traffic information and the advertised VHF frequencies, as there are frequent and useful navigation information broadcasts.

Km

0·0	Junction with the Dortmund-Ems-Kanal Km 108·4
0·6	Floodgates. VHF Ch 20
4·4	Entrance to old channel on south bank. Moorings for leisure craft on both sides of old channel.
7·5	Mooring place for leisure craft on both banks.
12·8	Marina Recke. Water, electricity, toilet, showers, slip. Restaurant 1km.
17·0	VHF Ch 78.
30·0	Mooring place for leisure craft on north bank.
30·4	Junction with the Stichkanal Osnabrück on south bank.

Stichkanal Osnabrück

Navigable distance 14·5km
Maximum draught 2·10m
Maximum height 4·00m
Current Nil
Locks 2
Hours 0600–2000 Mon–Fri, 0600–1600 Saturday, closed Sunday
Speed limit 12km/h

This short canal links the town of Osnabrück to the Mittellandkanal.

Km

0·0	Junction with Mittellandkanal Km 30·4
5·9	Yacht harbour on east bank. Yachthafen des Osnabrücker MYC. Depth 2m. Water, electricity, showers, clubhouse, washing machine, dryer, slip, diesel, 3-tonne crane.
7·2	*Schleuse Hollage* Rise 4·8m VHF Ch 78
12·7	*Schleuse Haste* Rise 4·8m VHF Ch 78
14·0	Hafen **Osnabrück**. Depth 3m. Commercial harbour, but may be possible to find a place to moor. 20 minutes from town centre.

Mittellandkanal (continued)

33·2	Mooring place for leisure craft on north bank.
33·8	Mooring place for leisure craft on north bank.
40·0	VHF Ch 79.
46·9	Mooring place for leisure craft on south bank.
47·5	Inlet with moorings for leisure craft on north bank.
53·9	Mooring place for leisure craft on north bank.
62·1	Yacht harbour in quiet basin on north bank. Motoryachtclub Mittelland Bad Essen. Depth 1·7m in 6·3m wide entrance. Water, electricity, toilet, showers, clubhouse, fuel, repairs, slip, 5-tonne crane. Shops 1·5km.
70·6	Yacht harbour in small bay on south bank. WSV Preußisch-Ol-dendorf. Depth 1·8m. Water, electricity, showers, clubhouse, repairs. Shops near by.

Motoryachtclub Bad Essen at 62.1km, Mittellandkanal

71·3	Mooring place for leisure craft on north bank. Shallows at eastern end.
80·4	Sportboothafen Lübbecke. Motor-Yacht-Club Lübbecke in small basin on south bank. Three guest moorings max length 18m. Depth 1·5m. Water, electricity, showers, toilets, clubhouse, fuel, slip, 15-tonne crane. Shops 2km.
83·0	VHF Ch 22.
89·0	Possible moorings on south bank.
97·0	Sportboothafen – Minder Yacht Club. Depth 1m. Water, electricity, toilets, showers.
100·6	Bunker boat for diesel on south bank.
101·4	VHF 25 Kanal Brücke Minden
101·6	Junction with Nordabstieg zur Weser (northern connection canal to Weser). Good bank-side mooring, no facilities before entrance to lock.

Sportboothafen, Motor Yacht Club Lubbecke, at 80.4km

MIDDLE

Nordabstieg zur Weser (Verbindungskanal Nord)

Navigable distance 1·2km
Maximum draught 2·10m
Maximum height 4·00m
Current Nil
Locks 1
Hours 0500–2100 Mon–Sat and 0800–1100 Sunday

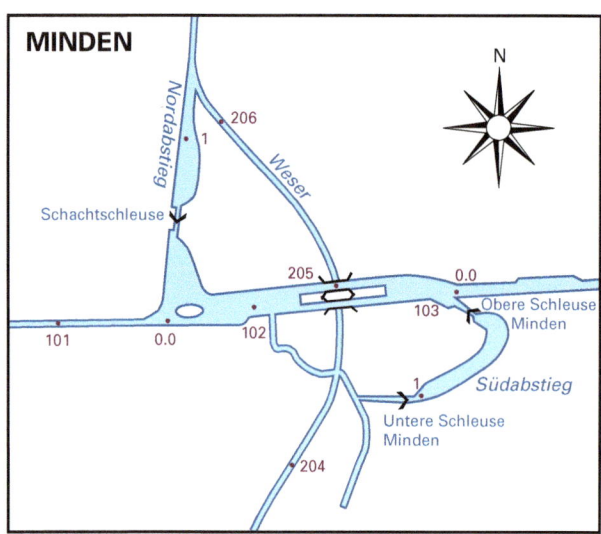

At the old town of Minden, the Mittellandkanal crosses the Weser by means of a high viaduct.

Ships can transfer from the canal to the river via either of two Verbindungskanäle (connecting canals) (see plan). The Nordabstieg has one lock, Schachtschleuse Minden, which is an interesting piece of canal engineering, having been one of the first locks to have its water inlets in the bottom of the chamber. This creates considerably less turbulence when the lock is filling than the more normal method of filling by means of sluices in the upper gates.

Km

0·0	Junction with Mittellandkanal Km 101·6.
0·1	Pleasant mooring to bank on west side above lock.
0·5	*Schachtschleuse Minden* Fall 13·2m VHF Ch 22
1·0	Mooring place below lock.
1·2	Junction with Weser Km 206·2.

Mittellandkanal (continued)

102·4	Aqueduct over the Weser River, depth 4·00m and width of channel 42·00m.
102·9	Junction with Südabstieg zur Weser (southern connecting canal to Weser).

Minden aqueduct over Weser river

Südabstieg zur Weser (Verbindungskanal Sud)

Navigable distance 1·4km
Maximum draught 1·90m
Maximum height 3·80m
Current Nil
Locks 2
Hours 0730–1600 weekdays, 0800–1200 Sat, closed Sun

As an alternative to the *Schachtschleuse*, traffic transferring from the MLK to the Weser or vice versa can use the Verbindungskanal Süd, with two conventional locks. It also provides access to Minden commercial harbour.

Km

0·0	Junction with Mittellandkanal Km 102·9
0·2	*Obere Schleuse* Fall 6·3m VHF Ch 25
0·5	Hafen **Minden**. Commercial harbour.
1·0	*Untere Schleuse* Fall 7·0m VHF Ch 23
1·4	Junction with Weser Km 204·5.

Schachtschleuse, Minden

MIDDLE

Mittellandkanal (continued)

107·5	Moorings for leisure craft on north bank.
110	VHF Ch 81.
123·3	Mooring place for barges and leisure craft on south bank. Village nearby.
130·0	VHF Ch 82.
135·2	Marina on north bank. Yachthafen Idensen. Depth 1·7m in 7m wide entrance. Water, electricity, showers, toilets, clubhouse, repairs, slip, 11t crane, restaurant. Shops 1km.
138·0	Moorings for leisure craft on south bank.
143·2	Moorings for leisure craft on south bank.
148·5	Moorings for leisure craft on north bank.
149·4	Bunker boat for diesel on south bank.
149·7	Junction with Stichkanal Hannover-Linden.

Stichkanal Hannover-Linden

Navigable distance 11·2km
Maximum draught 1·90m
Maximum height 4·00m
Current Nil
Locks 1
Hours 0900–1900 Mon–Fri, 0600–1200 Sat, closed Sun

Connecting canal between Hannover and the Mittellandkanal. Also links to a short navigable stretch of the Leine, chiefly to transport fuel to the power station situated there.

Km

0·0	Junction with Mittellandkanal Km 149·7.
0·4	Mariner Rasche-Werft. Showers, toilets, water, electricity. Bistro.
2·4	Motorboot-Sportclub Seelze. Depth 2m. Water, electricity, showers, fuel, repairs, slip, crane. Shops and restaurants 10 mins.

Yacht Harbour Hannover

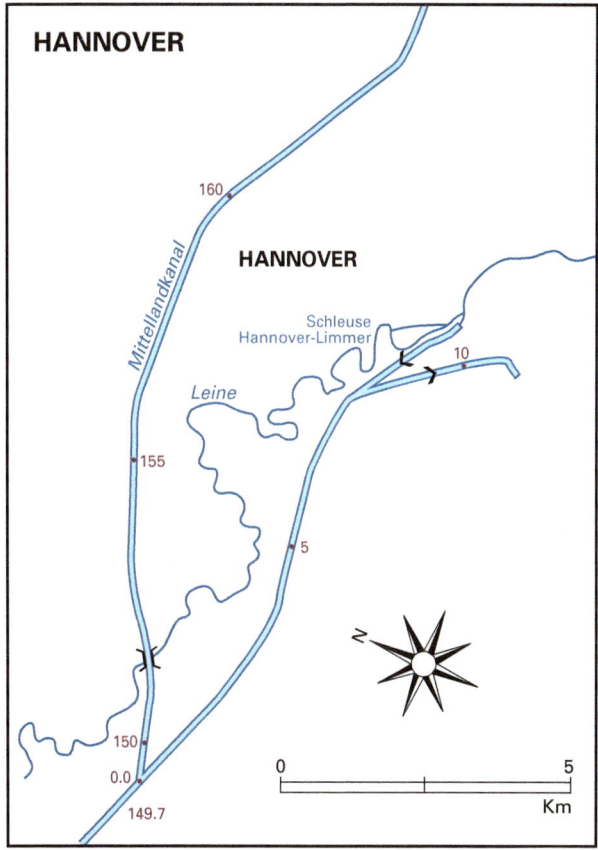

8·5	Niedersächsischer Motor-Boot-Club. Depth 1·5m. Water, electricity, toilets, showers, 4·5-tonne crane. Shops and restaurants Limmer, 25 minutes. Trams to Hannover from Limmer.
	Junction with Abstiegskanal zur Leine (linking canal to Leine). Not recommended for leisure craft beyond this junction.

Abstiegskanal zur Leine

Navigable distance 1·8km
Maximum draught 1·50m
Maximum height 4·00m
Current Nil
Locks 1
Hours Weekdays 0700–1430, by advance notice only

This short canal connects the Stichkanal Hannover-Linden and the short navigable stretch of the Leine. Its main purpose is to serve the nearby power station.

Km

0·0	Junction with Stichkanal Hannover-Linden.
0·6	*Schleuse Hannover-Limmer* Fall 2·0m VHF Ch 20
1·8	Junction with Leine.

MIDDLE

Stichkanal Hannover-Linden (continued)

9·5 *Hafenschleuse Hannover-Linden*
Rise 7·8m
VHF Ch 20

11·2 Linden commercial harbour. End of canal.

Mittellandkanal (continued)

152·8 Moorings for leisure craft on north bank. Shops. Beer garden.

153·7 Flood gates.

155·0 Moorings for leisure craft on south bank.

163·0 Mooring for small leisure craft south bank, beside road.

163·5 Yacht harbour on south bank. Yachtfahen Marine-Kameradschaft **Hannover**. Depth 1·5m. Water, electricity, showers, toilets, washing machine, dryer, clubhouse, diesel, repairs. Supermarket 1km. 15 minutes to Hannover by bus.

165·0 Moorings for leisure craft on south bank. VHF Ch 18.

171·2 Marina entrance, north side.

171·2 Junction with Stichkanal Misburg.

Stichkanal Misburg

> **Navigable distance** 3·5km
> **Maximum draught** 1·90m
> **Maximum height** 4·00m
> **Locks** 0

Entering Schleuse Anderten

Leaving Schleuse Anderten

A short canal leading past an oil terminal into quiet and rural surroundings. Beyond lies more industry.

Km

0·0 Junction with Mittellandkanal Km 171·2.

Ca1 Possible moorings on north bank.

2·0 Hannoverscher Motorboot-Club e V moorings, electricity, water, toilets, shower, washing machine, dryer, shop.

3·5 End of canal.

Mittellandkanal (continued)

174·2 *Schleuse Anderten*
Rise 14·7m
VHF Ch 18

Hours 0600–2200 daily. Exceptions are Easter Sunday, Whit Sunday and 1 May, when it operates 0800–1730.

Call up Schleusen Mister and register your presence on VHF Ch 18 or ☏ 0511 95085 2230. You will be invited to tie up on the north bank at the sports boat holding quay and you should wait your turn. You are likely to be called up on VHF Ch 18 and advised when to proceed into one of the two lock chambers. 217m long. 12m wide. Fixed crucible bollards. Leisure craft must lock with commercial vessels. Take care when exiting the lock as there will be numerous commercial vessels waiting to enter at the lock exit/entrance. Allow plenty of time to pass through lock, can be 3hrs or more.

174·9 To enter lock from the opposite side, the same applies.

183·2 Junction with Stichkanal Hildesheim.

Stichkanal Hildesheim

> **Navigable distance** 15·1km
> **Maximum draught** 2·0m
> **Maximum height** 4·00m
> **Locks** 1
> **Hours** 0600–2000 Mon–Fri and 0600–1600 Saturday
> **Speed Limit** 12km/h

Links the historic city of Hildesheim to the Mittellandkanal. There are no yacht clubs or harbours, but it is possible to lie alongside the quay at the end of the main harbour. No facilities. Shops and restaurants in the vicinity.

Leisure craft must lock with commercial vessels.

MIDDLE

Km	
0·0	Junction with Mittellandkanal Km 183·2.
0·6	*Schleuse Bolzum* Rise 8·0m VHF Ch 78
14·6–15·1	Hafen **Hildesheim**. Moorings at end of main harbour.

Mittellandkanal (continued)

184·6	Small yacht harbour on north bank. Motorboot Club Sehnde; depth 1·2m, berths max 8m long, longer boats moor alongside, water, electricity, toilets, showers, pump out, washing machine, restaurant, slip, 1·5-tonne crane.
195·0	Inlet on north bank. Possible overnight mooring.
197·0	Moorings for leisure craft on south bank.
199·0	Moorings for leisure craft on north and south bank.
200·4	Inlet on south bank. Possible overnight mooring.
201·1	Watersports club on north bank. 80m landing stage. Depth 1·5m. water, electricity, showers, clubhouse, 4-tonne crane. Closed in spring.
202·0	Inlet on north bank. Possible overnight mooring. VHF Ch 79.
210·9	Overnight mooring place with café on north bank.
213·5	Junction with Stichkanal Salzgitter.

Stichkanal Salzgitter

> **Navigable distance** 18·0km
> **Maximum draught** 2·20m
> **Maximum height** 4·20m
> **Locks** 2
> **Hours** Mon–Sat 0600 to 2200, Sunday 0800–1600. Closed 25/26 Dec & 1 Jan.
> **Speed Limit** 12km/h

This canal is heavily industrial, although the Heidanger yacht harbour is very pleasant. If leisure craft venture further along the canal they should use the eastern chamber at each lock and must lock with commercial vessels.

Km	
0·0	Junction with Mittellandkanal Km 213·5.
3·6	Heidanger yacht harbour on east bank. Depth 2m. Water, electricity, toilets, showers, clubhouse, washing machine, restaurant, repairs, slip, crane. Shops 1km.
4·6	*Schleuse Wedtlenstedt* Rise 8m VHF Ch 79
10·7	*Schleuse Fingen* Rise 9·0m VHF Ch 79
14·8	Bunker boat for diesel.
18·0	**Salzgitter**. End of canal.

Mittellandkanal (continued)

213·5	New yacht basin on south bank under construction entry via lifting bridge.
213·5	Moorings for leisure craft north side.
214·0	Moorings for leisure craft south side.
217·5	Yacht Harbour north side MBC Braunschweig. Depth 1·3m in 9m-wide entrance. Water, showers, toilets, electricity, diesel, Clubhouse, 1·6-tonne crane.
219·0	Moorings for leisure craft north side.
219·0	**Braunschweig**. Hafen Braunschweig for commercial vessels.
222·0	VHF Ch 20.
227·3	Small refurbished yacht harbour on south bank. Marina Abbesbüttel, depth 2·5m. Water, electricity, showers, clubhouse.
233·7	Junction with Elbe-Seitenkanal Km 0·0.
233·9	Moorings for leisure craft south side.
235·2	Yacht basin on south bank. YC-Hoffmannstadt Fallersleben depth 1·3m. max length 14m. Water, electricity, showers, toilets, slip. Shops 15 minutes.
236·9	*Schleuse Sülfeld* Fall 9·0m VHF Ch 20 Hours 24hrs a day, daily. Exceptions: closed 24–27 December and 31 December to 2 January; operates from 0600 on 27 December to 1200 on 31 December.

Floating bollards in Schleuse Sülfeld

MIDDLE

Volkswagen visitor building, Wolfsberg

Sportboothafen Haldensleben, Mittellandkanal

Call up Schleusen Mister on VHF Ch 20 or ☏ 05362 96112150 and register your presence. You will be invited to tie up on the north bank at the sports boat holding quay and wait your turn. You are likely to be called up on VHF Ch 20. Floating bollards. Leisure boats must lock with commercial vessels.

241·0	Possible mooring place on south bank.
Ca245	**Wolfsburg.** Volkswagen car plant.
245·6	Moorings for leisure craft south side adjacent to Wolfsburg Railway Station.
246·5	Yacht basin north side, next door to Wolfsburg football stadium. Motorbootclub Wolfsburg. Depth 1·4m in 8m wide entrance. Water, electricity, toilets, showers, pump-out, clubhouse, restaurant, 6-tonne crane, close to railway station.
Ca255	Mooring place on north bank. Water and café.
258·0	VHF Ch 24.
268·7	Moorings on good piles with 35m double sided landing platform for leisure craft on north side at the beginning of the 1km commercial piles. No facilities.
283·9	Moorings for leisure craft on south bank at far end of quay after commercial moorings.
293·4	Moorings on north bank.
294·7	**Bülstringen.** Moorings on north and south banks. Shops.
299·0	Moorings on south bank.
300·8	**Haldensleben.** Sportboothafen Wsf Haldensleben south side. 1·70m depth, 7m side-board berths, 9m back-board berths, guest berths max 15m. Water, toilets, showers, disabled access, slip, pump-out. Shops. Restaurant.
301·0	Possible moorings on north bank. Followed by Commercial Hafen Haldensleben.
302·4	Floodgates.
305·0	Upgraded section of Mittellandkanal. Depth 4·2m. Restricted speed limit 7km/h where works in progress.
309·0	VHF Ch 79.
315·3	Small Bootshaus Elbeu north side. Depth 1m. Water, toilets, showers, electricity, slip.
319·8	Junction with Rothenseer Verbindungskanal.
320·0	As you approach the 918m long Mittellandkanal Aqueduct call Brücke Mister on VHF Ch 26 or ☏ 039222/9517 200 and register your presence. Passage across the Aqueduct will take place in convoy. You will be invited to tie up on the south bank at the sports boat holding quay and wait your turn. The Mittellandkanal Aqueduct at Magdeburg is open 0600–2200 Mon–Sat and 0700–1900 Sunday and Bank Holidays.

Good moorings at 268.7 north bank of Mittellandkanal with landing platform for leisure boats

MIDDLE

Elbe Aqueduct, Mittellandkanal

Schleuse Hohenwarthe Entrance 19.5m deep

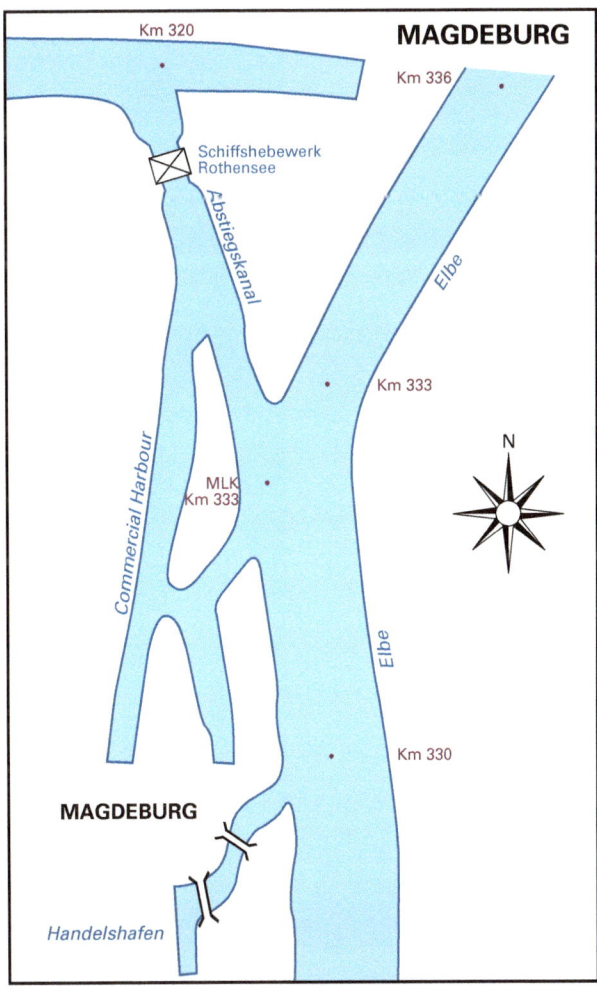

322·4 Exit to the Aqueduct.

325·1 *Schleuse Hohenwarthe*
Fall 19·5m
VHF Ch 26

Floating numbered bollards on south side only.

End of the Mittellandkanal at the entrance of the lock Schleuse Hohenwarthe and start of the Elbe-Havel-Kanal.

ELBE-SEITENKANAL

Navigable distance 115·2km
Maximum draught 2·50m
Maximum height 5·25m
Current Nil
Locks 2
Hours Mon–Sat 0600–2200, Sunday 0800–1730
Speed limit 12km/h

The Elbe-Seitenkanal, opened in 1976, was built to provide a link between Hamburg and the Mittellandkanal without passing through East Germany. It is straight and is flanked by banks just too tall to see over, which makes for a boring, albeit fast, journey. It is best to time one's journey to enable an overnight stop to be made at Uelzen, a pleasant, well equipped yacht harbour at a convenient point on the canal.

The difference in level of 61m between the MLK and the Elbe is accomplished with only two installations: the huge Lüneburg twin ship-lifts and a 23m-deep lock at Uelzen, both of which are very impressive engineering accomplishments. The experience of using them easily makes up for an otherwise boring journey. The layout of the ship-lift installation is shown on page 94.

The canal is operated by WSD-Mitte and use of it is free. The Uelzen lock has floating bollards.

Km

0·0 Junction with Mittellandkanal Km 233·7.

10·0 Osloss. Mooring for commercial vessels on east bank.

24·2 Siedlung Weisses Moor. Mooring for commercial vessels on east bank.

38·6 Hafen **Wittingen**. Commercial harbour on east side.

39·6 Possible mooring place on east bank.

50·0 Bodenteich. Overnight moorings on east bank.

60·6 *Schleuse Uelzen*
Fall 23·0m
VHF Ch 18

MIDDLE

65·9 **Uelzen.** Yacht harbour on east bank. Yachtclub Uelzen. Water, electricity, showers, clubhouse. Shop nearby.

71·1 Hafen Uelzen. Commercial harbour on west side.

79·6 Bad Bevensen. Overnight yacht moorings on west bank.

92·0 Wulfstorf. Overnight yacht moorings on east bank.

100·2 Hafen **Lüneburg**. Commercial harbour on west side.

106·1 *Schiffshebewerk Lüneburg,*
Fall 38·0m
VHF Ch 20

Twin ship-lifts. Moor to piled walls above and below lift whilst waiting.

115·2 Junction with Elbe Km 573·0.

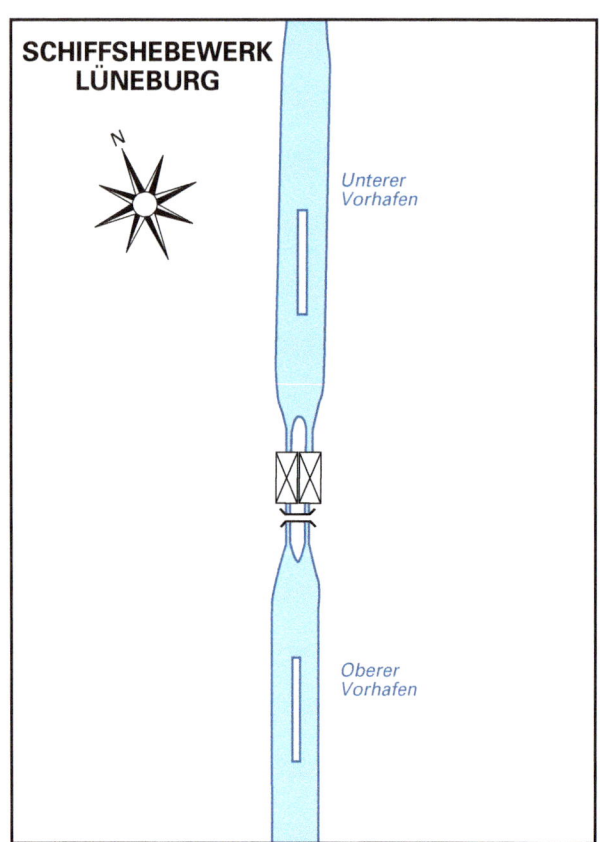

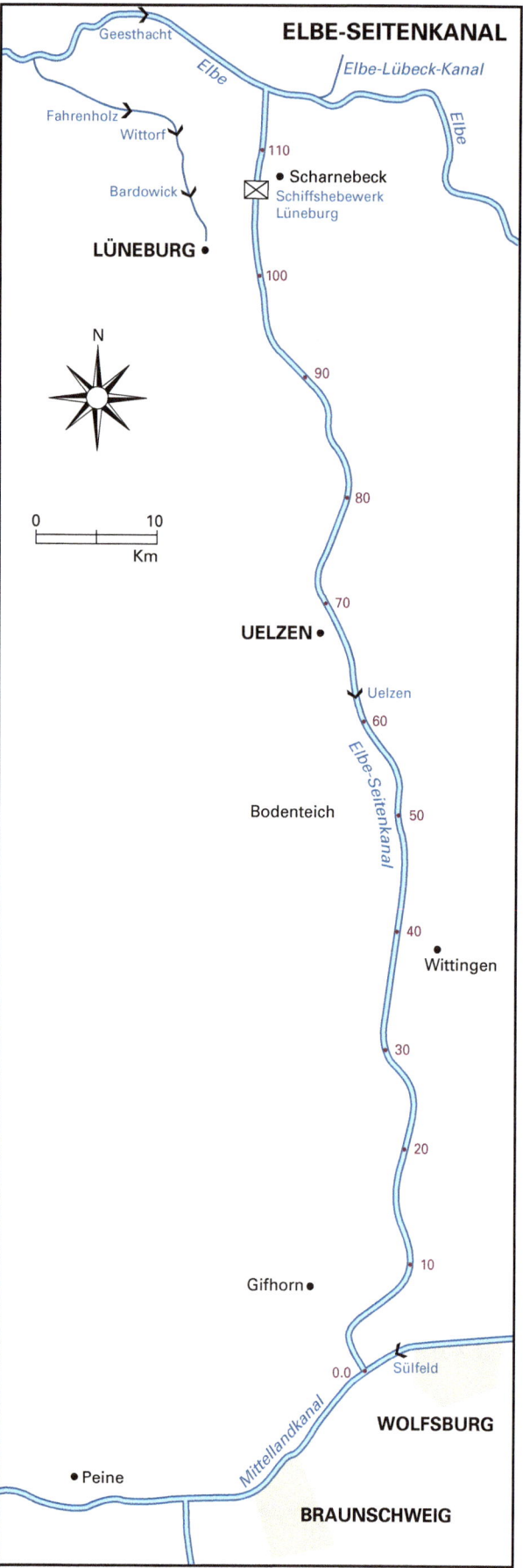

North

SCHIFFAHRTSWEG ELBE-WESER

Navigable distance 61·5km
Maximum draught 1·50m
Maximum height 2·60m
Current Negligible
Locks 3
Hours Varied. see route description
Speed limit 8km/h

Originally built in the late 19th century, the delightful little Schiffahrtsweg Elbe-Weser (Elbe-Weser shipping route) was reopened in 1962, linking the tidal Elbe with the tidal Weser. It comprises several waterways: the Medem, the Hadelner Kanal, the Aue, the Bederkesa-Geeste-Kanal and the Geeste. Between the picturesque and historic villages of Otterndorf and Bederkesa the route passes through fertile agricultural land. At Bederkesa it skirts the See von Bederkesa (Sea of Bederkesa) and continues towards Bremerhaven through a relatively marshy area, rich in wildlife. The waterway is quite narrow, and is suitable only for vessels under 33·5m long, 8m beam and 1·50m draught. At normal water levels the maximum permitted height of vessel is 2·60m. There is little commercial traffic, but meeting a barge can be a little hair-raising. Fortunately, the barge skippers are usually extremely helpful. Westbound vessels take priority over east-bound vessels when they meet.

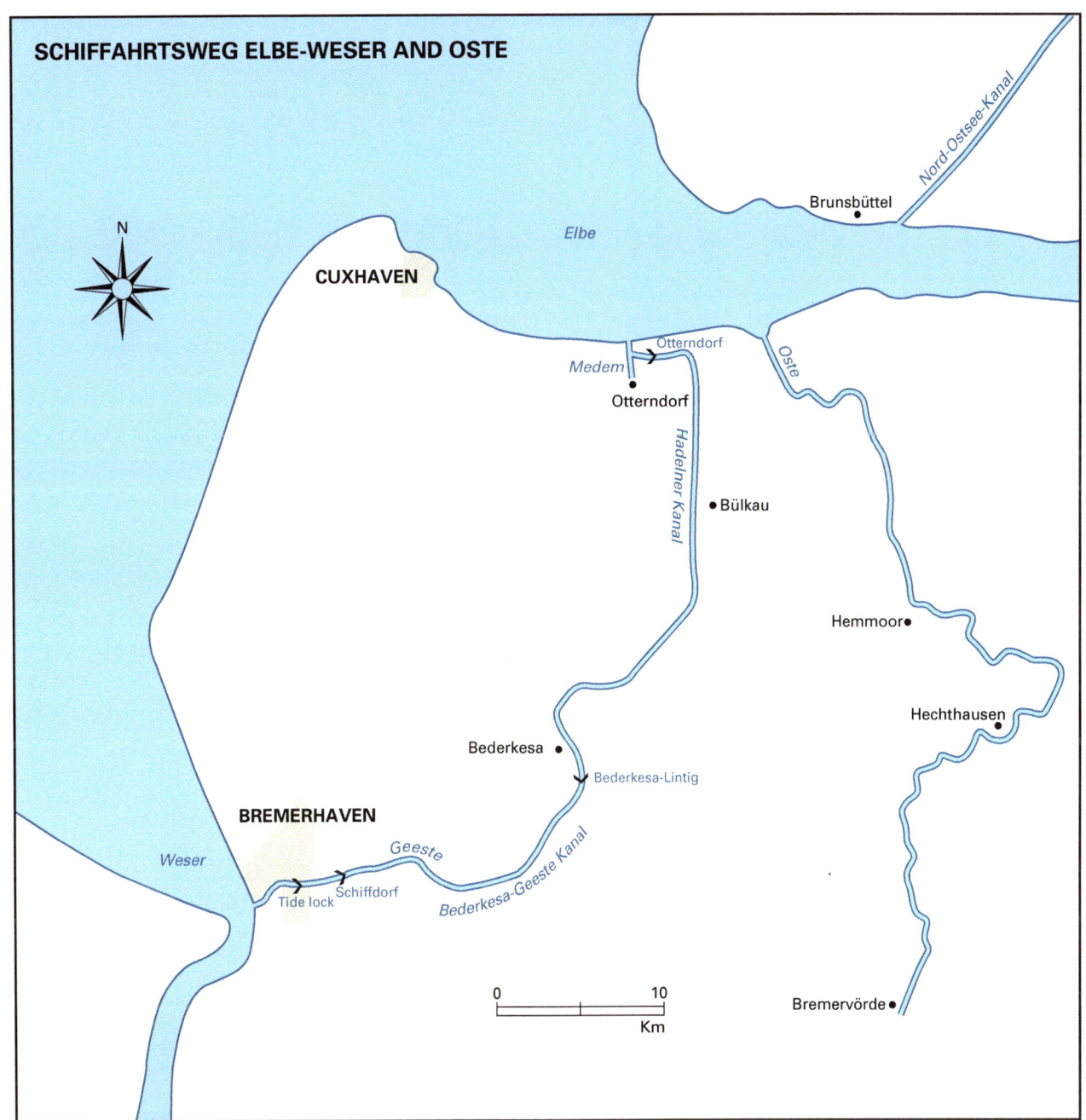

INLAND WATERWAYS OF GERMANY

NORTH

At Otterndorf access from the Elbe is via the mouth of the Medem, then via a lock through to the Hadelner Kanal. Timing a passage through this is a matter of judgement, as at HW there is insufficient headroom, whilst at LW the tidal part of the Medem dries. However, as the bottom of the tidal harbour is so soft that deep-keeled yachts sit up-right, running aground is unlikely to be disastrous. The harbourmaster will advise, and if necessary arrange access to the crane for removing or replacing masts.

At Bremerhaven the entrance to the Geeste is at Km 65·5 on the Unterweser, between a pair of light towers on the ends of the short moles guarding the entrance. Just inside, it is possible to lock into the fishing harbour, where there are good facilities for yachts. Alternatively, a vessel may proceed into the Geeste to the tide lock.

The waterway is not operated by WSD, but by the Land of Niedersachsen (Lower Saxony), and a charge is levied for using the canal and for each lock used. There is a strict speed limit of 8km/h on the waterway, and a vessel's speed is checked from the timed lock tickets.

Boats with a beam greater than 3·00m are required to fly flag N of the International Code of Signals on the bow.

Km

0·0	Junction with Elbe Km 712·5.
1·2	*Schleuse Otterndorf* Rise depends on tide in Elbe. Hours 0730–1730 4 hours around HW.
1·3	Possible mooring above lock on left bank.
1·4	Quiet mooring on left bank.
8·2	Railway bridge. Height 2·60m.
22·0	Possible overnight mooring.
ca31	**Bederkesa.** Pleasant overnight mooring. Water, electricity, showers. Shops and restaurants nearby.
34·0	*Schleuse Bederkesa-Lintig* Rise is very small. Hours Mon–Sat 0730–1730, Sunday 1000–1200 & 1500–1700. Overnight mooring. Fuel.
52·2	Former *Schleuse Schiffdorf.* Permanently open. Restaurant, mooring possible.
55·5	Yacht club. Water, electricity.
56·0	*Tidesperrwerk.* Fall depends on tide in Weser. Hours 0700–1830.
60·4	Flood barrier under bridge.
61·2	Tidal mooring place. Water, electricity, chandlery. Shops and restaurants nearby.
61·4	Entry to fishing harbour on left side via lock. Marina. Water, electricity, showers, restaurant.
61·5	Junction with Unterweser Km 65·5.

NORD-OSTSEE-KANAL (KIEL CANAL)

Navigable distance 98·2km
Maximum draught 9·50m
Maximum height 40m
Current None
Locks 2
Speed limit 15km/h

The Nord-Ostsee-Kanal is a heavily used commercial shipping route carrying the world's shipping between the North Sea and the Baltic. Throughout the day and night there is a constant stream of large seagoing vessels passing through it. Leisure craft without pilots may not transit the canal at night or in fog.

Negotiating the canal in a small boat is very easy. Approaching either lock, all that is necessary is to hover in view of the control tower (but out of the way of commercial shipping) outside the lock until the white lights flash. There is no need to speak to the lock-keepers on VHF, although this is of course possible in case of difficulty. The fees for using the canal are as follows:

The appropriate fee is payable at the Holtenau end of the canal (during locking) whichever direction the transit is made in. A ticket should be bought from the news stand on the north side of the old (north) lock at Kiel-Holtenau and taken to the lock-keepers in the control tower to be stamped. It is possible, however, that the system may soon be changed so that the ticket is actually bought from the lock-keeper. Mooring in the locks is to wooden pontoons floating low in the water. Fenders are required at water level.

It goes without saying that a small boat should stay close to the starboard bank, well clear of the heavy traffic of large seagoing ships. Sailing is theoretically not permitted in the canal, but as it is acceptable to motor-sail it is difficult to see how the authorities are to tell whether or not the engine is running. Anchoring in the canal is forbidden, and stopping is restricted to the places listed below in the route description.

The canal authorities can be contacted during transit by calling Kiel Canal 2 on VHF Ch 2 for the stretch from Brunsbuttel to Breiholz (Km 50) or Kiel Canal 3 on VHF Ch 3 for the stretch from Breiholz to Kiel-Holtenau.

It may be useful to know that British, German and Scandinavian charts and navigational books can be bought at the Kiel-Holtenau lock from Kapitan Stegmann, whose shop is on the small industrial estate immediately south of the new lock.

The transit, which can be accomplished in one day in most cruising boats, is on the whole lacking in interest, except for the wonderful old transporter bridge at Rendsburg - and of course the world's ships, which pass in a continuous stream.

NORTH

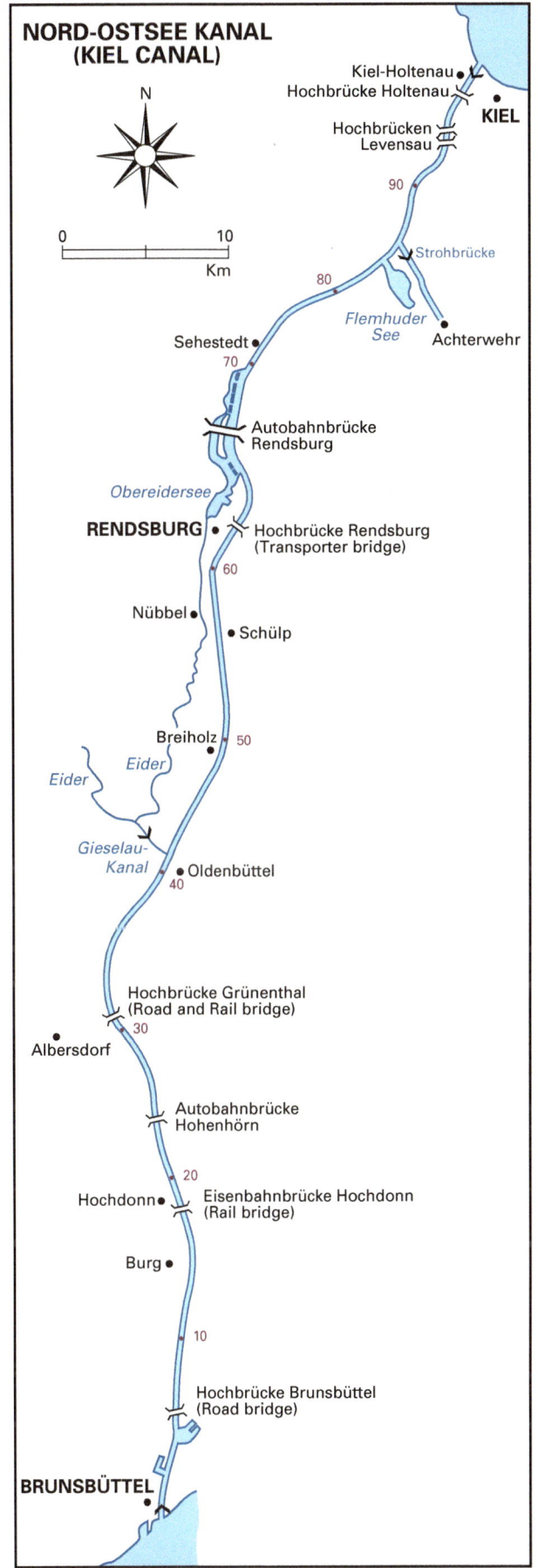

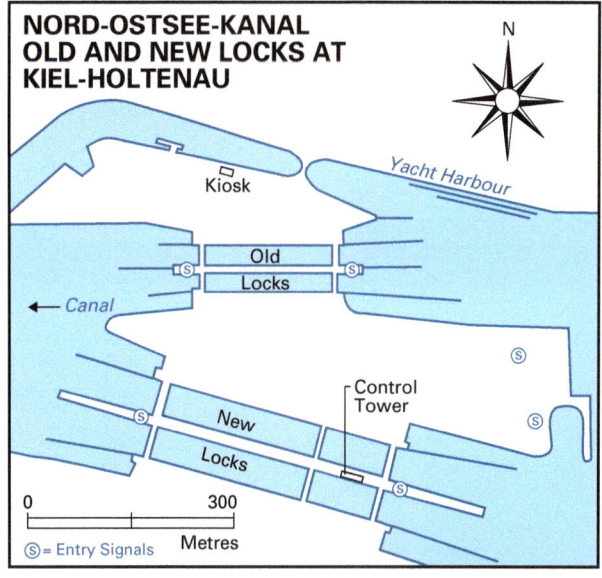

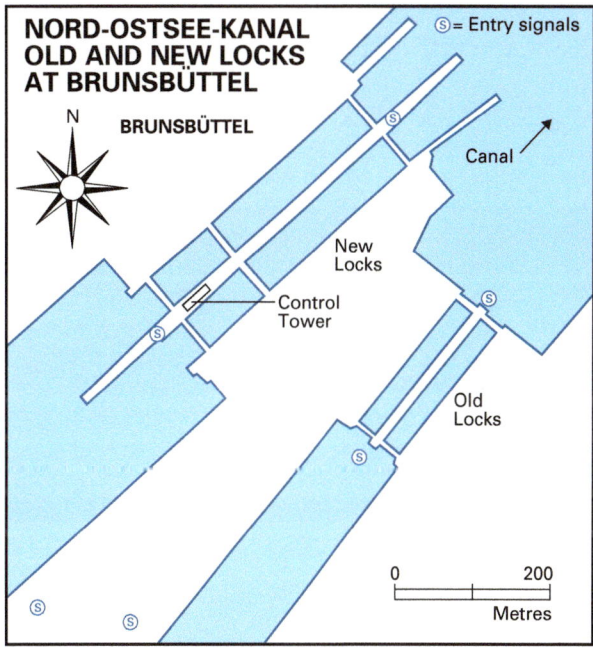

Km

0·0   Junction with Elbe Km 696·4.

1·5   *Neue Schleuse* und *Alte Schleuse* Brunsbüttel
Rise Depends on tide in Elbe.
VHF Ch 13 (call Kiel Canal 1).

Two old locks and two new locks.

1·8   Yachthafen **Brunsbüttel** on north bank.

2·7   Additional yacht moorings on north side of canal.

20·6 Possible overnight mooring on north side.

40·7 Junction with Gieselaukanal, linking to Eider. Mooring permitted before lock.

62·7 **Rendsburg**. Transporter bridge for cars. Trains cross at high level.

INLAND WATERWAYS OF GERMANY

NORTH

66·1	Entrance to Obereidersee (old Eider). Yacht harbour. Diesel.
70·0	Borgstedter Enge. Floating moorings on north side.
85·5	Entrance to the Flernhuder See. Pleasant tree-lined anchorage on south bank.
85·6	Entrance to Achterwehrer Schiffahrtskanal via Schleuse Strohbrücke. Max. draught 2m. Speed limit 8km/h.
98·0	*Neue Schleuse und Alte Schleuse Kiel-Holtenau* Fall is very small, probably 20cm. VHF Ch 12 (call Kiel Canal 4). Two old locks and two new locks.
98·5	**Kiel-Holtenau.** Yacht harbour on north side outside lock.
98·6	Junction with Kieler Forde (Kiel Fiord).

EIDER AND GIESELAUKANAL

For a boat heading for the Baltic via the Nord-Ostsee-Kanal (Kiel Canal), it is well worth considering the more leisurely route via the Eider as an alternative to braving the tides of the Elbe estuary and then slogging along the first part of the NOK. The home of the ubiquitous eider duck, the Eider is a little-used but quite delightful river, meandering in huge loops through pastoral countryside with cattle standing knee-deep at the banks, buzzards wheeling overhead, an abundance of herons and - of course - eider ducks by the thousand.

1. EIDER: NORTH SEA TO GIESELAU- KANAL

Km 110·0-Km 22·8
Navigable distance 87·2km
Maximum draught 2·50m, 2m in tidal section at LW
Maximum height Unlimited
Current Tidal to Nordfeld, then 2–3km/h
Locks 3
Hours Summer Mon–Sat 0800–1900, Sunday 0800–1000 & 1600–1800
Speed limit 15km/h upstream of Friedrichstadt

From the off-lying Eider buoy there is a clearly buoyed channel to the flood barrier with a two-way tide lock on the north side of the barrier. From there to Tönning, 11km from the flood barrier, the route crosses a wild salt-water mere before narrowing to a river which continues to the Nordfeld lock. The channel is tidal but well marked with buoys and withies and has a minimum depth of 2m. Nevertheless it is advisable to carry out this passage on a rising tide.

At Friedrichstadt, between Tönning and Nordfeld, it is possible to go through the Friedrichstadt lock into the Treene. There is a good yacht club for an overnight stay at Friedrichstadt, a picturesque mediaeval town.

Shortly after the Lexfahre lock the river swings to port towards Rendsburg, but the route to the NOK goes to starboard into the short Gieselaukanal.

Each lock has its own operating times. These are shown in the route description below. Only the lock

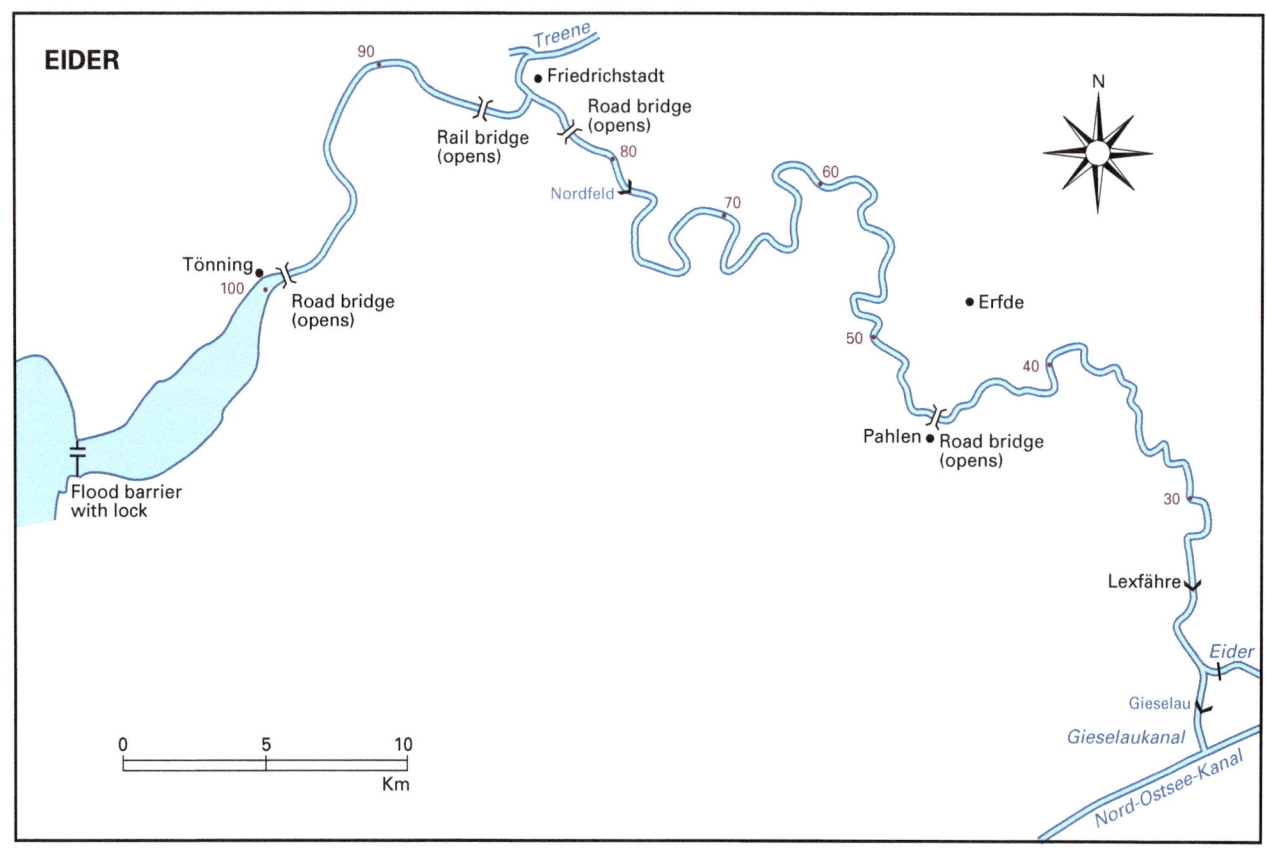

at the flood barrier is equipped with VHF radio. A fee is levied for using the locks.

Km

110·0	Eider flood barrier with lock Rise depends on tide. Hours Always available. VHF Ch 14.
100·2	Hafen Tonning, Dries at LW. Soft mud.
99·0	Opening road bridge. Closed height 5·60m above mean HW. Operates 0700–1900 daily during summer. On Sundays advance notice is required ☎ 04861 5690.
85·0	Opening railway bridge. Closed height 3·95m above mean HW. Operates Monday–Saturday 0430–2300 and Sunday 0600–2300.
83·7	**Friedrichstadt**. Junction with Treene via *Schleuse Friedrichstadt*. Approach to lock 1m deep at LW. Yacht harbour 1km into Treene.
83·0	Opening road bridge. Closed height 5·60m above mean HW. Operates 0700–1900 daily, but on Sundays advance notice is required ☎ 04881 260.
78·0	*Schleuse Nordfeld* Rise 0·20–1·60m
46·0	Opening road bridge. Closed height 3·50m above mean HW. Operates 0700–1900 daily, but on Sundays advance notice is required ☎ 04803 211.
26·0	*Schleuse Lexfahre* with opening bridge. Rise 0·10–0·20m
23·0	Junction with Gieselaukanal. Eider continues to Obereidersee, but through passage is not possible.

2. GIESELAUKANAL: EIDER TO NORD-OSTSEE-KANAL

Km 2·9–Km 0·0
Navigable distance 2·9km
Maximum draught 2·70m
Maximum height 21m
Current Nil
Locks 1
Hours Weekdays 0800–1300 & 1400–1800, Sunday 0800–1000 & 1600–1800
Speed limit 10km/h

The stretch of the Gieselaukanal between the lock and the Nord-Ostsee-Kanal is a convenient and peaceful overnight stop for small vessels passing through the Nord-Ostsee-Kanal.

Fees are vary according to length and increase above 12m. Navigation at night is forbidden.

Km

2·9	Junction with Eider Km 23·0
1·3	*Schleuse Gieselau* Rise 0·20–1·60m Mooring at bank. Junction with Nord-Ostsee-Kanal Km 40·7.
ca1	Mooring at bank.
0·0	Junction with Nord-Ostsee-Kanal Km 40·7.

ELBE-LÜBECK-KANAL AND TRAVE

Navigable distance 88·6km
Maximum draught 2·00m
Maximum height 4·20m
Current Negligible
Locks 7
Hours Summer, weekdays 0600–2100, Saturday 0600–1800 and Sunday 0700–1200
Speed limit 10km/h on ELK, 12km/h on Trave downstream from Km 5·6

The Elbe-Lübeck-Kanal links the Elbe to the Baltic at Travemünde. The section from the Elbe at Lauenburg to the beautiful seven-spired Hanseatic city of Lübeck is amongst lush countryside, partly wooded and partly agricultural, the home of herons, grebes and goldeneye. The canal joins the Trave near Lübeck, and from here onwards to the sea the river banks are mostly wooded until the busy ferry port of Travemunde is reached.

There is very little commercial traffic. The journey from Lauenburg to Lubeck normally takes about 12 hours, which makes an overnight stop desirable. The complex of old gravel pits at Guster, known as the Prüss-See and now converted into a leisure area, is a pleasant stopping-place. Alternatively, there are a number of places where it is possible to moor at the bank-side.

The canal is controlled by WSD-Ost, the Trave by WSD-Nord.

There is strict enforcement of the 10km/h speed limit on the canal. The lock-keepers check the running times between locks.

1. ELBE-LÜBECK-KANAL

Km

61·6	Junction with Elbe Km 569·2.
60·0	Hafen Lauenburg. Busy yacht harbour at staging on west side.
59·9	*Schleuse Lauenburg* Rise 4·8m VHF Ch 22
50·4	*Schleuse Witzeeze* Rise 3·3m VHF Ch 79

NORTH

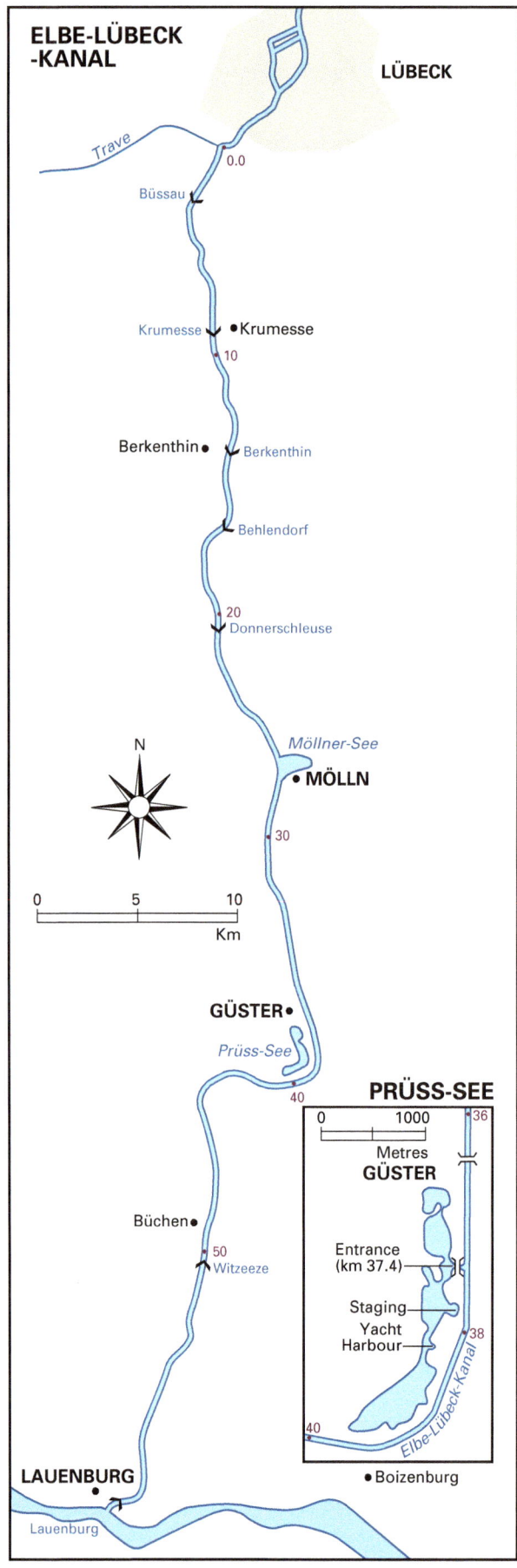

37·4	Entrance to Prüss-See. Privately owned leisure area, based on converted gravel pits. Yacht harbour and other mooring places. Campsite, restaurant, showers, shop. Depth in main parts varies 1·50–2·00m.
26·5	**Mölln.** Fuel and short-term mooring at town quay on Mollner-See on east side of canal. Depth 1·50m. 3 yacht clubs. Water, electricity, showers, clubhouse. Shops and restaurants nearby.
20·7	*Schleuse Donnerschleuse* Fall 4·2m VHF Ch 79
16·5	*Schleuse Behlendorf* Fall 1·7m
13·3	*Schleuse Berkenthin* Fall 1·8m
8·5	*Schleuse Krummesse* Fall 2·5m
3·4	*Schleuse Büssau* Fall 1·5m VHF Ch 78
0·0	Junction with Trave. Keep right into Trave for easiest through route.

2. TRAVE

0·0	Junction with Elbe-Lübeck-Kanal.
2·6	Yacht club on west side. Water, electricity, club-house. 2km from centre of Lübeck.
Ca5	**Lübeck.** Historic ship harbour in Holstenhafen. Close to city centre, but permission needed for mooring. Commercial *Hansahafen* beyond opening bridge. No facilities at either.
9·8	Yacht harbour on west side.
12·3	Yacht harbour on east side.
15·9	Fishing harbour, yacht harbour and boatyard on east side.
22–27	**Travemünde**
24·4	Scandinavian ferry quay on west side.
25·2	Marina Baltica on west side. All facilities.
25·4	Fuelling berth on west side.
25·8	Fuelling berth on east bank.
26·6	Passathafen on east side behind square-rigger *Passat*. All facilities, including crane for mast stepping and unstepping. Frequent ferry to town centre on west side of harbour.
27·0	Mouth of Trave. Access to Baltic Sea.

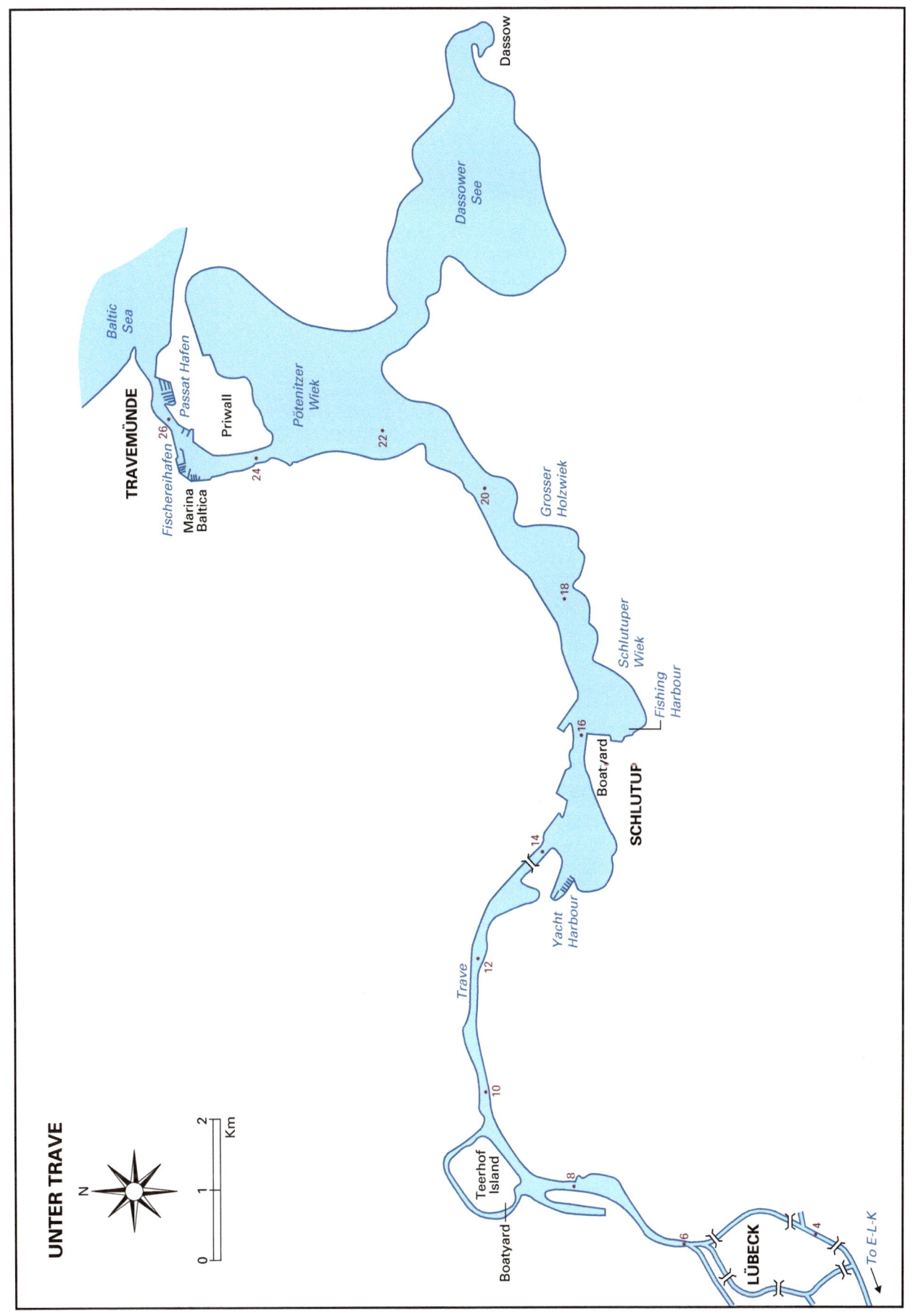

East

ELBE

The Elbe starts life as the Labe in the northern part of the Czech Republic. It is navigable for commercial shipping from Chvaletice, about 70km to the east of Prague. There are 15 locks from here to Melnik, where the Vltava (Moldau) joins the Labe from Prague. From Melnik to the border, where it flows into Germany as the Elbe, there are six locks. There are no locks in Germany except at Geesthacht, near Hamburg, where the river becomes tidal. The kilometering system in Germany is not contiguous with that within the Czech Republic, starting again with Km 0·0 at the border.

The river can be used by cruising boats from its mouth near Cuxhaven through to the interior of the Czech Republic, either to Prague and beyond on the Vltava or to Chvaletice (and possibly beyond) on the Labe. This gives a total cruising distance of some 950km, through scenery ranging from the wildness of the estuary to the towering sandstone cliffs of *die Bastei* in Sachsische Schweiz (Saxon Switzerland), the national park near the Czech border which embraces perhaps the most dramatic scenery in Germany.

Hydrology

Both the depth of the river and the strength of the current can vary widely. In normal conditions the minimum depth is in the range 1·50m to 3·00m and the strongest current is around 4 to 5km/h. However, when the river is in flood the current can become as much as 8 to 10km/h, whilst in dry seasons the depth can be as little as 0·70m in certain places. The trouble spots so far as depth is concerned are Torgau (Km 153·6–Km 154·8), Wittenberg (ea Km 217), Barby (Km 293·4–Km 312·1) and Magdeburg (Km 324·7–Km 333·6). The large hotel ships, drawing 1·15m, which operate between Prague, Hamburg and Szczecin (via the Havel-Oder-Wasserstrasse) are seldom unable to get through the whole length of the Elbe. The table below, based on 10 years' statistics, shows the monthly variations in minimum depth of water which might typically be expected in the Elbe between Lauenburg and the Czech border. As can be seen, the best time of the year for cruising on the Elbe is normally during May and June, when the probability of shoal depths is relatively low.

For convenience in publishing depth information, the river is considered as nine Strecken (stretches):

Elbe-Strecke 1	Schona to Dresden
Elbe-Strecke 2	Dresden to Riesa
Elbe-Strecke 3	Riesa to mouth of the Elster
Elbe-Strecke 4	Mouth of the Elster to Barby
Elbe-Strecke 5	Barby to Magdeburg
Elbe-Strecke 6	Magdeburg to Niegripp
Elbe-Strecke 7	Niegripp to Havelberg
Elbe-Strecke 8	Havelberg to Domitz
Elbe-Strecke 9	Dornitz to Lauenburg

With the exception of Strecke 6, the transit from the Mittelland-Kanal to the Elbe-Havel-Kanal, the Tauchtiefe (maximum permissible draught) for each Strecke is announced daily at 0755 and 1255 on Radio Aktuel (FM 89·0, 89·2 and 89·4MHz). For Strecke 6, the channel depth is announced, and ship captains are left to decide the weight of cargo which they can safely carry. Tauchtiefen can also be obtained over VHF from Geesthacht (Ch 22), Hitzacker (Ch 18) and Lauenburg (Ch 22). It is also possible to ask for the latest figures from WSA offices by VHF or by telephone (see *Appendix*).

Below Lauenburg there are no depth restrictions so far as cruising boats are concerned.

VHF radio

VHF frequencies are allocated as follows:

Ch	Purpose
10	Calling and safety channel (including police)
11	Ship to ship
12	Ship to land (including traffic control)
13	Ship to lock
14	Ship to land (including traffic control)
69	Tripper-boat channel
71	Ship to ship (including onboard communication)
73	WSA offices

The procedure is generally to use Ch 10 to establish the call, then to ask for the appropriate working channel. However, it may be found in many instances that direct calling on the working channel is usual.

ELBE MINIMUM DEPTHS
(Recorded depths over 10 years)

	Days under 1·0m	Days 1·00 to 1·50m	Days 1·50 to 2·00m	Days over 2·00m
May	0	3	5	23
June	0	6	11	13
July	3	15	9	4
August	4	13	6	8
Sept	1	14	12	3
October	1	14	9	7

EAST

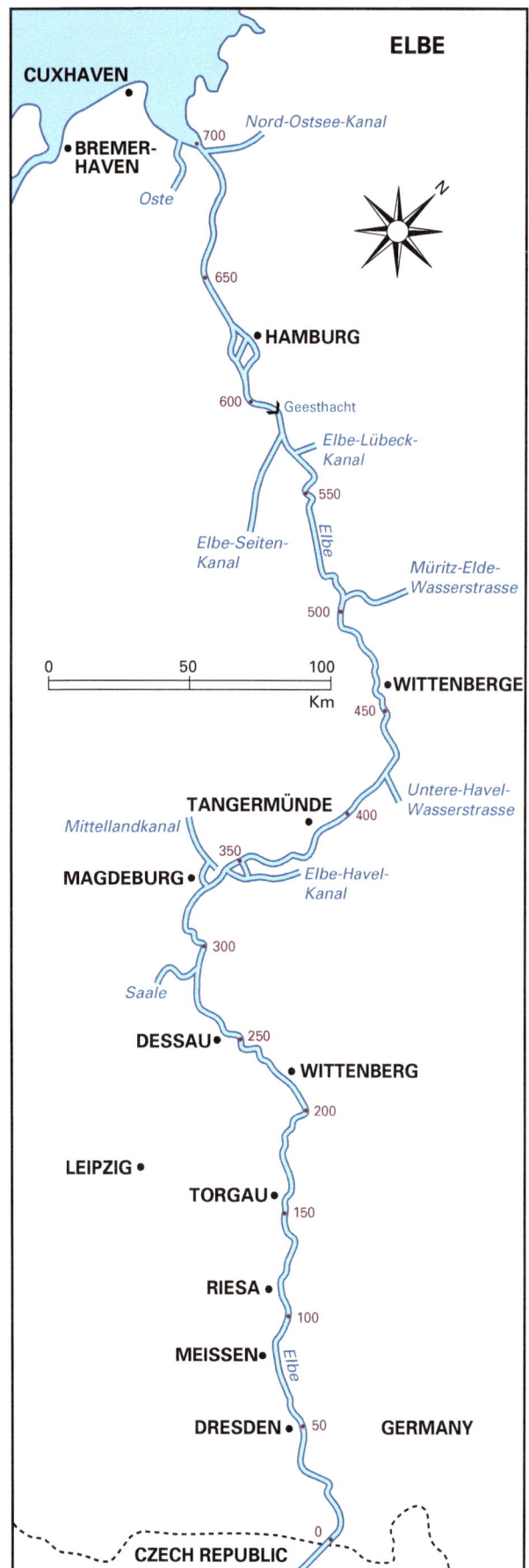

Fuel

The only diesel bunker stations on the Elbe above Geesthacht are at Wittenberg (Km 454·9), Magdeburg (Km 327·3 and Km 332·8) and Borschütz (Km 124·7). In general, therefore, it is necessary to buy fuel in cans from street filling stations, of which there are many within reasonable striking distance of mooring places.

Buoyage and markings

Buoyage along the whole length of the river is conventional: greens to the left and reds to the right heading downstream. Where the channel crosses from one side of the river to the other, it is marked by yellow crosses on the bank. Otherwise, internationally standard warning signs are placed as appropriate on banks and bridges (see Appendix VI). Kilometre marks are on the right bank.

1. CZECH BORDER TO GEESTHACHT

Km 0–Km 585·8
Navigable length 585·8km
Maximum draught See table
Maximum height 4·50m
Current 2–10km/h
Locks 1
Hours 0500–2200

The first stretch of the river is dramatic. From the frontier town of Schmilka, the river flows through the Sachsische Schweiz (Saxon Switzerland), an area of breathtaking beauty, past interesting old towns and villages such as Bad Schandau, Konigstein (with its spectacular mediaeval fortress hanging high above the river), Rathen and Wehlen, to the haunting city of Dresden.

For centuries Dresden was a major centre of culture and full of art treasures. It was a city of immense cultural importance and entirely without military significance, yet it was the scene of one of the worst atrocities of the Second World War. On the night of 13 February 1945 the British sent a force of 800 bombers to destroy it. Dresden was wiped out. 50,000 people, mostly women, children and the elderly, were massacred. For an Englishman, walking in the streets of Dresden is, to say the least, a thought-provoking experience. Unfortunately, the city has more recently become the centre of extreme nationalist activities, chiefly directed against foreign immigrant workers. It remains, however, a great Baroque city. The famous Zwinger palace has been beautifully reconstructed, as have Semper's magnificent opera house, the Catholic Hofkirche and the public buildings along the waterfront. It is a most interesting and attractive city.

Below Dresden the scenery loses much of its drama, but nevertheless the river runs through many interesting places. The old city of Meissen, for example, where the cathedral and the castle stand joined together high above the river, is famous the world over for its porcelain. Wittenberg, Luther's town and the birthplace of the Reformation and the

Protestant world, still has the austere feel of Luther's day. Dessau, where the famous Bauhaus school of art originated, is fascinating, even though it too was largely destroyed by Allied bombing in the Second World War.

Magdeburg, although in times past an important religious and scholastic centre, is badly scarred by some of the worst architectural atrocities of the Communist era, but further downstream Tangermunde, the old Hanseatic town on the left bank of the river, is something of a jewel of mediaeval buildings. From here onwards the river meanders through low-lying agricultural land as far as Geesthacht, where a lock marks the beginning of the tidal part of the Elbe.

The Elbe above Magdeburg is an extremely interesting area in which to cruise, but the higher reaches of the river do perhaps present a number of practical problems. Depths can be a serious problem in a dry season during July, August and September, and the currents, although normally in the region of 4–5kn, can vary widely according to the volume of water coming down the river. Recognised overnight mooring places are also somewhat few and far between, and finding a quiet place to tie up for the night may sometimes call for the exercise of some degree of ingenuity.

The depth of the river at Magdeburg has always been a problem for east/west shipping passing from the Mittellandkanal to the Elbe-Havel-Kanal, and most people had given up all hope that the viaduct to carry the MLK over the Elbe, on which work was abandoned at the outbreak of the Second World War, would ever come to fruition. However, the project has now been re-established, and there is every hope that in the not too distant future shipping will bypass the Rothensee lift and continue over the top of the Elbe to a new lock, Doppelschleuse Hohenwarthe, which will have a rise of 18·5m and provide a direct connection to the EHK behind Schleuse Niegripp. The new layout is shown on page 107.

Km

0·0	Border with Czech Republic on left bank.
2·7	Customs post on right bank.
3·4	Border with Czech Republic on right bank.
3·9	Schmilka.
8·0	Mooring place on right bank. Water, toilets. Provisions and restaurants 2km.
9·0	Shipyard on right bank.
11·0	Bad Schandau. Quay near railway station.
13·2	Hafen Prossen on right bank. Water authority harbour. Mooring not normally allowed.
15·5	Filling station near to left bank.
17·2	Konigstein, public harbour. No facilities. Possible depth problems when water levels low.
17·5	Festung Konigstein on left bank.
221	Rathen. Possibility of mooring at ferry landing on right bank.
23·5	Bastei. Towering sandstone cliffs on right bank.
26·0	Wehlen. Possibility of mooring at ferry landing.
33·5	Hafen Copitz. Shallow: 1·00m when *Pegel* Dresden reads 190. Access to Pirna. Showers. Shops and restaurants nearby.
45·6	Possible mooring place on left bank.
43·0	Schloss Pillnitz on right bank.
47·2	Sailing club on right bank. Clubhouse. Shops and restaurants nearby.
48·5	Possible mooring at staging on left bank.
50·5	Hafen Dresden-Loschwitz. City centre 5km. Enter carefully - possibly subject to silting. Water, electricity, showers, clubhouse, slip. Shops and restaurants nearby. Filling station 1km.
55·0	**Dresden**. Possibility of mooring amongst passenger ships on left bank close to city centre.
57·3	Hafen Dresden-Neustadt. Harbour for passenger ships on right bank. Sport boats prohibited.
58·5	Hafen Pieschen on right bank. Water, clubhouse, provisions, fuel nearby. City centre 2km. Shallow-draught boats only.
60·5	Hafen Dresden-Friedrichstadt. Commercial harbour.
68·1	Yachthafen Kotzschenbroda (Radebeul) on right bank. Showers, provisions, clubhouse, repairs.
72·9	Yachthafen Coswig on right bank. Water, electricity, showers, clubhouse, provisions 1km.
73·9	Schloss Gauernitz on left bank.
74·3	Entrance to backwater on right bank. Possible mooring, but depth uncertain.
80·5	Yacht moorings at staging on right bank. Showers, clubhouse. Shops and restaurants nearby. Filling station 150m. Meissen centre 2km.
82·5	**Meissen**. Albrechtsburg palace/ cathedral/ castle on left bank. Busy passenger quay.
83·3	Winterhafen Meissen on right bank. Filling station nearby, but no other facilities.
89·7	Possible mooring at ferry landing.
96·2	Schloss Hirschstein on left bank.
102·0	Possible mooring on right bank above mill.

103·8	Possible mooring in small harbour on right bank at entrance to Grodel-Elsterwerdaer Flosskanal.	261·5	**Dessau**. Entrance to Leopoldhafen near 'Regatta Tower' on left bank. Two yacht clubs. Water, electricity, showers, slip, clubhouse. Shops and restaurants nearby.
107·1	Entrance to Promnitzer Lache on right bank. Possible mooring, but depth uncertain.	264·2	Hafen Rodleben. Commercial harbour on right bank.
107·6	**Riesa**. Commercial quay on left bank.	274·8	Hornhafen Aken. Commercial harbour on left bank.
109·4	Groba, Entrance to commercial harbour (Hafen Riesa) on left side.	276·0	Aken. Mooring on left bank at staging.
116·0	Hafen Lorenzkirch. Possible mooring.	276·6	Mooring at sailing club on left bank. Showers, slip, repairs. Provisions and restaurants in town.
124·7	Entrance to Baggersee Borschutz on right bank. Working gravel pit. Anchorage possible, but noisy day and night. Diesel bunker station.	277·3	Verkehrshafen Aken. Commercial harbour on left bank. Possible mooring at rowing club at end of harbour.
127·1	Hafen Mühlberg. Water authority harbour on right bank. Possible mooring, with permission. Clubhouse of rowing club, with showers. Shops and restaurants nearby.	290·7	Junction with Saale.
		291·5	Ronney. Possible mooring near ferry on left bank.
		293·5	Barby
139·6	Hafen Belgem on left bank. Possible mooring.	294·1	Barby railway bridge. Choice of arch depends on water level at *Pegel* Barby. When *Pegel* Barby reads less than 140 only one vessel is permitted to pass through the bridge at anyone time.
140·5	Belgem
150-165	Navigation difficult due to narrow channel and protruding groynes. Do not go outside channel markers.
		295·5	Hafen Barby. Commercial harbour. Mooring, but no facilities.
154·1	Hafen **Torgau**. Access forbidden to private leisure craft.	309·8	Schönebeck, Yacht harbour on left bank. Showers. Shops and restaurants nearby.
154·6	Torgau road bridge. When *Pegel* Torgau is 315 or less, all traffic must use the left (west) arch.	311·8	Schönebeck road bridge. When *Pegel* Barby shows less than 200 only left (west) arch is used.
154·7	Schloss Hartenfels.	312·0	Possible mooring on left bank.
155·2	Mooring to left bank. No facilities.	314·6	Hafen Schonebeck-Frohse. Commercial harbour on left bank. Yacht moorings in harbour. Clubhouse, showers, shops, crane.
155·5	Torgau railway bridge. Upstream traffic must use right (east) arch and downstream traffic must use left (west) arch.
		317–333	**Magdeburg**
184·8	Possible mooring below ferry on left bank. Restaurant nearby.	317–318	Stony shallow patch stretches from left bank almost to centre of stream.
185·0	Schloss Pretzsch.	318·0	Possible mooring on left bank near ferry.
198·6	Junction with Schwarze Elster. Possible anchorage if depth allows.	322·0	Yacht harbour Magdeburg-Sudost on left bank. Water, electricity, clubhouse, showers, slip, repairs. City centre 5km. Shops and restaurants within 1km.
200·2	Elster. Possible mooring on right bank above ferry. Shops and restaurants.
213·0	**Wittenberg**. Mooring at staging on right bank. No facilities.	322·8	Yacht clubs in old (east) branch of Elbe. Useable only when water level adequate: depth 0·50m when *Pegel* Magdeburg-Strombrücke reads 120. No facilities.
216·5	Hafen Wittenberg. Commercial harbour. Possible mooring.
236·6	Yachthafen Coswig on right bank. No facilities, but shops and restaurants nearby.	324·1	Sülzehafen, Commercial harbour on left bank. Possible mooring place.
		324·8–329·9	Stromstrecke Magdeburg. Special regulations and control system for commercial shipping only. Vessels under 33m in length are not subject to control.
257·9	Rosslau. Possible mooring on right bank. Filling station 300m.

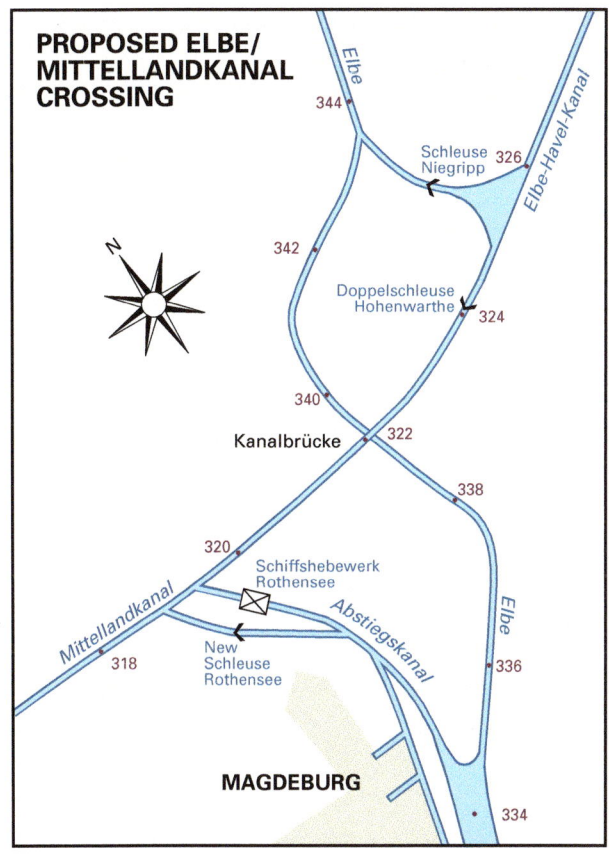

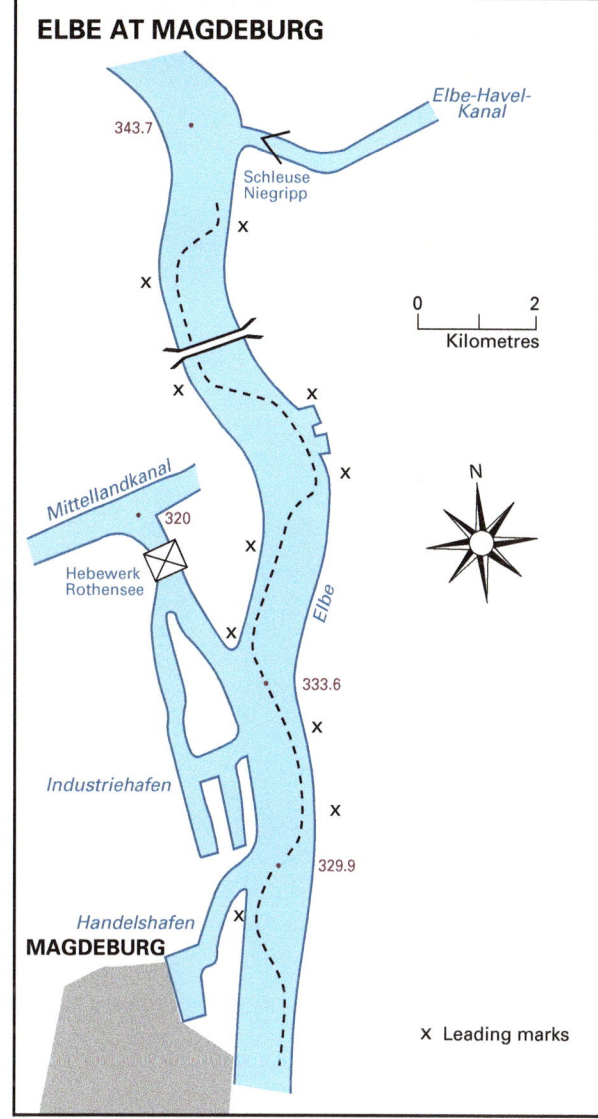

325·1	Signal station on left bank. Traffic control point for passage through Domfelsen.
325·7	Domfelsen. Strong current and shallow patch stretching from left bank almost to centre of river.
327·2	Signal station on right bank. Traffic control point for passage through Domfelsen.
327·3	Zollhafen. Marina Magdeburg on right bank. Convenient for city centre. Water, electricity, clubhouse, showers, fuel, repairs. Shopping centre nearby.
328–343	Channel zigzags due to shallows. Course indicated by yellow crosses on both banks. Current normally 3–4km/h, but can vary considerably according to volume of water. See plan.
329·9	Handelshafen. Commercial harbour on left bank. Mooring, but no facilities. Shops nearby. Close to city centre.
332·8	Industriehafen. Commercial and water authorities harbours. Two bunker boats for diesel, but no facilities for yachts.
333·6	Junction with Mittellandkanal (via Abstiegskanal Rothensee and ship-lift) on left bank.
339·7	Unfinished canal crossing from Mittellandkanal to Elbe-Havel-Kanal. Work abandoned during the Second World War.
343·7	Junction with Elbe-Havel-Kanal (via Niegripper Verbindungskanal and Schleuse Niegripp) on right bank.
346·1	Entrance to Hafen Niegripp on right bank. No facilities.
350·6	Rogätz. Possible mooring at staging on left bank near ferry. No facilities, but shops and restaurants nearby.
354·2	Entrance to gravel pit on left bank. Good anchorage in rural surroundings, but no facilities of any sort.
365·5	Gravel quay on right bank. No facilities.
371·5	Junction with Pareyer Verbindungskanal, linking with Elbe-Havel-Kanal Km 351·4.
374·3	Ship repair yard on right bank in entrance to Baggerelbe. No facilities.
388·2	Hafen **Tangermünde** on left bank. Commercial harbour with yacht harbour. Clubhouse, showers. Shops and restaurants in town. Filling station 800m.

EAST

403·6	Water authority harbour on left bank. No mooring.
422·8	Havelberg. Junction with Untere Havel-Wasserstasse Km 148·5.
438·1	Junction with Gnevsdorfer Vorfluter on right bank. Link to Untere Havel-Wasserstrasse via Schleuse Gnevsdorf and Schleuse Quitzobel. Depth 1m. Information from lock-masters at Gnevsdorf ☏ 038791 2098 or Quitzobel ☏ 039387 391.
454·9	Hafen **Wittenberg**. Two yacht harbours and commercial harbour. Water, showers, shops, restaurants. Diesel bunker station in commercial harbour.
469·5	Moorings in former frontier-control harbour on right bank. No facilities.
474·6	Hafen Schnackenburg on left bank. Mooring possible in commercial harbour. Water, electricity, shops.
484·6	Hafen Lenzen. Harbour for commercial ships on right bank. No facilities for yachts.
493·0	Gorlebener Haken on left bank. Water authority harbour. No facilities for sport boats.
504·1	Junction with Müritz-Elde-Wasserstrasse on right bank. Hafen Dömitz at entrance. No facilities. Shops and restaurants nearby.
509·0	Staging on left bank suitable for small boats. No facilities.
509–569	Dömitz to Lauenburg depth normally 2–4m, but in dry periods can reduce to 0·90m.
522·8	Sportboothafen Hitzacker on left bank. Motor-Yacht-Club Oberelbe Hitzacker. Water, electricity, slip. Filling station, shops and restaurants nearby in town.
528·1	Tiessau. Harbour on left bank for tankers. No entry except in emergency.
536·5	Neu Darchau. Yacht harbour in town centre. Water, electricity, showers, slip, shops, restaurants.
543·3	Alt Garge. Yacht harbour at end of backwater on left bank. Water, electricity, slip.
550·0	Hafen Bleckede on left bank. Commercial harbour with yacht moorings. Water, slip. Filling station, shops and restaurant nearby.
559·5	Hafen Boizenburg on right bank. Commercial harbour with yacht moorings. No facilities, but filling station, shops and restaurants close by.
569·2	Staging on left bank. Junction with Elbe-Lübeck-Kanal Km 61·6. Yacht harbour 1·5km inside canal at Lauenburg. Good facilities. See Elbe-Lübeck-Kanal.
569·2–585·8	Underwater obstructions outside channel markers. Stay inside channel. Minimum depth in channel 3·60m.
573·0	Junction with Elbe-Seitenkanal Km 115·2.
574·5	Artlenburg. Yacht harbour on left bank. Entrance subject to silting. Deepest water on starboard side of entrance. Artlenburger Boots Club. Water, electricity, showers, slip, repairs. Filling station, shops and restaurants nearby.
579·0	Tesperhude. Possible mooring on right bank.
584·5	Yacht moorings in old harbour on right bank. Motor-Yacht-Club Geesthacht. No facilities.
585·8	*Schleuse Geesthacht* *Fall 4·50m at LW* *VHF Ch 22*

Note Water inlets at both ends of chambers: avoid last 20m either end. N wall of N chamber is piled. Other side of N chamber and both sides of S chamber are smooth. No floating bollards. Level of water below lock can be higher than level above lock under certain tidal conditions.

2. GEESTHACHT TO CUXHAVEN

Km 585·8–Km 724·9
Navigable length 139·1km
Maximum draught 3·20m at mid-tide
Current Tidal
Locks 0

The tidal part of the river, the Unterelbe, from Geesthacht to Cuxhaven and beyond to the North Sea, carries a considerable traffic of shipping, has strong tidal streams and can become dangerously rough in bad weather. It would be inadvisable to attempt to navigate this part of the river without detailed charts and a vessel suitable for sea passages. Hamburg, 35km below Geesthacht, is Germany's biggest port and one of the ten most important container ports in the world. It is a maze of harbour basins and connecting waterways covering 100km². The port provides employment for 100,000 people.

Apart from the many attractions of this major city, be they historical, maritime, cultural, sporting, gastronomic or social, it may be useful to know that the best maritime book shop in the world is situated in Hamburg: Hanse Nautic, www.hansenautic.de, Herengraben 31.

In the port area the Elbe splits into the Norderelbe and the Suderelbe (part of which is known as the Kohlbrand), which come together again on the seaward side of the port as the Unterelbe. Below Hamburg the low-lying banks become once again rural, and the tidal mudflats and sandbanks of the estuary have a wildness which is in complete contrast to the bustle of the busy city. Cuxhaven, a pleasant resort and fishing harbour, provides an excellent staging point when working the tides into or out of the estuary.

Km

590·0	Elbstorf. Mooring on left bank. Shops and restaurants nearby.
599·0	Junction with Ilmenau Km 25·6. Marina 300m into Ilmenau. Water, electricity, showers, slip, provisions nearby.
	Note The Ilmenau is navigable for 28km to Lüneburg for vessels drawing less than 0·90m. There are three locks: *Fahrenholz*, *Wittorf* and *Bardowick*.
601·8	Staging on left bank. Water, electricity, restaurant.
607·2	Mooring possible in commercial harbour on right bank. Boat yard.
608·5	River divides into Suderelbe/Kohlbrand and Norderelbe.

Süderelbe/Köhlbrand

612·0	Wilhelmsburger Motor Boot Club.
615·0	Yacht harbour and boatyard.
615·6	Lock on left bank leading to Binnenhafen. Mooring possible for private craft by permission from harbourmaster.
	Entrance via *Ernst-August-Schleuse* to Motor-Yacht-Club Dove-Elbe Wilhelmsburg on right bank. Water, electricity, slip. Locking Mon–Sat 0800–1600. Bridge clearance 3·70m.
621·5	Süderelbe becomes Kohlbrand.
624·6	Kohlbrand rejoins Norderelbe and becomes Unterelbe.

Norderelbe

615·0	Junction with Dove-Elbe.
	The Dove-Elbe is 14km in length and has two locks, *Tatenberg* at Km 1·6 and *Krapphof* at Km 12·5. Between the two locks there are two boatyards and three yacht clubs, including the Hamburger Yacht-Club with its attractive harbour, good facilities and bus links to the city centre. The channel can be used by vessels drawing up to 1·80m and with a maximum height above the water of 4·15m. *Schleuse Tatenberg* operates Mon–Fri 0630–2000 and weekends 0630–2100. A small locking fee is payable. Speed limit 8km/h.
618·0	Entrance on right hand to Billwerder Bucht and Tiefstackschleuse, leading into the Bille, which has three well equipped yacht clubs. Depth 2m. Good bus and U-Bahn connections to city centre. Diesel bunker boat near entrance.
618·9	Entrance on right hand to Binnenhafen via the Oberhafenkanal, Oberhafen and Zollkanal, emerging again in the Norderelbe at Km 622·2. This route passes the Motor-Yacht-Club von Deutschland Hamburg, right in the city centre. Junction with Bille via Brandshofer Schleuse in Oberhafenkanal.
622·2	Entrance to Hamburg City-Sporthafen (for short-term visitors) and Binnenhafen on right side. Junction with Alster just beyond yacht haven through Schaartor and Rathaus locks.
623·0	St Pauli landing stages. Passenger ferries to England and other destinations. Close to main shopping centre. Floating bunker station for diesel.
625·7	Norderelbe converges with Kohlbrand to form the Unterelbe Km 624·6.

Unterelbe

625·7–642·5	Three yacht harbours on south side and four on north side.
641·3	Schulau yacht harbour on right bank. Dries at LW.
642·5	Hamburger Yachthafen at Wedel on right bank.
	All facilities, including fuel, but very busy.
643·2	Buoyed channel to Este on left bank. Navigable 12km to Buxtehude. Minimum depth 1·00m. No locks but two flood barriers (VHF Ch 10). Yacht harbour.
644·0	Entrance to Hahnöfer Nebenelbe. Small yacht harbour. Depth 1·5m.
645·5	Junction with Lühe on left bank. Navigable 12km to Homeburg using the tide.
654·7	Diesel bunker station on left bank.
654·8	Junction with Schwinge. Navigable for 5km to Stade. Minimum depth 1·50m. Motor- und Yachtclub Stade in town centre. Water, electricity, showers, slip, crane, repairs.
657·8–666·3	Pagensand island on right bank. The stream running east of the island, the Pagensander Nebenelbe, has a drying harbour and entrances to the rivers Pinnau

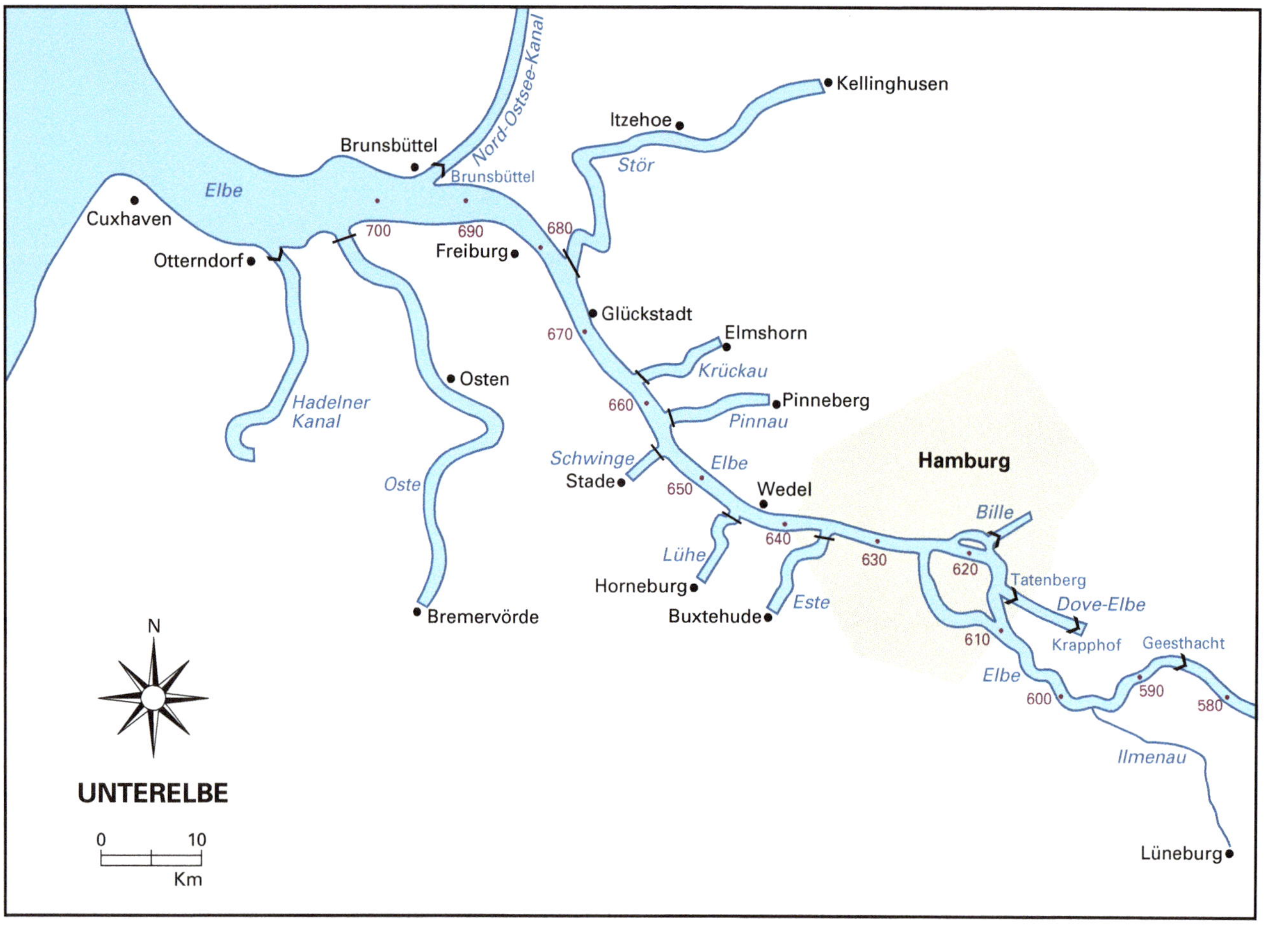
UNTERELBE
Kellinghusen
Itzehoe
Stör
Nord-Ostsee-Kanal
Brunsbüttel
Brunsbüttel
Elbe
Cuxhaven
Otterndorf
700
690
680
Freiburg
Glückstadt
670
Elmshorn
Krückau
Osten
Hadelner Kanal
Oste
660
Pinneberg
Pinnau
Schwinge
Stade
Elbe
650
Wedel
Hamburg
Bille
640
630
620
Lühe
Horneburg
Este
Buxtehude
Bremervörde
Tatenberg
Dove-Elbe
610
Krapphof
Geesthacht
Elbe
600
590
580
Ilmenau
Lüneburg
N
0
10
Km

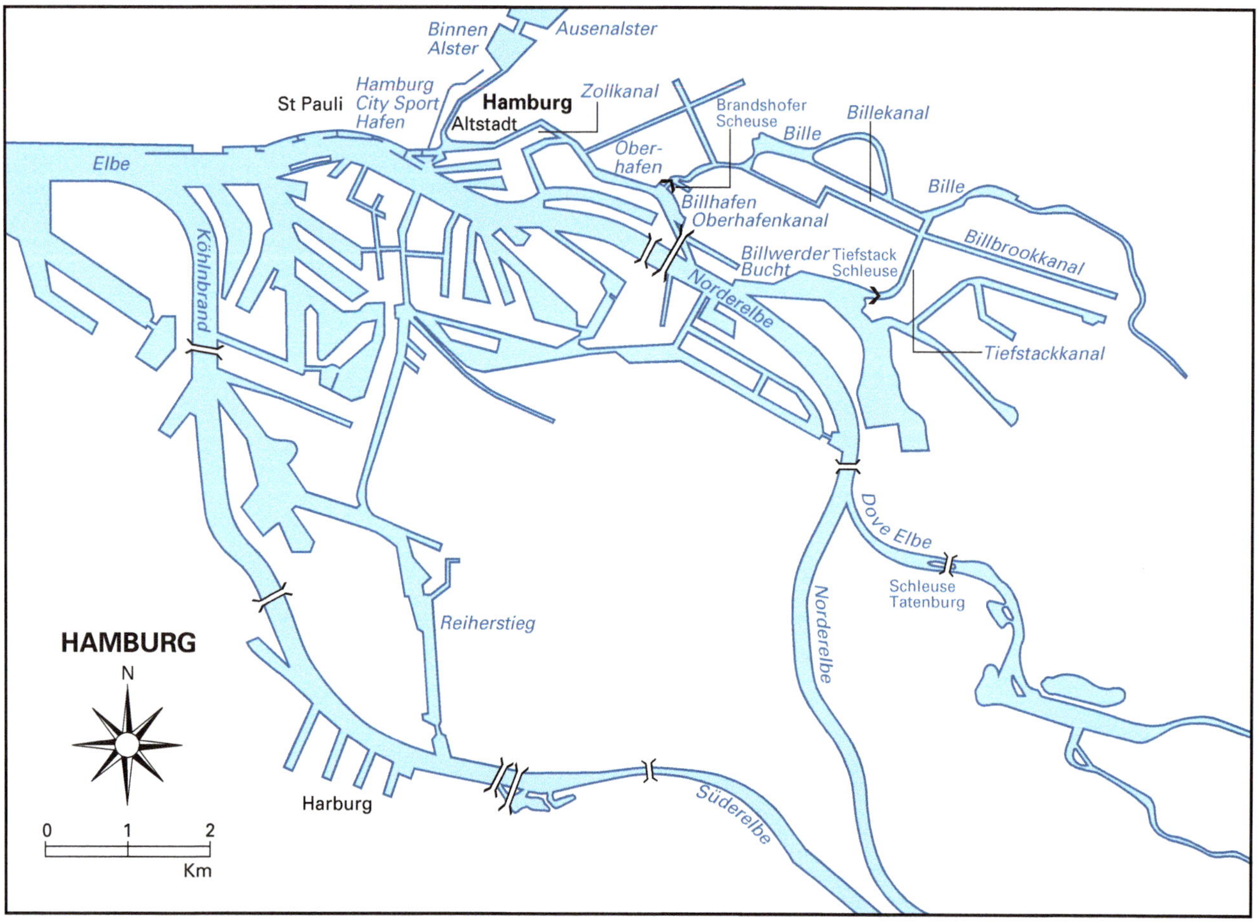
HAMBURG
Binnen Alster
Ausenalster
Hamburg City Sport Hafen
St Pauli
Hamburg
Altstadt
Zollkanal
Brandshofer Scheuse
Bille
Billekanal
Elbe
Ober-hafen
Billhafen
Oberhafenkanal
Bille
Billbrookkanal
Billwerder Bucht
Tiefstack Schleuse
Köhlbrand
Norderelbe
Tiefstackkanal
Dove Elbe
Schleuse Tatenburg
Reiherstieg
Norderelbe
Harburg
Süderelbe
N
0
1
2
Km

and Krückau. The Pinnau is navigable for 19km, and at low water has a minimum depth of 0·80m. The Krückau is navigable for 11·6km, but effectively dries at low water. However, at high water it is possible to reach the harbour at Elmshorn, the head of navigation.

669·8	Junction with Glückstadter Nebenelbe on right bank. Rejoins Elbe at Km 678. Entrance to Aussenhafen and Binnenhafen Glückstadt.
670·0	Junction with Ruthenstrom on left bank. Mooring place with water and electricity.
679·3	Junction with Stör (Km 50·6) on right bank. Buoyed channel. The Stör is tidal, but it is possible to reach Itzehoe (Km 23·6) at any state of tide. To reach Kellinghusen, the head of navigation (Km 0·0), it is necessary to use the tide, but entry from the Elbe can be at any time.
695·7	**Brunsbüttel**. Junction with Nord-Ostsee-Kanal on right bank.
696·9	Hafen Brunsbüttel on right bank.
707·0	Junction with Oste. The Oste is navigable for 74·6km to Bremervörde, passing through flat green agricultural land. Craft drawing not more than 1·70m can reach Bremervörde, but deeper-draught vessels can easily reach Osten, some 20km from the Elbe, where the mid-tide depth is around 4m. The flood barrier at the junction with the Elbe is closed only for high tides in the Elbe. There are two opening bridges. The Oste was once connected to the Hamme, which is a tributary of the Weser, by the Hamme-Oste-Kanal, but there is no longer any connection.
712·5	Junction with Medem and Hadelner Kanal on left bank.
724·5	Cuxhaven Alter Hafen. New marina under construction.
724·9	Cuxhaven yacht harbour. All facilities.

SAALE

Navigable length 160·6km
Maximum draught 1·40m (but see note below)
Maximum height 3·20m
Current 2–5km/h
Locks 17
Hours Varied. See end of Saale introduction
Speed limit 12km/h

The Saale, especially in its higher reaches, is a very attractive river, flowing in beautiful countryside and through picturesque and interesting old towns and villages where very little has changed over the years. Heading upstream for the last 30km (from Bad Dürrenberg to Naumburg) the river runs along an idyllic wooded valley full of wildlife and providing from time to time dramatic glimpses of castles perched high on the hill tops. Apart from tripper boats, which are fairly numerous in the summer months, commercial shipping has no reason to go above Halle, leaving the upper stretches of the river to leisure craft. Unfortunately, the lower reaches have not yet recovered from the pollution which was allowed to develop during the years of Communism.

The largest town on the river is Halle, the birthplace of Handel. Although a major industrial centre, Halle is one of Germany's oldest towns. It escaped damage during the Second World War, and in spite of suffering somewhat from neglect whilst under Communist control, most of its cobbled streets and gabled houses still survive. An important collection of German paintings is housed in Moritzburg Castle, near the cathedral.

Merseburg, a little further upstream, suffers from having two large chemical works on its outskirts and was also badly damaged in the war. Nevertheless it possesses a number of historic buildings, including a splendid Renaissance castle and an 11th-century cathedral.

Unfortunately, the depth of the water limits the size of vessel which can enjoy the delightful scenery of the river above Merseburg. Early in the summer months it is possible for craft drawing 1·40m to reach Naumburg, but later, especially in dry years, no vessel drawing more than 1·00m can reach this far upstream, let alone venture beyond this point into the lovely but shallow River Unstrut, which is navigable for small boats with a draught of 0·80m to Karsdorf.

Official information on depths is made available daily over Radio Aktuel, on VHF and by telephone, along with the data provided for the Elbe. For the purposes of these announcements, the lower part of the river is divided into two stretches: *Strecke 1* from Trotha to Calbe and *Strecke 2* from Calbe to the junction with the Elbe. When water levels are low, special care should be taken in the lock cut below Schleuse Trotha and also that below Schleuse Meuschau. If in doubt consult one of the lock keepers.

EAST

From the mouth to Merseburg (Km 124·2) the river is administered by WSD-Ost, and no fees are demanded for using it. Above Merseburg, for many years there was disagreement over which body should be responsible, WSD-Ost or the Land. It has now been decided, however, that the upper Saale should become a *Landeswasserstrasse*, although as yet no fees are being demanded.

Above Merseburg there are several ferries which use a rope across the river a metre or so above the water. These are indicated in the route description, but a good lookout needs to be kept as they are not easy to see. A blast on the ship's horn will usually bring the ferryman out to remove the line, provided of course the ferry is not about to cross.

The locks are not equipped with VHF. Lock working times are as follows:

Schleuse Calbe to *Schleuse Wettin*
Mon–Sat 0700–1700; Sunday 0700–1500

Schleuse Trotha to *Schleuse Rischmuhle*
Mon–Tue closed; Wed–Thu 0800–1200 & 1245–1600; Fri–Sun 0800–1200 & 1245–1845

Schleuse Bad Dürrenberg to *Schleuse Oeblitz*
Mon–Tue closed; Wed–Sun 0800–1200 & 1300–1800

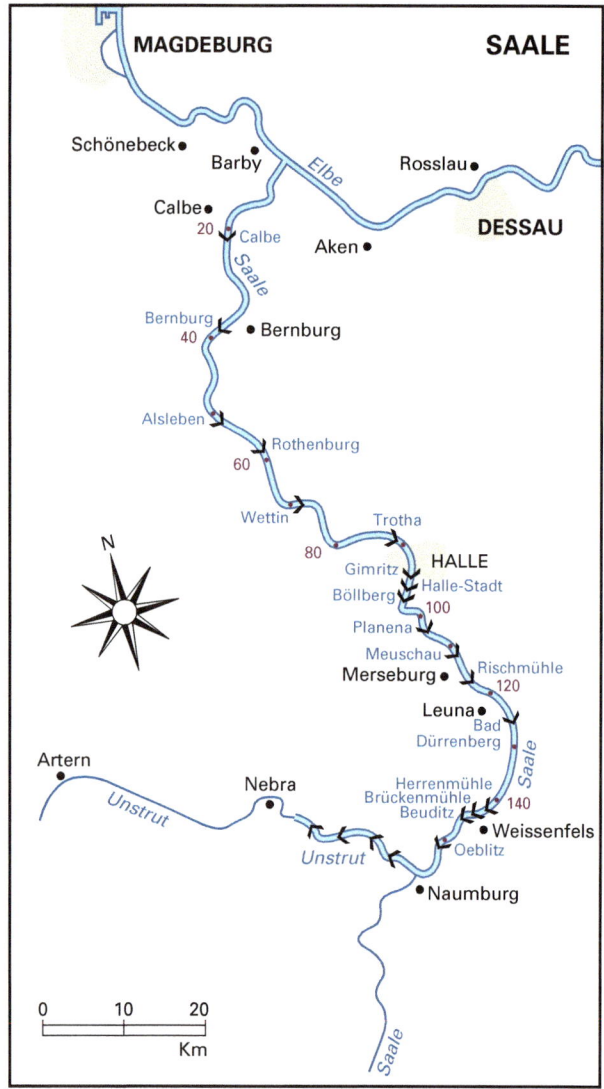

Km	
0·0	Junction with Elbe Km 290·8.
0·4	Possible mooring on right bank.
0·5	Junction with old river on right bank. Possible anchorage for shallow-draught boats.
15–17	Channel very narrow. Observe signs.
19·5	Junction with weir stream on left bank. Possible mooring place for shallow-draught boats.
20·0	*Schleuse Calbe* Rise 3·4m
20·9	Junction with weir stream on left bank. Possible mooring place for shallow-draught boats.
21·5	**Calbe**
22·0	Junction with old river on right bank. Possible anchorage, but depth uncertain.
27·2	Nienburg. Possible mooring on left bank.
27·6	Junction with Bode on left bank. Possible mooring place.
34·6	Possible mooring place on left bank.
36·0	**Bernburg**. Possible mooring on left bank. Filling station in street.
36·1	*Schleuse Bernburg* Rise 3·2m
36·4	Weir on left bank. Beware strong undertow.
37·0	Possible mooring at staging on right bank.
41·0	Gröna, Possible mooring on right bank.
50·3	*Schleuse Alsleben* Rise 3·5m
50·8	Weir stream on left bank. Possible mooring at quay.
51·1	Alsleben. Possible mooring on right bank.
58·4	Entrance to weir stream on right bank. Possible anchorage for shallow-draught boats.
58·7	*Schleuse Rothenburg* Rise 2·5m
60·0	Rothenburg
70·4	*Schleuse Wettin* Rise 2·3m
70·9	Entrance to upper part of weir stream on right bank. Possible mooring.
71·1	Wettin. Possible mooring on right bank.
71·6	Possible mooring on right bank near ferry.
78·5	Salzmünde. Possible mooring on left bank.

86·5	Entrance to Hafen Halle-Trotha on right bank. Commercial harbour. Possible mooring.
88·7	*Fangschleuse Trotha* on left side. Used when water levels are low to avoid shallows below main lock. If in doubt, telephone Schleuse Trotha (① 0345 25588) before reaching this point.
89·1	Signal for upstream traffic.
89·2	*Schleuse Trotha* Rise 2·5m
89·3	Trotha
89·4	Signal for downstream traffic.
90·4	Sailing club on left bank. Clubhouse. Provisions nearby in Halle. Filling station in street.
89·2	*Schleuse Gimritz* Rise 0·8m
92·9	Sophienhafen on left bank. Possible mooring.
93·5	**Halle.** Old town on right, new town on left.
93·6	*Schleuse Halle-Stadt* Rise 1·0m
95·9	*Schleuse Böllberg* Rise 1·0m
96·0	Beware weir at entrance to lock cut above lock.
96·2	Wörmlitz. Yacht club on right bank. Clubhouse, water, electricity. Shops and restaurants nearby.
97·2	Possible mooring at camp site on right bank.
104·5	*Schleuse Planena* Rise 2·0m
104·7	Possible mooring place in weir stream above lock.
113·5	*Schleuse Meuschau* Rise 2·5m
114·0	**Merseburg**
115·2	*Schleuse Rischmühle* Rise 1·2m
120·0	Ferry with rope across river. Beware!
124·2	End of Bundeswasserstrasse and start of Landeswasserstrasse.
126·4	*Schleuse Bad Dürrenberg* Rise 1·5m
126·4	Bad Dürrenberg.
132·5	Possible mooring at staging on right bank.
132·6	Ferry with rope across river. Beware!
141·0	*Schleuse Herrenmühle* Rise 3·0m
142·5	*Schleuse Brückenmühle* Rise 1·0m Beware sloping walls.
142·6	Beware undertow at weir above lock.
143·2	*Schleuse Beuditz* Rise 1·0m Beware sloping wall.
143·3	Beware undertow at weir above lock.
147·9	Ferry with rope across river. Beware! Possible mooring on right bank near ferry.
150·6	*Schleuse Oeblitz* Rise 1·4m Beware sloping walls.
156·9	**Naumburg.** Possible mooring on right bank.
160·5	Ferry with rope across river. Beware!
160·6	Junction with Unstrut. Navigation by small boats is possible for a further 25km, with 4 locks to Karsdorf.

ELBE-HAVEL-KANAL

Navigable distance 58km
Maximum draught 3·0m
Maximum height 4·20m
Current Nil
Locks 3
Hours Mon–Sat 0600–2200 and Sunday 0700–1900.
1 May to 31 August Schleuse Parey also operates Sunday 0800–2000
Speed limit 9km

The Elbe-Havel-Kanal is a continuation of the Mittellandkanal which is reflected in the kilometre numbering. A key east-west link in the European water transport system and a quick busy route for both commercial vessels and leisure craft. Its course is virtually through attractive countryside, bustling with wildlife such as deer, kites, golden orioles and of course swans and ducks.

Km

325·1	End of the Mittellandkanal and the commencement of the Elbe-Havel-Kanal.
325·1	*Schleuse Hohenwarthe* Fall 19·5m VHF Ch 26 Floating numbered bollards on south side only.
326·0	Junction with the Niegripper Verbindungskanal linking the Elbe-Havel-Kanal with the River Elbe

EAST

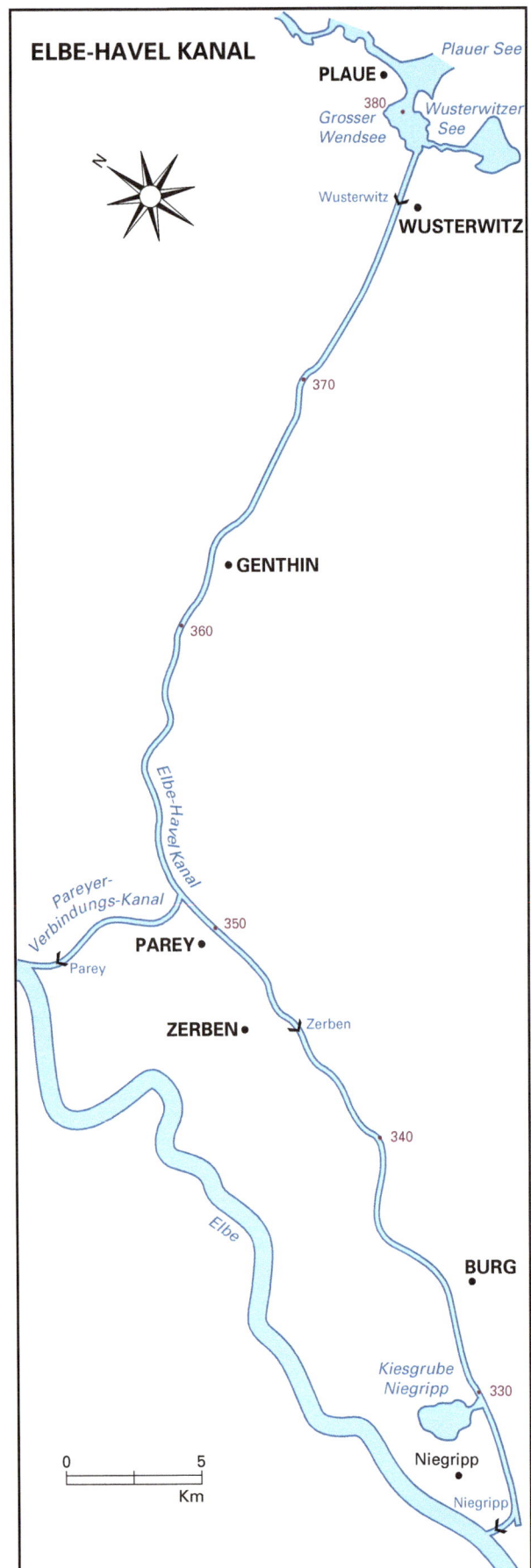

ELBE-HAVEL KANAL

Entering and exiting Schleuse Hohenwarthe. 19.5m deep

Niegripper Verbindungskanal

Navigable distance 1·8km
Maximum draught Check water level in River Elbe normally 2·00m plus
Maximum height 4·00m
Current Nil
Locks 1
Hours Mon–Sat 0600–2200, Sunday 0700–1900
Speed limit 9km/h

This short canal links the Elbe-Havel-Kanal to the River Elbe its maximum depth being totally dependent upon the Elbe, which, in exceptionally dry periods can be as low as 1·00m.

114 INLAND WATERWAYS OF GERMANY

Km		
0·0	Junction with Mittellandkanal Km 326·0	
0·5	*Schleuse Niegripp* Fall 1·5 to 5·0m VHF Ch 22	
1·8	Junction with the River Elbe at Km 343·7	

Elbe-Havel-Kanal (continued)

329·7	**Niegripp.** Entrance to old gravel pit (Kiesgrube Niegripp) on west side. Caution Depth 0·5m to 1·5m.	
331·2	Junction with the Niegripper Altkanal on west side. A short canal, Depth 1–2m with Sportboothafen der TUS-Empor Burg e.V. Eight guest moorings, water, electricity, shower, slip. Moorings on north side opposite the entrance to the Niegripper See. The Niegripper See is an old gravel pit, depth 0·5m to 1·5m. Camping. Shops and restaurants in Niegripp.	
332·2	New Yachthafen Brug on east side for leisure craft. Call for entry. Electricity, water, showers, toilets.	
333·0	Mooring places on east bank.	
334·0	**Burg.** Yacht harbour on west side. Sportboothafen des WSF BURG Depth 1–2m. Water, electricity, showers, toilets, slip. Shops and Restaurants.	
338·5	VHF Ch 20.	
342·0	VHF Ch 5 at narrow bridge speed 6km/h	
345·1	*Schleuse Zerben* Fall 5·2m VHF Ch 20 Elbe *Pegel* information displayed at lock.	
349·0	VHF Ch 78.	
349·0	Mooring for leisure craft west side	
350·0	**Parey**	
351·0	Junction with 3·5km long Pareyer-Verbindungskanal leading to the River Elbe on west side. Max draught 1·8m. Speed limit 9km/h. Depth after lock depends on level in Elbe.	
0·8	*Schleuse Parey* Rise 1m to 5m VHF Ch 78	
351·5	Mooring for leisure craft east side.	
355	Junction with short Bergzower Altkanal on east side, for small leisure craft. Moorings at 1km, max depth 1·4m.	
359·8	Junction with Altenplathower Altkanal north side. Depth 0·6m to 1·0m. Rejoins EHK at 361·4km	
362·0	**Genthin**	
362·1	Mooring for leisure craft north side.	
363·0	Small yachthafen on south side. Water, electricity, toilets, showers, pump-out, crane. Depth 2m. Restaurants in town.	
363·8	Junction with 6·8km long Roßdorfer Altkanal, north side. Max draught 1·5m. Max height 3m. Speedlimit 5km/h.	
376·7	*Schleuse Wusterwitz* Fall 2·5 to 5·0m VHF Ch 18	
379·0	Entrance to Grosser Wendsee. Channel swings NE across lake follow navigation buoys. Access southwards to Wusterwitzer See. Good anchorage, but beware of fishing posts. Two small Yachthafens with 'Gastliegeplätze' on west side. Both have Max depth 0·9m	
382·0	**Plaue.** Junction with Untere Havel-Wasserstrasse Km 66·7	

UNTERE HAVEL-WASSERSTRASSE

The Havel starts its journey as the Obere Havel, about 100km to the northeast of Berlin in the beautiful Mecklenburg Lake District. The river flows southwards to join the Havel-Oder-Wasserstrasse where it turns south to Spandau on the north western outskirts of Berlin. Here it becomes the Untere Havel, with kilometering starting from zero at the point where the Havel-Oder, the Spree and the Untere Havel all meet.

South of Spandau the river widens into an enormous and beautiful lake, largely surrounded by woods. A wonderful play area for numerous types of vessels on hot summer days. At Potsdam, the waterway splits into the Potsdamer Havel and the Sacrow-Paretzer-Kanal. The former through Potsdam and continues through a very attractive area with wooded banks, pleasant anchorages and friendly yacht clubs. The latter bypasses Potsdam and provides a shorter more rural, but less interesting route towards the west. In the Göttin See, near Ketzin, the two routes converge with the Havelkanal; popular with vessels wishing to bypass the Berlin area and travel onwards to Poland. Once again, as the Untere-Havel, the waterway continues westwards towards the old Hanseatic town of Brandenburg.

To avoid Brandenburg, commercial barges and some leisure craft use the larger straight Silokanal and the Vorstadtschleuse, a standard big-ship lock. Small vessels can, however, go through the centre of Brandenburg on the smaller Brandenburger Niederhavel or the older small limited 2·5m height Stadtkanal using the little Stadtschleuse which avoids the larger double Vorstadtschleuse.

EAST

Brandenburg Church

A Potsdam Steam Driven Tripper Boat

Before and after Brandenburg the route crosses a number of meres or lakes (not unlike the Norfolk Broads) which is abundant with bird life: reed warblers, marsh harriers, bittern, stork, cranes and fearless herons, can all be seen by the determined birdwatcher.

West of Brandenburg, at Plaue, the Elbe-Havel-Kanal branches off to the west and the Untere Havel turns northeast, winding through flat but pleasant agricultural land to Havelberg, where it joins the River Elbe.

Berlin is, of course, a city of enormous interest from many points of view, and to arrive by water – and perhaps to move around the city on the labyrinth of the waterways – is a fascinating experience. A few of the waterways of Berlin are industrial, but most are attractive tree-lined canals and rivers which provide a superb mini cruising ground. Well equipped yacht clubs are far too numerous to list in detail, but some have been included as being of special interest to cruising boats seeking convenient places for overnight stops. There is good access to the efficient public transport system and several facilities for fuel, shopping and repairs. In order to explore the city, there are a variety of short-stay mooring facilities at Spandau, Potsdam or the Grosser Wannsee.

Spandau is one of the oldest parts of Berlin, but has an excellent modern shopping centre. Potsdam is definitely worthy of several days to visit the numerous historical sites and palaces: The Cecilienhof, where Churchill, Truman and Stalin met after the Second World War to agree the division of Germany and its surrounding countries; followed by the signing of the Potsdam Agreement in 1945. The Cecilienhof is now an Hotel, but during the day, a museum is open to the public where one can view the famous conference room where the Potsdam

Potsdam

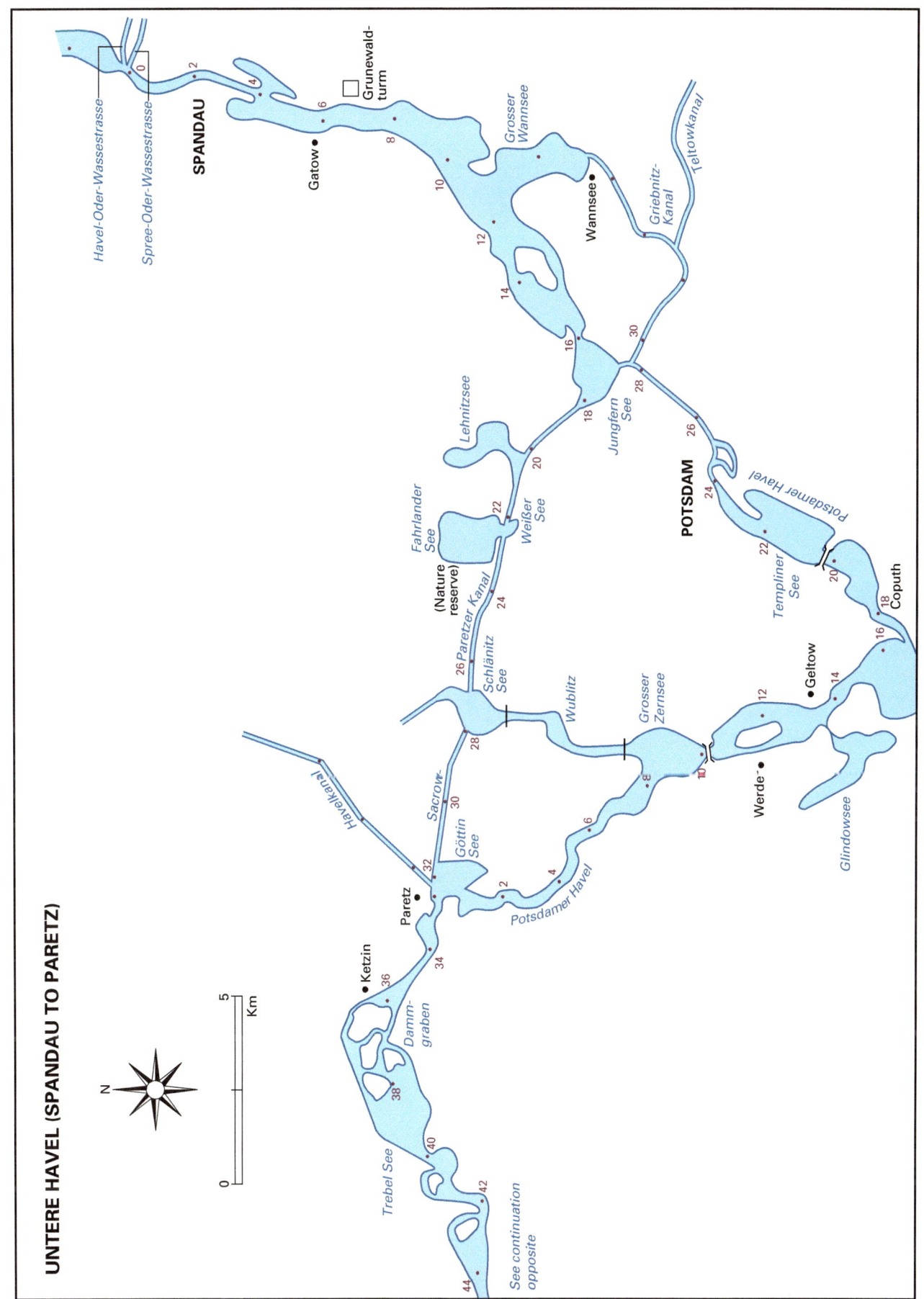

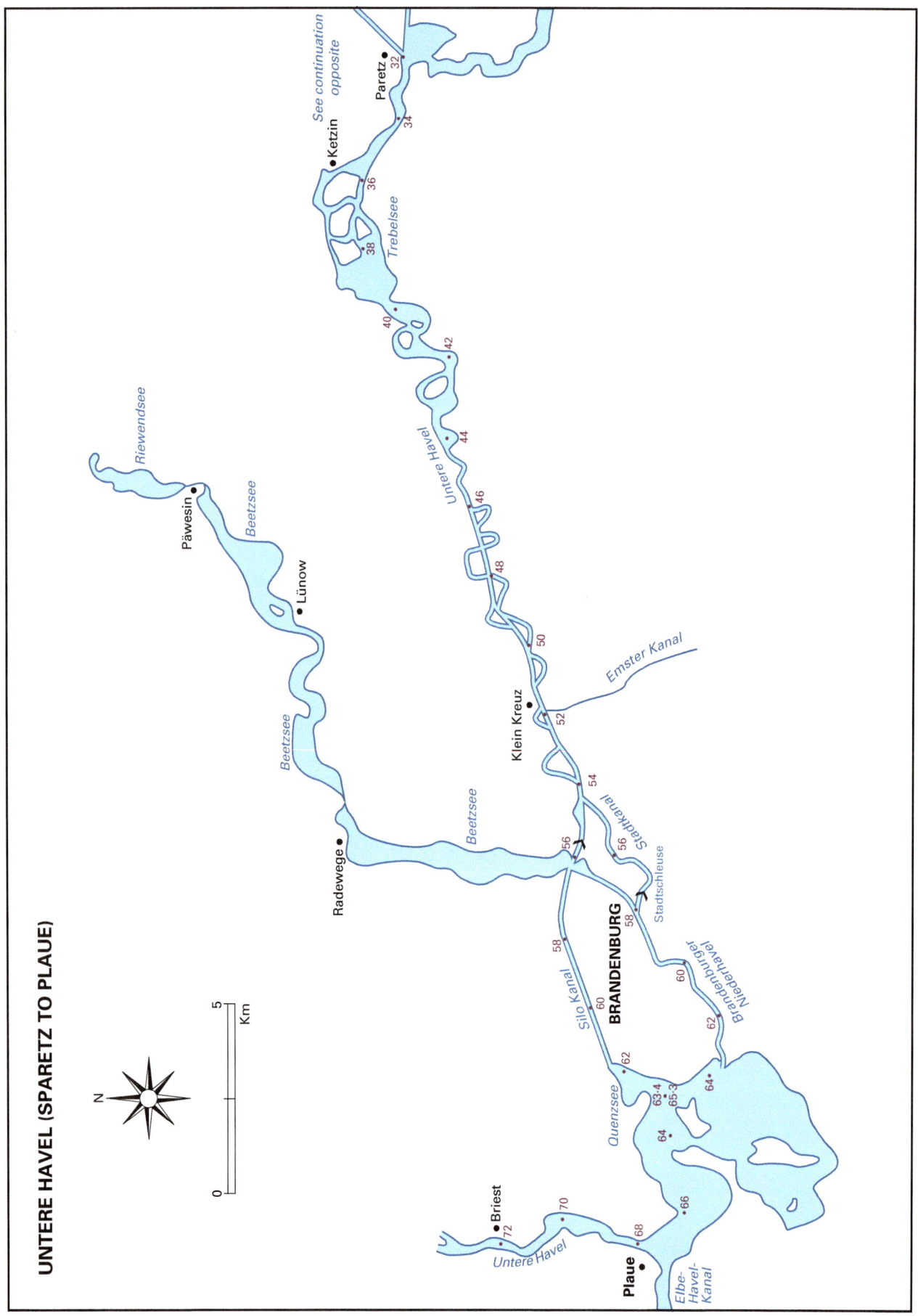

Agreement was signed. Frederick the Great's elegant rococo style Sanssouci Palace and garden complex is well worth a visit too. The list of historical buildings, sites and vibrant modern architecture are too many to include here, but a cultural tour of Potsdam and Berlin is illuminating. The navigational passage is predominantly across various size lakes with well buoyed channels: red to starboard and green to port when heading down stream.

As with other rivers of variable depth in Germany, the Untere Havel is notionally divided into stretches, and the Tauchtiefe for each stretch is made available daily via signs at the sides of locks and over VHF radio. The *Strecke* used for this are set out in the table below:

Strecke 1	Havelberg to Rathenow
Strecke 2	Rathenow o Bahnitz
Strecke 3	Bahnitz to Plaue
Strecke 4	Plaue to Brandenburg
Strecke 5	Brandenburg to Spandau

1. SPANDAU TO PLAUE

Km 0·0 to Km 66·7
Navigable distance 66·7km
Maximum draught 2·20m (possibly less in dry season)
Maximum height 4·10m
Current Slight
Locks 1
Speed limit 9km/h

Km

0·0 **Spandau.** Junction with Spree (Km 0·0) and the Havel-Oder-Wasserstrasse (Km 0·0).

0·1 Mooring for leisure craft east side, max stay 24hr.

1·0 VHF 23.

1·6 Mooring for all vessels on west side.

3·5 Yachthafens with guest moorings.

4–6·2 Speed limit 12km/h.

4·1 Several Yacht Clubs immediately behind the point where the Untere Havel-Wasserstrasse widens out into a lake to the south of Spandau. All facilities. Convenient for major shopping centre in Spandau and for access to central Berlin by U-Bahn.

Marina Lanke Werft, 4.3km Untere Havel-Wasserstrasse

4·3 Marina Lanke Werft. West side. Moorings for guest boats. Water. electricity, WC, shower, pump out. Slip, 50-tonne crane. Fuel ☎ 030 3610014.

6·2–12 Speed limit 25km/hr.

7·4 Grunewaldturm: Prominent red-brick tower high amongst trees on east bank.

9·0 YC on west bank amongst the trees.

10·0 Entrance to Grosser Wannsee on the east side. Entrance shallow: observe buoyage. Speed limit 12km/hr. At 3km into the Grosser Wansee in the SE corner is the Potsdamer Yacht Club, good facilities and convenient for the S-Bahn.

10·3 The Deutsch-Britscher YC on the west side welcomes guests, Clubhouse with most facilities.

14·0 12km/h.

Pfaueninsel Island (Peacock Island) on east side, which can only be accessed via ferry. Pretty island with folly castle created as a summer palace by Friederich-Wilhelms II.

16·5 Heilandskirche 'church' on west side.

The Deutsche-Britischer Yacht Club 10.3km Untere Havel-Wasserstrasse

EAST

Ferry to Pfaueninsel Island

Heilandskirche 16.5km Untere Havel-Wasserstrasse

16·8   Route divides: Potsdamer Havel to the left and Sacrow-Paretzer-Kanal to right. Kilometre markings follow Sacrow-Paretzer-Kanal.

Sacrow-Paretzer-Kanal (right branch)

17·8   Lookout tower now used by Quantum Sails and a section of the Berlin Wall.

18·2   Moorings for leisure craft against steel quay on west side. No facilities. Walking distance to the Cecilienhoff.

Cecilienhof

18·5–32   No overnight mooring places. Anchorage permitted close to canal side but care to be taken as a thoroughfare for heavy commercial traffic.

20·7   Entrance to Lehnitzsee. Speed limit 12km/h on lake.

22·5   Entrance to Fahrlander See. Nature reserve.

32·6   Junction with Havelkanal Km 34·9 on north side.

33·0   Junction with Potsdamer Havel Km 0·0 on south side.

Potsdamer Havel (left branch)

The Potsdamer Havel is a very attractive waterway with many places of interest and good facilities for visiting boats. The minimum depth at normal water levels is 1·90m. There is a speed limit of 12km/h throughout the busy waterway including the lakes and care should be taken as there are numerous tripper boats, water taxis, commercial vessels and various types of leisure craft all using the waterway.

28·6   The Glienicker Brücke. Limited daytime mooring for leisure craft under west side of bridge, easy access to visit the Marble Palace and the Cecilienhof.

28·4   Junction with Teltowkanal on the east side.

27·1   Buchardi-Werft Wassersport-Servicezentrum. West side. Guest moorings, water, electricity, WC, shower, 20-tonne crane, pump out.

26·7   Fuel. West side. ✆ 0331 292022

25·26   Hafen for hotel barges and tripper boats on east side, NOT for leisure craft.

25·0   Follow buoyed channel

24·3   Yacht harbour on west bank. Motor-Club Potsdam on island amongst trees. Depth 1·50–2·00m. Water, electricity, clubhouse. Shops and restaurants close by. Good centre for visiting the Sanssouci Palace complex and a short walk Potsdam Stadt railway station for trains to the centre of Berlin.

23·9   Kiewitt bunker station on west side.

Glienicker bridge with short term public mooring - easy access to Marble Palace

120   INLAND WATERWAYS OF GERMANY

EAST

Sanssouci Palace

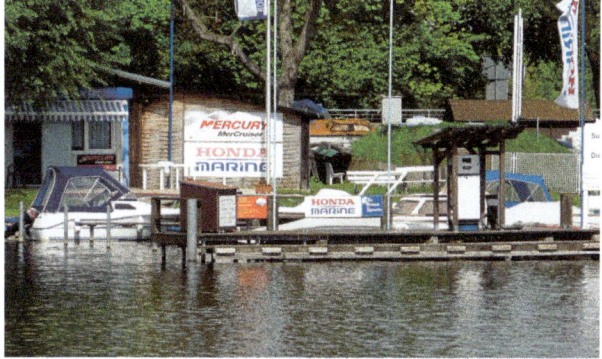

Kiewitt bunker station at 23.9Km Potsdamer Havel

Km	Description
23·8	Chain ferry.
22·7	Yachthafen Potsdamer, west side. Guest moorings, good facilities, pump out, repairs, slip and 25-tonne crane. Convenient access to Sanssouci complex and shops.
21·0	Railway bridge (6·6m headroom).
20·8	Yacht harbour on west bank immediately after railway bridge. Good facilities. Shops, restaurants and railway station near at hand.
18·2–16·8	Narrow channel linking Templiner See and Schwielowsee. On exit into Schwielowsee, channel swings sharply northwards and is well buoyed. The remainder of the Schwielowsee is navigable, but there are many shoals outside the buoyed channel. It is possible to moor at Ferch, at the southwestern end of the lake.
18·0	Boatyards on each side of river. Repairs, Facilities for overnight mooring.
17·4	Chain ferry.
16·5	Follow narrow channel under railway, bridge height 4·2m then continue on, bearing right into Schwielowsee. Follow buoyed channel.
15·0	Schlosshafen on east side. Schwielowsee Resort on west side, with guest moorings for leisure craft, Restaurant and good facilities.
14·7	Narrow channel under road bridge, height 5·9m, into Zernsee.
13·5	Entrance to Glindowsee on west side. Bridge height 4·1m.
11·5	Moorings at staging on west side at Inselstadt Werder, MC Werder. Often busy. Possible to anchor in vicinity.
10·3	Motorbootclub Werder on west bank. Attractive setting. Water, electricity, showers. Shops, chandlery and restaurant nearby.
10·1	Under railway bridge height 4·5m into Grosser Zernsee.
7·4	Marina Zernsee west side. Good facilities for leisure craft.
7·1	Boatyard on east side just before autobahn bridge. Repairs. Facilities for overnight mooring.
4·2	Phöben. Moorings at staging on east bank for small craft.

Chain ferry on Potsdamer Havel

Werder - Moorings

Brandenburg Havel Marina 54.9

Moorings at Ketzin

4·1	Follow buoyed channel.
0·0	Junction with Sacrow-Paretzer-Kanal Km 33·0.

Untere Havel-Wasserstrasee (continued)

33·1	**Paretz**. Possible mooring on west bank.
34·5	Chain Ferry.
35·8	Entrance to Ketziner Havel on north side. Depth 2m. Mooring possible at Ketzin. Ketziner Havel rejoins Untere Havel-Wasserstrasse at Km 36·8.
38–40	Trebelsee. Follow buoyed channel.
Ca 40	Garbage mountain and processing plant on south bank.
43·0	Fitchener Marina on south side.
51·5	Eden campsite on north side, harbour for small boats, depth 1m.
54·3	Channel divides. Right for Silokanal (for commercial ships and large leisure craft) and left for Brandenburger Stadtkanal (for leisure craft drawing under 1·5m and max height 2·70m, which links into Niederhavel below Stadtschleuse (Bootschleuse) Brandenburg.
54·7	Lock holding quay for sports boats on south side.
54·9	New Brandenburg Havel Marina with guest moorings, north side. Electricity, water, showers, WC, restaurant, winter moorings outside and winter storage inside large hangar.

Silokanal (right branch)

55·6	*Vorstadtschleuse Brandenburg* Double chamber Fall 1·2m Length 167·0m Breadth 12·1m VHF Ch 20 Hours Mon–Sat 0600–2200, Sunday 0700–1900.
56·00	Lock. Holding quay for sports boats on north side.
56·2	Junction with Brandenburger Niederhavel (south).
	Junction with Beetzsee (north). The Beetzsee is navigable for 18km to Päwesin for boats drawing 1·70m, where there are several possible mooring places and anchorages. Speed limit 6km/h.
	On the connecting Riewendsee motorboats are forbidden.
58·9	Fuel bunker barge.
61·6	Moorings with guest places on right bank. Some with facilities.
63·1	Junction with Brandenburger Niederhavel (south).

Brandenburger Stadtkanal (left branch)

Leisure boats with a height above water level of 2·70m or less must use this route in preference to the Silokanal. Speed limit 6km/h.

54–56	Winding channel (depth 1·70m), not well marked. Care required (but bottom soft).
56·0	North side branch (depth 0·8m) leads to Marinestation Schoners with 10 guest moorings, water, electricity, WC, showers, pump out. Not suitable for large boats.

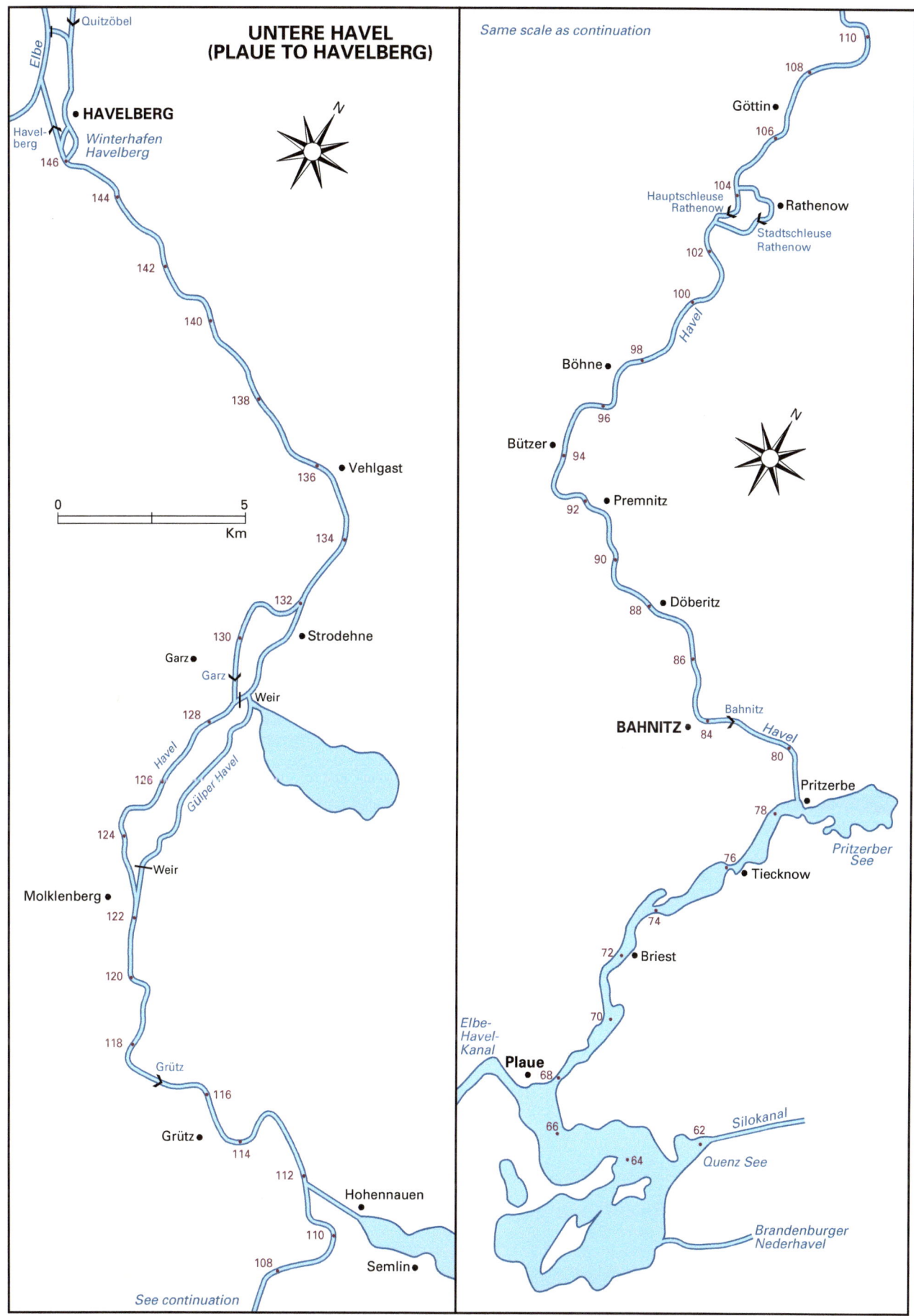

EAST

New bridge on Brandenburger Niederhavel

57·0 Possible mooring against wall on left bank. Easy access to town centre, but no facilities.

57·4 Stone bridge. Height 2·75m.

57·5 *Stadtschleuse Brandenburg*
Fall 1·0m
Hours Mon–Sat 0700–1900, Sunday 0700–1900

58·0 Junction with Brandenburger Niederhavel.

Brandenburger Niederhavel

56–65 Depth 1·80m. Passes through the town centre, then through woodlands and pastures to Plauer See. Speed limit 6km/h.

New Homeyen Brücke now 5·5m.

56·8 Yachtclub on left bank, clubhouse, shops and restaurants in town.

57·6 Pontoon moorings for guest boats with water, electricity, WC, showers.

57·8 Fuel.

58·0 Junction with Brandenburger Stadtkanal.

Public Moorings at Brandenburg

58·8 Guest moorings for 20 leisure boats, water, electricity, WC, showers.

59·0 Fuel bunker.

63·4 Junction with Untere Havel-Wasserstrasse Km 63·4.

Untere Havel-Wassertrasse (continued)

63–66 Plauer See. Follow buoyage.

66·7 Plaue. Junction with Elbe-Havel-Kanal Km 382·0.

2. PLAUE TO HAVELBERG

Km 66·7 to Km 148·5
Navigable distance 81·8km
Maximum draught 1·80m (see below)
Maximum height 4·70m
Current Slight
Locks 5
Hours Varied. See route description
Speed limit 9km/h

This stretch of the Havel is far less heavily used than the Berlin-Brandenburg section. On average only about 10 to 20 barges pass through a day, and during the late summer months in a dry year this number may be even less when the water levels can be as low as 1·20m.

Km

66·7 **Plaue**

67·9 Quay side moorings on west side for leisure boats. No facilities, close to supermarket and shops. Freshly caught fish for sale from local fish stalls.

68·2 WBF Yacht harbour on right bank. Water, electricity, pump out.

68·4 Boatyard on left bank. Facilities for mooring. Thomas Brauckman, marine engineering ✆ 03381 890660.

78·6 Entrance to Pritzerber See on right hand side under road/rail bridge height 3·2m. Navigable for 3km. Depth 1·20m

78·7 Moorings for 10 guest boats on east side. Water, electricity, WC, showers, pump out, near village.

78·8 Ferry.

81·5 Start of lock cut. Small boat lock in weir stream. Max length 11·5m.

81·9 *Schleuse Bahnitz*
Fall 1·3m
Length 215·0m
Breadth 10·0m
VHF Ch 4
Hours 1 May to 31 August, Mon–Sat 0800–2100, Sunday 0800–2000;
1 September to 30 April, Mon–Sat 0600–1900, Sunday 0700–1800.

Beware sloping walls.

83·9	End of lock cut.
90·8	**Premnitz**. Yacht harbour on east side. Depth 1·2m. Restaurant in floating clubhouse. Shops in village.
92·7	Yacht harbour on northeast side. Depth 1·0m. Clubhouse. WC, shower.
92·8	Boatyard on left bank. Attractive mooring. Shops and restaurants nearby.
102·8	**Rathenow**. Speed 8km/h. River divides. Left to Vorstadtschleuse Rathenow, right to Stadtschleuse Rathenow (Stadtkanal).

Left branch

103·3	*Hauptschleuse (Vorstadtchleuse) Rathenow* Fall 1·2m Length 220·0m Breadth 9·5m VHF Ch 3 Hours Mon–Sat 0600–2200, Sunday 0700–1900 Beware sloping wall. Leisure craft drawing 1m or less are forbidden when Stadtschleuse is operating.
104·2	Junction with right branch.

Right branch

104·0	Mooring on east side.
104·2	Mooring in Stadthafen above Stadtschleuse. Depth 1·5m.
104·3	*Stadtschleuse Rathenow* Fall 1·2m Length 71·5·0m Breadth 8·4m Hours 1 May to 30 June, Fri 1200–2000 and Sat/Sun 0900–2000; 1 July to 31 August, Fri–Sun 0900–2000, Mon–Thur 0900–1800; 1 September to 30 April, closed. Mandatory for sports boats drawing under 1m and less than 2·3m high.
Ca105	Stadtkanal depth possibly only 1m.
105·5	Jederitzer Brücke. Height 2·3m.
106·0	Junction with left branch.

Untere Havel-Wasserstrasse (continued)

111·9	Junction with the beautiful Hohennauener Kanal on right bank. Navigable 10km to Ferchesar. Depth normally 1·7m, but may reduce considerably during dry periods. Berthing bows to, on north side Hohennauen. Mooring also at Semlin on south side of Hohennauener See. Depth 1·2m.
115·0	**Grütz**
115·2	Boat hafen with two guest moorings. Water, electricity, shower, WC, 8-tonne crane, slip. Fuel Mon–Fri 0700–1500.
116·5	Start of lock cut. Small-boat lock (maximum beam 2·4m) in weir.
117·0	*Schleuse Grütz* Fall 0·6m Length 219·0m Breadth 10·0m VHF Ch 2 Hours as per Schleuse Bahnitz (Km 81.9). Beware sloping walls.
117·5	End of lock cut. Weir stream rejoins.
122·4	Junction with Gülper Havel on right bank. Depth 1·3m at normal levels. Two small-boat locks (in very bad condition), Maximum beam 2·0m. Gülper Havel reunites with Untere Havel-Wasserstrasse at Km 129·0 below weir at Garz.
122·5	Hafen Molkenberg on left bank. Moorings to quay. No facilities. Depth 1·0m.
129·0	*Schleuse Garz* Fall 0·69m Length 215·0m Breadth 10·0m VHF Ch 1 Hours as per Schleuse Bahnitz (Km 81.9). Beware sloping walls.
130·2	Entrance to channel on west side to Hafen Garz for leisure boats, 15 guest moorings, water, electricity, WC, Shower, Pump out, Slip.
131·4	Entrance to weir stream and moorings at Strodehne. Four guest moorings, water, electricity, WC, shower. Depth 1·2m.
135·5	Vehlgast. Possible mooring in old river entrance on right bank. Depth uncertain.
145·8	Havelberg. Entrance to Winterhafen Havelberg on right bank. Basic facilities only, but harbour is in a pleasant village with shops.
146·0	Channel branches. Route to Elbe via Schleusenkanal, speed 6km/h straight on. Entrance to Havel Mündungsstrecke, speed 9km/h on right which connects via Schleuse Quitzöbel (canoes only) to the Gnevsdorfer Vorfluter, which passes through another small lock, Schleuse Gnevsdorf, and joins the Elbe at Km 438·0. The depths of these waters can be less than 1m in dry seasons.

EAST

147·1 *Schleppzugschleuse Havelberg*
Fall 1·4m
Length 225·0m
Breadth 12·0m
VHF Ch 21
☏ 03385 53980 / 53971
Hours as per Schleuse Bahnitz (Km 81.9)

148·5 Junction with Elbe Km 422·8

HAVELKANAL

Navigable distance 34·9km
Maximum draught 2·0m
Maximum height 4·30m
Current Nil
Locks 1
Hours Weekdays 0600–2000, weekends 0700–1900
Speed limit 8km

Following the division of Germany by the Allies after the Second World War, the East German canal link from the Elbe to the Oder required a passage through West Berlin. Cold War politics dictated that a new canal should be constructed to avoid this necessity, and therefore the Havelkanal came into existence in 1952, having taken only 13 months to build.

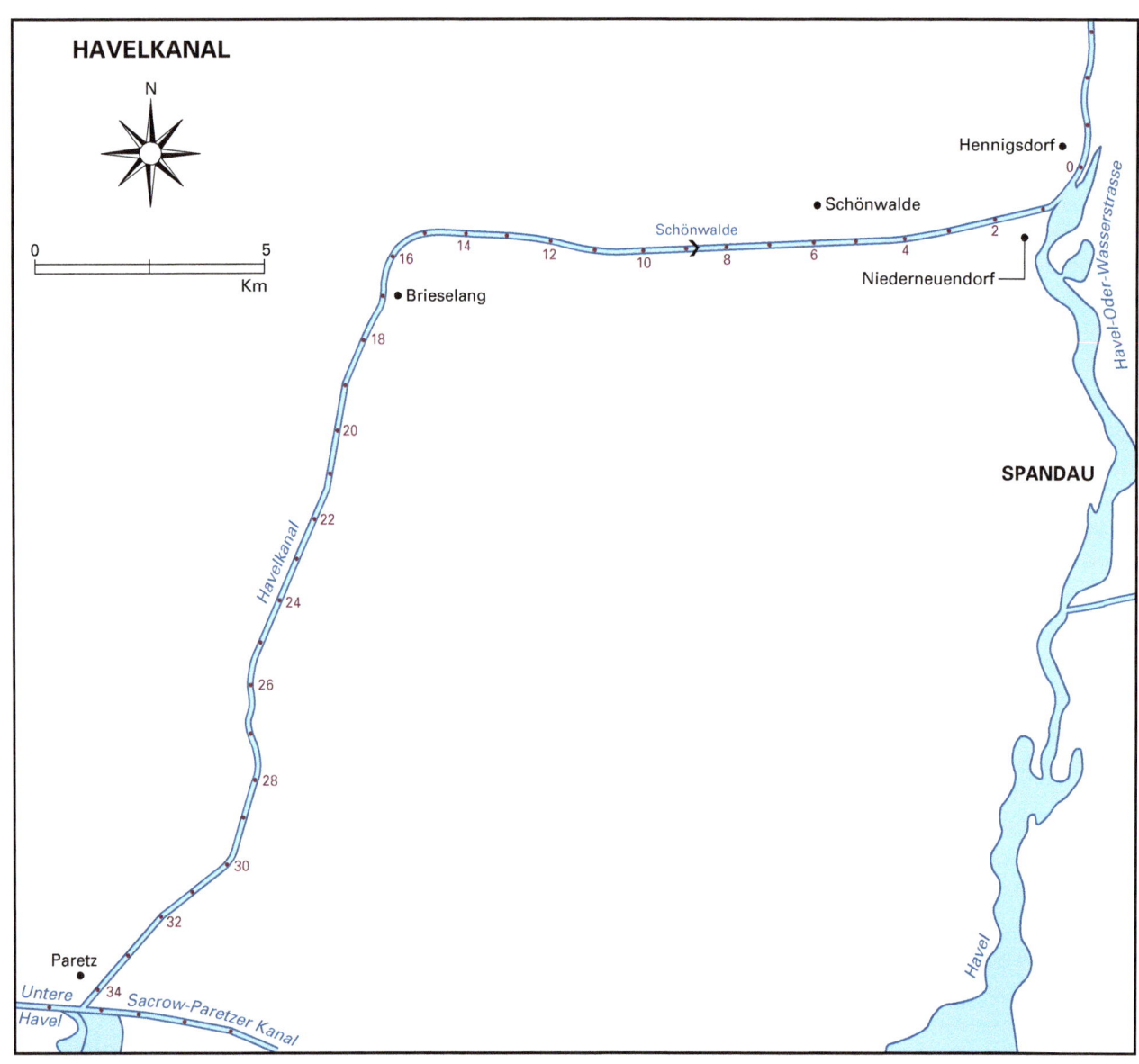

126 INLAND WATERWAYS OF GERMANY

Being relatively straight and featureless, the canal is somewhat uninteresting to travel along. Nevertheless, it certainly provides the fastest route from the Elbe to the Oder, as not only is it shorter bypassing Berlin and Potsdam, but it also avoids a considerable wait during busy times at the Spandau lock.

It has only one lock, Schönwalde.

Km

0·0	Junction with the Havel-Oder-Wasserstrasse Km 10·5.
0·9	Mooring at Niederneuendorf at Yachtzentrum Nordwest am Südufer on south bank, Depth 2m. 10 Guest berths, water, electricity, WC, shower, bump out, dustbins, slip, 25-tonne crane. Clubhouse.
0·9	Mooring at Hennigsdorf at Bootscenter Rittmann am Nordufer on north bank, depth 1·2m. Five guest berths, water, electricity, WC, shower, pump out, dustbins, slip, 16-tonne crane. Shops and restaurants in Hennigsdorf and Niederneuendorf.
8·8	*Schleuse Schönwalde* Rise 2·0m Length 85·0m Breadth 12·0m VHF Ch 19
18·1	Brieselang. MC Birkenwerder on east side.
18·1	Moorings for sports boats depth 1·5m west side. Water, electricity, WC, shower, slip.
23·6	Moorings for sports boats depth 1·5m east side
27·1	Moorings for sports boats depth 2·0m west side
34·4	**Paretz**. Entrance to old lock on east side. Guest moorings available. Shower, WC. ☎ 0172 1583 592
34·9	Junction with Untere-Havel-Wasserstrasse Km 32·6.

HAVEL-ODER-WASSERSTRASSE

Spandau Km 0 to Hohensaaten Km 93·0
Navigable distance 93·0km
Maximum draught 2·3m
Maximum height 4·10m
Current Slight
Locks 4 (including ship-lift)
Hours The locks operate Mon–Sat 0600–2200, Sunday 0700–2200. Schiffshebewerk Niederfinow (ship-lift) operates 24hrs
Speed limit 12km/h from Km 0·0–10·4 (including lakes), 9km/h from Km 10·4–93·0

Strictly speaking, the Havel-Oder-Waserstrasse comprises several connected waterways. The first 3·5km from Spandau is the Spandauer Havel. From Km 3·5 the Havel-Oder-Wasserstrasse cuts across to Hohensaaten (Km 93·0). At Hohensaaten the notional direction of flow reverses and the waterway becomes the Hohensaaten-Friedrichsthaler-Wasserstrasse, the end of which (Km 135·3) connects to the West-Oder close to the Polish border. For the sake of simplicity, the Hohensaaten-Friedrichsthaler-Wasserstrasse is described separately in this book and the Havel-Oder-Wasserstrasse is considered to end at Hohensaaten.

Schleuse Spandau was something of a bottleneck in this very busy waterway, and waiting times for barges were often very long. It was therefore decided to completely close the lock in 1993 and rebuild it. The new lock is now fully operational.

After leaving Spandau, which was part of West Berlin, the waterway soon passes evidence of industrial decay at Hennigsdorf, in what used to be East Germany. Beyond this, however, open country is reached and the canal lies amongst unspoilt rural countryside and woodlands.

The need to negotiate the massive ship-lift at Niederfinow (Km 77·9) in a small boat amongst the massive 1,500-tonne barges seems at first sight a

Old lock at Paretz - guest moorings at entrance to old lock 34km Havelkanal

Bathers in the heat of the summer on the banks of Havel-Oder-Wasserstrasse

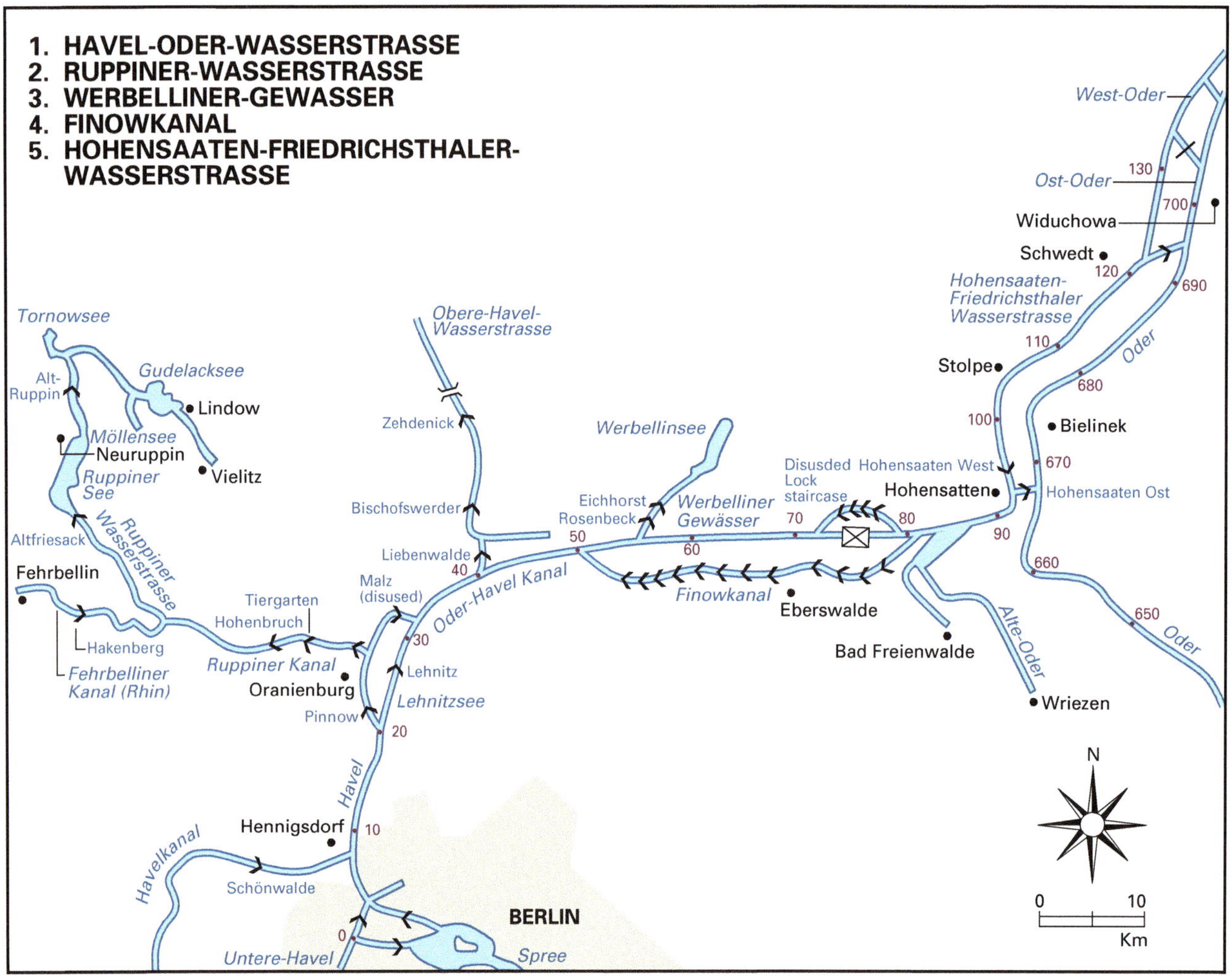

EAST

1. **HAVEL-ODER-WASSERSTRASSE**
2. **RUPPINER-WASSERSTRASSE**
3. **WERBELLINER-GEWASSER**
4. **FINOWKANAL**
5. **HOHENSAATEN-FRIEDRICHSTHALER-WASSERSTRASSE**

fearsome prospect. In the event, however, the experience proves to be interesting rather than frightening, and on the whole less problematic than using one of the large commercial locks. If time is on your side, the alternative route would be to take the much slower but pretty Finowkanal with its 12 locks, thus avoiding the ship-lift.

At Hohensaaten, where the waterway turns to the north to run parallel with the Ost-Oder, (which is also the Polish border), storks nest on chimney top platforms, agriculture appears to be more primitive and the land seems wilder. Good places to stop for the night are few and far between in this stretch, but it may be possible to find comfortable mooring at Km 76·6 in the entrance to the disused lock staircase above the Niederfinow ship-lift, though there is a huge engineering project on at the present time (2016) with the building of a new and larger ship lift adjacent to the existing one. This is unlikely to be completed before Autumn 2017 at the earliest. There are moorings at Oderberg and possible mooring places at Hohensaaten.

If heading down the Oder towards Szczecin it is possible either to use the Ostschleuse and travel down the Ostoder, or to use the Westschleuse and the Hohensaaten-Friedrichsthaler-Wasserstrasse. On the whole it is better to use the latter route because of more reliable depths.

Km

0·0 Junction with Untere-Havel-Wasserstrasse (Km 0·0) and the Spree-Oder-Wasserstrasse (Km 0·0)

0·4 Waiting area for lock on east side. Traffic lights.

0·6 *Schleuse Spandau*
Fall 2·8m
Length 115m
Breadth 12·5m
VHF Ch 23

Schleuse Spandau Km 0.60 Havel-Oder-Wasserstrasse

128 INLAND WATERWAYS OF GERMANY

1·0	Free mooring for leisure craft on west side max. 24hrs.
1·00–10·00	The waterway is a series of interlinked lakes, but the through channel is well buoyed and navigation is straightforward. The banks and inlets are lines with yacht and boat clubs, although not all have space or facilities to cater for visitors.
2·8	Free moorings for leisure craft on east side max. 24hrs.
3·4	Junction with Berlin-Spandauer-Schiffahrtskanal (Hohenzollern-Kanal) on east bank.
3·9	Entrance to Tegeler See on east bank. Navigable for 4km. Depth 2–4m. Many yacht clubs. Some restricted areas, no sports boats in SE corner bathing areas.
4·2	Ferry. Restaurant on east bank.
8·1	Marina Papenberge, mooring for leisure craft on west side, new facilities: electricity, water, showers, toilets, shops 1km walk.
10·5	Junction with Havelkanal (Km 0·0) on west bank.
12·3	Stadthafen Hennigsdorf on west bank. Commercial harbour. Steelworks nearby.
16·8	Marina for small leisure craft on west bank.
18·3	Marina Havelbaude on east bank with moorings for leisure craft. Showers, toilets, water and electricity.
20·8	Junction with Oranienburger Kanal on west bank, leading to Ruppiner Kanal.
25·0	Junction with Oranienburger Havel on west bank. No through passage. Depth 1·50m at entrance. Moorings possible at Marina Oranienburg. VHF Ch 18.
25·5–28	Lehnitzsee. Channel well buoyed
26·1	Staging on west bank of lake. Depth 1·50m. Also possible to anchor off. Shops and restaurants close by.
28·2	Waiting point for sports boats on west bank below lock. Traffic lights.
28·6	*Schleuse Lehnitz* (two chambers) Rise 6·0m Length 125·0m Breadth 11·9m VHF Ch 18
28·8–29·1	Waiting quay for sports boats on east bank above lock. Traffic lights.
32·4	Entrance to (disused) Malzer Kanal. Mooring overnight possible above Schleuse Malz.

Restaurant at Km 4.2 on left side of Havel-Oder-Wasserstrasse

Marina Havelbaude at Km 18.3

Marina Wassersportszentrum Oranienburg

EAST

Schleuse Lehnitz on Havel-Oder-Wasserstrasse

Tripper Boat on Havel-Oder-Wasserstrasse

Floodgates at Km 55.1

Modern industry between Km 65 and Km 70 Havel-Oder-Wasserstrasse

40·5	Junction with Malzer Kanal (first section of Obere-Havel-Wasserstrasse) on north bank.
41·5	Section of one-way traffic for commercial vessels.
50·4	Junction with Finowkanal on south bank.
54·9	Junction with Werbellinkanal on north bank.
55·1	Floodgates
55·3	Marina Marienwerder mooring for leisure craft on south bank: electricity, water, showers, toilets, 10-tonne crane.
57·8	Possible moorings on right bank.
71·0	Possible mooring place in entrance to old canal on north bank. Depth 2m.
78·0	*Schiffshebewerk Niederfinow* Fall 36·0m. Length 85·0m Breadth 12·0m VHF Ch 22. No fee. Waiting point for small boats close to entrance above ship-lift on north bank. Below ship-lift the waiting point for small boats is on north bank. Contact lift on VHF Ch 22 to advise presence and await instructions. An additional ship-lift is currently under construction.
78·5	VHF Ch 20.
79·0	Junction with Finowkanal on south bank.
81·8	Restaurant with mooring for guests.
82·5–84·0	Oderberger See. Buoyed channel along north side. Depth outside channel 1·00m.
84·6	Junction with Alte Oder on south bank.
85·6	Oderberg. Free mooring for leisure craft max 24hrs.
86·4	Wasserwanderastplatz on north bank for small leisure craft depth 1·9m.
87·0	Marina Oderberg mooring for leisure craft; electricity, water, toilets, shower, 12-tonne crane, slip. Depth 1·9m.
87·0	Follow buoyed channel.
91·2	Bootsanleger Hohensaaten mooring with electricity, water.
91·9	**Hohensaaten.** Water authority harbour on north bank. Mooring not officially allowed but possible if permission given.
92·6	Mooring to dolphins before Ostschleuse.

92·7 *Ostschleuse Hohensaaten* (to Oder River)
Rise 1·9m.
Length 170·0m
Breadth 11·9m
VHF Ch 20

92·8 Boats drawing under 1·20m can moor to staging on the right (west) bank above Westschleuse.

92·9 *Westchleuse Hohensaaten*
Fall 0·9m
Length 170·0m
Breadth 11·5m
VHF Ch 20

93·0 Junction with the Ost-Oder and Polish border.

HOHENSAATEN-FRIEDRICHSTHALER-WASSERSTRASSE

Navigable distance 42·3km
Maximum draught 1·80m
Maximum height 5·00m
Current Negligible
Locks 0
Speed limit 6km/h

This waterway, actually part of the Havel-Oder-Wasserstrasse, runs parallel to the Oder through pleasant agricultural countryside. The bird life in this area is very interesting: kingfishers, herons, storks, golden orioles, grebes and geese are much in evidence.

For vessels bound to or from Szczecin in Poland, this is an easier route than that via the Oder (Ostoder) itself, as there is less variation in depth. It should be noted that the direction of buoyage changes at Hohensaaten. From here northwards red buoys are to starboard and greens to port.

There are two options for vessels heading towards Szczecin. The normal route is to leave the Hohensaaten-Friedrichsthaler-Wasserstrasse at Schwedt and cross via the Schwedter Querfahrt to the Ostoder. This means using Schleuse Schwedt, as at this point the level of the Oder can be anything up to a metre above that of the Hohensaaten-Friedrichsthaler-Wasserstrasse. The alternative is to continue to the end of the Hohensaaten-Friedrichsthaler-Wasserstrasse at Km 135·3 and into the Westoder, clearing German customs (left bank) and Polish customs (right bank) at Mescherin. There are no locks to negotiate on this route. The Westoder route may be somewhat less busy with commercial traffic, but otherwise there is little to choose between the two options.

Km

93·0 Junction with Havel-Oder-Wasserstrasse (Km 93·0). Kilometre markings continue.

95·8 Loading quay for gravel.

98·9 Possible bank-side mooring at Lunow on left bank. Depth 2m. No facilities.

105·6 Stolpe. Mooring on left bank in 1·80m. No facilities but restaurant nearby.

120·7 Schwedt. Possible mooring on left bank. Depth uncertain.

121·4 Bootshafen Schwedt. Yacht harbour on left bank. Depth 1·8m, but varies slightly. Water, electricity, showers, slip. Shops and restaurants nearby.

Schwedter Querfahrt

123·3 Junction with Schwedter Querfahrt (length 3·5km) on right bank. Connects to Ostoder via *Schleuse Schwedt*.

Rise Around 1m, according to water level in Oder.
VHF Ch 79.
Hours Mon–Sat 0600–2000, Sunday 0700–1900.

No fee.

Mooring on left bank after lock immediately before junction with Oder. Use stem anchor and tie bow line to tree. No facilities.

Hohensaaten-Friedrichsthaler- Wasserstrasse (continued)

125·0 Industrial quay on left bank.

128·0 Gatow. Possible mooring on left bank. Depth uncertain.

133·6 Friedrichsthal. Possible mooring on left bank.

Depth uncertain.

135·3 Junction with Westoder (Km 3·0). 14km to German/Polish border. Speed limit on Westoder 12km/h.

RUPPINER WASSERSTRASSE

> Navigable length 71·4km
> Maximum draught 1·40m
> Maximum height 3·00m
> Current Negligible
> Locks 5
> Hours Mon–Thur 0800–1200 & 1400–1700, Fri–Sun 0800–1200 & 1400–1900. See route description for Schleuse Pinnow and Schleuse Hakenburg hours
> Speed limit 6km/h, on Ruppiner See 25km/h, on Vielitz-See 12km/h

The Ruppiner See and its connecting waterways form part of the original canal system of Germany, although nowadays, of course, there is no commercial shipping. It is an area of great charm and an excellent cruising ground.

The waterway system basically comprises the Oranienburger Kanal and the Ruppiner Kanal, leading to the Rhin river and continuing upstream through a series of lakes (including the 15km-long Ruppiner See) as far as Lindow. Boats drawing less than 1·10m can go 10km beyond Lindow to Vielitz. It is also possible to take the delightful lower part of the Rhin in a downstream direction; the river is navigable for 17km as the Fehrbelliner Kanal for boats drawing up to 1·3m. The old Rhin Kanal shown on some maps as an extension of the Fehrbelliner Kanal across to the Untere Havel at Garz is only a drainage canal.

Km

Oranienburger Kanal

Km	
20·8	Junction with Havel-Oder-Wasserstrasse Km 20·8.
22·5	*Schleuse Pinnow* Rise 2·4m Hours 0730–1700
28·8	Junction with Ruppiner Kanal Km 0·0 (and disused sections of Havel).

Ruppiner Kanal

0·0	Junction with Oranienburger Kanal Km 28·8.
2·1	*Schleuse Tiergarten* Rise 0·8m
7·2	*Schleuse Hohenbruch* Rise 0·7m
22·0	Junction with Rhin. Straight on upstream towards Ruppiner See and left for downstream Rhin and Fehrbelliner Kanal.

Fehrbelliner Kanal

0·0	Junction with Ruppiner Kanal.
8·0	*Schleuse Hakenberg* Fall 1·1m Hours 0800–1800 on request (☏ 033913300)
17·5	Fehrbellin. End of waterway.

Ruppiner Wasserstrasse (continued)

28·7	*Schleuse Altfriesack* Rise 1·1m. Dangerous lock with high sill. Boats with a draught of over 1·00m should insist on using the third lock gate and should stay in the southern part of the double lock during locking.
29·6–43·5	Ruppiner See. Numerous possible mooring places and anchorages.
40·5	**Neuruppin**. Several possible mooring places on west bank.
43·7	Alt Ruppin.
45·1	*Schleuse Alt Ruppin* Rise 2·0m.
45·3–47·0	Molchowsee. Possible anchorages.
47·5–49·7	Teetzensee. Possible anchorages.
50·3–53·0	Zermützelsee. Possible anchorages.
51·2	Entrance to Tornowsee (4km diversion).
59·5–60·5	Möllensee. Possible mooring place at southern end.
61·3–65·0	Gudelacksee. Mooring at staging on west side at Gühlen.
65·0	Lindow. Yacht harbour on lake.
65·3–66·6	Vielitz-Kanal. Maximum draught 1·00m.
66·6–71·4	Vielitz-See.
71·4	End of navigation.

FINOWKANAL

Navigable distance 32·2 km
Maximum draught 1·20m
Maximum height 3·80m
Current Negligible
Locks 12
Hours Daily 0900–1700 from 1 May to 30 September
Speed limit 6km

This attractive canal was once the main commercial route from the Elbe to the Oder and is now a very pleasant alternative route to the fast link on the Havel-Oder-Wasserstrasse, thus avoiding the Niederfinow Ship-Lift. The Finowkanal was built in 1605 and contributed to the evolution of the surrounding industry. It was noted to have had over 15,000 ships pass through it in 1890, but fell into disuse as a through route in the late 1900s. Now the canal is fully operational as a leisure canal, with modernised locks and operated by lock keepers, some of whom may operate more than one lock. The beautiful waterlily-lined canal meanders its way through the charming Naturepark Barnim countryside, with its pleasant villages on a journey that is likely to take you at least one and a half days and longer if your interest level dictates several sightseeing stops en-route. There are many mooring places along the canal though they are limited in both space and size. Considerable canalside maintenance is taking place; however, there is some concern over the depth and the amount of water weed restricting the canal in the summer.

The WSA Eberswalde contact number for the Finowkanal is ✆ 03335 45160.

There are no fees charged for this canal.

Km
57·2 Junction with Havel-Oder-Wasserstrasse Km 50·4.
59·2 *Schleuse Ruhlsdorf* Fall 1·7m
61·1 *Schleuse Leesenbrück* Fall 2·5m
62·0 Possible limited mooring at Bootsangler Marienweder.
63·3 *Schleuse Grafenbrück* Fall 3·6m
65·3 Possible limited mooring at Marina Eisvogel with electricity, water, toilet, shower, restaurant.
67·3 Possible limited mooring at Wasserwanderrastplatz Finowfurt with electricity, water, toilet, shower.
67·5 *Schleuse Schöpfurth* Fall 3·6m
70·3 Possible limited mooring at Wasserwanderrastplatz Messingwerkhafen.
71·0 *Schleuse Heegermühle* Fall 2·6m
72·9 *Schleuse Wolfswinkel* Fall 2·6m
73·5 **Eberswalde** Lifting bridge operates every two hours from 0800 to 1800 every day throughout the season.
74·0 *Schleuse Drahthammer* Fall 3·6m
      Possible limited mooring at the Anlegestelle Familiengarten – below the lock.
75·9 *Schleuse Kupferhammer* Fall 4·0m
      Possible limited mooring at the Anlegestelle Finowkanal-Park with electricity, water, restaurant, hiring of canoes and bicycles.
77·8 Mooring at Wasserwanderrastplatz Eberswalde.
77·9 *Schleuse Eberswalde* Fall 3·5m
81·0 *Schleuse Ragöse* Fall 2·3m

Finowfurt

Lifting bridge in Eberswalde km 73.5

EAST

Niederfinow ship-lift, opened in 1934

81·1	Mooring below Schleuse Ragöse.
84·4	*Schleuse Stecher* Fall 3·0m
86·4	**Niederfinow** lifting bridge. Operates daily throughout the season in consultation with the two locks either side.
88·9	*Schleuse Liepe* Fall 2·4m
89·4	Junction with the Havel-Oder-Wasserstrasse Km 78·8.

WERBELLINER GEWÄSSER

Navigable length 16·6km
Maximum draught 1·20m
Maximum height 4·00m
Current Negligible
Locks 2
Hours 0700–2000
Speed limit 6km/h (25km/h on lake if at least 100m from shore)

From Km 54·9 on the Havel-Oder-Wasserstrasse the attractive Werbellinkanal, 3·50m deep as far as the second lock, runs northwards to the Werbellinsee, a beautiful lake some 10km long and up to 50m deep. The waterway runs through woodland and heath rich in wildlife: kites, eagles, cranes, otters and beavers can all be seen from time to time. Much of the area is in fact a nature reserve. There are excellent anchorages and mooring places around the shores of the Werbellinsee, the largest being at the village of Altenhof (Km 14 on the east bank).

In the canal above Schleuse Eichhorst the depth of water can be a problem for deeper-draught boats, but a word with the friendly lock-keeper may well result in a temporary adjustment in level to overcome the problem.

Navigation on the lake is prohibited at night 2200–0500. On Saturdays, Sundays and holidays from May to September motorboats are prohibited from navigating on the lake from 1200–1500.

Km

3·4	Junction with Havel-Oder-Wasserstrasse Km 54·9.
6·0	Schleuse Rosenbeck Rise 3·1m.
8·5	Schleuse Eichhorst Rise 3·1m.
10·5–20·0	Werbellinsee.

OBERE HAVEL-WASSERSTRASSE

Navigable distance 94·4km
Maximum draught 1·2m
Maximum height 3·5m
Current Negligible
Locks 11
Hours Varied. See route description
Speed limit 9km/h from Havel-Oder-Wasserstrasse to Km 23·5; 6km/h above Km 23·5

The Obere Havel and its network of lakes, rivers and canals forms a major part of a beautiful area, generally known as the Mecklenburg lake district, to the north and northwest of Berlin. This area has become available to cruising boats since the reunification of Germany.

The main through route is basically the upper part of the Havel, which together with its major branches, the Wentow Gewässer, the Templiner Gewässer and the Lychener Gewässer, forms a magical waterway system set in an area of outstanding natural beauty. It is also an area rich in history, and the many picturesque towns and villages all have stories to tell; from medieval rivalries, to the concentration camps of the Second World War, to the desperate plight of the population during the cold war. The north western end of the waterway links with the Müritz-Havel-Wasserstrasse, which in turn links with Lake Müritz and eventually, via the Müritz-Elde-Wasserstrasse, to the lower Elbe.

One of the attractive features of this area is that there are many tranquil, out-of-the-way places in which to moor and anchor. There are a few yacht harbours, but such is the attraction of this less known area, that in the main most people find it preferable to lie in some peaceful corner of a lake. The kilometering is a little confusing, as the beginning of this stretch of water still reflects the

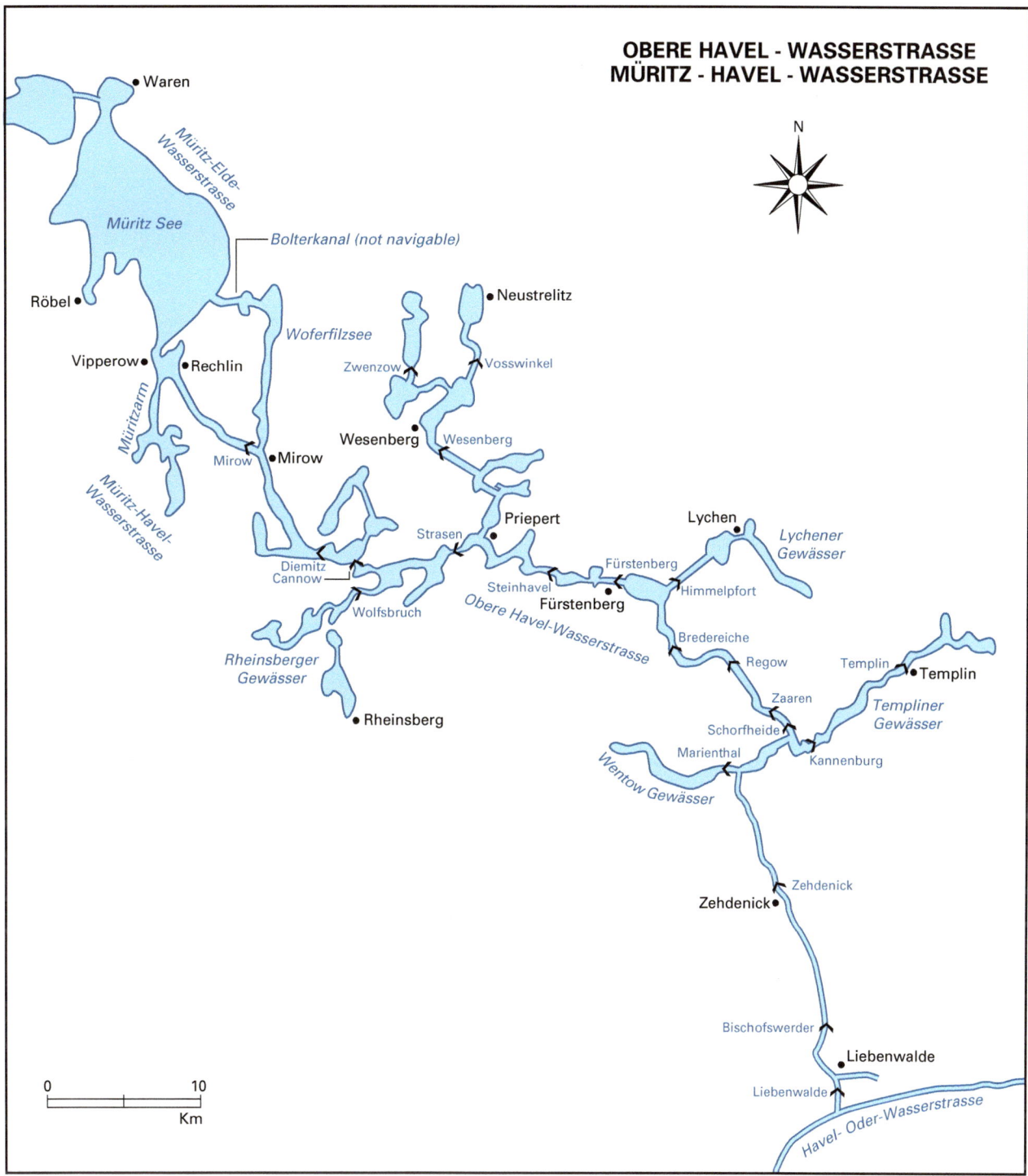

original waterway system, starting with 0·0 at the junction with the defunct northwest extension of the Finowkanal; now used as a marina for small boats. The 2·9km section between this point and the Havel-Oder-Wasserstrasse is technically the Malzer Kanal and is numbered from Km 44.0 at the junction with the Havel-Oder-Wasserstrasse to Km 46·9 at the junction with the old section of the Finowkanal.

At normal times the main through-route is available to boats drawing 1·5m, but in dry seasons the depth may be a little less than this.

Of the 17 locks in the area as a whole, 11 are on the through route and six are on branches; the majority of which are operated automatically by self-activation of the locking through process.

There are no fees.

EAST

Km	
44·0	Junction with the Havel-Oder-Wasserstrasse Km 40·4
45·3	*Schleuse Liebenwalde* Rise 2·0m Length 51·3m Breadth 10·5m Hours 1 April to 30 September, daily 0700–2000; 1 October to 30 November, daily 0800–1800; 1 December to 31 March, daily 0800–1600. Automatic lock ☏ 033054 602669.
46·9	Junction with old defunct section of Finowkanal now Marina Liebenwalde with guest moorings for boats less than 14m long. Water, electricity, WC, shower.
0·0	**Liebenwalde**
4·5	*Schleuse Bischofswerder* Rise 3·3m Length 85·0m Breadth 10·6m Hours as per Schleuse Liebenwalde (Km 45·3) Automatic lock ☏ 03307 60640.
15·5	Public free mooring just before lifting bridge on Westside. Max 12 hours, max boat length 15m, no facilities. Close to town centre, shops and restaurants.
15·7	**Zehdenick**. Lifting bridge which operates in tandem with the lock. Semi-automatic activation from staging pontoon on left side. One pull on the activation rod activates the lifting bridge and cycles lock ready for entry. Repeat rod activation in the lock when all boats are secure and ready for the lock cycle to commence. *Note* If there is any current in the river Havel south of Zehdenick, there will be a left to right cross-flow in the lock entrance channel.
15·9	Lock bridge max height 4·2m *Schleuse Zehdenick* Rise 3·0m Length 44·9m Breadth 9·5m Hours as per Schleuse Liebenwalde (Km 45·3) Automatic lock ☏ 03307 2705.
16·0	*Note* right-angled bend to the right on exiting the lock.
16·1	Zehdenick Stadthafen on east side. Guest moorings, water, electricity, WC, shower. Pumpout.
16·2	Marina Zehdenick on east side. Guest moorings, water, electricity, WC, shower. Restaurant. Fuel. Yacht service.

Lifting bridge and lock entrance in background, Zehdenick

Entrance to Zehdenick Lock on right angled bend - southbound

21·7	New spacious Museumhafen west side. Guest moorings, water, 16A electricity, WC, shower. Fuel.
22·0	Marina in Ziegeleipark west side. 15 guest moorings, water, electricity, WC, shower. Restaurant. Yacht service.
24·2	Burgwall. 10 guest moorings along river bank east side. Water, electricity, restaurant; free mooring only if you dine at the restaurant.
24·9	Junction with Wentow Kanal.

Marina Zehdenick with guest moorings Km 16.3

Moorings at Burgwall east side Km 25.2 Obere-Havel-Wasserstrasse

Wentow Gewässer

Navigable distance 11·0km
Maximum draught 1·0m
Maximum height 3·5m
Current Negligible
Locks 1
Hours 1 to 30 April, daily 0700–1800;
1 May to 30 September, daily 0700–2000;
1 October to 30 November, daily 0800–1600;
1 December to 31 March, closed
Speed limit 6km/h and 10km/h lake stretch

This short waterway, comprising the Wentow Kanal and the Wentowsee, lies amid very pretty countryside. There are several anchorages and mooring places.

Km

0·0	Junction with the Obere Havel-Wasserstrasse Km 24.9.
0·1	*Schleuse Marienthal* Rise 1·9m Length 44·0m Breadth 5·3m Automatic lock ✆ 033054 60239.
2·5–7·9	Grosser Wentowsee.
9·2	Road and railway bridges max height 3·5m. Only small boats can continue beyond this point.
9·6–11·0	Kleiner Wentowsee.

Obere Havel-Wasserstrasse (continued)

32·1	Junction with the Templiner Gewässer on the east side.

Templiner Gewässer

Navigable distance 20·0km
Maximum draught 1·2m
Maximum height 3·6m
Current Negligible
Locks 2
Hours 1 to 30 April, daily 0700–1800;
1 May to 30 September, daily 0700–2000;
1 October to 30 November, daily 0800–1600;
1 December to 31 March, closed
Speed limit 6km/h

The Templiner Gewässer is a string of small beautiful lakes connected by canals and canalised rivers. The countryside is very pleasant and passes through what used to be an area that was frequented by Russian troops for exercises and is therefore largely unspoilt. An idyllic location for just anchoring, bathing and relaxing.

Km

0·0	Junction with the Obere Havel-Wasserstrasse Km 32·1.
2·6	Enter Grosser Kuhwallsee.
3·5	Good holding quayside on north side before lock.
3·6	*Schleuse Kannenburg* Rise 1·4m Length 42·5m Breadth 5·3m ✆ 0171-6742196
3·8	Good holding quayside on north side before lock.
5·8–9·0	**Rödelinsee**
8·0	Floating pontoon attached to restaurant grounds on west side of the Rödelinsee; no facilities.
8·1	Jetty guest moorings on far east side of the Rödelinsee, water, electricity, pumpout.

Schleuse Kannenburg Km 3.5 Templiner Wasser

EAST

Guest moorings on east side of the Rodelinsee

Upperstream entrance to Schleuse Templin Templiner Kanal Km 11.8

9·0	Entrance to Templiner Kanal at northwest corner of the Rödelinsee. Take care, restricted vision at entrance to channel, due to high reeds and overgrown vegetation. A scenic winding narrow kanal. Beware, channel used by a local tripper boat.
9·8	Sound horn before railway bridge. *Note* one-way traffic at a time at this bridge.
10·5	Low bridge, Ziegeleibrücke max height 3·6m.
11·4	Tripper boat mooring.
11·5	**Templin**
11·8	Lock holding stage on right side. Activate automatic lock.
11·9	*Schleuse Templin* Rise 4·0m Length 25·0m Breadth 4·9m Recently rebuilt automatic lock. The recently rebuilt automatic lock at Templin is operating well and is a vast improvement on its predecessor.
12·1	Lock holding stage on east side. Activate automatic lock.
12·2	Moorings for small boats
12·9	Stadthafen Templin on east side. Guest moorings, water, electricity 16amp, WC, shower, cafe, pump out, gated, slip nearby. Close to pretty walled town centre, shops and many restaurants.
13·0– 16·0	Templiner See. Possible anchorages on both sides.
16·1	Road and railway bridges max height 3·9m, max breadth 5·5m, leading to Fährsee.
16·2– 20·0	Fährsee, leading to Zaarsee. End of navigation.

Lock activator - turn green pole - at holding area and in lock

Templin town

Entrance to lock at Templin

138 INLAND WATERWAYS OF GERMANY

Guest moorings - Stadthafen Templin

Schleuse Bredereiche 47.8km Obere-Havel-Wasserstrasse

Obere Havel-Wasserstrasse (continued)

32·7 *Schleuse Schorfheide*
Rise 0·6m
Length 51·5m
Breadth 5·45m

Hours 1 April to 30 September, daily 0700–2000; 1 October to 30 November, daily 0800–1600; 1 December to 31 March, closed.

Automatic lock ✆ 0171 6742195.

36·2 *Schleuse Zaaren*
Rise 1·1m
Length 44·3m
Breadth 5·6m
Hours as per Schleuse Schorfheide (Km 32.7).

Automatic lock.

42·5 *Schleuse Regow*
Rise 1·0m
Length 43·6m
Breadth 5·5m
Hours as per Schleuse Schorfheide (Km 32.7)

Automatic lock ✆ 033087-52318.

47·7 *Schleuse Bredereiche*
Rise 2·6m
Length 55·0m
Breadth 6·5m
Hours as per Schleuse Schorfheide (Km 32.7).

Automatic lock ✆ 033087 52223.

47·8 Guest moorings west side, water, electricity, WC, shower, slip.

48·1 Moorings west side, electricity.

48·1 Possible moorings east side, no facilities.

54·3– Stolpsee. Junction with Lychener
57·5 Gewässer.

Mooring at Bredereiche 48.3km Obere-Havel-Wasserstrasse

EAST

Lychener Gewässer

Navigable distance 9·5km
Maximum draught 1·2m
Maximum height 3.5m
Current Negligible
Locks 1
Hours 1 April to 30 September, daily 0700–2000;
1 October to 30 November, daily 0800–1600;
1 December to 31 March, closed
Speed limit 6km/h

This is another pleasant detour from the main through route, suitable for boats drawing no more than 1·2m. The Woblitz river leads through the pretty village of Himmelpfort into the Grosser Lychensee lake, at the north eastern corner of which lies the small holiday resort of Lychen. Although badly damaged by bombs in the Second World War, Lychen is still extremely attractive, and is a very pleasant centre from which to explore the surrounding neighbourhood. The Grosser Lychensee is generally around 5m in depth and has three small islands. Anchor in the lake or moor at the small staging on the foreshore at Lychen.

Km

0·0	Junction with Stolpsee Km 55·0.
0·1	Srassenbrücke Himmelpfort. Low bridge max height 3·5m.
0·2	*Schleuse Himmelpfort* Rise 1·2m Length 42·0m Breadth 5·3m Automatic lock.
0·3–1·7	Hausee. Anchoring possible, mooring at staging in top eastside corner.
4·0–5·1	Very tight oxbow bends with one way moving traffic at a time, sound horn.
5·3–8·3	Grosser Lychensee.
8·4	Railway bridge max height 3·2m
8·5–9·5	Stadtsee.
8·9	**Lychen**. Sailing club jetty. Guest moorings, limited facilities.
9·5	End of navigation.

Obere Havel-Wasserstrasse (continued)

54·3–57·5	Stolpsee.
59·4	Railway ferry, historical technical monument.
59·9	Junction with Schwedtsee. Yacht harbour at Fürstenberg on north side. Guest moorings, with all facilities, restaurant, close to town centre.
60	**Fürstenberg**

Passage from Baalensee to entrance of Schwedtsee with Furstenberger YC in background, Obere Havel-Wasserstrasse

60·1	Passage to Baalensee. Anchoring possible.
60·5	Holding piles for lock on west side, activate lock to indicate presence.
60·6	*Schleuse Fürstenberg* Rise 1·9m Length 42·6m Breadth 11·0m Hours 1 April to 30 September, Mon–Sun 0700–2000; 1 October to 30 November, Mon–Sun 0800–1600; 1 December to 31 March, closed. Lock keeper attended/automatic. New double width lock, lock gates diagonally opposite. Busy lock, probable queuing at peak times, often shared with canoeists, engines OFF ✆ 033093 32244.
60·8	Guest moorings, north side, no facilities, close to town centre, shops, restaurants.
60·9	Holding piles for lock, south side, activate lock to indicate presence.
60·9	Guest moorings, north side, water, electricity, WC, shower, pump out, close to town centre, shops, restaurants.
61·4–63·2	Röblinsee. Buoyed channel. Possible anchorage.
62·2	Bootsstege Röblinsee with guest moorings, south side. Water, electricity 16amp, WC, shower, pump out.
63·3	Exit channel on northside into Steinhavel is a tight right turn, turning very close to the reed bed.
64·6	*Schleuse Steinhavel* Rise 1·6m Length 41·9m Breadth 5·3m Hours as per Schleuse Fürrstenberg (Km 60.6). Lock keeper attended ✆ 033093 32095.
66·6	Entrance to Menowsee on west bank. Possible anchorage.

Scleuse Steinhavel - 64.6km Obere Havel-Wasserstrasse

66·7	Entrance to channel NE, leading to Ziernsee
67·0–68·6	Ziernsee. Mooring at camp site at north end of lake.
68·6	Entrance to channel on west side of lake, leading to Ellbogensee.
69·0–74·5	Ellbogensee and continuation west onto the Müritz-Havel-Wasserstrasse.
72·5	Entrance north side for the continuation of the Obere Havel-Wasserstrasse.
72·6	**Priepert.** Guest moorings south of town, water, electricity, WC, shower.
73·0–75·2	Grosser Priepert See.
75·4–75·6	Wagnitzsee. Motorboats forbidden to go east of marked channel.
75·8	Entrance to OHW channel west side.
77·8	Entrance to Drewensee. Motorboats forbidden to go east of marked channel.
77·8	Entrance north west side channel for the continuation of the OHW.
78·5	Ahrensberg.
81·3	*Schleuse Wesenberg* Rise 2·4m Length 55·6m Breadth 6·6m Hours as per Schleuse Fürrstenberg (Km 60·6) Lock keeper attended ☏ 039832 20124.
82·3–86·7	Woblitzsee. Anchorage possible. Take care with variable depth outside of the channel markers.
86·2	Entrance NW, to upper reaches of the Havel river and Grosser Labussee to Km 5·3. Navigation further upstream forbidden to motorboats.
86·8	Entrance north east side channel for the continuation of the OHW.
88·0	*Schleuse Vosswinkel* Rise 1·8m Length 43·1m Breadth 5·3m Hours as per Schleuse Fürrstenberg (Km 60·6). Lock keeper attended. ☏ 03981 200549
89·5	Railway bridge max height 3·5m
91·5–94·4	Zierker See. Follow buoyed channel.
93·0	**Neustrelitz.** Four marinas all with guest moorings, depth 1·1m to 1·5m all with facilities. Close to town centre, shops, restaurants.
94·4	End of waterway.

MÜRITZ-HAVEL-WASSERSTRASSE

Navigable distance 31·8km
Maximum draught 1·4m
Maximum height 3·8m
Current Negligible
Locks 4
Hours 1 April to 30 September, daily 0700–2000;
1 October to 30 November, daily 0800–1600;
1 December to 31 March, closed.
Speed limit 9km/h except on lakes more than 250 metres wide 25km/h

The Müritz-Havel-Wasserstrasse cuts through the heart of the Mecklenburg lake district. Although only 31km in length, it passes through a labyrinth of lakes, rivers and canals, which are a paradise to boat users and has now become one of Germany's holiday playgrounds. A large proportion of the gently rolling landscape is covered with woodland, and there are many charming and interesting small towns and villages. For example, the small town of Mirow has a history which can be traced back to the 7th century.

The main branches from the main route are the Rheinsberger Gewässer to the south and the chain of small lakes leading north from Mirow (at one time with an exit via the Bolter Kanal to the Müritz See).

There are four locks on the main route and a further one on the Rheinsberger Gewässer all of which are likely to be busy and will be shared with canoes and other small vessels. All locks are attended. There are no fees.

EAST

Schleuse Strasen Km 2·7 Muritz-Havel-Wasserstrasse

Km

0·0   **Priepert.** Junction with the Obere Havel-Wasserstrasse Km 72·5

2·7   *Schleuse Strasen*
      Rise 1·5m
      Length 41·5m
      Breadth 5·1m
      ☎ 039828 20484

2·8   Strasen-Priepert. Mooring places immediately above lock in centre of village.

2·8–4·2   Grosser Pälitzsee. Channel goes south for 1km then turns sharp right in a westerly direction into the Kleiner Pälitzsee. Anchoring possible in both lakes.

7·4   Junction with Rheinsberger Gewässer on south side of lake.

Rheinsberger Gewässer

Navigable distance 13·1km
Maximum draught 1·4m
Maximum height 3·65m
Current Negligible
Locks 1
Hours 1 April to 30 September daily 0700–2000;
1 October to 30 November daily 0800–1600;
1 December–31 March closed
Speed limit 9km/h

This is a short waterway which connects to the upper reaches of the Rhin at Rheinsberg. The Rhin becomes navigable lower down (see Ruppiner Wasserstrasse), but at this point it is useable only by canoes only. The cruise up to Rheinsberg is very worthwhile, with pole position views of Schloss Rheinsberg from the Grienericksee at the end of the navigation channel.

The area has been developed for holiday homes, but there are many pleasant moorings and anchorages at Rheinsberg. There are also very pleasant anchorages and mooring places, in the Zechliner Gewässer, which branches off at Km 5·2.

Km

0·0   Junction with the Müritz-Havel-Wasserstrasse Km 7·4

2·4   *Schleuse Wolsbruch*
      Rise 0·4m
      Length 42·6m
      Breadth 5·2m
      ☎ 033921 70240

2·9   Yachthafen Wolfsbruch south side, 50 guest moorings, water, electricity, WC, shower, pump out, 20-tonne crane, restaurant, hotel.

4·0   Prebelowbrucke rebuilt in 2005. Height 4·5m.

5·2   Junction with Zechliner Gewässer on west side. The tree-flanked Zechliner Gewässer is 8·2km long, ending at the village of Flecken Zechlin. Can be used by vessels with max 1·4m draught of and 3·5m height.

6·6   Zechliner Hütte. Small village on east side with mooring place.

6·8   Entrance to Dollgowsee on west side under bridge. The delightful Dollgowsee, which is a 3km diversion, is bordered by a nature reserve and provides good opportunities for secluded anchoring.

9·0–10·9   Rheinsberger See. Good anchoring places. Depth 2·5–30·0m

10·9   Hafendorf Rheinsberg, a large yacht harbour at the south eastern corner. Guest moorings, water, electricity, WC, shower, restaurant, slip, 20-tonne crane, pump out. Hafen Office ☎ 033931 80545 or 0176 10039393.

11·8   Guest moorings.

Hafendorf Rheinsberg Km 10.8 Rheinsberger Gewasser

142   INLAND WATERWAYS OF GERMANY

Schloss Rhiensberg Km 12.8 Rheinsberger Gewasser

12·5 Motorwassersportclub Rheinsberg, guest moorings, water, electricity, WC, shower, pump out. Close to town centre, shops, restaurant. Walking distance to visit Schloss Rheinsberg and evening concert performances in palace grounds.

Müritz-Havel-Wasserstrasse (continued)

9·5 *Schleuse Canow*
Rise 1·3m
Length 41·6m
Breadth 5·3m
☏ 039828 20255

10·0–
12·5 Labussee. Channel turns west after leaving Canow. Interesting diversion for small boats to the north (but forbidden to motorboats) through Dollbeck to the Gobenowsee and from there through to the Drosedower Bach under the 1·9m high bridge to the Rätzsee. The passage from Gobenowsee eastwards under the bridge into the Klenzsee can be 0·5m deep.

13·2 *Schleuse Diemitz*
Rise 1·4m
Length 42·0m
Breadth 5·3m
☏ 039827 30450

The lock bridge, Schleusenbrücke Diemitz, is 4·3m high.

Anchoring/mooring above and below the lock in Kleiner Peetschsee and Grosser Peetschsee. Take care, watch out for new cardinal buoys.

14·0–
15·5 Vilzsee. Channel passes through eastern end of lake turning northwards after approx. 0·6km. Take care of cardinal buoy markings. Can be choppy in strong westerly winds. A 2km diversion westwards along the lake is possible, and non-motorised vessels drawing 1·3m can then enter the Schwarzer See.

18·0–
19·7 Zotzensee

21·8 Main route branches northwest as the Mirower Kanal, north branch, and under the 4·0m road bridge, leads to the waterfront of Mirow, with several guest mooring places with good facilities and shops, restaurants ashore. Continuing northwards, the route of the old Müritz-Havel-Wasserstrasse passes through several delightful small lakes and finishes in the Woterfilzsee, which was connected to the Müritz by the now defunct Bolter Kanal.

Note Motorboats are forbidden to navigate north of the Mirower See.

22·3 Continuing on the main northwest route

Lock holding piles with small platforms on west side before and after the lock. A very busy lock, long queues, can take half a day to get through at peak times. Separate canoe track.

Schleuse Mirow
Rise 3·1m
Length 56·0m
Breadth 6·6m
☏ 039833 20259

29·0–
30·0 Sumpfsee. Buoyed channel.

31·8 End of waterway. Exit to Kleine Müritz Km 172·0

Schleuse Mirow Km 22.5, Müritz-Havel-Wasserstrasse

EAST

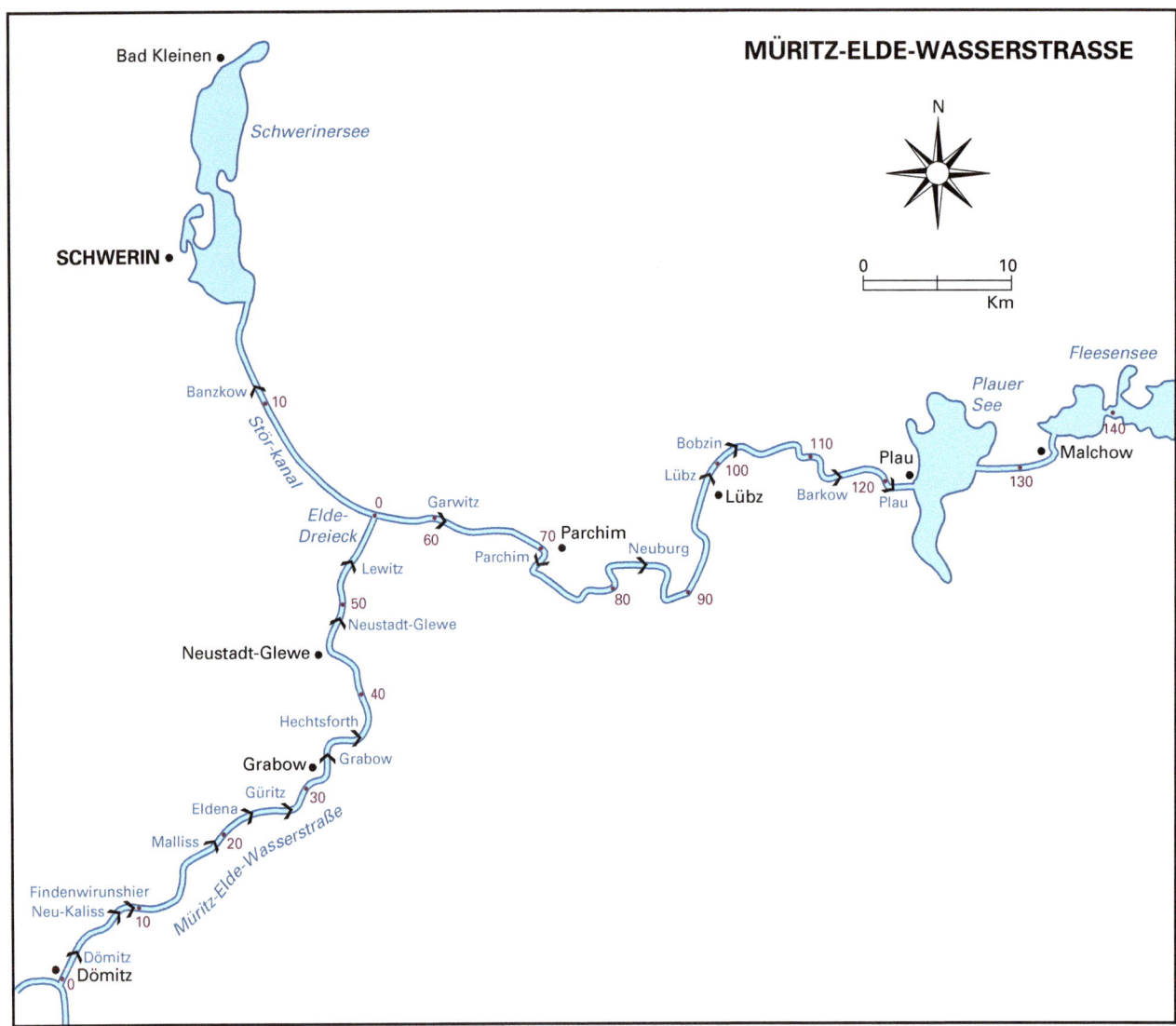

MÜRITZ-ELDE-WASSERSTRASSE

Navigable distance 180·0km
Maximum draught 1·2m
Maximum height 3·8m
Current Negligible
Locks 17
Hours 1 April to 30 September daily 0900–2000;
1 October to 30 November daily 0900–1600
1 December to 31 March closed
Speed limit 6km/h in canal, 9km/h along lake inside 250m from the coastline, 25km/h in lake outside 250m from the coastline.

This waterway provides an interesting and attractive route from the Elbe to the Müritz Lake in the beautiful Mecklenburg lake district. From here it is possible to continue via the Müritz-Havel-Wasserstrasse and the Obere Havel to join the Havel-Oder-Wasserstrasse north of Berlin. The 44km Stör-Wasserstrasse, including the second biggest lake in the area, the Schweriner See, makes an interesting detour.

From the Elbe, the first 120km of the Müritz-Elde-Wasserstrasse, to the Plauersee, the waterway is the canalised Elde River. At first, it runs through very pleasant low-lying agricultural land, but from Parchim (Km 72) the landscape becomes more picturesque. There are yacht harbours, secluded places to moor or anchor and enjoy the scenery, to talk to the friendly locals and to see the wildlife for which the area is famous. A major part of the shores of the Müritz is in fact a huge nature reserve, a breeding ground for white-tailed eagles and black storks as well as many other species. The woods abound with deer, and there are large numbers of interesting flora, including orchids and gentians. Müritz is also famous for its water lilies during the summer months.

The towns of Waren, Malchow and Plau were all well established as health resorts by the middle of the 19th century. The beautiful old city of Schwerin has a 12-century cathedral, many half-timbered houses dating from mediaeval times and a spectacular castle built on an island. The city was one of the few that escaped damage from British bombs during the Second World War.

The 17 locks and the many opening bridges survived the 44 years of Communist rule remarkably well and are generally in good working order. The waterway is well buoyed where necessary; travelling eastwards from the Elbe is the upstream direction so reds are to port and greens to starboard, as convention dictates. It should be noted that in bad weather, owing to the size and shallowness of the Müritz (and other lakes), dangerous navigation conditions can develop, often very rapidly. It is as well to be aware of the weather forecast before setting out to cross any of the large lakes. There are several websites for checking the last minute wind, wave height and weather information, such as www.tide-forecast.com and www.windfinder.com

There are some places for repairs in this area, but their suitability for all types of craft cannot be confirmed. Should problems occur which call for professional assistance, the most likely places to find service are at Dömitz, Grabow, Schwerin, and Rechlin. At the time of writing, fuel could be found at several of the mooring places listed below. However, it should be noted that following recent changes to the EU legislation, some establishments are ceasing to provide this service.

Km

0·0	Junction with the Elbe Km 504·1
0·6	**Dömitz**. Mooring possible in harbour area before lock.
0·8	Swing bridge.
1·0	*Schleuse Dömitz* (with lift bridge) Rise 1·5–2·9m Length 53·2m Breadth 8·7m ☏ 038758 22725
1·2	Moorings on west side, water, electricity, WC, shower, pump out, slip, crane, fuel.
4·9	*Schleuse Neu Kaliss* Rise 2·1m Length 40·3m Breadth 5·4m ☏ 038758 26318
5·8	*Schleuse Findenwirunshier* (with lift bridge) Rise 2·1m Length 41·8m Breadth 5·3m ☏ 038758 24112
6·0	Moorings east side, water, electricity, WC, shower, slip.
9·5	*Schleuse Malliss* Rise 2·0m Length 41·1m Breadth 5·3m ☏ 038750 20424
9·6	Mooring in inlet on west side. Depth 1·2m. Electricity, WC, shower, pump out.
12·0	Mooring on east side. Depth 1·5m water, electricity, WC, shower, pump out, fuel.
17·8	Mooring on west side. Depth 1·4m, water electricity, WC, Shower, fuel.
18·0	*Schleuse Eldena* Rise 1·7m Length 46·7m Breadth 6·4m ☏ 038755 20304
22·7	*Schleuse Güritz* Rise 3·3m Length 56·8m Breadth 6·6m ☏ 038755 20268
27·9	Mooring on west side. Depth 1·2m, water, electricity, WC, shower, restaurant.
28·5	**Grabow**
28·6	Stadhafen Grabow guest mooring on east side. Depth 1·5m, water, electricity, WC, shower, pump out.
29·8	*Schleuse Grabow* Rise 1·9m Length 40·8m Breadth 5·3m ☏ 038756 22339
29·0	*Rehberger Hubbrücke* New lifting bridge height closed 3·5m; bridge height open 4·3m. Bridge opens daily at 0900, 1030, 1200, 1330, 1500. From 1 April–30 September it also opens at 1630, 1800, 1930.
34·6	Possible mooring. Water, electricity, WC.
34·8	*Schleuse Hechtsforth* Rise 3·2m Length 44·7m Breadth 6·6m ☏ 038756 22473
46·0	**Neustadt-Glewe**
46·0	Restaurant east side with mooring. Depth 0·9m.
46·0	Guest mooring on west side close to town centre. Depth 1·2m, water, electricity, WC, shower, restaurant, pump out, fuel.
46·2	*Schleuse Neustadt-Glewe* Rise 2·2m Length 53·9m Breadth 6·6m ☏ 038757 22578
49·5–55·5	Extensive fish farms on both sides.

50·6 *Schleuse Lewitz*
Rise 3·7m
Length 53·3m
Breadth 6·5m
☏ 038757 22684

56·7 Elde-Dreieck. Junction with Stör-Wasserstrasse (Störkanal). Müritz-Elde-Wasserstrasse turns southeast, Stör-Wasserstrasse turns northwest.

Stör-Wasserstrasse

Navigable distance 44·0km
Maximum draught 1·2m
Maximum height 4·2m
Current Negligible
Locks 1
Speed limit 6km/h in canal, 9km/h along lake inside the 250m from coastline, 25km/h in lake outside 250m from coastline

Schloss Schwerin, viewed from the harbour

This waterway comprises the Störkanal and the Schweriner See. The first 10km of the canal are relatively straight and featureless, but then it takes a more meandering route and passes through several pleasant villages before entering the Schweriner See, which is a major centre for water sports and recreation. It is divided into two parts, north (Aussensee) and south (Innensee), which are separated by a narrow channel over which there is a road bridge with a height of 4·3m.

The historic city of Schwerin has many interesting features, the most famous being the splendid castle and the 12th century cathedral.

Km

0·0 Junction with Müritz-Elde-Wasserstrasse Km 56·7

10·9 *Schleuse Banzkow*
Rise 0·9m
Length 47·8m
Breadth 5·4m
☏ 03861 7232

11·0 Swing bridge.

14·8 Plate. Hubbrücke Plate, bridge closed height 1·7m.

Bridge opens daily 1000, 1130, 1300, 1430, 1500.

Also from 1 April–30 September at 1600, 1730, 1900.

14·9 Restaurant Störkrug with guest mooring. Electricity, WC, shower.

20·0 Raben. Entrance to Schwerin See. Mooring place on east side campsite. Water, electricity, WC, shower.

20·0– Schweriner See. Check weather conditions before entering the lake. Follow buoyed channel. Beware of cardinal buoys marking shallows. There are two islands in the southern part of the lake both of which are nature reserves, forbidden areas, no access.

24·0 **Schwerin** on west side.

Segelclub Schlossbucht Schwerin, guest moorings, water, electricity, WC, shower, restaurant, clubhouse. Depth 1–1·5m.

Schweriner Yacht Club, Kalkwerder, water, electricity, WC, shower, slip, pump out. Depth 1–1·3m.

Schwerener Segler Verein v. 1894, Marstall, guest moorings, water, electricity, WC, shower, clubhouse, guestrooms, camping, slip, pump out. Depth 1–1·3m.

Clubhouse at Schwerin Yacht Club

	SV-Meclenburgisches Staatstheatre (SVTh), guest moorings, water, shower, WC, shower, camping, slip, pump out. Depth 1·5m.
25·2	Stangengraben. Entry into Stangengraben channel on west side of the Schweriner See. Port buoy 30, follow buoyed area into the Heiden-See.
	Marina Nord, guest moorings with facilities, depth 1·6m.
	Onwards to the Ausserer Ziegal-see.
	Yachtclub Frankenhorst in northwest corner, guest moorings, restaurant, hotel. Depth 1·2–2·5m.
	The 2km long Langer Graben exit to Paulsdamm is only 0·9m deep with exit bridge height 2·6m.
30·0	Paulsdamm. Bridged entry channel at top of northwest corner of the Schweriner See into Schweriner See (Aussensee). Port buoy 24, starboard buoy 29. Bridge height 4·3m, depth 1·4m in normal conditions. Follow buoyed channel. Beware of cardinal buoys marking shallows in the lake. Nature reserve area.
34·5	Ferienpark Seehof, campsite at Lübstorf on west side, mooring, water, electricity, WC, shower restaurant, slip, pump out.
38·0	Hotel Gallentin, west side, guest moorings, restaurant.
40·1	Marina Ziegenwiese, west side, guest mooring, water, electricity, WC, shower, pump out.
42·8	Segelverein at Hohen Viecheln, north side, mooring.
43·0	Fischerei Priegnitz at Hohen Viecheln, north side, possible mooring.
43·2	End of navigation. Forbidden beyond.

Müritz-Elde-Wasserstrasse (continued)

56·7	Junction with Stör-Wasserstrasse, turn right in an easterly direction.
60·7	Garwitz. Mooring on south side, water, WC, shower, slip, boat service, pump out, fuel. Depth 1·5m.
60·8	*Schleuse Garwitz* Rise 4·3m Length 38·5m Breadth 6·6m ☏ 038722 20020
60·9	Possible mooring north side, water, electricity. Depth 1·5m.
61·2	Mooring south side, water, WC, slip, pump out.
64·7	Possible mooring by Malchow village, depth 1·0m.
68·6	Possible mooring, north side on outside of bend, no facilities, depth 1·2m.
70·8	Mooring at cafe on south bank. Depth 1·2m.
72·0	**Parchim**. Main channel turns sharp right and southwards under Srassenbrücke Parchim, height 4·5m. and into lock.
72·1	*Schleuse Parchim* Rise 3·1m Length 56·2m Breadth 6·9m ☏ 03871 444104
	Mooring above and below the lock in centre of town, depth 0·9m and 1·2m.
76·0	Rundtörn Marina, west side, guest mooring, water, electricity, WC, shower, washing machine, slip, pump out, fuel.
82·0	Neuburg, mooring place on east side. Water, electricity, WC, shower. Depth 1·2m.
83·3	*Schleuse Neuburg* Rise 3·8m Length 57·5m Breadth 6·6m ☏ 038724 20220
	Automatic lock operation.
91·4	Burow. Mooring in channel west side. Water, electricity, WC, shower, depth 1·0m.
98·3	**Lübz**. Stadt-Marina-Lübz, east side. Guest moorings, water, electricity, WC, shower, slip, crane, service, pump out. Depth 1·2m.
98·9	*Schleuse Lübz* Rise 2·9m Length 55·0m Breadth 6·6m ☏ 038731 22114
99·9	Basin on west bank above town, possible mooring, car fuel station close.
103·8	*Schleuse Bobzin* Rise 6·9–7·3m Length 55·0m Breadth 6·9m ☏ 038731 22922
	Strong turbulence due to water inlets in lock chamber bottom.
108·5	Kuppentin. Moorings north side above bridge, water, electricity, WC. Depth 1·2–1·9m.
114·0	*Schleuse Barkow* Rise 3·2m Length 55·0m Breadth 6·6m ☏ 038735 42712

EAST

119·9	**Plau.** *Schleuse Plau* Rise 1·4m Length 41·5m Breadth 5·1m ☏ 038735 44364
120·4	Lifting bridge height closed 2·2m, and height open 4·3m.
120·6	Wasserwanderrastplatz Plau, 80 guest moorings, water, electricity, WC, shower, slip, 6-tonne crane, pump out.
121·0	Entrance to Plauer See. This 15km-long lake is a popular sailing centre and offers numerous quiet anchorages and mooring places, especially in the southern half. There are several shallow patches marked by cardinal buoys. Marina Plau am See, just south as entering Plauer See. Guest moorings, water, electricity, WC, shower, camping, boat service, slip, 3-tonne crane, depth 1·5m.
126·0	Exit from Plauer See to Petersdorfer See. Mooring possible inside entrance to Petersdorfer See.
126·2	Lenzer Hafen, west side, guest moorings, water, electricity, WC, shower, service, 7-tonne crane, pump out, fuel. Depth 1·6m.
126·7– 129·6	Petersdorfer See. Buoyed channel. Speed limit 9km/h.
130·8– 135·0	Malchower See divided in half by the opening road bridge in the centre of Malchow.
131·8	Yachtclub Malchow, south side, guest mooring, water, electricity, WC, shower, slip, depth 1·5m.
131·8	Malchow-Boot Kock & Klien, boat service.
131·0	**Malchow**
131·8	Stadthafen Malchow, west side, guest moorings, ☏ 039932 80893, water, electricity, restaurants, shops, depth 1·5m.
131·9	Opening road bridge in town centre. Operates 1 April to 30 September daily 0900–2000; 1 October to 30 November daily 0900–1600; 1 December to 31 March opens on request. ☏ 039932-1640 Fee €2–3 per passage through.
132·5	Wasserwanderrastplatz Erddamm, south side, guest moorings, water, electricity, WC, shower, restaurant, depth 1–3m.
133·1	Bootswerft Max Thiele, north side, guest moorings, water, electricity, WC, shower, boat service, slip, 3·2-tonne crane
133·2	Bootsbau D. Thiele, north side, guest moorings, water, electricity, WC, shower, boat service, slip, fuel.
134·0	Seglerhafen, north side, guest moorings, water, electricity, WC, shower, washing machine.
135·0– 139·0	Fleesensee. Popular for all water sports. Follow buoyed channel into open water, then head ENE for exit on east side of lake, into the Göhrener Kanal channel.
139·3– 147·0	Kölpinsee. 0·6km to the north of the entry point is a very narrow channel, 1·4–2·0m deep, leading through to the Jabelscher See. An idyllic lake for boats small enough to enter, although landing is forbidden other than at Maribell Yachthafen on the northwest side, 1km from village shop in Jabel. Very pleasant guest moorings,

Entrance to Stadthafen Malchow

Malchow road bridge opening to allow through cruising on the Malchower See Km 132

Marina Maribell at Jabel on the Jabelscher See

water, electricity, WC, shower, restaurant, slip, pump out.

Otherwise, follow buoyed channel across the Kölpinsee to exit on the east side; anchorage possible on north side only, west of Schloss Schwenzin, shallow waters.

147·0–
149·7   Reekkanal, Strassenbrücke Eldenburg, bridge height 3·8m, leading to Binnen Müritz.

148·5   Marina Eldenburg, north side before bridge. Guest moorings, water, electricity, WC, shower, boat service, winter storage, pump out.

149·7   Binnen Müritz. A semi-enclosed bay about 2km wide at the northern extremity of the **Müritz** itself. Directly opposite the entrance lies the historic and beautiful town of Waren. There are several possible places to moor along the elegant Riviera style waterfront, but the 4–9m-deep town harbour is the most convenient, close to shops and restaurants.

Müritz-Marina, guest mooring, water, electricity, WC, shower, pump out.

Sailpoint Wassersportzentrum, guest moorings. Pump out.

WSV Stille Bucht, Guest moorings, water, electricity, WC, shower.

Bootswerft Christen. Guest moorings, WC, shower, boat service, slip, 3-tonne crane. Depth 0·8m.

Stadthafen **Waren**, town centre, restaurants, guest moorings, water, electricity, WC, shower, boat service, 6·5-tonne crane, pump out, fuel.

Müritz-Marina Waren, water, boat service, pump out, fuel.

151–
169·0   **Müritz**. The second largest lake in Germany, and a wonderful expanse of water for sailing on a good day, but it should be noted that storms can whip up extremely quickly and can create very dangerous conditions. Check weather forecast before navigating on the Müritz. There are several interesting towns and villages to visit around the west and south shores of the Müritz, some with good sheltered moorings. Nature reserves along east side of the lake, shallow waters which have been clear by the line of offshore restricted zone buoys, therefore anchoring is forbidden. Follow buoyed channels and be aware of shallow areas clearly marked by cardinal buoys.

Waren town on the north side of Binnen-Müritz

EAST

Aerial view of Muritz See taken from Röbel church tower

Schloss Klink on northwest side of Die Muritz

152·4 Hafen Müritz Hotel in Klink, hotel, restaurant, guest moorings, water, electricity, WC. Shower, slip. Depth 1–1·8m.

153·0 Schloss Klink. Marina am Schloss, hotel, restaurant, guest moorings, water, electricity, WC, shower, slip. Depth 1–1·4m.

159·0 Sietow Dorf. In Seearm Sietow bay.

Müritz Mariner Höcker, restaurant, guest moorings, water, electricity, WC, shower, boat services, slip, 12-tonne crane, fuel, pump out.

162·0 The Binnen See. Channel entry from the Muritz See is between green starboard channel buoys 23 and 21·0; there is a small middle ground buoy which marks the centre of the entrance to the channel to Röbel. Then follow the 'R' numbered buoyed channel to the town of Röbel.

Röbel. A picturesque town with a Scandinavian influence and an attractive town harbour. Shops and restaurants.

Stadthafen Röbel, town centre, guest moorings, water, electricity, WC, depth 1–1·8m.

RSV Müritz, Regattahafen, guest moorings, water, electricity, WC, shower, boat services, 6-tonne crane, slip, campsite.

Wasser-Service-Centre in Röbel, guest moorings, water, electricity, WC, shower, boat services, slip, fuel, pump out.

166·0 Bolter Kanal on south east shore, restaurant, guest moorings, water, electricity, WC, shower. Depth 1·0m.

Moorings at Röbel on the west side of Die Muritz

Aerial view of Röbel Harbour on the Muritz See from Röbel church tower

168·0　Rechlin Nord. Southern bottom end of Müritz.

Rundtörn Marina im Claassee, restaurant, 100 guest moorings, water, electricity, WC, shower, boat services, 90-tonne crane, slip, fuel, pump out. Depth 1·2–1·5m.

171·0　**Rechlin**. Shops in town.

Müritz-Segel-Verein Rechlin. Guest moorings, water, electricity, WC, shower, boat services, 7-tonne crane, slip, fuel, pump out. Depth 1·5m.

Ferienananlage Yachthafen Rechlin. Restaurant, guest moorings, water, electricity, WC, shower, boat services, 7-tonne crane, slip, fuel, pump out. Depth 1·5m.

172–179·5　Müritzarm. 9km/h. This is the 11km-long and 300m-wide southern extension of the Müritz. Follow buoyed area under 4·0m high bridge. It is flanked by low-lying marshland and woodland, and is a glorious backwater to explore, especially for those interested in wildlife. It ends at the village of Buchholz, where there is a good mooring place.

Buchholz. Yachthafen Buchholz, café, guest moorings, water, electricity, WC, shower, pump out. Depth 1·5m.

172·0　Junction with Müritz-Havel-Wasserstrasse Km 31·8

Guest moorings at Rechlin on southeast side of Kleine Muritz

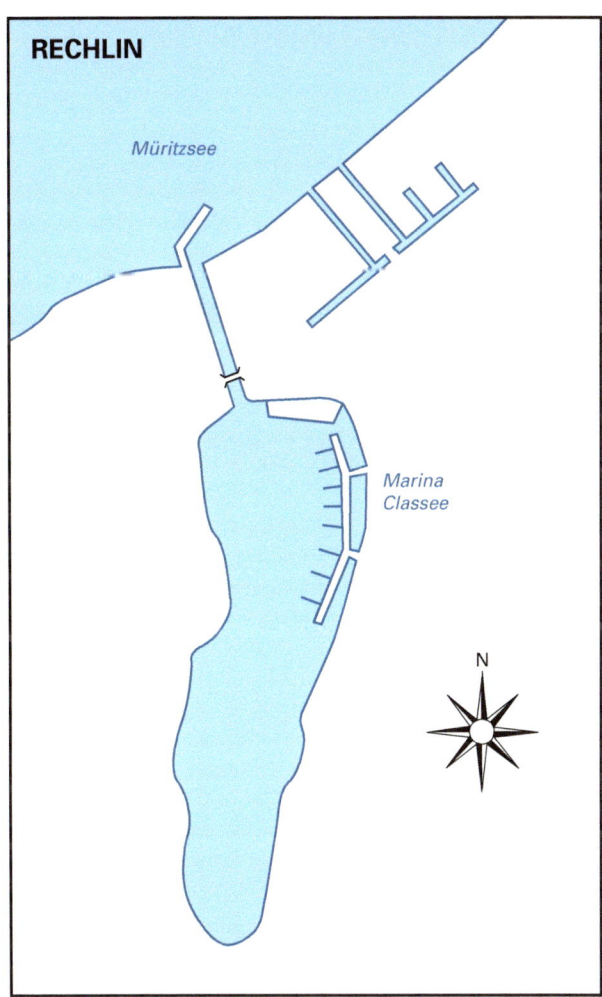

Boathouses along the Muritzarm

Guest moorings at Yachthafen Buchholz at the far end of Muritzarm

EAST

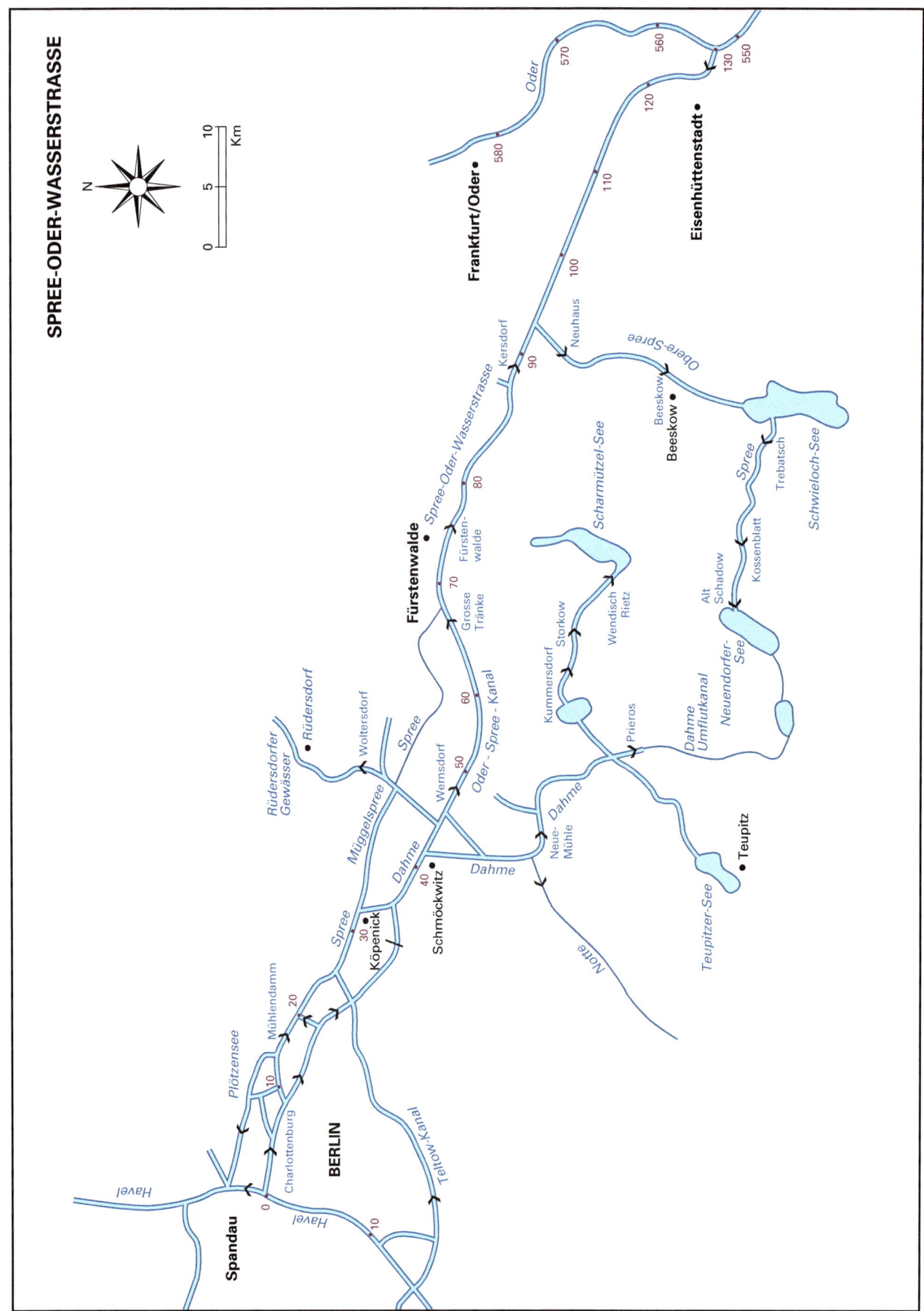

SPREE-ODER-WASSERSTRASSE

Navigable distance 130·2km
Maximum draught 1·75m
Maximum height 4·00m
Current Negligible
Locks 7
Hours Varied. See route description
Speed limit 9km/h (12km/h from Km 0·0–6·3; 9km/h from Km 6·3–23·5; 10km/h from Km 23·5–33·34)

This waterway is the second main traffic route from Berlin to the Oder and the Polish waterway system, although compared to the Havel-Oder-Wasserstrasse it carries only a small volume of commercial traffic. Starting at the point the Spree links with the Havel at Spandau, the waterway is at first the Spree, but branches upstream into the Dahme where this runs into the Spree to the southeast of the city. After only a few kilometres the Oder-Spree-Kanal then cuts eastwards away from the Dahme, back to follow the course of the Spree for a short distance before leaving the river once again and heading directly eastwards to the steel town of Eisenhüttenstadt, where it joins the Oder. In the Berlin area, there are a number of branch and connecting canals forming a maze of waterways.

The first few kilometres upstream from the junction with the Havel are through a somewhat industrial area, but approaching the city centre the route becomes more interesting: Schloss Charlottenburg with its surrounding gardens; followed by many overlooking waterside-beach cafes, biergartens, bistros; restaurants; modern architecture; the Tiergarten; the Reichstag building and many other well known places. Continuing upstream the route lies in what used to be East Berlin past Berlin Cathedral (The Dom), Museum Island to the double chamber Schleusen Mühlendamn, then passing by the memorial section of the Berlin Wall on the north side just before Oberbaumbrücke. Then the waterway passes through pleasant parkland and then another relatively industrial area. At Köpenick, where the waters leave the Spree and turns up the Dahme, it becomes a reasonably wide lake (the Langer See) with yacht clubs, beaches and watersports centres of all kinds. At Wernsdorf, the upstream part of the Dahme branches off southwards; the Spree-Oder-Wasserstrasse continues to the east as the Oder-Spree-Kanal, tree-lined but otherwise relatively featureless. At Schleuse Grosse Tränke, however, the downstream course of the Müggelspree is rejoined and the waterway becomes alive again until it reaches Schleuse Kersdorf. Here it again leaves the course of the river, and its last 35km is somewhat lacking in character.

The pure canal sections of the waterway are not well endowed with suitable places to moor for the night, but where the route follows the Spree or the Dahme, there is no shortage of places where a small boat can lie. In the centre of Berlin there are several attractive stretches of river bordered by parks, but it is unwise to moor there and prudent to avoid such places overnight. Official 24 hour free mooring places for leisure craft have been provided throughout the city, but these are limited both in number and size. It would be unwise to exceed the 24 hour free mooring period.

Note that on the 25km stretch between Wernsdorf and Fürstenwalde it is forbidden to moor along the canal banks, but as there are no satisfactory mooring places anyway this is no great hardship.

Km

0·0 Junction with Untere-Havel-Wasserstrasse (Km 0·0) and Havel-Oder-Wasserstrasse (Km 0·0).

6·3 *Schleuse Charlottenburg*
Rise 1·2m
Length 115·0m
Breadth 12·5m
VHF Ch 82.
Hours Mon–Sat 0600–2400, Sunday 0700–2400.

6·5 Junction with Westhafenkanal on left (north) bank for Commercial Barges.

Westhafenkanal

Navigable distance 3·1km
Maximum draught 2·00m
Maximum height 4·40m
Locks 0
Speed limit 7km/h

This short canal for commercial barges, connects the Spree and the Spandauer Schiffahrtskanal. It is straight, partly tree-flanked and partly industrial.

Spree-Oder-Wasserstrasse (continued)

Km

7·7 Schloss Charlottenburg on the left (south) bank.

8·0 Free max 24hr mooring for leisure craft on south bank.

9·1 Junction with Charlottenburger Verbindungskanal on north bank and with the Landwehrkanal on south bank.

9·6 Free max 24hr mooring for leisure craft on north bank. Walking distance to the Schloss Charlottenburg, shops and restaurants. Good metro system for central Berlin.

EAST

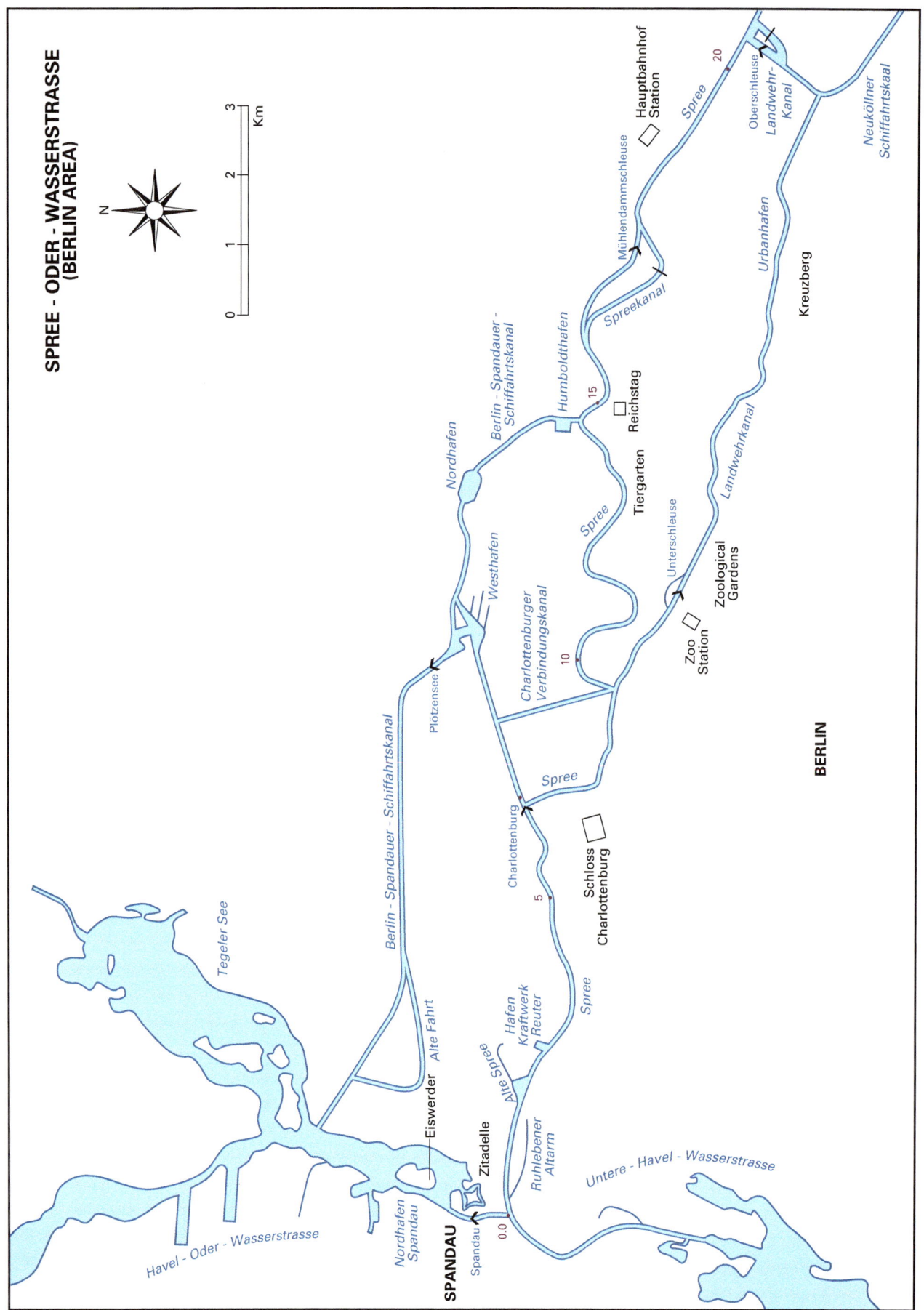

Charlottenburger Verbindungskanal

Navigable distance 1·6km
Maximum draught 2·00m
Maximum height 4·80m
Locks 0
Speed limit 8km/h southend and 6km/h northend

Another connecting canal which is straight, mainly tree-lined and somewhat lacking in character.

Landwehrkanal

Navigable distance 10·7km
Maximum draught 1·65m
Maximum height 3·40m
Locks 2
Speed limit 7km/h

This canal is a loop, with both ends connected to the Spree. It passes through the centre of West Berlin, between the Zoological Gardens and the Tiergarten.

Km

0·0	Junction with Spree-Oder-Wasserstrasse Km 9·1
1·7	*Unterschleuse* Rise 1·4m. VHF Ch 81
9·5	Junction with Neuköllner Kanal (see page 158).
10·6	*Oberschleuse* Rise 0·2m
10·7	Junction with Spree-Oder-Wasserstrasse Km 21·2.

Spree-Oder-Wasserstrasse (continued)

12·4	Free max 24hr mooring for leisure craft on north bank. Moor with care, the tripper boats pass at speed and work until about 2200.
13·0	VHF Ch 10.
13·1	Lutherbr. Low bridge on bend with three arches, use single middle arch. Take care, tripper boats approach very quickly and have priority.
13–14	Tiergarten on south bank.
14·2	Hauptbanhof, the main railway station, on north bank.
14·5	Junction with Berlin-Spandauer Schiffahrtskanal on north bank. Prohibited to Leisure Craft.
15·0	Reichstag building on south bank. Brandenburg Gate beyond it.
15·8	Free max 24hr mooring for leisure craft on north bank.

Berlin-Spandauer Schiffahrtskanal (Hohenzollernkanal)

Navigable distance 12·2km
Maximum draught 2·00m
Maximum height 3·90m
Locks 1
Speed limit 12km/h

PROHIBITED TO LEISURE CRAFT

The canal connects the Havel-Oder-Wasserstrasse directly to the Spree, avoiding the congestion at Schleuse Spandau. Part of it is flanked by trees and part of it is industrial.

Km

0·0	Junction with Havel-Oder-Wasserstrasse Km 3·5
0·9 & 2·8	Entrances to loop of old canal.
7·5	*Schleuse Plötzensee* Fall 0·7m. VHF Ch 22
8·0 & 8·8	Junction with Westhafenkanal.
12·2	Junction with Spree-Oder-Wasserstrasse Km 14·5. End of canal.

Spree-Oder-Wasserstrasse (continued)

16·3	Entrance to Spreekanal (loop) behind Museum Island. No through passage.
16·8	Passing the Dom cathedral on the south bank.
17·6	Sports Boat holding quay on north bank. Traffic lights for lock. Take care with tripper boats some of which turn around in the channel just before the lock.
17·8	*Schleusen Mühlendamm* Two chambers Rise 1·5m Length 136·0m Breadth 11·9m VHF Ch 20 Hours 1 April to 31 October Mon–Sun 0600–2400; 1 November to 31 March Mon–Sat 0600–2000, Sunday 0700–1900.
18·0	Junction with Spreekanal (loop). Navigable channel 0·5km long, width 22m. Two bridges, max height restriction 3·3m dependent upon water level and current in this channel. Limited free mooring for leisure craft on east bank behind Museum Island max 24hr. No through passage and boats will need to be able to turn around in the 22m channel.
21·2	Junction with Landwehrkanal on south bank.

Km	Description
23·4	Limited free mooring for leisure craft on south bank, max 24hr behind Insel der Jugend. Restaurant.
23·8	Entrance to Rummelsburger See, 1·2km long on north side. Yacht Club for small leisure craft on left side just inside 25m entrance passage to the See. Beyond, on right hand side limited free mooring for leisure craft, max 24hr. Water only 1m deep.
26·4	Junction with Britzer Verbindungskanal (Km 31·8) on south bank.
29·8	Netto supermarket with mooring on southside.
28·5– 33·0	Few moorings available at various small yacht and motor boat clubs.
31·4	Motorwassersportclub Oberspree, south side, possible mooring for small leisure craft, water.
32·8	Waterway turns south into Dahme through the Lange Brucke Height 4·3m. Upstream Spree (Muggelspree) branches off eastwards through Dammbrucke Height 4·9m.
35·0	Entrance to Teltowkanal Km 37·83
33·6– 43·3	Langer See. Numerous possibilities for mooring with facilities. Anchoring possible. Observe buoyage and markings.
43·1	Entrance to Grosse Krampe on north side. Mooring possible at southern end, Depth 1·5m. Speed limit 12 km/h on lake. Propellor driven boats forbidden in upper lake.
43·9	**Schmöckwitz.** Watersports centre. Upstream Dahme branches south. Spree-Oder-Wasserstrasse continues in Seddinsee to entrance of Oder-Spree-Kanal. Seddinsee continues 3km beyond entrance of Oder-Spree-Kanal to start of Gosener Kanal (entry via buoyed channel).
45·1	Start of Oder-Spree-Kanal.
47·1	Entrance to Krossinsee on south bank, leading to Grosser Zug and hence Dahme. Depth uncertain. Speed limit 12km/h on lake.
47·6	*Schleuse Wernsdorf* Rise 4·6m. Length 115·0m Breadth 9·8m VHF Ch 20 Hours 1 April to 31 October Mon–Sat 0600–2000, Sunday 0830–1800; 1 November to 31 March daily 0800–1730.
68·8	*Schleuse Grosse Tränke* Rise 0·0m (stands open).
73·5	Mooring at north bank.
74·8	*Schleuse Fürstenwalde* Rise 0·9m. Length 67·0m Breadth 8·4m VHF Ch 22 Hours as per Schleuse Wernsdorf (Km 47·6). Mooring places above lock on both sides of the channel. Entrance to Drahendorfer Spree on south side, navigable by limited draft vessels for 1km. Possible mooring.
89·7	*Schleuse Kersdorf* Rise 2·9m. Length 57·0m Breadth 9·5m VHF Ch 82 Hours as per Schleuse Wernsdorf (Km 47·6).
96·2	Junction with Obere Spree (via Speisekanal Neuhaus). Also Drahendorfer Spree via Schleuse Wergensee. Limited vessel length, bridge height and water depth.
103·9	South bank entry to Kleiner Müllroser See with Yacht moorings for guests. Water, electricity, WC. Shops and restaurant nearby. Last mooring place before Eisenhüttenstadt.
107·0	Junction with defunct Brieskowkanal, which at one time provided a direct route to Frankfurt.
125·1	Eisenhüttenstadt. Mooring place on west bank.
127·3	*Schleuse Eisenhüttenstadt* Fall 14·0m Length 127·0m Breadth 12·0m VHF Ch 20 Hours as per Schleuse Wernsdorf (Km 47·6). Twin chambers operate alternately, with the same water being transferred backwards and forwards. Both locks are equipped for floating bollards, but they may not always be working. Check before entry.
127·9	Mooring place on east bank. Also, possibility of mooring alongside water authority vessels stationed here. Seek permission first.
130·2	Junction with the Oder Km 553·4.

TELTOWKANAL

Navigable distance 37·83km
Maximum draught 3·00m
Maximum height 4·40m
Current Negligible
Locks 1
Hours Mon–Sat 0600–2200, Sunday 0700–2200
Speed limit 7km/h (12km/h Km 0·0–3·1)

The Teltowkanal starts in the Glienicker lake on the Potsdamer Havel and cuts across Berlin, south of the city centre to join the Spree-Oder-Wasserstrasse via either continuing on the Teltowkanal or via the short Britzer Verbindungskanal.

Apart from the first 3km, which are a natural waterway, the canal is rather uninteresting. It is, however, the quickest route for vessels wishing to get from the Untere-Havel-Wasserstrasse to the Spree-Oder-Wasserstrasse without spending time in Berlin.

The canal meandered across what was East and West Berlin and witnessed several East Berliner escapees successfully swim to the west, but, also many more unsuccessful and tragic scenes.

Km

0·0	Junction with Potsdamer Havel Km 28·4
0·0–3·1	Glienicker Lake and Griebnitzsee. Speed limit 12km/h.
3·3	Junction with Griebnitzsee-Kanal on north side. This short canal linking the Teltowkanal to the Grosser Wannsee. The max permitted draught is 1·30m, max beam is 2·0m and max bridge clearance is 5·0m. The southernmost half-kilometre is subject to one-way traffic system, alternating half-hourly. Speed limit 5km/h.
8·2	Waiting area for lock on south side. Traffic lights.

Polish commercial barge on the Telltowkanal

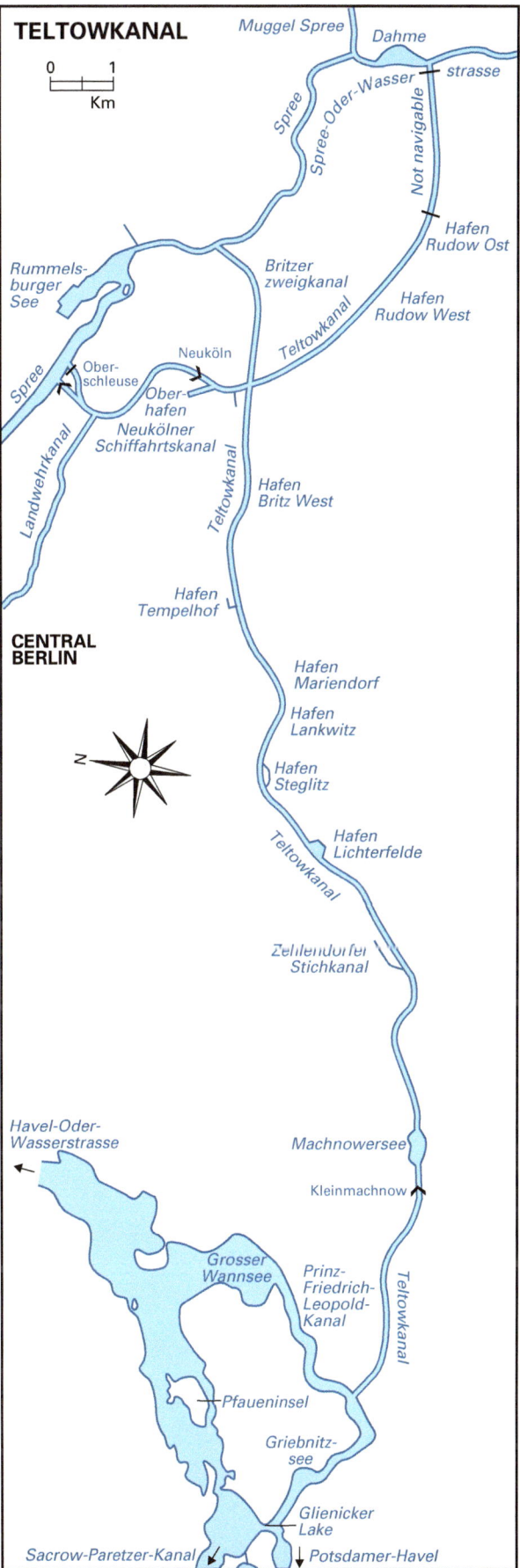

INLAND WATERWAYS OF GERMANY

EAST

Schleuse Kleinmachnow

8·3	*Schleuse Kleinmachnow* Three Chambers Rise 2·86m Length 82m Breadth 12m VHF Ch 18
13·5	Zehlendorfer Stichkanal on north side. Industrial harbour.
15·4	Free mooring for leisure craft max. 24hrs north bank.
16·7	Industrial quay south bank.
18·6	Motor Rennboot Club Berlin mooring south side.
18·7	Small industrial harbour on south side.
19·0	Channel narrows. Commercial traffic one-way alternate working, listen on VHF Ch 10 and announce your presence.
21·6	Small industrial harbour on south side.
23·4	New Yachthafen, Hafen Tempelhof mooring on north side.
23·5–25·5	Works on upgrade of channel, one-way traffic system with traffic lights.

MRC Berlin

28·3	Junction with the 3·4km long Britzer Verbindungskanal (Zweigkanal) – tree lined canal leading to the Spree-Oder-Wasserstrasse at Km 26. Max height 4·5m.
28·3	Junction with the 4·1km long Neuköllner Schiffahrtskanal which joins the Landwehrkanal at Km 9·5 It can be entered by vessels with a draught of not more than 1·75m and a maximum height of 3·6m. It has one lock, Schleuse Neukölln, with a fall of 0·2m (going northwards). The lock operates Mon–Fri 0630–1900, Saturday 0630–1400 and is closed on Sundays. VHF Ch 73 or ☏ 030 68092067. Speed limit 8km/h.
28·3–34·3	The Teltowkanal runs parallel to the Autobahn A113.
35·5	Possible mooring on northside.
37·83	Junction with the Spree-Oder-Wasserstrasse at Km 35.

MÜGGELSPREE

Navigable distance 11·4km
Maximum draught 1·7m
Maximum height 4·7m
Current Negligible
Locks 0
Speed limit 8km/h in canal, (25km/h in Grosser Müggelsee, Km 4·0–7·0)

Although the main route of the Spree-Oder-Wasserstrasse through the Langer See (Dahme) is attractive, the alternative route via the Müggelspree, through the beautiful Müggelsee and then back south through the Gosener Kanal is even more so. It also offers the possibility of a diversion into Löcknitz and the chain of pretty lakes which runs eastwards from the Rüdersdorfer Gewässer. The longer expedition to the northern part of the Rüdesdorfer Gewässer around Rüdersdorf itself is somewhat industrial and less interesting.

Km

0·0	**Köpenick.** Junction with the Spree-Oder-Wasserstrasse Km 32·8.
0·5	Cöpenicker Seglerverein. Mooring for small boats, WC.
1·7	Café Bistro Evelin, mooring depth 1·2m.
2·5	Friedrichshagen. Wassersportzentrum Berlin, with boatyard on north bank. Guest moorings, water, electricity, WC, shower, boat services, 15-tonne crane, pump out. Depth 1·5m. Windrose Restaurant, Hotel and Chandlery. Winter moorings.

EAST

Entrance to Muggelspree at Km 0.0

Wassersportzentrum Berlin Km 2.5

Anchoring in the Kleiner Muggelsee

Restaurant Neu Helgoland with guest mooring, Km 8.0

Entrance to Dameritzsee at Km 11.39

3·0	Berliner Bürgerbräu. Guest mooring Monday–Friday, WC.
3·8–7·4	Grosser Müggelsee. Yacht harbour immediately south of entrance. Keep to buoyed channel across the centre of the lake. Motorboats are forbidden to leave the channel. Immediately north of exit is entrance to attractive small bay known as Die Bäanke. Depth 1·2m. Beautiful yacht anchorage, narrow entrance – no facilities.
7·3	Exit from Grosser Müggelsee. Speed limit 8km/hr.
7·8	Kleiner Muggelsee, on south side. Another beautiful bay and ideal for anchoring.
7·9	Cafe L+B mooring.
8·0	Restaurant Neu Helgoland, guest mooring, WC.
8·2	Eva+Horst Krause, mooring for small boats, water, electricity, WC, shower.
8·6	Fresh fish stall.
9·0	Entrance channel to 'Little Venice' for very small vessels only.
10·1	Exit channel to 'Little Venice'.
11·0	Bootswerft Sturzbecher, mooring, WC, boat service, depth 1·0m, 2·5t-crane, 7m-slip
11·4	Entrance to Dämeritzsee. Junction with Gosener Kanal immediately to starboard.

Access from eastern end of Dämeritzsee to Rüdersdorfer Gewässer.

INLAND WATERWAYS OF GERMANY 159

EAST

Rüdersdorfer Gewässer

Navigable distance 14·5km
Maximum draught 1·65m
Maximum height 4·2m
Current Negligible
Locks 1
Hours 1 April to 31 October Mon–Sat 0600–2000, Sunday 0700–1900; 1 November to 31 March Mon–Sat 0800–1600, Sunday closed
Speed limit 10km/h in canal (6km/h upstream of Km 9·8)

Km	
0·0	Entrance from Dämeritzsee.
0·8	Mooring for sport boats, max 24hr on south side. Depth 0·7m.
1·0	Bootshaus Burchard. Depth 0·8m, mooring, water, electricity, WC, shower, boat service, 10m-slip, pump out.
2·6	Junction with Löcknitz and access for boats drawing up to 1·7m for a further 10·6km eastwards to Werlee, Peetzsee and Möllensee. Various attractive mooring places and anchorages.
3·8	*Schleuse Woltersdorf* with lifting bridge. Rise 2·1m Length 65·0m Breadth 9·6m VHF 18 ☏ 03362 50334
7·5	Fuel at garage 100m from mooring.
9·7	Junction with Langerhans-Kanal to Kriensee. Industrial.
11·3	Entrance to Stienitzsee. Mooring places on each bank.
14·3	End of Stienitzsee.

Gosener Kanal

Navigable distance 2·8km
Maximum draught 2·0m
Maximum height 4·3m
Current Negligible
Locks 0
Speed limit 8km/h

Km	
5·7	Exit Dämeritzsee.
2·9	Entrancee to Seddinsee. Speed limit 25km/h on lake.
0·0	Junction with Oder-Spree-Kanal Km 44·9.

DAHME-WASSERSTRASSE

Navigable distance 26·0km
Maximum draught 1·6m
Maximum height 3·9m
Current Negligible
Locks 3
Hours Varied. See route description
Speed limit 10km/h, and 12km/h after Km 3·8, (8km/h along inside 100m on lake, 25km/h in lake outside 100m from the bank)

The Dahme south of Schmöckwitz, together with its branches, forms an interesting network of natural waterways set in a pleasant, mainly wooded landscape, with many interesting places to visit and plenty of attractive spots in which to moor or anchor. Deeper-draught boats, however, need to take care in some of the remote parts of the waterway, as depth can be a problem.

For the purpose of this book, the waterway is assumed to end at Prieros, but except when water levels are low, vessels drawing 1·5m could venture through Schleuse Prieros and Schleuse Hermsdorfer Mühle to Märkisch Buchholz.

There are two main side arms to the Dahme: the Storkower Gewässer, which gives access to the Scharmützelsee, and the Teupitzer Gewässer, which leads to the Teupitzer See.

On the main route to Prieros, there is only one lock, Neue Mühle. The Storker Gewässer has three locks, but there are none in the Teupitzer Gewässer.

Km	
0·0	**Schmöckwitz**
	Junction with Spree-Oder-Wasserstrasse Km 43·9. Follow the channel marker buoys.
0·2	Sports boat mooring max 24hr on west side after bridge. Depth 0·7m.
1·4	Zeuthener Yachtclub, guest mooring, water, electricity, WC, boat service, slip.
0·5–4·6	Zeutherner See. Numerous moorings on west side for small boats.
3·0	Bootshaus Roll. Guest mooring piles, stern on. Water, electricity, WC, shower, slip. Depth 2m.
3·8	Bootshaus Zeuthen. Guest moorings, water, electricity, WC, pump out.
4·5	Entrance to Grosser Zugsee and Krossinsee on east side. Mooring on east side. Very pretty alternative route back to Spree-Oder-Wasserstrasse, but depth 1·8m in places through channel to Wernsdorf.
4·7	Moorings for small boats on west bank.
5·2	Guest mooring hotel, restaurant, west side.

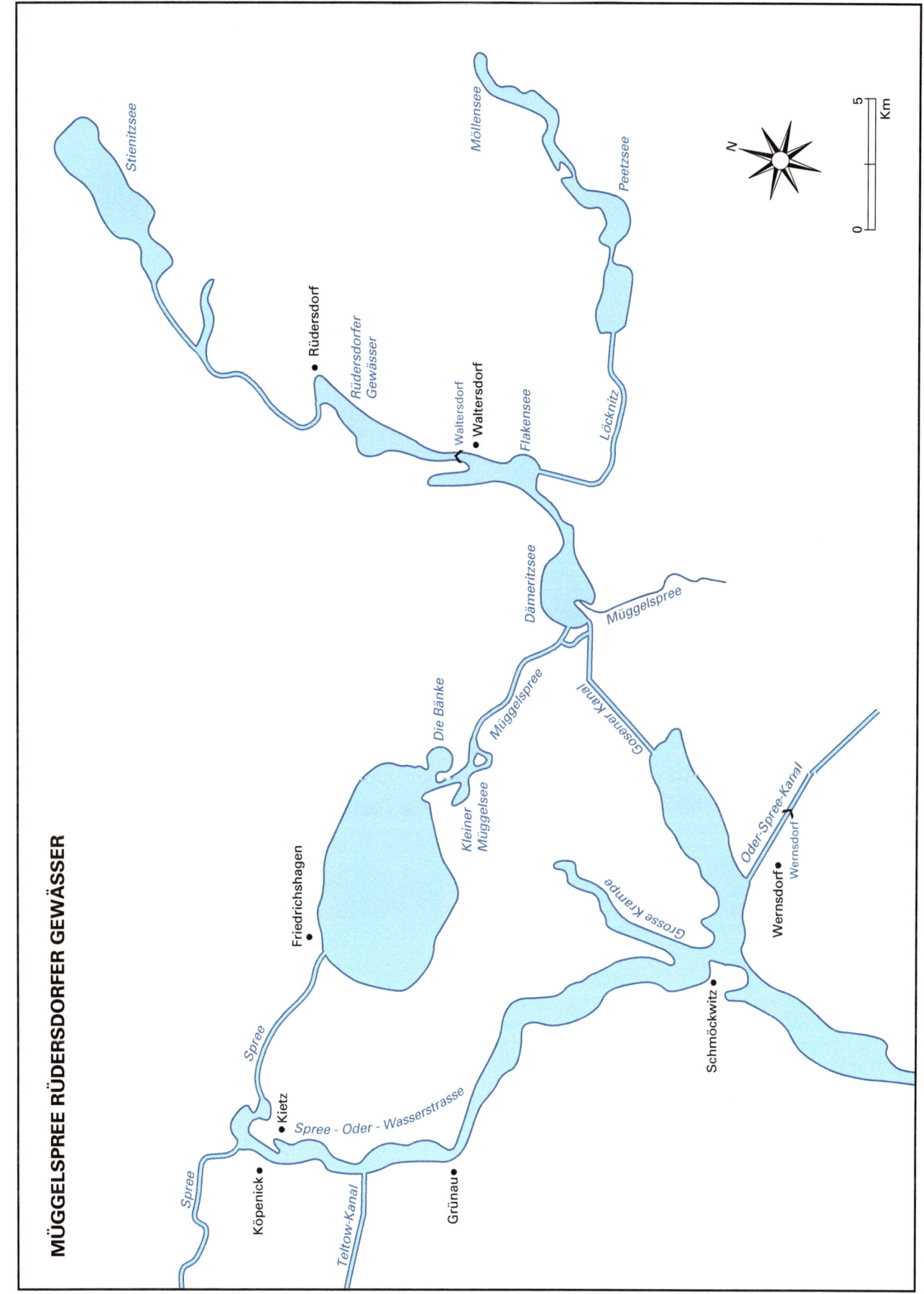

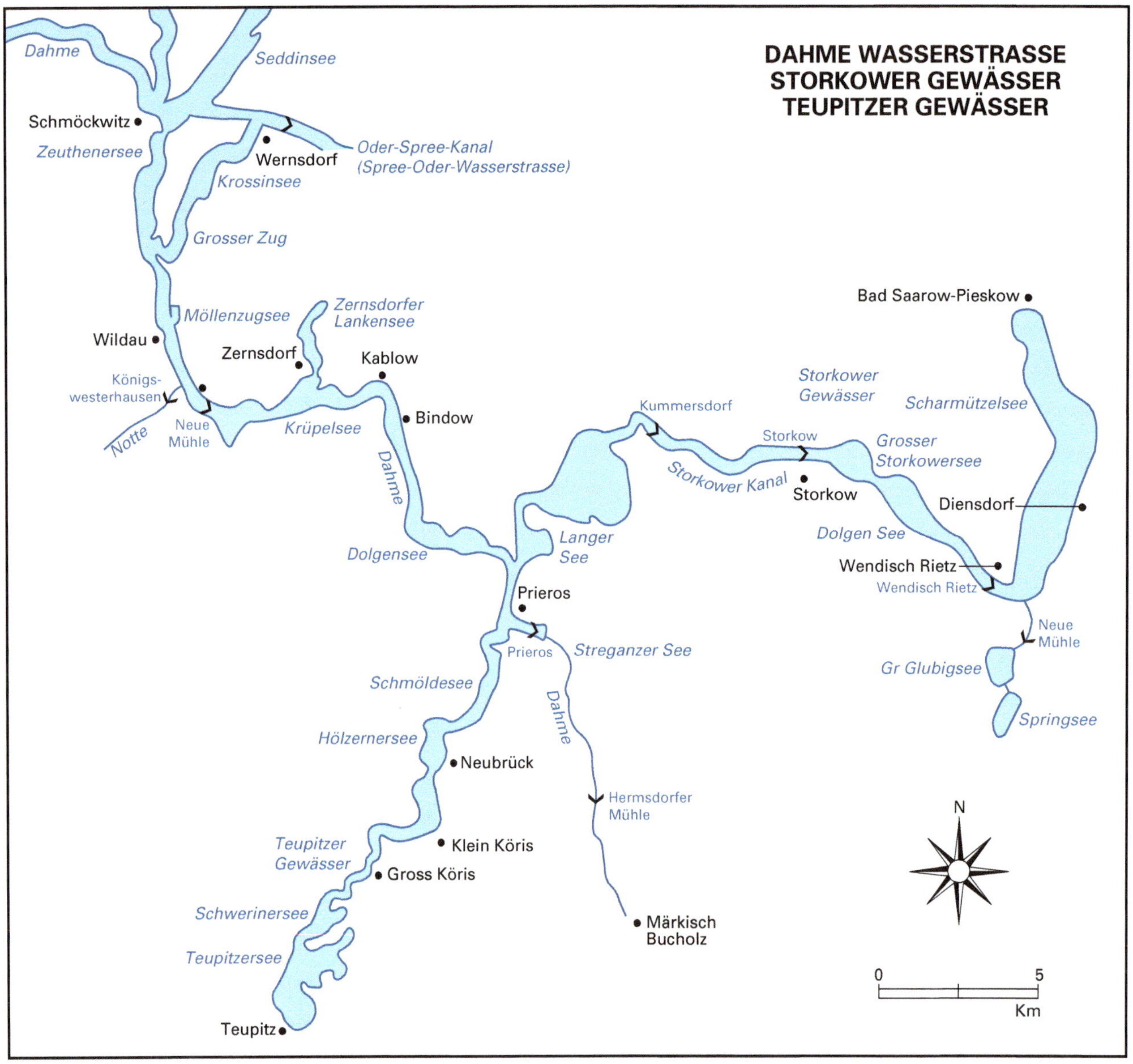

EAST

DAHME WASSERSTRASSE
STORKOWER GEWÄSSER
TEUPITZER GEWÄSSER

6·7 Entrance to Möllenzugsee on east side. Quiet anchorage, depth 2·2m.

7·0 Marine Service Niederlehme. Guest pontoon on east side, water, electricity, WC, shower, boat service, crane, fuel.

8·2 Königswusterhausen. Junction with Notte on west side. Small 22km river with depths around 1·0 and 1·1m high at Telz bridge. It has a branch canal, the Galluner Kanal, which has depths of only 0·6m.

8·2 Yachtvertrieb Niedelehme, east side. Boat service, crane, slip, water, electricity, WC, shower.

8·6 Fuel. New *tankstelle* on east side below bridge and lock.

Tankstelle Km 8.6 Dahme-Wasserstrasse

Schleuse Neue Muhle Km 9.5

Public mooring at Km 19.5

9·5	*Schleuse Neue Mühle* Rise 1·4m Length 38·0m Breadth 5·3m Hours 1 April to 31 October Mon–Sat 0700–2000, Sunday 0700–2100 1 November to 31 March Mon–Sun 0800–1600, Sunday closed. ☎ 03375-293686
10·3– 14·8	Krimnicksee and Krüpelsee. Follow buoyed channel. Speed limit 12km/h. Interesting mooring places and anchorages, including in the Zernsdorfer Lankensee, a superb 2km-long fjord accessed through railway bridge (max height 3·5m).
11·5	Yachthafen Seeblick, guest mooring, water, electricity, WC, pump out.
13·0	Seebrücke Senzig, restaurant with guest mooring, water, electricity, WC, pump out.
17·6	Bootswerft Bindowbrüke, guest mooring, water, electricity, WC, boat service, 3-tonne crane, 8·5m slip, fuel.
19·5	Public mooring. Max 24hr.
20·7	Sport-Boot-Centre, guest mooring, water, electricity, WC, shower, 8m slip, pump out.
20·7– 23·3	Dolgensee. Follow buoyed channel. Anchoring permitted.
23·3	Kuddel's Lustige Stube, south side, guest mooring, WC. Depth 1·6m.
23·4	Haus Dolgensee, north side, restaurant with small guest mooring, WC, shower. Depth 0·9m.
23·9	Yachtwerft Jacko and Sportbootcentre, north side, boat service, pump out. Depth 1·5m.
24·9	Entrance to Langer see and Storkower Gewässer on east side.
26·0	**Prieros.** Junction with Teupitzer Gewässer. Dahme contintues eastwards through *Schleuse Prieros* and *Schleuse Hermsdorfer Mühle*, a link (for canoes only) to the Obere Spree via the Dahme-Umflutkanal. Both locks operate daily 29 April to 03 October 1000–1230 & 1330–1900.

Storkower Gewässer

Navigable distance 33·6km
Maximum draught 1·4m
Maximum height 3·6m
Current Negligible
Locks 3
Hours 1 April to 31 October Mon–Sun 0700–2000;
1 November to 31 March closed
Speed limit 8km/h

Km

0·0	Junction with Dahme Wasserstrasse Km 24·9. Follow buoyed channel to Langer See.

Seebrücke Senzig restaurant with mooring, Km 13.0

EAST

Exit Wolziger See Km 6·8 channel entry on Storkower-Wasserstrasse

Schleuse Kummersdorf, Storkower Kanal

Lifting bridge at Storker, Km 15.7 Storkower Kanal

0·7–2·7	Langer See. Follow buoys into Sauwinkel.
4·0–6·8	Wolziger See. Follow buoyed channel to Storkower Kanal.
4·5	Blossin. Fish Stall and café with mooring. Depth 1·0m.
5·0	Yacht harbour and water sports centre on west bank of lake. Mooring, water, electricity, WC. Depth 1·7m.
6·4	Follow Buoys into Storkower Kanal, narrow entrance, shallows both sides.
9·8	Mooring south side for restaurant guests. Depth 0·8m.
10·2	*Schleuse Kummersdorf* Rise 1·2m Length 34·25m Breadth 5·3m ☏ 033678 433041
12·9	Strassenbrücke at Philadelphia. Max height 3·6m.
15·4	Mooring before lock. Depth 1·5m.
15·6	*Schleuse Storkow* Rise 1·9m Length 36·0m Breadth 5·3m ☏ 033678 72088
15·7	Storker. Public moorings south side, no facilities, close to shops and restaurants.
15·8	Lifting bridge.
16·2–21·1	Grosser Storkower See and Dolgen See.
16·4	SV *Ciconia*, mooring, water, electricity, WC, shower, slip, 5-tonne crane. Depth 0·5–1·0m.
16·9	Hotel Restaurant Karlslust. Mooring south side. Depth 2·0m
17·2	Storker Ruderverein, mooring north side, water, WC, shower. Depth 1·5m
18·4	Schloss Hubertushöhe, south side, depth 1·8m. Hotel, Restaurant (booking essential), guest mooring, water, electricity 16 amp, WC, shower. Beautiful grounds, close to train, regular service to Berlin.
22·6	*Schleuse Wendisch Rietz* Rise 1·2m Length 34·0m Breadth 5·3m ☏ 033678 215
22·9	Wedisch Rietz. Harbour and several good anchorages near entrance to Scharmützelsee.
	The very attractive and secluded short canal to the south through automatic Glubig Schleuse is only 0·6m deep and max height 1·5m.

22·8	Wendisch Rietz. Marina Wendisch Rietz. Mooring south west side, water, electricity, WC, shower, boat service, 20 tonne crane, 8m slip. Depth 1·5m.
22·9–33·6	Scharmützelsee.
	Ring Marina 1 and 2. Mooring southern end, close to railway station, water, electricity, WC, shower. Depth 1·5m.
27·8	Yachtakademie Axel Schmidt. Mooring west side, water, electricity, WC, shower, pump out. Depth 2·0–3·0m.
28·0	Yachtclub Diensdorf. Mooring east side, water, electricity, WC, shower. Depth 2·0m.
28·6	Marina am Cafe Dorsch. Guest mooring west side, water, electricity, WC. Depth 2·5m.
29·0	Sportbootclub Scharmützelsee. Mooring west side, WC, shower, boat service. Depth 1·8m.
32·4	Shallow area marked by buoys.
32·5	Bad Saarow. Sportboothafen Fontanepark. Mooring north east side, electricity, WC, shower, pump out. Depth 1·0–2·0m.
33·2	Sportboothafen Freilichtbühne. Mooring north, water, electricity, WC, depth 0·9–1·5m.
33·4	Bad Saarow-Pieskow. End of waterway.

Teupitzer Gewässer

Navigable distance 18·2km
Maximum draught 1·4m
Maximum height 3·8m
Maximum width 4·0m
Current Negligible
Locks 0
Speed limit 8km/h

This waterway is a chain of small lakes which make it a wonderland for cruising, with many quiet anchorages. There is a low lifting road bridge at Gross Köris.

Km

0·0	Junction with Dahme Wasserstrasse Km 26·0
0·7–6·7	Schmöldesee and Hölzerner See. Many places for anchoring.
4·9	Erholungszentrum Hölzerner See, mooring, water, electricity. Depth 3·0m.
5·7	Marina Leg. Mooring, water, electricity, WC, shower, pump out. Depth 2·9m.

Lifting bridge at Gross Köris Km 11.4 Teupitzer Gewasser

6·6	Sportboothafen Hölzerner See. Guest moorings, water, electricity, WC, shower, boat service, 8m slip, pump out. Depth 1·0–2·0m.
7·0–10·0	Kleinköriser See. Observe buoyage.
8·6	Klein Köris. Hotel Lindengarten, restaurant, guest mooring.
11·4	Opening bridge. Sound horn five minutes before the hour, bridge opens on the hour. Beware the bridge does not open fully. Max width 5·5m. No fee.
11·7	Marina Gross Köris. Mooring, water, electricity, WC, shower, boat service, pump out.
12·4	Road bridge Max width 4·0m.
13·2	Rankenhof, mooring, depth 0·8m.
14·0–18·2	Teupitzer See.
14·5	Gasthaus am See, guest mooring, depth 1·2m.
16·6	Schlosshotel Teupitz, guest mooring, depth 2·0m.
16·9	Hafen Teupitz, mooring, water, electricity, WC, shower, pump out. Depth 1·6m.
18·2	Teupitz. End of waterway.

OBERE SPREE WASSERSTRASSE

Navigable length 40·9km
Maximum draught 1·30m
Maximum height 2·70m
Current 1–3km/h
Locks 5
Hours Varied. See route description
Speed limit 6km/h

It is a great pity that depth limits the use of the Obere Spree to boats drawing only 1·30m, as it is a most attractive waterway in which to cruise. The Spree meanders lazily through swamp, moor and woodland, there are plenty of secluded anchorages and there is wildlife in abundance.

At Beeskow there are two locks side by side, but the smaller, the Sportbootschleuse, is not in operation. At the time of writing, Schleuse Kossenblatt is undergoing major repair and is likely to be out of action for some time. As Schleuse Trebatsch normally stands open, there are in effect only two locks on the waterway, Neuhaus and Beeskow. When Schleuse Kossenblatt is eventually back in action the waterway will extend a further 17·5km to Leibsch, the limit of navigation for all but very small boats. South of Leibsch lies the Spreewald, a labyrinth of swamp, woodland and waterway, famous for its wildlife and for the punts which are used to transport both goods and people. It is also an area which still has its own language, Sorbian, brought there by the Sorbs, a Slavic tribe which settled in the area many centuries ago.

Note that in dry summers the water level may fall below the designated minimum depth of 1·30m.

Km

0·0	Junction with Spree-Oder-Wasserstrasse Km 96·2.
2·8	*Schleuse Neuhaus* (with lift bridge) Rise 1·10m Hours 0800–1600.
3·4	Drahendorfer Spree on west side via Schleuse Wergensee. Depth 1·0m. No through route.
16·9	*Schleuse Beeskow* Rise 0·40m Hours 0700–1900 Boat lock out of operation.
25·2– 28·5	Leissnitz See and Glower See. Follow buoyed channel. Beware weeds.
28·5	Entrance southwards to Schwielochsee. 10km long. Several good anchorages at southern end. Yacht harbour at Goyatz.
31·6	*Schleuse Trebatsch* Rise Stands open.
35·6	Lift bridge.
40·9	*Schleuse Kossenblatt*. Temporary end of waterway.

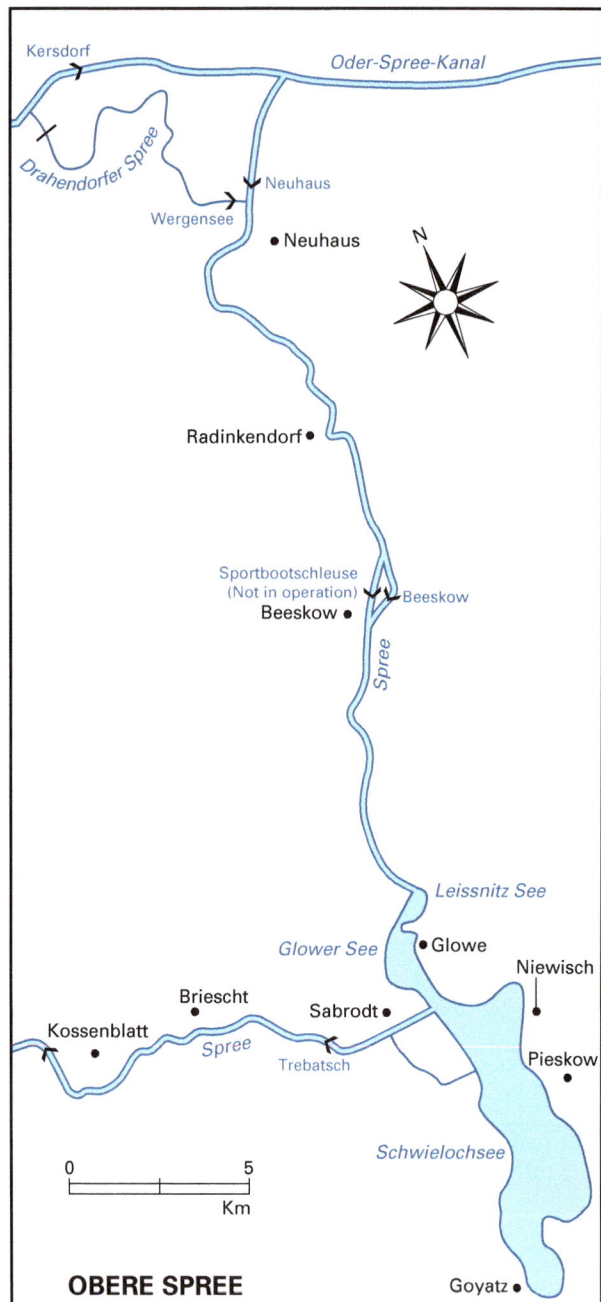

OBERE SPREE

ODER

Navigable distance 161·7km
Maximum draught 0·80–2·50
Maximum height 4·20m
Current 2–10km/h
Locks 0

The potential of the Oder for cruising has not yet been fully explored. The river is navigable for 800-tonne barges from Kozle in southern Poland to its mouth at Swinoujscie on the Baltic Sea, around 850km. It also has a major link via the Warta and the Notec to the Wisla (Vistula), which flows into the Baltic near Gdansk; upstream the Wisla leads to Warsaw, and at one time it was connected to the Dniepr, which flows into the Black Sea.

The landscape along the Oder is undramatic, being mostly flat and either agricultural or wooded. Apart from the old Hanseatic town of Frankfurt/Oder, there are few towns of any size.

From Ratzdorf, to the southeast of Eisenhüttenstadt, to Widuchowa, a short distance south of Szczecin, the Oder is the border between Germany and Poland. This is the section described in this book, but it should be understood that there is much still to be learned about the river from the point of view of leisure cruising.

The timing of a cruise on the Oder is important. From Ratzdorf to Hohensaaten at mean water level the depth of water is normally sufficient for boats drawing 1·30m, and the current is likely to be in the region of 4km/h. During the second half of a dry summer, however, the depth in this stretch can reduce to well under a metre. In the spring, when the river is in flood, the depth may be considerably greater but the current may reach 9–10km/h (5kn). In the stretch from Hohensaaten to Szczecin at mean water level the depth is unlikely to fall below 1·50m, even in a dry summer, and the current is much less than higher up the river. Information on water levels can be obtained from Wasser- und Schiffahrtsamt Eberswalde, Grabowstrasse 1, 16225 Eberswalde-Finow 1 ✆ 03334 22053.

There are also water authority offices along the river at Frankfurt/Oder (Km 584·5), Gozdowice (Km 645·3) and Widuchowa (Km 701·8) where information on conditions may be available. Similar information is broadcast at 1155 daily over Polish radio. The official Strecke are:

Strecke 1 Ratzdorf–Frankfurt
Strecke 2 Frankfurt–mouth of Wartha
Strecke 3 Mouth of Wartha–Hohensaaten
Strecke 4 Hohensaaten–Widuchowa

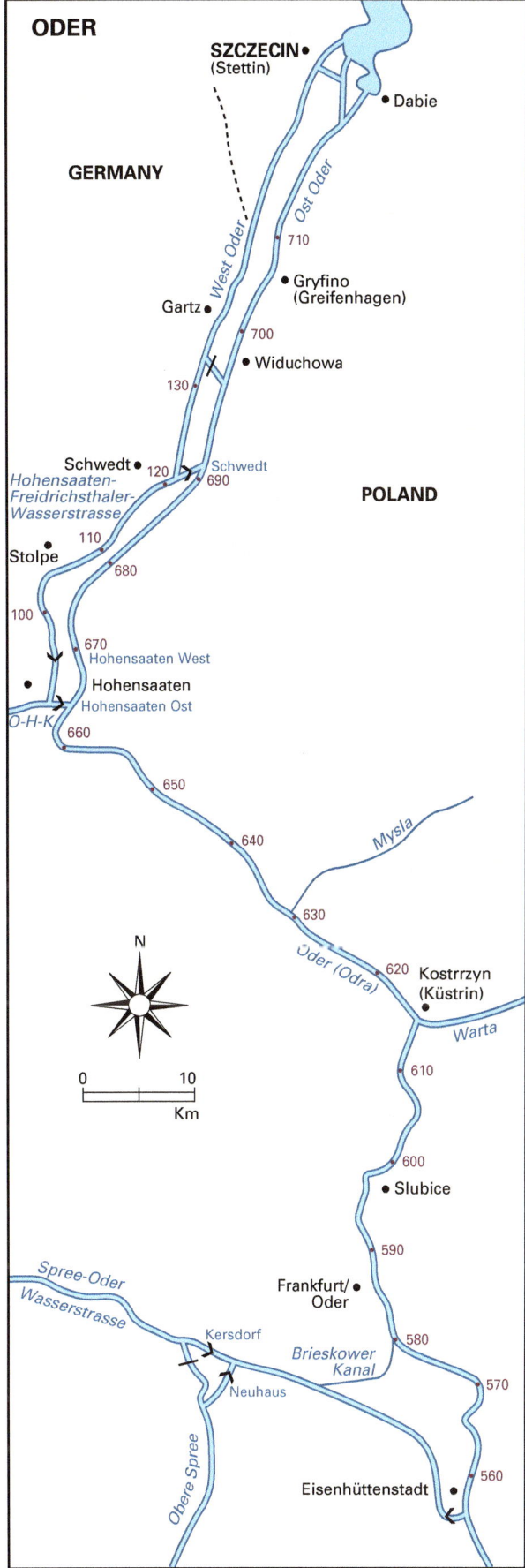

EAST

Finding a place to moor for the night is a problem. There are no yacht harbours, and mooring is permitted only at certain designated points (listed below). There are also no refuelling points suitable for small boats.

The river is well buoyed, and in addition there are leading marks where the channel runs at an angle to the course of the river. Commercial traffic is relatively light, perhaps amounting to around 20 barges per day. The Oder is policed by the Wasserschutzpolizei, not by the Polish authorities. Navigation by leisure craft is prohibited between 1 November and 31 March and at night throughout the year.

Km

Km	
542·4	Junction with Lausitzer Neisse. Polish border.
542·8	Ratzdorf. Official mooring place on left bank.
553·4	Eisenhüttenstadt. Official mooring place in entrance to Spree-Oder-Wasserstrasse.
576·8	Official mooring place in entrance to Brieskower See.
582·6	Frankfurt/Oder. Official mooring place on left bank.
593·8	Lebus. Official mooring place on left bank.
617·1	Neu-Bleyen. Official mooring place on left bank.
617·5	Junction with Warta on right bank. Connects to River Wisla (Vistula).
632·8	Winterhafen Kienitz. Official mooring place at far end of harbour.
651·1	Zollbrücke. Official mooring place in inlet on left bank.
664·9	Hohensaaten. Official mooring place in inlet on left bank.
667·2	Junction with Havel-Oder-Wasserstrasse (Ostschleuse Hohensaaten).
697·0	Schwedter Querfahrt. Connects with Hohensaaten- Friedrichsthaler- Wasserstrasse. Official mooring place in entrance.
702·6	German customs post on left bank.
702·7	Widuchowa. Polish customs post on right bank.
704·1	Junction with West-Oder (weir - no through passage).

PEENE

Navigable length 98km
Maximum draught 1·80m
Maximum height 4·10m
Current Negligible
Locks 0
Speed limit 12km/h

The Peene, with adequate depths, no locks, and interesting places to visit and to moor, is a very pleasant river to explore by boat. The rural countryside is a mixture of agriculture, swamp and woodland, and the visitor feels that nothing has changed in these parts for many years.

Although there are no locks, there are three opening bridges, at Anklam, Loitz and Demmin. The Peene continues upstream in a northwesterly direction from the Kummerower See, but only boats with a draught of less than 1·00m can reach Neukalen. The navigable route goes southwest through the Peenekanal to Malchin, the end of navigation for most cruising boats. Very shallow-draught boats can use the Dahmer Kanal and visit the charming Malchiner See.

Km

Km	
104·0	Mouth of Peene. Junction with Peenestrom. Nature reserve.
96·5–94·7	Anklam. Mooring places on right (south) bank (partly commercial harbour).
95·1	Railway lift bridge. Opens according to schedule, normally every 2–3 hours.
94·0	Yacht moorings on right bank.
85·7	Stolpe. Quay.
78–71	Several isolated mooring places and anchorages.
67·7	Jarmen. Quay and boathouses.
57·0	Alt Plestlin. Quay.
52·9	Sophienhof. Quay.
48·9	Loitz. Quay.
48·8	Low swing bridge. Opens on request 0800–1600.
40·6	Ferry. Beware rope across river.
34·3	Entrance to Trebel. Navigable only by canoes.
34·0–33·0	Demmin. Quay. Low lift bridge. Opens on request 0800–1600.
15·0	Entrance to Kummerower See. Several possible mooring places.
15–4·7	Kummerower See. Buoyed channel across centre, but anchoring off possible near several small villages around lake. Depth questionable at several small jetties. Entrance to Neukalener Kanal leading to Neukalen. Depth 1·8m.

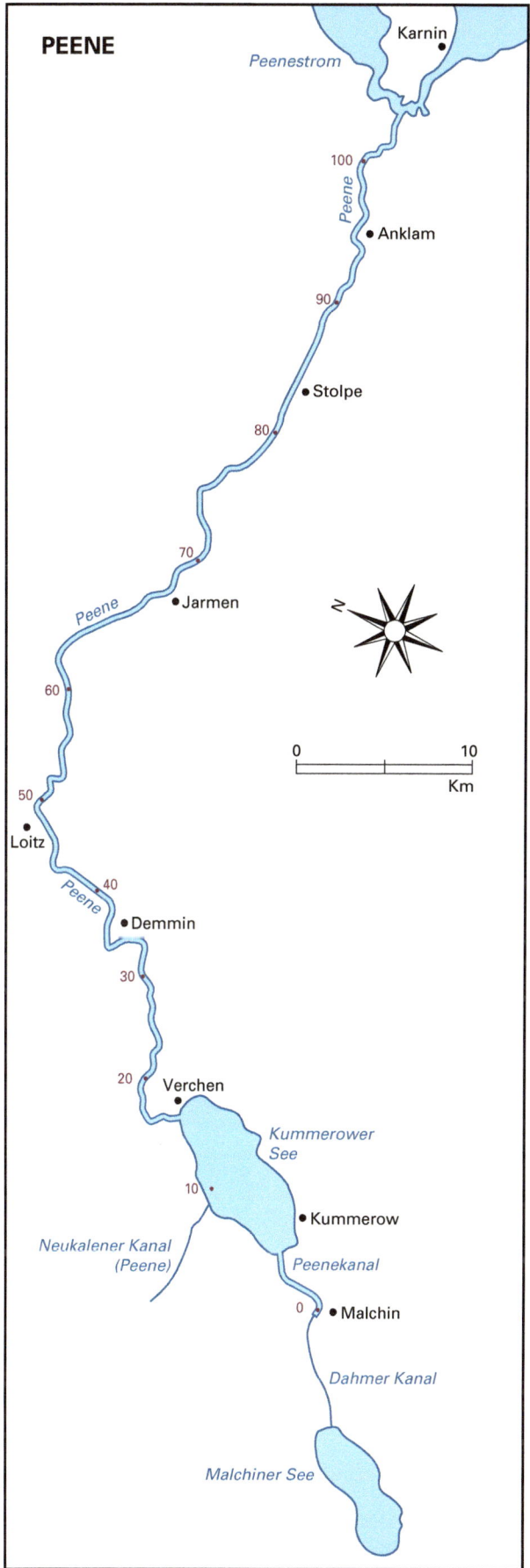

4·5	Entrance to Peenekanal.
3·0	Bank-side mooring place at restaurant.
0·0	Malchin. Several mooring possibilities on north side of canal. Canal continues as Dahmer Kanal, leading to Malchiner See. Depth 1·0m.

UECKER

Navigable length 11·0km
Maximum draught 3·00m to Ueckermunde, 1·30m above Ueckermünde.
Maximum height Unlimited
Current Negligible
Locks 0
Speed limit 6km/h

This small river is not dissimilar in character to the Peene. Flowing out into the Stettiner Haff (which lies half in Germany and half in Poland – it is known as Zalew Szczecinski in Polish) just inside the Polish border, the tree-lined river leads upstream 2·5km to

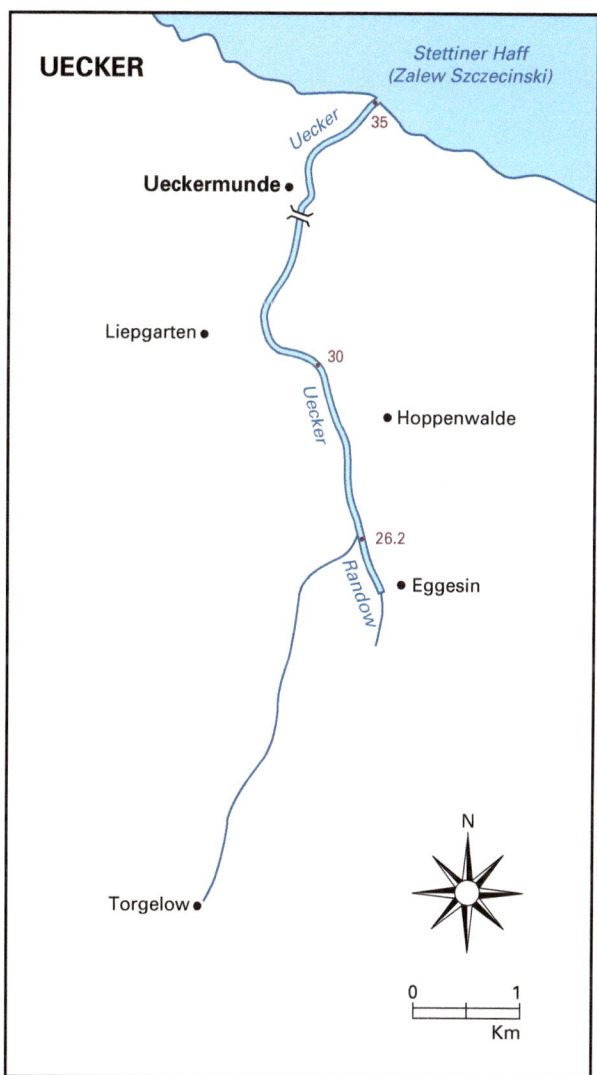

INLAND WATERWAYS OF GERMANY 169

Ueckermünde, where there is a Stadthafen in the town centre. 7km further upstream the Uecker itself swings southwest and the main route continues in the Randow for a further 1·5km to Eggesin.

There is an opening road bridge at Ueckermünde.

Km

0·0	Eggesin.
1·5–26·2	Junction of Randow and Uecker.
33·2	Ueckermünde. Stadthafen on east bank.
34·2	Yacht harbour on west bank.
35·7	Entrance to Stettiner Haff.

STRELASUND AND THE BODDEN

The northeastern corner of Mecklenburg-Vorpommern has always been remote and mysterious. An atmosphere of wildness pervades the air, and although the district is largely agricultural, there are large expanses of unspoilt saltmarsh and meadow where many species of flora and fauna flourish – and where it is easy to believe that secret activities are going on. It comes as no surprise that it was here, at Peenemünde on the island of Usedom, that the deadly V2 was developed during the Second World War. After visiting Berlin, it is a very interesting cruise (for boats capable of navigating in coastal waters) to go down the Oder to Szczecin in Poland, cross into Germany in the Zalew Szczecinski (Stettiner Haff) and travel through the Peenestrom, the winding channel between the desolate island of Usedom and the mainland. If time allows, it is worth diverting into the Uecker and the Peene and stopping to explore some of the interesting old towns and villages along the route. From the northern end of the Peenestrom a buoyed channel leads westwards across the huge Greifswalder Bodden and into the Strelasund. This channel divides the holiday island of Rügen from the mainland. Halfway along the Strelasund lies the lovely old Hanseatic city of Stralsund, which suffered considerable neglect during its 44 years of Communist government, but is now recovering rapidly.

Continuing northwards in the Strelasund, it is possible to branch either east or west into great expanses of enclosed and sheltered water forming a series of lakes known as Bodden. This whole area supports a great variety of wildlife, and part of it is a breeding ground for swans and geese, which can often be seen in thousands. Following several days at least exploring the Bodden, a series of short coastal hops leads to Travemünde, and back into the inland waterway system via the Elbe-Lübeck-Kanal. It is beyond the scope of this book to give detailed information on navigating in coastal waters, but appropriate charts and guide books are readily available.

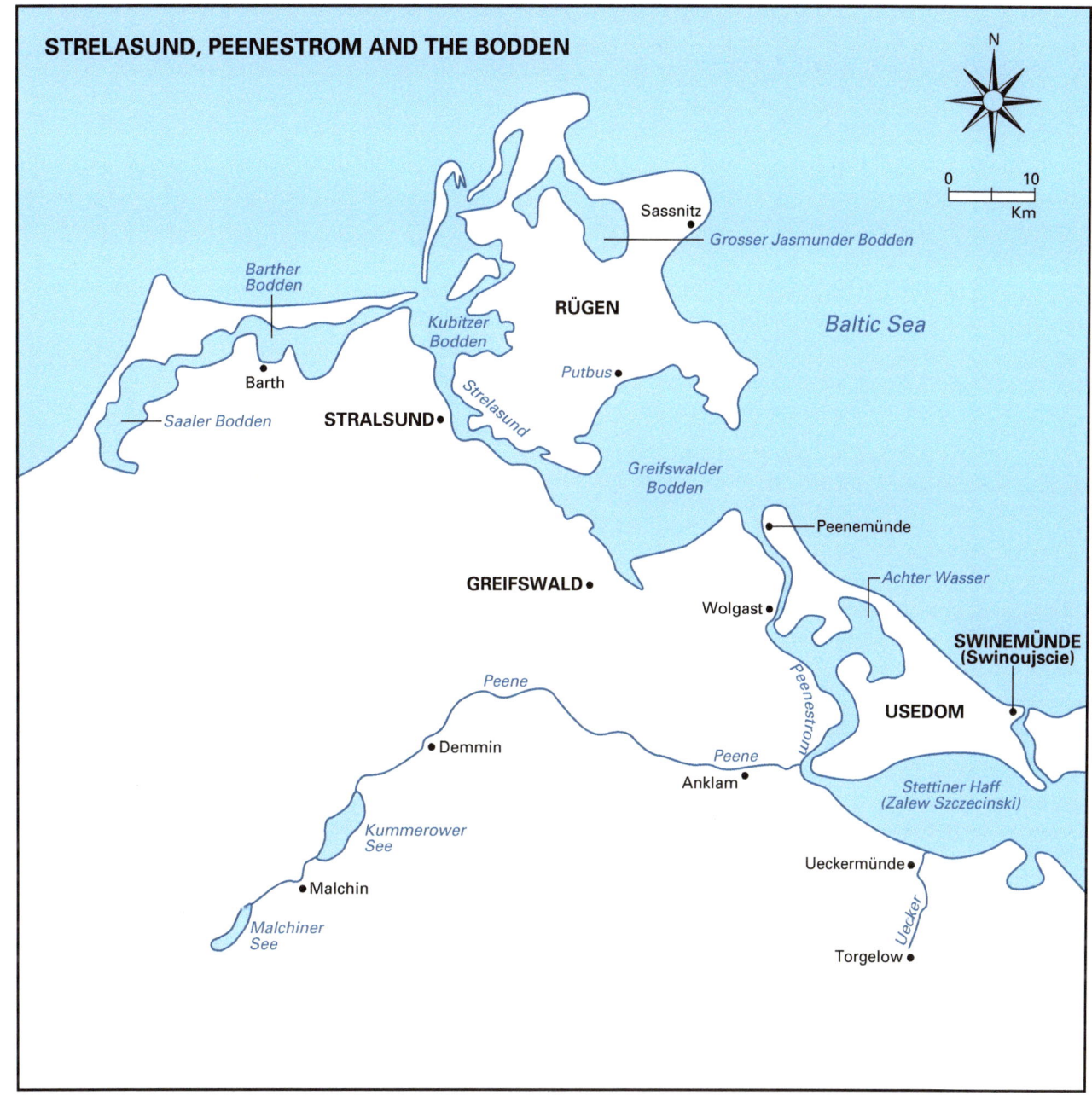

Appendix

I. GUIDES AND CHARTS

Guides in English

Slow Boat Through Germany Hugh McKnight (Adlard Coles)
The Danube - A river guide Rod Heikell (Imray)
The Baltic Sea RCC Pilotage Foundation Imray
Through the German Waterways Phillip Bristow (Adlard Coles)
Cruising Guide to Germany and Denmark Brian Navin (Imray)

German published maps and guides

Various publishers produce detailed maps and guides of the German waterways and the best source of information and supplier is **HanseNautic**:

Hamburg - Herrengraben 31 – 20459
info@hansenautic.de.
www.hansenautic.de

Their website is comprehensive and very helpful. They stock publications from the publishers below whose maps and guides are particularly recommended.

Delius Klasing, based in Bielefeld, publish a range of chart guides in book form and the most recent ones are supplemented by CD-ROMs. Delius Klasing acquired the Edition Maritim range of guides several years ago, and now only the older guides are published under the Edition Maritim label.

DSV Verlag published a useful set of 20 guides to German Inland Waterways in the 1990s, but these are now out of print and although a few still appear in bookshop lists, they are likely to be out-of-date.

Nautische Veröffenlichung of Eckernförde publish 5 inland cruising guides covering almost all of the area east of Hamburg and north from Berlin (as well as guides to Poland and also the Swedish Göta canal).

Verlag Rheinschiffahrt of Bad Soden (between Mainz and Frankfurt) publish 8 guides, primarily to the Rhine and its tributaries and the Danube.

Binnenschiffahrt-Verlag of Duisburg offer a range of about a dozen guides including some on CD rom also covering the Rhine region and the Danube.

II. USEFUL ADDRESSES

German National Tourist Office
60 Buckingham Palace Road, London SW1W 0AH
office-britain@germany.travel
www.germany.travel

German Embassy
23 Belgrave Square, London SWIX 8PZ
☏ 020 7824 1300
www.uk.diplo.de

For general enquiries and information on yacht and sailing clubs:
Deutscher Motoryachtverband eV
www.dmyv.de
Deutscher Segler-Verband (DSV)
www.dsv.org

For technical enquiries relating to specific waterways:
Wasser und Schifffahrtsverwaltung des Bundes (WSV)
Bundesministeriums für Verkehr und digitale Infrastruktur.

Head office and information on licensing:
Generaldirektion Wasserstraßen und Schifffahrt
Ulrich-von-Hassell-Straße 76, 53123 Bonn
info@wsv.de

Regional offices

Nord
Kiellinie 247, 24106 Kiel
☏ 0431/33940
ast-nord.gdws@wsv.bund.de

Nordwest
Schloßplatz 9, 26603 Aurich
☏ 04941 6020
ast-nordwest.gdws@wsv.bund.de

Ost
Postfach 1320, 39003 Magdeburg
Gerhart-Hauptmann-Straße 16, 39108 Magdeburg
☏ 0391 28870
ast-ost.gdws@wsv.bund.de

Mitte
Am Waterlooplatz 5, 30169 Hannover

West
Cheruskerring 11, 48147 Münster
☏ 0251 27080
ast-west.gdws@wsv.bund.de

Südwest
Postfach 31 01 60, 55062 Mainz

Brucknerstraße 2, 55127 Mainz
☎ 06131 9790
ast.suedwest.gdws@wsv.bund.de

Süd
Wörthstraße 19, 97082 Würzburg
☎ 0931 41050
ast-sued.gdws@wsv.bund.de
www.ast-sued.gdws.wsv.de

III. SPEED AND DISTANCE TABLE

Time to cover 1km	Speed over the ground	
Min:sec	*km/h*	*knots*
2:00	30	16·2
2:30	24	13·0
3:00	20	10·8
3:30	17	9·2
4:00	15	8·1
5:00	12	6·5
6:00	10	5·4
7:00	8–6	4·6
8:00	7–5	4·0
10:00	6	3·2
12:00	5	2·7
15:00	4	2·2
20:00	3	1·6
30:00	2	1·1

APPENDIX

IV. INTERNATIONAL WATERWAY MARKS, SIGNS AND SOUNDS

LIGHTS AT LOCKS

  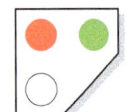  

Wait | Lock being prepared | Get ready | Enter now | Lock not in operation

OTHER LIGHTS

No entry to basin or channel indicated by white arrow

MANDATORY & WARNING SIGNS

No entry | No overtaking | No meeting or overtaking (i.e. single lane) | No mooring or anchoring | No anchoring | No mooring | No turning (winding) | Do not create wash | Motor boats forbidden

Proceed in direction indicated | Stop | Do not exceed speed limit | Give a sound signal | Danger - keep a sharp lookout | Major waterway ahead | Headroom limited | Width of passage or channel limited | Keep this distance from bank

       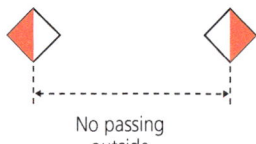

Make radio contact with waterway staff* | Cross channel to pass boats starboard to starboard | Cross channel to pass boats port to port (normal) | Keep to port | Keep to starboard | Channel moves to port | Channel moves to starboard | No passing outside marked limits

* Note that channel 10 is the ship-to-ship channel on inland waterways throughout the continent.

OTHER SIGNS (RECOMMENDATORY OR INFORMATIVE)

    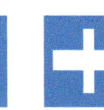   

Weir | Ferry | Chain ferry | Side turning | Tributary waterway | Priority waterway | Berthing permitted | Anchoring permitted | Making fast permitted | Turning

Recommended direction | Electricity cable | End of prohibition or restriction

SIGNS ON BRIDGES

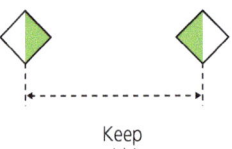  

Keep within limits (green) | Recommended channel (in both directions) | Passage only in direction indicated (other direction prohibited)

SOUNDS

```
—        Attention                                    ••••••    (6 very short) Imminent danger of collision
•        I am coming to or holding to starboard       — — —     (repeated) Distress signal
••       I am coming to or holding to port            — •       I am turning to or coming round to starboard
•••      I am going astern                            — ••      I am turning to or coming round to port
••••     I am incapable of manœuvre
```

174 INLAND WATERWAYS OF GERMANY

V. GERMAN VOCABULARY

German	English
Abwasser	sewage
Abwassertank	holding tank
Anhalten	to stop
Anker	anchor
Anherplatz	anchorage
Anlegestelle	mooring place
Ausfahrt	exit
Backbord	port side
Bake	beacon
Benzin	petrol
Berg	mountain
Bergfahrer	upstream vessel
Betreiben	to operate
Binnengewässer	inland waterways
blau	blue
Bodden	saltwater lagoons
Boje	buoy
Boot	small boat
Bootshöhe über Wasser	height of boat
Bootstankstelle	filling station for boats
Bootstreppe	boat ramp
Bootsvermietung	charter company
Bootswerft	boatyard
braun	brown
Breite	width
Brücke	bridge
Bug	bow
Bundeswasserstrassen	national waterways
Bunkerboot	bunker boat
Burg	castle
Charterfirma	charter company
Dalben	dolphin
Diesel	diesel
Doppelschleuse	double lock
Durchfahrthöhe	headroom
Duschen	showers
Einfahrt	entrance
Eisenbahnbrücke	railway bridge
Fähre	ferry
Fahren	to travel
Fahrrinne	channel
Fahrrinnentiefe	channel depth
Fahrt	journey
Fallhöhe	fall of lock
Fender	fender
Festmachen	to tie up
Flagge	flag
Fluss	river
Führer	guide
Führerschein	permit
Funk	radio
Gasthof	guesthouse
Gaststätte	pub/restaurant
Gelb	yellow
Geschwindigkeit	speed
Gesperrt	closed
Gewässer	waterways
grün	green
Hafen	harbour
Hafenbecken	harbour basin
Hafenverwaltung	harbour administration
Hebewerk	ship-lift
Heck	stern
Hinweise	reference material
Hochwasser	high water
Höhe	height
Hubhöhe	rise of lock
Insel	island
Jacht	yacht
Kai	quay
Kanal	canal, VHF channel
Karte	map
Knoten	to tie
Kraftstoff	fuel
Kraftwerk	power station
Kran	crane
Land	state or region
Länge	length
Langsam	slowly
Lebensmittel	groceries
Liegebühren	mooring fees
Liegemöglichkeit	possibility of mooring
Liegeplatz	mooring place
Liegeverbot	mooring forbidden
Liegezeit	mooring period
Mast	mast
Müll	garbage
Mündung	mouth of river
Niedrigwasser	low water
Nord	north
Notfall	emergency
Nullpunkt	zero point
Öl	oil
Ost	east
Pegel depth	gauge
Pegelstand	water level at Pegel
Poller	bollard
Propeller	propeller
rot	red
Rückwärts	astern
Ruhig	quiet
Rundfunk	broadcast radio
Schachtschleuse	shaft lock
Schiff	ship
Schifffahrt	shipping
Schiffsbedarf	chandlery
Schleppzug	convoy
Schleuse	lock
Schleusengruppe	multiple lock
Schleusenkammer	lock chamber
Schleusentor	lock gate
Schleusenwärter	lock-keeper
Schloss	castle
Schnell	fast
Schutzhafen	safety harbour
schwarz	black
Schwimmen	to swim
Schwimmpoller	floating bollard
Schwimmweste	lifejacket
Segel	sail
Sicherheit	safety

INLAND WATERWAYS OF GERMANY

APPENDIX

German	English	English	German
Sperrtor	flood barrier	anchor	Anker
Sportboot	leisure craft	anchorage	Ankerplatz
Sportboothafen	yacht harbour	association	Verein
Sprechfunk	radio telephone	astern	Rückärts
Stadt	town	bank of river or canal	Ufer
Stark	strong	beacon	Bake
Steganlage	staging	black	schwarz
Steuerbord	starboard side	blue	blau
Stoppen	to stop	boat ramp	Bootstreppe
Strassenbrücke	road bridge	boatyard	Bootswerft
Strassentankstelle	roadside filling station	bollard	Poller
Strecke	stretch of river	bow	Bug
Strom	electrical current	branch canal	Zweigkanal
Stromabwärts	downstream	bridge	Brücke
Stromaufwärts	upstream	broadcast radio	Rundfunk
Strömung	current in river	brown	braun
Süd	south	bunker boat	Bunkerboot
Supermarkt	supermarket	buoy	Boje, Tonne
Tal	valley	canal, VHF channel	Kanal
Talfahrer	downstream vessel	castle	Burg, Schloss
Tankstelle	filling station	chandlery	Schiffsbedarf
Teilstrecke	stretch of river	channel	Fahrrinne
Tief	deep	channel depth	Fahrrinnentiefe
Tiefe	depth	charter company	Bootsvermietung, Charterfirma
Tiefgang	draught		
Toiletten	toilets	closed	Gesperrt
Tonne	buoy	connecting	Verbindung
Treibstoff	fuel	convoy	Schleppzug
Trinkwasser	drinking water	crane	Kran
Ufer	bank of river or canal	current in river	Strömung
UKW	VHF	customs	Zoll
Umschlagstelle	loading place	deep	Tief
Unbefahrbar	unnavigable	depth	Tiefe
Untief	shallow	depth gauge	Pegel
Verbindung	connecting	diesel	Diesel
Verboten	forbidden	dockyard	Werft
Verein	association	dolphin	Dalben
Versorgung	provisions	double lock	Doppelschleuse
Wassersportler	leisure boater	downstream	Stromabwärts, zu Tal
Wasserstand	water level	downstream vessel	Talfahrer
Wasserwanderer	person who cruises	draught	Tiefgang
WC	WC	drinking water	Trinkwasser
Wehr	weir	East	Ost
weiss	white	electrical current	Strom
Wendestelle	turning place	emergency	Notfall
Werft	dockyard	entrance	Einfahrt
West	west	exit	Ausfahrt
Zoll	customs	fall of lock	Fallhöhe
zu Berg	upstream	fast	Schnell
zu Tal	downstream	fender	Fender
Zweigkanal	branch canal	ferry	Fähre
		filling station	Tankstelle
		filling station for boats	Bootstankstelle
		filling station in street	Strassentankstelle
		flag	Flagge
		floating bollard	Schwimmpoller
		flood barrier	Sperrtor
		forbidden	verboten
		fuel	Kraftstoff, Treibstoff
		garbage	Müll
		green	grün

APPENDIX

English	German
groceries	Lebensmittel
guesthouse	Gasthof
guide	Führer
harbour	Hafen
harbour administration	Hafenverwaltung
harbour basin	Hafenbecken
headroom	Durchfahrthöhe
height	Höhe
height of boat	Bootshöhe über Wasser
high water	Hochwasser
holding tank	Abwassertank
inland waterways	Binnengewässer
island	Insel
journey	Fahrt
length	Länge
lifejacket	Schwimmweste
loading place	Umschlagstelle
lock	Schleuse
lock chamber	Schleusenkammer
lock gate	Schleusentor
lock-keeper	Schleusenwärter
low water	Niedrigwasser
map	Karte
mast	Mast
mooring fees	Liegebühren
mooring forbidden	Liegeverbot
mooring period	Liegezeit
mooring place	Anlegestelle, Liegeplatz
mountain	Berg
mouth of river	Mündung
multiple lock	Schleusengruppe
national waterways	Bundeswasserstrassen
North	Nord
oil	Öl
to operate	betreiben
permit	Führerschein
person who cruises	Wasserwanderer
petrol	Benzin
leisure boater	Wassersportler
leisure craft	Sportboot
port side	Backbord
possibility of mooring	Liegemöglichkeit
power station	Kraftwerk
propeller	Propeller
provisions	Versorgung
pub/restaurant	Gaststätte
quay	Kai
quiet	ruhig
radio	Funk
radio telephone	Sprechfunk
railway bridge	Eisenbahnbrücke
red	rot
reference material	Hinweise
rise of lock	Hubhöhe
river	Fluss
road bridge	Strassenbrücke
safety	Sicherheit
safety harbour	Schutzhafen
sail	Segel
saltwater lagoons	Bodden
sewage	Abwasser
shaft lock	Schachtschleuse
shallow	Untief
ship	Schiff
ship-lift	Hebewerk
shipping	Schiffahrt
showers	Duschen
slowly	Langsam
small boat	Boot
South	Süd
speed	Geschwindigkeit
staging	Steganlage
starboard side	Steuerbord
state or region	Land
stern	Heck
to stop	anhalten, stoppen
stretch of river	Strecke, Teilstrecke
strong	stark
supermarket	Supermarkt
to swim	schwimmen
to tie	knoten
to tie up	festmachen
toilets	Toiletten
town	Stadt
to travel	Fahren
turning place	Wendestelle
unnavigable	unbejahrbar
upstream	Stromaufwärts, zu Berg
upstream vessel	Bergfahrer
valley	Tal
VHF	UKW
water level	Wasserstand
water level at Pegel	Pegelstand
waterways	Gewässer
WC	WC
weir	Wehr
west	west, Westen
white	weiss
width	Breite
yacht	Jacht
yacht harbour	Sportboothafen
yellow	gelb
zero point	Nullpunkt

INLAND WATERWAYS OF GERMANY

Index

Note *j* preceding a name means 'junction with'

Abstiegskanal zur Leine, 89
accommodation, 10
Achterwehrer Schiffahrtskanal, 98
addresses, 172-3
administrative matters, 13-14
Alf, 54
Alken, 54
Aller, 84-5
   j Leine, 85
   j Mittelweser, 83, 85
Alte Oder, *j* Havel-Oder-Wasserstrasse, 130
Altenhof, 134
Altenplathower Altkanal, *j* Elbe-Havel-Kanal, 115
Altmühl, 25
Altrhein (Old Rhein), 34
Andernach, 41
Anklam, 168
architecture, 9
Aschaffenburg, 29
ATIS function, 18-19
Aue, 95
Aurich, 75
Austrian border, 23, 25

Baalensee, 140
Bad Abbach, 23, 24
Bad Dürrenberg, 111, 113
Bad Ems, 50
Bad Saarow, 165
Bad Schandau, 104, 105
Bad Wimpfen, 47
Baldeney-See, 61
Balduinstein, 51
Baltic Sea, 20, 100, 167-71
Bamberg, 25, 26, 31
bank holidays, 10
banks, 10
Barby, 103, 106
Basel, 32, 34, 35
Bech-Kleinmacher, 57
Bederkesa, 95, 96
Bederkesa-Geeste-Kanal, 95
beer, 11
Beeskow, 166
Beetzsee, *j* Silokanal, 122
Beilngries, 27
Beilstein, 54
Beinheim, 37
Bergzower Altkanal, *j* Elbe-Havel-Kanal, 115
Berlin, 17, 20, 116-19, 152-5
Berlin-Spandauer-Schiffahrtskanal, 153, 155
   j Havel-Oder-Wasserstrasse, 129, 155
   j Spree-Oder-Wasserstrasse, 153, 155
   j Westhafenkanal, 153, 155
Bernburg, 112
Bernkastel-Kues, 55
Besch, 57
bicycles, 10, 19-20
Bille, *j* Norderelbe, 109
Binau, 47

Bingen, 39
birds, 12
Black Sea, 20, 167
boat & equipment, 14, 19-20
Bodden, 7, 12, 20, 170, 171
Bode, *j* Saale, 112
Bodensee, 32
Bolter Kanal, 141, 143, 150
Bonn, 32, 42
Boppard, 40
Borschütz, 104
Brandenburg, 115-16, 122-4
Brandenburger Niederhavel, 115, 122, 124
   j Brandenburger Stadtkanal, 124
   j Silokanal, 122
   j Untere Havel-Wasserstrasse, 124
Brandenburger Stadtkanal, 116, 122-4
   j Brandenburger Niederhavel, 124
   j Untere Havel-Wasserstrasse, 122
Braunschweig, 85, 91
Breiholz, 96
Breisach, 32, 35
Bremen, 81, 83-4
Bremerhaven, 84, 95, 96
Bremervörde, 111
bridges, signs on, 174
Brieskower See, 168
Brieskowkanal, 156
Britzer Verbindungskanal (Zweigkanal), 156
   j Spree-Oder-Wasserstrasse, 156, 157
   j Teltowkanal, 157, 158
Brodenbach, 54
Brunsbüttel, 96, 97, 111
Budenheim, 39
Bullay, 54
Bülstringen, 92
Bundeswasserstrassen, 13, 14
Burg, 115
Buxtehude, 109

Calbe, 111, 112
Canal de la Marne au Rhin, *j* Rhein, 36
Canal du Rhône au Rhin, *j* Rhein, 35, 36
Canow, 143
cash machines (ATMs), 10
Celle, 84
certificates of competence, 13
channel depths, 18
charges, 14, 17, 22
Charlottenburger Verbindungskanal, 153, 155
   j Spree-Oder-Wasserstrasse, 153
chartering, 19
charts, maps & guides, 21, 96, 172
Chvaletice, 103
climate, 12
Cochem, 52, 54
Colmar, 35
Constance, Lake, 32
cost of living, 12
cranes, 19
credit & debit cards, 10

cruising grounds, 20
culture, 12
Cuxhaven, 103, 108, 109, 111
cycling, 10, 19-20
Czech border, 20, 103, 104, 105

Dahme Umflutkanal, 163
Dahme-Wasserstrasse, 153, 156, 160-65
   j Notte, 162
   j Spree-Oder-Wasserstrasse, 156, 160
   j Storkower Gewässer, 163
   j Teupitzer Gewässer, 163, 165
Dahmer Kanal, 168, 169
Dämeritzsee, 159-60
   j Gosener Kanal, 159, 160
   j Rüdersdorfer Gewässer, 159, 160
Danube *see* Donau
Datteln, 63, 64, 65
Datteln-Hamm-Kanal, 63-4
   j Dortmund-Ems-Kanal, 63, 65
Dausenau, 50
Deggendorf, 23, 25
Dehrn, 48, 52
Delfzijl, 69
Demmin, 168
Dessau, 105, 106
diesel fuel, 18
Dietkirchen, 51
Diez, 51
Dillingen (Donau), 22
Dillingen (Saar), 60
distance & speed table, 173
Ditzum, 20, 69
Dniepr, 167
documents, 13-14
Dollbeck, 143
Dömitz, 108, 145
Donau, 19, 20, 21-5
   j Main-Donau-Kanal, 23, 24, 28
Donaudurchbruch, 22
Donauwörth, 21, 22
Dorpen, 78
Dortmund, 62, 64, 65
Dortmund-Ems-Kanal, 20, 64-8
   j Datteln-Hamm-Kanal, 63, 65
   j Ems Vechte Kanal, 66
   j Haren-Rütenbrock-Kanal, 68, 71
   j Küstenkanal, 64, 68, 79
   j Mittellandkanal, 64, 66, 85, 86
   j Obere Ems, 66
   j Rhein-Herne-Kanal, 64, 65
   j Unter Ems, 69
   j Wesel-Datteln-Kanal, 63, 65
Dörverden, Schleusenkanal, 83
Dove-Elbe, *j* Norderelbe, 109
Drahendorfer Spree, *j* Obere Spree, 156, 166
Drakenberg, Schleusenkanal, 83
draughts (general), 18, 21
Dresden, 104, 105
Dreyschlot, 77
   j Jümme, 77, 78
   j Leda, 77

INDEX

Drosedower Bach, 143
Duisburg, 42, 43-4, 62
Dusseldorf, 42, 43
Dutch border, 20, 45, 69, 71

eating out, 11
Eberbach, 47
Eberswalde, 133
Eggesin, 170
Eibelstadt, 30
Eider, 20, 97, 98-9
   j Gieselaukanal, 99
Eisenhüttenstadt, 153, 156, 167, 168
Elbe, 20, 86, 95, 103-111, 126, 134
   j Elbe-Havel-Kanal, 107, 113, 114, 116
   j Elbe-Lübeck-Kanal, 99-100, 108
   j Elbe-Seitenkanal, 93, 94, 108
   j Gnevsdorfer Vorfluter, 108, 125
   j Grodel-Elsterwerdaer Flosskanal, 106
   j Ilmenau, 109
   j Mittellandkanal, 107
   j Müritz-Elde-Wasserstrasse, 108, 134, 144, 145
   j Niegripper Verbindungskanal, 107, 113, 115
   j Nord-Ostsee-Kanal, 97, 111
   j Pareyer Verbindungskanal, 107, 115
   j Saale, 106, 111, 112
   j Schiffahrtsweg Elbe-Weser, 96
   j Schwarze Elster, 106
   j Untere Havel-Wasserstrasse, 108, 125-6
   see also Norderelbe; Schiffahrtsweg Elbe-Weser; Süderelbe
Elbe-Havel-Kanal, 20, 113-15, 116
   j Altenplathower Altkanal, 115
   j Bergzower Altkanal, 115
   j Elbe, 107, 113, 114, 116
   j Mittellandkanal, 85, 93, 105, 113
   j Niegripper Altkanal, 115
   j Niegripper Verbindungskanal, 113
   j Rossdorfer Altkanal, 115
   j Untere Havel-Wasserstrasse, 115, 124
Elbe-Lübeck-Kanal, 20, 97-8, 170
   j Elbe, 99, 108
   j Trave, 100
Elbe-Seitenkanal, 17, 20, 93-4
   j Elbe, 93, 94, 108
   j Mittellandkanal, 93
Elbe-Weser shipping route *see* Schiffahrtsweg Elbe-Weser
Elde, 144
Elde-Dreieck, 146
electricity, 19
Elisabethfehn, 79
Elisabethfehnkanal, 76, 78-9
   j Küstenkanal, 78, 79
   j Sagter Ems, 77, 79
Ellbogensee, *j* Müritz-Havel-Wasserstrasse, 141
Elmshorn, 111
Elsfleth, 79
Eltmann, 31
Embassy (German), 172
Emden, 65, 68, 69-70, 73-4
Emmerich, 45
Ems Vechte Kanal, *j* Dortmund-Ems-Kanal, 66
Ems-Jade-Kanal, 69, 70, 73-6
   j Ems-Seitenkanal, 70

   j Jümme, 76
   j Nordgeorgsfehnkanal, 75, 76
   j Unter Ems, 70
Ems-Seitenkanal, 65, 68, 70
   j Ems-Jade-Kanal, 70
   j Unter Ems, 70
Ems, *see also* Obere Ems; Sagter Ems
equipment, 14, 19-20
Erlangen, 27
Erlau, 25
Erlenbach, 29
Essen, 62
Essen-Rellinghausen, 61
Essing, 28
Este, *j* Unterelbe, 109
etiquette, 12

Fahrlander See, 120
Fehrbelliner Kanal, 132
fendering, 19
Ferchesar, 125
festivals, 12
Finowkanal, 128, 1333-4
   j Havel-Oder-Wasserstrasse, 130, 133, 134
   j Obere-Havel-Wasserstrasse, 135, 136
flags, 13, 14
food, 11
Forchheim, 27
formalities, 13-14
Frankfurt (Main), 28, 29
Frankfurt (Oder), 156, 167, 168
French border, 20, 35-7, 57-8, 60
Friedrichstadt, 98, 99
Friendrichsthal, 131
fuel, 18
Fulda, 80, 81
Fürstenberg, 140
Fürstenwalde, 153
Fürth, 27

Galluner Kanal, 162
Garstadt, 31
Garz, 132
gas, 19
Gatow, 131
Gdansk, 167
Geeste, 95, 96
   j Unterweser, 84, 96
Geesthacht, 103, 105, 108
Gemünden, 30
Genthin, 115
geography, 7
German language, 10, 13, 15, 175-6
Gieselaukanal, 99
   j Eider, 99
   j Nord-Ostsee-Kanal, 97, 98, 99
Giessen, 48
Gleesen-Papenburg, Seitenkanal, *j* Küstenkanal, 79
Gleichwertiger Wasserstand-Fahrinnentiefe, 18
Glindowsee, 121
glossary, 175-6
Glückstadter Nebenelbe, *j* Unterelbe, 111
Gnevsdorfer Vorfluter, *j* Elbe, 108, 125
Gobenowsee, 143
Goldkanal, 37
Gosener Kanal, 156, 158, 160
   j Dämeritzsee, 159, 160

   j Müggelspree, 159, 160
   j Oder-Spree-Kanal, 160
Göttin See, 115
Goyatz, 166
Gozdowice, 167
Grabow, 145
Grand Canal d'Alsace, 35
Grevenmacher, 57
Griebnitzsee-Kanal, *j* Teltowkanal, 157
Griefswalder Bodden, 170
Grienericksee, 142
Grodel-Elsterwerdaer Flosskanal, *j* Elbe, 106
Grosser Labussee, 141
Grosser Wannsee, 116-19, 157
   j Untere Havel Wasserstrasse, 119
Grosser Wendsee, 115
Grütz, 125
Güdingen, 60
Gülper Havel, *j* Untere Havel-Wasserstrasse, 125
Gundelsheim, 47
Günzburg, 22
Güster, 99, 100

Hadelner Kanal, 84, 95
   j Medem, 96, 111
   j Unterelbe, 111
   j Unterweser, 84, 94
Hafenkanal Duisburg, 62
Hahl, 29
Haldensleben, 92
Halle, 111, 113
Hamburg, 103, 108-9, 110
Hameln, 81
Hamm (Ruhr), 64
Hamm (Saar), 59
Hamme, 111
Hanau, 29
Hannover, 85, 89-90
Hannover-Linden, Stichkanal, 89
Hannoversch-Münden, 80, 81
harbours, 17
Haren, 68, 71
Haren-Rütenbrock-Kanal, 71
   j Dortmund-Ems-Kanal, 68, 71
   j Ter Apelkanaal, 71
Hassfurt, 31
Hassmersheim, 47
Hatzenport, 54
Hauptfehnkanal, *j* Leda, 77
Havel, 115, 134, 141, 144, 153
Havel Mündungsstrecke, 125
Havel-Oder-Wasserstrasse, 20, 103, 115, 127-31, 135
   j Alte Oder, 130
   j Berlin-Spandauer-Schiffahrtskanal, 129, 155
   j Finowkanal, 130, 133, 134
   j Havelkanal, 127, 129
   j Hohensaaten-Friedrichsthaler-Wasserstrasse, 131
   j Obere-Havel-Wasserstrasse, 135, 136
   j Oder, 131, 168
   j Oranienburger Kanal, 129, 132
   j Ost-Oder, 131
   j Spree, 119
   j Spree-Oder-Wasserstrasse, 128, 153
   j Untere Havel-Wasserstrasse, 115, 119, 128

INLAND WATERWAYS OF GERMANY *179*

INDEX

j Werbellinkanal, 130, 134
Havelberg, 108, 116, 125-6
Havelkanal, 115, 126-7
　j Havel-Oder-Wasserstrasse, 127, 129
　j Sacrow-Paretzer-Kanal, 120, 127
　j Untere Havel-Wasserstrasse, 115, 120, 127
Hebewerke see *ship-lifts*
Heidanger, 91
Heidelberg, 45, 46
Heilbronn, 45, 47
Heining, 25
Hennigsdorf, 127, 129
Henrichenburg, 64
　ship-lifts, 64, 65
Herbrum, 68
Hermannsdorf, 24
Hildesheim, 85, 90-91
Hilpoltstein, 27
Himmelpfort, 140
Hirschhorn, 46
history, 8-9
Hofkirchen, 25, 125
Hohenauen, 125
Hohennauener Kanal, 125
Hohensaaten, 127, 128, 130-31, 167, 168
Hohensaaten-Friedrichsthaler-Wasserstrasse, 127, 128, 131
　j Havel-Oder-Wasserstrasse, 131
　j Oder, 168
　j Schwedter Querfahrt, 129, 168
　j West-Oder, 131
Hohenzollernkanal see Berlin-Spandauer-Schiffahrtskanal
holding tanks, 14, 18
holidays, public, 10
Holtenau, 96, 97, 98
Homeburg, 109
Hostenbach, 60
Hunte, 84

Iffezheim, 20, 32, 35, 36
Ilmenau, 109
　j Elbe, 109
Ingelheim, 39
Ingolstadt, 21-2
Inn, 23, 25
Itzehoe, 111

Jümme, 69, 76, 78
　j Dreyschlot, 77, 78
　j Ems-Jade-Kanal, 76
　j Leda, 77, 78
　j Nordgeorgsfehnkanal, 76, 78

Kachlet, 23
Kampe, 78
Karlsruhe, 37
Karlstadt, 30
Karsdorf, 111, 113
Kassel, 80
Kasteler Arm (Rhein), 38
Kaub, 32, 39
Kelheim, 21, 22, 23, 25, 28
Kellinghusen, 111
Kersdorf, 153, 156
Ketzin & Ketziner Havel, 115, 122
Kiel Canal see Nord-Ostsee-Kanal
Kiel-Holtenau, 96, 97, 98
Kieler Forde (Kiel Fiord), *j* Nord-Ostsee-Kanal, 98

Kitzingen, 31
Kleine Müritz, 143
Kleinostheim, 28
Klenzsee, 143
Kloster Weltenburg, 22
Klotten, 54
Koblenz, 32, 40, 52, 53
Köhlbrand/Süderelbe, 109
Köln, 32, 42-3
Konigstein, 104, 105
Konstanz, 32
Konz, 56
Köpenick, 153, 158
Kozle, 167
Kröv, 55
Krückau, *j* Unterelbe, 111
Kues, 55
Kummerower See, 168
Küstenkanal, 79, 84
　j Dortmund-Ems-Kanal, 64, 68, 79
　j Elisabethfehnkanal, 78, 79
　j Seitenkanal Gleesen-Papenburg, 79
　j Untere Hunte, 79
　j Unterweser, 84

Labe, 103
Labusee, 143
Lahn, 20, 32, 48-52
　j Rhein, 40, 48, 49
Lahnstein, 49
Länd/Länder, 14
Landesbergen, Schleusenkanal, 82-3
Landwehrkanal, 155, 158
　j Neuköllner Schiffahrtskanal, 155
　j Spree-Oder-Wasserstrasse, 153, 155
Langer See, 153, 156, 163-4
Langerhans-Kanal
　j Müggelspree, 160
　j Rüdersdorfer Gewässer, 160
Langwedel, Schleusenkanal, 83
Lauenburg, 20, 99, 100, 103, 108
laundry, 11
Laurenburg, 50
Lausitzer Neisse, *j* Oder, 168
laying-up, 18
Leda, 69, 76, 77, 78
　j Dreyschlot, 77
　j Hauptfehnkanal, 77
　j Jümme, 77, 78
　j Sagter Ems, 77
　j Unter Ems, 69, 77
Leer, 69, 77
Lehnitzsee, 120, 129
Leibsch, 166
Leine, 89
　j Aller, 85
Leiwen, 56
Lesum, *j* Unterelbe, 84
Lexfähre, 98, 99
Liebenwalde, 136
lights, 174
Limburg, 48, 51
Linden, 89-90
Lindow, 132
Lingen, 67
Linz, 41
Listrum, 66
Little Venice (Klein Venedig), 26, 159
Lobith Tolkamer, 45
Löcknitz, 158, 160
locks, 15-17, 19, 21, 174

Lohr, 30
Loitz, 168
Lorch, 39
Loreley Rock, 39, 40
Lübeck, 99, 100, 101
Lübz, 147
Ludwig-Donau-Main-Kanal, 23, 26
Ludwigshafen, 38
Lühe, *j* Unterelbe, 109
Lüneburg, 109
ship-lifts, 93, 94
Luxembourg, 52, 56-7
Lychen, 140
Lychener Gewässer, 134, 139-40
　j Obere-Havel-Wasserstrasse, 139, 140

Magdeburg, 20, 103, 104, 105, 106-7
　Aqueduct, 86, 92-3
　Rothensee ship-lift, 86, 105, 107
Main, 16, 20, 26, 28-31, 32
　j Main-Donau-Kanal, 25, 31
　j Rhein, 28, 38
Main-Donau-Kanal, 16, 17, 20, 21, 25-8
　j Donau, 23, 24, 25, 28
　j Main, 25, 31
Mainstockheim, 31
Mainz, 38
Malchin, 168, 169
Malchiner See, 168, 169
Malchow, 144, 147
Malzer Kanal, 129, 130, 135
Mannheim, 38
maps & guides, 21, 172
Mariaposching, 24
marinas, 17
markets, 10
Märkisch Buchholz, 160
marks, signs & sounds, 174
Marktbreit, 30
Mecklenburg lake district, 7, 13, 20, 115, 134, 141, 144
Medem, 95
　j Hadelner Kanal, 96, 111
　j Unterelbe, 111
Meissen, 104, 105
Melnik, 103
Menowsee, 140
Meppen, 67
Merseburg, 111, 112, 113
Merzig, 60
Mescherin, 131
Metten, 24
Mettlach, 59
Miltenberg, 29
Minden, 81-2, 85, 86, 87-8
　Aqueduct, 86, 88
　Schachtschleuse (Lock), 82, 86
　Viaducts, 81, 82, 86
Mirow, 141, 143
Mirower Kanal, 143
Misburg, Stichkanal, 90
Mittellandkanal, 20, 81, 82, 85-93
　j Dortmund-Ems-Kanal, 64, 66, 85, 86
　j Elbe, 107
　j Elbe-Havel-Kanal, 85, 93, 105, 113
　j Elbe-Seitenkanal, 93
　j Niegripper Verbindungkanal, 113, 115
　j Nordabstieg zur Weser (Verbindungskanal Nord, Minden), 87, 88

180 INLAND WATERWAYS OF GERMANY

j Rothenseer Verbindungskanal, 92
j Stichkanal Hannover-Linden, 89
j Stichkanal Hildesheim, 91
j Stichkanal Misburg, 90
j Stichkanal Osnabrück, 86, 87
j Stichkanal Salzgitter, 91
j Südabstieg zur Weser
  (Verbindungskanal Süd, Minden), 88
j Weser, 81, 88
Mittellandkanal Aqueduct (Magdeburg), 86, 92-3
Mittellandkanal Aqueduct (Minden), 86, 88
Mittellandkanal Viaduct (Minden), 81, 82
Mittelweser, 81, 82-4
  j Aller, 83, 85
  j Nordabstieg zur Weser
    (Verbindungskanal Nord, Minden), 82, 88
  j Schleusenkanal Dörverden, 83
  j Schleusenkanal Drakenberg, 83
  j Schleusenkanal Landesbergen, 82, 83
  j Schleusenkanal Langwedel, 83
  j Schleusenkanal Petershagen, 82
  j Schleusenkanal Schlusselburg, 82
mobile phones, 11
Moldau (Vltava), 103
Möllenzugsee, 162
Mölln, 100
money, 10
mooring in locks, 16
mooring overnight, 17-18
Mosel, 14, 16, 20, 32, 52-7
  j Rhein, 40, 52, 53
  j Saar, 56, 58
motor cruisers, 19
Müggelsee, 158, 159
Müggelspree, 153, 156, 158-60, 161
  j Gosener Kanal, 159, 160
  j Langerhans-Kanal, 160
  j Spree-Oder-Wasserstrasse, 158, 160
Mühlham, 25
Mülheim, 61
Münster, 64, 66
Müritz, 149-50
Müritz See, 134, 135, 141, 144, 149-51
Müritz-Elde-Wasserstrasse, 134, 144-51
  j Elbe, 108, 134, 144, 145
  j Stör-Wasserstrasse, 146, 147
Müritz-Havel-Wasserstrasse, 134, 135, 141-3
  j Ellbogensee, 141
  j Müritz-Elde-Wasserstrasse, 144, 151
  j Obere-Havel-Wasserstrasse, 141, 142, 151
  j Rheinsberger Gewässer, 142, 143

Nackenheimer Mühlarm (Rhein), 38
Nassau, 48, 50
Naumburg, 111, 113
navigation, 14-15
navigation marks, signs & sounds, 174
Neckar, 20, 32, 45-8
  j Rhein, 45, 46
Neckargemünd, 46
Neckargerach, 47
Neckarmühlbach, 47
Neckarsteinach, 46
Nesserland, 73, 74
Neuburg, 22

Neuhaus, Speisekanal, 156
Neukalen, 168
Neukalener Kanal, 168
Neuköllner Schiffahrtskanal, 155, 158
  j Landwehrkanal, 155
  j Teltowkanal, 158
Neumagen-Dhron, 56
Neuruppin, 132
Neustadt (Donau), 22
Neustadt-Glewe, 145
Neustrelitz, 141
Neuwied, 41
Niederfinow ship-lift, 127-8, 130, 134
Niegripp, 105, 107, 115
Niegripper Altkanal, *j* Elbe-Havel-Kanal, 115
Niegripper Verbindungskanal, 114-15
  j Elbe, 107, 113, 115
  j Elbe-Havel-Kanal, 113
  j Mittellandkanal, 113, 115
Nienburg, 83
Nierstein, 37, 38
Niffer, 20, 35
Nord-Ostsee-Kanal (Kiel Canal), 20, 96-8
  j Elbe, 97, 111
  j Gieselaukanal, 97, 98, 99
  j Kieler Forde, 98
  j Unterelbe, 111
Nordabstieg zur Weser (Verbindungskanal Nord, Minden), 82, 87, 88
Norderelbe, 109
  j Bille, 109
  j Dove-Elbe, 109
Nordfeld, 98, 99
Nordgeorgsfehnkanal, 76
  j Ems-Jade-Kanal, 75, 76
  j Jümme, 76, 78
Nordhorn, 66
North Sea routes, 20
Notec, 167
Notte, *j* Dahme, 162
Nürnberg (Nuremberg), 26, 27

Obere Ems, *j* Dortmund-Ems-Kanal, 66
Obere Havel, 115, 141, 144
Obere Havel-Wasserstrasse, 130, 134-41, 144
  j Finowkanal, 135, 136
  j Havel-Oder-Wasserstrasse, 135, 136
  j Lychener Gewässer, 139, 140
  j Müritz-Havel-Wasserstrasse, 141, 142, 144, 151
  j Schwedtsee, 140
  j Templiner Gewässer, 137
  j Wentow Gewässer, 136, 137
Obere Spree, 156, 163, 166
Obere Spree Wasserstrasse, 166
  j Drahendorfer Spree, 156, 166
  j Spree-Oder-Wasserstrasse, 156, 166
Obereidersee, 99
Obereisenheim, 31
Oberwesel, 39
Oberweser, 20, 80, 81
  j Fulda & Werra, 81
  j Mittellandkanal, 81
Obrigheim, 47
Ochsenfurt, 30
Ochtum, *j* Unterelbe, 84
Odenwald (Oden Forest), 45
Oder, 20, 126, 128, 153, 156, 167-8

j Havel-Oder-Wasserstrasse, 131, 168
j Hohensaaten-Friedrichsthaler-Wasserstrasse, 168
j Lausitzer Neisse, 168
j Spree-Oder-Wasserstrasse, 153, 156
j Warta, 167, 168
see also Ost-Oder; West-Oder
Oder-Spree-Kanal, 153
  j Gosener Kanal, 160
  j Spree-Oder-Wasserstrasse, 156
Oderberg, 128, 130
Offenau, 47
Offenbach, 29
Oldau, 84
Oldenburg, 78, 79
Oldersum, 69
Oppenheim, 37, 38
Oranienburg, 129
Oranienburger Kanal, 132
  j Havel-Oder-Wasserstrasse, 129, 132
  j Ruppiner Kanal, 132
Osnabrück, 85, 87
Ost-Oder, 128, 131
  j Havel-Oder-Wasserstrasse, 131
Oste, *j* Unterelbe, 111
Osten, 111
Osterhofen, 23
Otterndorf, 95, 96
overnight stops, 17-18
overtaking, 15
overwintering, 18

Pagensander Nebelelbe, 109
Papenburg, 68, 69
paperwork, 13-14
Parchim, 144, 147
Paretz, 122, 127
Parey, 115
Pareyer Verbindungskanal, *j* Elbe, 107, 115
Passau, 21, 23, 25
Päwesin, 122
Peene, 168-9, 170, 171
  j Peenestrom, 168
Peenekanal, 168, 169
Peenemünde, 170
Peenestrom, 171
  j Peene, 168
Pegels, 18
Petershagen, Schleusenkanal, 82
petrol, 18
Pfelling, 24
phones, 11
Pieskow, 165
Piesport, 56
Pinnau, 109-111
  j Unterelbe, 109-111
Plau, 144, 148
Plaue, 115, 116, 124
Plochingen, 45, 48
police (Wasserschutzpolizei), 13, 14
Pölich, 56
Polish border, 20, 128, 131, 167, 169-70
Potsdam, 115, 116-19
Potsdamer Havel, 115, 120-22
  j Sacrow-Paretzer-Kanal, 120, 122
  j Teltowkanal, 120, 157
  j Untere Havel Wasserstrasse, 120
Prague, 103
Premnitz, 125
Priepert, 141-2

INDEX

Prieros, 160, 163
Pritzerber See, 124
provisioning, 10-11
Prüss-See, 99, 100
public holidays, 10
Pünderich, 54

Quitzobel, 108, 125

radar, 19
radio, 11, 18-19
Randow, 170
   j Uecker, 170
Rathen, 104, 105
Rathenow & branches, 125
Ratsdelft, 74-5
Rätsee, 143
Ratzdorf, 167, 168
Rechlin, 145, 151
Rednitz, 25
refuelling, 18
Regensburg, 21, 23, 24
registration, 14
Rellinghausen, 61
Remich, 57
Rendsburg, 96, 97
restaurants, 11
Rhein, 14, 17, 18, 19, 20, 25, 26, 32-45
   j Canal de la Marne au Rhin, 36
   j Canal du Rhône au Rhin, 35, 36
   j Lahn, 40, 48, 49
   j Main, 28, 38
   j Mosel, 40, 52, 53
   j Neckar, 45, 46
   j Rhein-Herne-Kanal, 44, 62
   j Rhein-Kleve-Kanal, 45
   j Ruhr, 44, 61
   j Wesel-Datteln-Kanal, 44, 63
Rhein Gorge, 20, 32, 39
Rhein-Herne-Kanal, 20, 62
   j Dortmund-Ems-Kanal, 64, 65
   j Rhein, 44, 62
   j Ruhr, 44, 61
Rhein-Kleve-Kanal, *j* Rhein, 45
Rhein-Marne-Kanal, 20
Rhein-Seitenkanal, 35
Rheinfall (Rhine Falls), 32
Rheinfelden, 32, 34
Rheinsberg, 142-3
Rheinsberger Gewässer, 141, 142-3
   j Müritz-Havel-Wasserstrasse, 142, 143
   j Rhin, 142
Rheinschiffahrtsdirektion, 14
Rheinschiffahrtspolizeiverordnung, 14
Rhin, 132
   j Rheinsberger Gewässer, 142
   j Ruppiner Kanal, 132, 142
Rhin Kanal, 132
Rhine *see* Rhein
Rhône-Rhein-Kanal, 20
Riedenburg, 28
Riesa, 106
Riewendsee, 122
Rinteln, 81
river police (Wasserschutzpolizei), 13, 14
Röbel, 150
Rödelinsee, 137-8
Rossdorfer Altkanal, *j* Elbe-Havel-Kanal, 115
Rote-Mühle, 61
Rothensee ship-lift (Magdeburg), 86, 105, 107

Rothenseer Verbindungskanal, *j* Mittellandkanal, 92
routes, 20
Rüdersdorf, 158
Rüdersdorfer Gewässer, 158, 160, 161
   j Dämeritzsee, 159, 160
   j Langerhans-Kanal, 160
Rüdesheim, 39
Rügen, 170
Ruhr, 61
   j Rhein, 44, 61
   j Rhein-Herne-Kanal, 44, 61
rules of the road, 14
Ruppiner Kanal, 129, 132
   j Oranienburger Kanal, 132
Ruppiner See, 128, 132
Ruppiner Wasserstrasse, 128, 132
   j Fehrbelliner Kanal, 132
   j Oranienburger Kanal, 132
   j Rhin, 132, 142
Rütenbrock, 71
Ruthenstrom, *j* Unterelbe, 111

Saale, 111-13
   j Bode, 112
   j Elbe, 106, 111, 112
   j Unstrut, 111, 113
Saar, 20, 57-60
   j Mosel, 56, 58
Saar-kanal, 60
Saarbrücken, 57, 58, 60
Saarburg, 58-9
Saarlouis, 60
Sacrow-Paretzer-Kanal, 115, 120
   j Havelkanal, 120, 127
   j Potsdamer Havel, 120, 122
   j Untere Havel-Wasserstrasse, 120, 122
safety equipment, 14, 19
Sagter Ems, 76, 77
   j Elisabethfehnkanal, 77, 79
   j Leda, 77
sailing boats, 19
St Goar, 40
Salzgitter, 91
Sarreguemines, 60
Scharmützelsee, 160
Schengen, 57
Schengen agreement, 13
Schiffahrtsweg Elbe-Weser, 95-6
   j Elbe, 96
   j Unterweser, 96
Schlutup, 101
Schmilka, 104, 105
Schmöckwitz, 156, 160
Schönwalde, 127
Schwarze Elster, *j* Elbe, 106
Schwarzer See, 143
Schwebsange, 57
Schwedt, 131
Schwedter Querfahrt, 131, 168
Schwedtsee, *j* Obere-Havel-Wasserstrasse, 140
Schwerin, 144, 145, 146
Schweriner See, 144, 146-7
Schwielochsee, 166
Schwielowsee, 121
Schwinge, *j* Unterelbe, 109
Seddinsee, 156
See von Bederkesa, 95
Semlin, 125

ship-lifts (Hebewerke), 16-17, *see also* Henrichenburg; Lüneburg; Niederfinow; Rothensee
shopping, 10-11
signs, sounds & marks, 174
Silokanal, 122
   j Beetzsee, 122
   j Brandenburger Niederhavel, 122
   j Untere Havel-Wasserstrasse, 122
Small Ships Register, 14
sounds, marks & signs, 174
Spandau, 115, 116-19, 127, 128-9, 153
Spandauer Havel, 127
Spandauer-Schiffahrtskanal *see* Berlin-Spandauer-Schiffahrtskanal
speed & distance table, 173
speed limits, 14, 15, 21
Speisekanal Neuhaus, 156
Speyer, 37
Sportboot, 13
Spree, 153
   j Havel-Oder-Wasserstrasse, 119
   j Untere Havel-Wasserstrasse, 115, 119
   see also Müggelspree; Obere Spree; Spreekanal
Spree-Oder-Wasserstrasse, 20, 152-6, 157, 168
   j Berlin-Spandauer-Schiffahrtskanal, 153, 155
   j Britzer Verbindungskanal, 156
   j Charlottenburger Verbindungskanal, 153
   j Dahme-Wasserstrasse, 156, 160
   j Havel-Oder-Wasserstrasse, 119, 128, 153
   j Landwehrkanal, 153, 155
   j Müggelspree, 158, 160
   j Obere Spree Wasserstrasse, 156, 166
   j Oder, 153, 156
   j Oder-Spree-Kanal, 156
   j Spreekanal, 155
   j Teltowkanal, 156, 157, 158
   j Untere-Havel-Wasserstrasse, 119, 153
   j Westhafenkanal, 153, 155
Spreekanal, 155
   j Spree-Oder-Wasserstrasse, 155
Spreewald, 166
Stade, 109
Stettiner Haff (Zalew Szczecinski), 169, 170
Stienitzsee, 160
Stolpe, 131
Stolpsee, 139, 140
stopping places, 17-18
Stör, *j* Unterelbe, 111
Stör-Wasserstrasse, 144, 146-7
   j Müritz-Elde-Wasserstrasse, 146, 147
Störkanal, 146
Storker, 164
Storkower Gewässer, 160, 162, 163-5
   j Dahme Wasserstrasse, 163
Storkower Kanal, 164
Stralsund, 170
Strasbourg, 32, 35
Straubing, 21, 24
Strelasund, 170, 171
Strücklingen, 77
Stuttgart, 45, 48
Südabstieg zur Weser (Verbindungskanal Süd, Minden), 81, 88
Süderelbe/Köhlbrand, 109

INDEX

Sumpfsee, 143
Swinoujscie, 167
Swiss border, 32, 34, 35
Szczecin, 20, 103, 128, 131, 167, 170

Tangermünde, 105, 107
Tauchtiefen, 18, 21
Tegeler See, 129
telecommunications, 11
Teltowkanal, 157-8
   j Britzer Verbindungskanal, 157, 158
   j Griebnitzsee-Kanal, 157
   j Neuköllner Schiffahrtskanal, 158
   j Potsdamer Havel, 120, 157
   j Spree-Oder-Wasserstrasse, 156, 157, 158
Templin, 138
Templiner Gewässer, 134, 137-8
   j Obere-Havel-Wasserstrasse, 137
Templiner Kanal, 138
Templiner See, 121, 138
Ter Apelkanaal, *j* Haren-Rütenbrock-Kanal, 71
Teupitzer Gewässer, 160, 162, 165
   j Dahme, 163, 165
through routes, 20
Tolkamer (Lobith), 45
Tönning, 98, 99
Torgau, 103, 106
Tourist Office (German), 172
Traben, 55
transport & travel, 9-10
Trarbach, 55
Trave, 99, 100, 101
   j Elbe-Lübeck-Kanal, 100
Travemünde, 20, 99, 100, 101, 170
Treene, 98, 99
Trier, 56
Trittenheim, 56
Trotha, 111, 113

Uecker, 169-70
   j Randow, 170
Ueckermünde, 170
Uelzen, 93-4
Ulm, 21, 22
Unstrut, *j* Saale, 111, 113
Unter Ems, 65, 68-70, 76, 77
   j Dortmund-Ems-Kanal, 69
   j Ems-Jade-Kanal, 70
   j Ems-Seitenkanal, 70
   j Leda, 69, 77
Unter Trave, 99, 100, 101
Untere Havel-Wasserstrasse, 115-26, 132, 157
   j Brandenburger Niederhavel, 124
   j Brandenburger Stadtkanal, 122
   j Elbe, 108, 125-6
   j Elbe-Havel-Kanal, 115, 124
   j Grosser Wannsee, 119
   j Gülper Havel, 125
   j Havel-Oder-Wasserstrasse, 115, 119, 128
   j Havelkanal, 115, 120, 127
   j Hohennauener Kanal, 125
   j Ketziner Havel, 122
   j Potsdamer Havel, 120
   j Sacrow-Paretzer Kanal, 120, 122
   j Silokanal, 122
   j Spree, 115, 120
   j Spree-Oder-Wasserstrasse, 153

Untere Hunte, 79
   j Küstenkanal, 79
   j Unterweser, 79, 84
Unterelbe, 109-111
   j Este, 109
   j Glückstadter Nebenelbe, 111
   j Hadelner Kanal, 111
   j Krückau, 111
   j Lühe, 109
   j Medem, 111
   j Nord-Ostsee-Kanal, 111
   j Oste, 111
   j Pinnau, 109-111
   j Ruthenstrom, 111
   j Schwinge, 109
   j Stör, 111
Unterweser, 81, 84
   j Geeste, 84, 96
   j Hadelner Kanal, 84, 96
   j Küstenkanal, 84
   j Lesum, 84
   j Ochtum, 84
   j Schiffahrtsweg Elbe-Weser, 84, 96
   j Untere Hunte, 79, 84
Usedom, 170

Verden, 85
VHF radio, 18-19
Vielitz Kanal, 132
Vielitz-See, 132
Vilshofen, 23, 25
Vilzsee, 143
Vistula (Wisla), 167, 168
Vltava (Moldau), 103
Völklinger, 60

Walhalla, 23, 24
Waltrop, 64
Waren, 144
Warsaw, 167
Warta, *j* Oder, 167, 168
Wasser-und-Schiffahrtsamt (WSA), 14
Wasser-und-Schiffahrtsdirektion (WSD), 14
Wasser-und-Schiffahrtsverwaltung des Bundes (WSV), 172-3
Wasserbillig, 56
Wasserschutzpolizei (police), 13, 14
Wasserstände, 32-4
water, 18
waterways (general), 13-20, 21
weather, 12
websites, 172-3
Weener, 69
Wehlen, 104, 105
Weilburg, 48
Weissenburg, 25
Wentow Gewässer, 134, 136, 137
   j Obere-Havel-Wasserstrasse, 136, 137
Werbelliner-Gewässer, 128, 134
Werbellinkanal, *j* Havel-Oder-Wasserstrasse, 130, 134
Wernsdorf, 153, 156, 160
Werra, 80, 81
Wertheim, 30
Wesel, 20, 44, 62-3
Wesel-Datteln-Kanal, 20, 62-3
   j Dortmund-Ems-Kanal, 63, 65
   j Rhein, 44, 63
Weser, 20, 64, 79, 80, 81-4, 95
   j Fulda & Werra, 80
   j Mittellandkanal, 81, 87, 88

see also Mittelweser; Oberweser; Schiffahrtsweg Elbe-Weser; Unterweser
West-Oder, 127, 131, 168
   j Hohensaaten-Friedrichsthaler-Wasserstrasse, 131
Westhafenkanal, 153
   j Berlin-Spandauer-Schiffahrtskanal, 153, 155
   j Spree-Oder-Wasserstrasse, 153, 155
Widuchowa, 167, 168
Wiesbaden, 32, 38
wildlife, 12
Wilhelmsburg, 109
Wilhelmshaven, 76
Windorf, 23
wines, 11
Winningen, 53
Wisla (Vistula), 167, 168
Wittenberg, 103, 104-5, 106
Wittenberge, 104, 108
Wittingen, 93
Woblitzsee, 140, 141
Wolfsburg, 92
Wormeldange, 57
Worms, 37, 38
Wöterfilzsee, 143
Würzburg, 28, 30
Wusterwitzer See, 115

yacht & equipment, 14, 19-20
yacht clubs (general), 11, 12, 17, 18, 19

Zalew Szczecinski (Stettiner Haff), 169, 170
Zechliner Gewässer, 142
Zehdenick, 136
Zell, 54
Zernsee, 121
Zotzensee, 143